Picture Post 1938-50

The Happy Elephants – a photographic cartoon. It was the work of the now famous John Heartfield. *Picture Post* used it to puncture optimism over Chamberlain's Munich agreement with Hitler. 'The elephants are happy because they have got peace. But for how long have the elephants got peace?'

Picture Post 1938-50

Edited and with an Introduction and Foreword

by Tom Hopkinson

Chatto & Windus · The Hogarth Press   London

Published in 1984 by
Chatto & Windus · The Hogarth Press
40 William IV Street, London WC2N 4DF

British Library Cataloguing in Publication Data
Picture Post 1938-50.
1. Great Britain – Social life and customs –
20th century – Pictorial works
I. Hopkinson, *Sir* Tom
941.084'022'2 DA566.4

ISBN 0 7011 2858 5

This selection was first published by Penguin Books Ltd and Allen Lane The Penguin Press in 1970
Introduction and selection copyright © Tom Hopkinson 1970
Foreword copyright © Tom Hopkinson 1984

Printed in Great Britain by
Redwood Burn Ltd, Trowbridge, Wiltshire

Acknowledgement

The editor and publishers wish to thank the writers and photographers who have kindly granted permission for the articles and photographs which appeared in the original issues to be reproduced in this selection.

Every effort has been made to trace copyright holders, but in a few cases this has proved impossible. The publishers therefore wish to thank the writers or copyright holders of those articles and photographs not acknowledged.

To the Editorial Staff of *Picture Post* around
whose varied talents and idiosyncrasies
a much longer book than this might
have been written

Contents

Foreword

The Golden Age of the Picture Magazines

For a short period of three decades in the mid nineteenth century – from 1928 to the late 1950s – picture magazines were the most popular source of information and entertainment throughout much of the Western world. *Life* and *Look* in the United States; *Vu* and later *Paris-Match* in France; *Picture Post* and *Illustrated* in Britain; *Berliner Illustrirte, Münchner Illustrierte,* with a host of others in Germany and almost as many again in Italy, provided the favourite viewing and reading for tens of millions every week. In Germany political parties published their own weekly picture magazines; there were others devoted to sport, fashion and the cinema. Journalists and photographers in Western countries coveted the opportunity of working for one of the picture magazines as eagerly as today they pursue the chance of employment with an important television programme.

And then, as suddenly as the Golden Age had dawned, it faded, to be superseded by a medium in which the pictures move, the programme changes continually and can be watched by the whole family at the same time. Figures tell the story. In Britain before World War II television was no more than an experiment. By 1953 there were just over two million television licences.* Thirty years later there would be 18.5 million television licences in Britain, 80 per cent of them for colour; the picture magazines had died long since, and a number of their most talented staff had moved across to work for television.

It was in Germany, during the turbulent years following her disastrous defeat in World War I, that the picture magazines came into being. The consequences of that defeat – the exile of the Imperial family, the discrediting of the powerful and prestigious military clique, the breakdown of the banking system, raging inflation with consequent loss of capital and widespread unemployment – induced in the German people a bitter cynicism on the one hand and, on the other, an eager search for whatever was new and different. In theatre and cinema; in architecture, design and decoration; in art and literature, a new spirit manifested itself, demanding a complete break with the past and its moral, social and political values.

The Twenties were not to be merely the decade which followed the two previous ones. They were to mark the beginning of a new era, an era of experiment and self-expression, through which a new attitude to life, surely indeed a new kind of man and woman, would emerge from the shadows of the past into a sunlit future. Clearly the new spirit of the age demanded a new form of

*At this time it was a joint radio-television licence. There were also in that year 10.7 million licences for radio alone.

journalism through which to spread its message. But before this could come into existence there had to be the journalists, and there had to be the instrument. That instrument proved to be a new kind of camera.

From before the first World War experiments had been going on in Germany to combine the advantages of the film camera with those of the single-shot cameras used by newspaper photographers. Press cameras such as the Speed Graphic and Speed Graflex, popular in Britain, and the Contessa Nettel in Germany, used large negatives giving sharp definition and affording good newspaper reproduction. But they were ponderous and heavy; one or two pictures were often all that could be obtained by operating with such a camera.

'What's the picture?' the Fleet Street photographer of the Twenties would ask when sent out on an assignment, and, once having carried out the instruction, would make haste back to the office without waiting to see if anything more pictorially interesting or newsworthy developed.

Noisy, conspicuous, dependent on strong lighting, press cameras almost up to World War II required in general 'photography by consent' – posed arrangements of the type known to journalists as 'firing squad pictures' in which the subjects line themselves up and affix their toothy smiles. One could no more 'steal' pictures with a speed Graphic than you could ride a motor-cycle unnoticed into a cathedral.

The cameras of the cinema industry, using much smaller film drawn rapidly past the lens, produced hundreds of pictures in rapid succession. They could capture movement, facial expression, the drama of events, the flow of life. But in each individual frame the movement was blurred and the result unsuitable for reproduction as still pictures. Only in the mid-1920s, with the development of small format cameras, did the photo-journalist begin to acquire the equipment needed for his job – that of telling a story in pictures in much the same way that the reporter tells it with his pen. The first of these cameras, the Ermanox, was superseded before long, but during its short lifespan its remarkable lens made photography by 'available light' possible under conditions which would hitherto have required the use of flash. However it was the Leica, first produced in 1924 and perfected over the next years, which launched the era of the picture magazine.

The Leica, with its small format, thirty-six pictures on a film, ease of operation and quiet mechanism – to which before long was added a wide range of interchangeable lenses – brought photography out of the studio and into the stream of everyday life. It was now possible to photograph statesmen in angry argument,

actors in actual stage productions, operations in hospital or athletes straining for a record. Equally important, cameramen could now steal pictures in places where photography was not permitted, and in the decade following 1928 a new breed of cameraman came on the scene, through whom the Leica's possibilities began to be exploited. *

Press photographers hitherto had been technicians. They were not ranked as journalists but occupied a no man's land just above chauffeurs and office messengers, but well below reporters.

'D'you mind if I bring in my photographer?' the political correspondent would enquire, once he had got on sufficiently easy terms with the important Minister.

'All right – provided he doesn't stay too long,' the great man would assent. And the photographer, after exposing a plate or two, would be hustled out of the room as though he were some wet shaggy dog, liable to shake itself over the furniture.

But the cameramen appearing now in Germany were sophisticated and well-educated, equally able to hold their own, or to pass unnoticed, in any company. The first and most renowned of these was Dr Erich Salomon, a doctor of law and a skilled linguist. Salomon started taking news pictures only in 1928, but within two years his pictures of political conferences and his stolen pictures of murder trials had won him a European reputation. Until 1932 Salomon operated with an Ermanox before switching to the Leica. For trial scenes he used such devices as secreting his camera inside a bowler hat or small attaché case, and he would at times gain entry to a discussion among high-ranking diplomats disguised as a waiter or house painter. But his finest disguise was his own cool assurance, enabling him to attach himself to the train of some eminent personage entering the buildings – he was always immaculately dressed – or to occupy the seat of a missing delegate. Once inside he would operate his cameras with such confidence and tact that everyone assumed he had full official authority in his pocket.

Other cameramen who were quick to develop the new possibilities included many names now famous – André Kertesz, Martin Munkacsi, Wolfgang Weber, Walter Bosshard, Felix Man (then known as Hans Baumann), Kurt Hutton (Kurt Hübchmann), 'Umbo' whose real name was Otto Umbehr, and Alfred Eisenstadt. It was the cameramen whose skill and daring attracted public

* 'The Leica was the first miniature camera which the new photo reporter could use as an extension of his eye, instead of his eye being the slave of the instrument'. Tim Gidal. Article in *Creative Camera*, July-August 1982.

notice, but the picture magazines were essentially a cooperation between them and the editors, who often planned the assignments as well as selecting the photographs and laying out the pages. Notable editors in these early days were Kurt Korff of the *Berliner Illustrirte Zeitung* and his managing director Kurt Szafranski, and Paul Feinhals and Stefan Lorant of the *Münchner Illustrierte Presse.* Managers of certain of the picture agencies, such as Simon Guttman (Dephot) and Rudolph Birnback (Weltrundschau), also made valuable contributions to the success of the new journalism.

From 1928 onwards the rise of the picture magazine was dramatic. The biggest and most successful publishing house in Europe was that of Ullstein in Berlin. The flagship of their wide range of publications was the *Berliner Illustrirte Zeitung,* whose sales by 1930 had reached an impressive two million copies a week. Of its many rivals and imitators the most successful was the *Münchner Illustrierte Presse;* others included the *Kölnische Illustrierte,* the *Leipziger Illustrierte* and the *Hamburger Illustrierte,* each with a strong following particularly in its own area. Based on political parties were the magazines *AIZ* (Arbeiter Illustrierte Zeitung) for the Communists and, before long, the *Illustrierte Beobachter* for the Nazis. Other existing journals soon changed from the old style of posed photographs to exploit the advantages of the new photography in covering home life, fashion, the cinema, industry and sport.

From Germany the fashion spread rapidly across Europe, a movement which was greatly speeded up by Hitler's seizure of power, culminating in his becoming Chancellor of the German Reich in January 1933. This was the death knell for Ullsteins, a Jewish firm. Many of the most talented journalists and cameramen were also Jewish or had Jewish relatives, and over the next two years there was an exodus. Painful as this uprooting must have been, it brought to London the talents of Stefan Lorant, who had been imprisoned under the Nazis, Felix Man, who was not himself Jewish and Kurt Hutton, who had a Jewish mother, while Eisenstadt, Kertesz, Munkacsi, Korff, Szafranski and others went to the United States. There before long began the rise of the most successful of all picture magazines, *Life,* whose sales in 1969 – shortly before its collapse under its own weight – had climbed to a fantastic eight-and-half million copies a week, while the cost of a single page of colour advertising had been pushed to $43,000.

Two years after the launch of *Life* in 1936, the first copy of *Picture Post* went on sale in this country. Its editor was Stefan Lorant, and the bulk of its early picture stories were the work of Felix Man and Kurt Hutton. The Golden Age of the picture magazines had dawned in Britain. It would be all over in less than twenty years.

Though *Picture Post* has been dead now for nearly thirty years, an extraordinary interest in the magazine and its history still continues. In the Introduction which follows I have told the magazine story as I saw and lived it at the time. This is also set out in more personal detail in the first part of my autobiography *Of This Our Time,* published by Hutchinson in 1982. Other useful sources for those who want to dig deeper are an article by Stuart Hall, 'The Social Eye of Picture Post' in *Working Papers in Cultural Studies,* No. 2., spring 1972. (Centre for Contemporary Studies, University of Birmingham). Another article in *The Listener* (September 1, 1977) was based on the B.B.C. Television programme 'The Life and Death of Picture Post'. This programme was the work of the distinguished producer John Ormond, who was a reporter on *Picture Post* in the late 1940s. The magazine *Creative Camera* published a special number, 'Fifty Years of Picture Magazines', as its issue for July/August 1982; and the history of picture magazines in Germany has been described by Tim N. Gidal, who was a pioneer in this field, in his book *Modern Photojournalism: Origin and Evolution, 1910-1933,* published in 1973.

Lastly, a word about this book. It was first published in 1970 by Penguin Books in a soft cover, and simultaneously in a hard cover by Allen Lane The Penguin Press. In 1978 the soft cover edition was reprinted, and it is now brought out again by Chatto & Windus with a new cover and a Foreword. After much consideration it was decided to leave the body of the book unchanged and so keep it more truly representative of its period, or periods. The reader should therefore bear in mind when reading certain of the Hindsights – those for example by Tom Driberg (p.44) and Fyfe Robertson (p.61) – that he is reading words written in the very different political and social climate of fifteen years ago.

Introduction

Picture Post folded in May 1957. But in one sense it continues to remain very much alive. There is certainly no dead newspaper or magazine which is so much talked about, or which continues to exercise such influence on the minds of its former readers – in particular on those who were boys and girls, or young men and women, during the years 1938 to 1950.

As an ex-editor I am often asked – twenty years after my connexion with the magazine was broken off – 'Why did the paper die?' 'Could it have been kept alive?' 'Why doesn't someone start another *Picture Post*?' 'If *Paris-Match* and *Life* survive, why couldn't a picture magazine survive in Britain?' and other questions of the sort. When Penguin Books set out to collect two complete sets of the magazine for the purpose of this book, it appeared that there are hundreds, perhaps thousands, of homes in Britain in which anything from a handful of copies to almost complete files are still being cherished.

The basic reason for this is plain. *Picture Post*, for a great part of its life, applied itself to the issues which most concerned the young and thoughtful people of its time. Such issues were dealt with far less adequately in the press of the forties and fifties than they would be today. There was also virtually no television. *Picture Post* thus became, for millions of young men and women, the magazine which handled the subjects they talked and argued about among themselves. Equally, in my time as editor, I was never happy unless I could see in every issue some topic which was going to be discussed and argued over. I was convinced that in order to survive the magazine had to be provocative and controversial.

This was not so much a matter of morals or ethics as of journalistic common sense, of knowing what niche the paper filled. By following its own path it would appeal to a distinct section of the community whose interests no one else was catering for, and whether from a publishing point of view this was right or wrong, that clearly-defined attitude is certainly what has made the present book possible. Here is a social history of Britain for the years 1938–50, as seen through the pages of a single magazine. It is obviously not a complete social history, nor anything like it. It is a vivid and compelling series of glimpses into a period of intense crisis in our country's life, followed by the five post-war years when Britain was recovering, taking stock, and trying to adapt itself to its new position in the world.

In going through the old volumes, I have been astonished to find how many of the issues which trouble us today were already troubling us then. The editorial problem has been to choose. It would have

been easy to fill the 250 pages of the body of this book three times over with picture-stories, all of which would have seemed directly relevant to this moment. It is as if we are watching the history of the sixties and seventies being roughly sketched out in the forties and fifties – and being sketched by many of the figures familiar to us today, but in a younger and more prepossessing form.

The idea of *Picture Post* – most British of magazines – came from abroad. Its first editor, Stefan Lorant, was a Hungarian Jew – one of a small and brilliant band who left their country after the First World War because they found its political climate oppressive, and Hungary too small to give scope to their talents; and the paper's two first cameramen, Hans Baumann (or Felix H. Man as he signed himself) and Kurt Hubschmann (K. Hutton), were both Germans who had mastered their craft on magazines in Berlin and Munich.

The original conception owed everything to Lorant. I met him first, four years before *Picture Post* was launched, when he turned up at Odhams Press where I then worked, with a suggestion for starting a picture magazine. This was in June 1934, and he arrived at one of very few moments in Odhams' history when an original idea had a chance of being accepted. The firm had just experienced a disastrous failure with a magazine called *Clarion*, a tiny socialist journal with a backing among cycling clubs, which they had attempted to turn into a 'poor man's *New Statesman*' on a giant scale. Launched in the manner which had proved successful with the *Daily Herald* – the offer of lavish gifts to all who signed on as 'registered readers' for ten weeks or so – the *Clarion* stubbornly refused to take off. It established indeed a circulation record, but – despite the advantages of having Bob Fraser (later Sir Robert Fraser of I.T.V.) as editor, myself as assistant editor, and a weekly page of comment from Claud Cockburn – the record was an inverted one. The circulation *fell*, from a ludicrously inflated starting figure of 400,000, to 40,000 in ten weeks.

Some important reputations on the managerial side were involved in this collapse, and Lorant's proposal of a picture magazine was seized on as a means of salvaging what little remained of *Clarion*. Under these lowering auspices *Weekly Illustrated* was launched in June 1934. But it was not long before Lorant's originality – an independence of outlook which extended to his ideas about office hours – proved too much for Odhams. When he left, I went to see John Dunbar, the managing editor, and said that I thought the magazine was being sacked as well as the editor. Firmly but not unkindly, Mr Dunbar

The Founder. Edward Hulton, who founded *Picture Post* at the age of 32, was son and grandson of newspaper proprietors.

asked me if I wished to keep my job. Having a wife and two small children, I answered that I did.

'In that case,' he said, '*shut up!*'

I took his advice and remained shut up for the next four years. But in the early summer of 1937 I once more came across Stefan Lorant. We were both walking across Covent Garden, picking our way among the squashed fruit and cabbage stalks.

'How are you getting on, Stefan?'

'*Not* well. Not enough editors buy my articles. There is only one thing for me to do. I become an editor myself!'

A few weeks later, on £1,200 lent him by a girl-friend, he launched his brilliant and delightful pocket-magazine *Lilliput*. It was an immediate success, but it carried no advertising, and cost more to produce than he got back from sales. When the first £1,200 was almost gone, Lorant met a young journalist named Sidney Jacobson, recently back from India with a gratuity from some years on the *Statesman*. Jacobson put in the gratuity and became assistant editor. One year later still, in June 1938, I was due to lunch with Lorant to discuss an article for *Lilliput*. But on the day fixed I got a message not to call at his little office in Chancery Lane, but to go to the *Evening Standard* offices in Shoe Lane, where a new firm called Hulton Press had set up. So here I was waiting at the foot of the lift for Stefan to appear. It was a long wait, and when he finally turned up he seized my arm and hurried me out of the building in a conspiratorial manner. Only when we were well clear did he speak.

'Tom, I am a very rich man! The very rich men lunch only at the Savoy. We go to the Savoy.'

Once there he told me he had sold *Lilliput* to the new firm (for a price which was generally said to be £20,000) and was planning to start for them a new picture magazine.

'In that case,' I said, 'I shall join it. I insist on being taken on.'

Neville Chamberlain . . . the Beautiful Llama. One of the famous 'picture comparisons' from the magazine *Lilliput* founded by Stefan Lorant.

The Editor Plans the Next Issue. Stefan Lorant, *Picture Post*'s first editor, was a Hungarian refugee who had been imprisoned in Munich by the Nazis.

Lorant seemed less enthusiastic than I could have wished, but later when I met the General Manager, Maxwell Raison, it was agreed that I should be the assistant editor of the still unnamed magazine. Lorant would be responsible for the picture side, and I would take charge of the text. I happily sent in my month's notice to Odhams Press.

The first issue was planned for early September – and finally came out on 1 October. Already we were in July, but all that seemed to be happening was the taking of sets of photographs by Baumann and Hubschmann. I was anxious for dummies to be made up, for advertising to be collected, for advance orders to be booked by the circulation. But that was not the way Lorant worked. He could only work when he had generated a head of excitement and enthusiasm. There was also a sharp division inside the firm as to what kind of magazine this was to be. For Lorant and myself the main interest was that it should be strongly political, 'anti-Fascist' in the language of the time; we also believed that the magazine's success depended on its taking such a line. But being 'anti-Fascist' meant being 'left-wing' – and our proprietor, Edward Hulton, was a staunch Conservative.

When we finally got round to producing a dummy, it was far from winning general approval. Mr Hulton told us that the cover for the first number had got to show a battleship. When I said privately to Lorant that there

Editorial Conference on the New Magazine. Looking over the editor's shoulder (left to right): John Langdon-Davies (science), W. H. Pearson (picture library), Lionel Birch (writer), Richard Darwall, Honor Balfour, H. E. Bewick (lay-out) and Tom Hopkinson (assistant editor).

could only be one thing on the cover of the first number, and that was a girl, he replied, 'Tom, there will be two girls!'

The advertising agent, Donald Gillies, had prepared some brilliant advertising for the paper, but he was convinced that its title should be 'Lo!' 'Buy Lo! See and Know' was to appear on all the buses, together with those wide-open eyes on the front spaces of the upper deck which seemed, when the magazine at last appeared, to follow one all over London. Lorant alone refused to accept 'Lo!', and from pages of scribbled suggestions we finally put 'Picture' and 'Post' together to form the title. But there was little confidence in the project. W. H. Smith, on whom so much depended, would give a firm order for only 30,000 copies. At a despondent meeting the management agreed that we might go ahead, but Lorant and I were asked to give our assurance that the new magazine would sell a quarter of a million copies. Having nothing but a small overdraft and a spare suit, I was willing to guarantee anything, but I thought Lorant — with a presumed £20,000 from *Lilliput* — rash to join in the undertaking.

At the last moment, with everything ready for the printer, came the scare of war. Chamberlain had gone to meet Hitler for the third time. Could any new project be launched successfully in such an atmosphere of crisis? We argued, however, that if war came everyone would want war pictures, so the magazine would quickly find a public: and if there was peace, *Picture Post* could get away to a flying start on the general feeling of relief. Edward Hulton accepted the argument — and we were off. As we drove down to the printing works at Watford

to put the first issue to bed, searchlights and anti-aircraft guns were being sited on rising ground. Convoys of troops and guns held up our journey.

On the morning that first issue went on sale, I called in at the office of Vernon Holding, the circulation manager. He had performed prodigies in forcing a print order of three quarters of a million on to an unwilling trade. We should all have been delighted with a sale of half that amount.

'How's it going?' I asked.

'I don't know,' Holding told me. 'Come back later.'

By midday I was back: 'How's the paper going?'

'It's gone!' he told me thankfully. 'Over the whole South and East of England you can't buy a copy.'

To me, Lorant's way of working was both a revelation and a nightmare. He would let picture stories accumulate while I pleaded with him to tell me which ones he meant to use so that I could get the articles written.

'How can I tell you which ones I am using when I don't know what's going in the paper?' he would snort and glare.

Then suddenly late one evening he would gather

A Car Loses its Wheel. A dramatic stunt picture from the first issue of the new magazine. Query: how was it taken?

the whole bundle of material under his arm and migrate to the little *Lilliput* office in Chancery Lane which he had retained. After a couple of hours a rain of rough lay-outs would start pouring out, covered with scribbled instructions. 'Tom – get H. G. Wells to write this article. Explain to him what we want!' 'This one must be very funny (underlined).' 'Hore-Belisha (Minister of War) has to see these pictures. He will help you with the captions,' and so on.

Often there was no time to find anyone to write articles, and I would cook up whatever I could myself. Of the first three writers I found to help me out on the staff, one took an hour to write half a page: one couldn't do any useful work after eight o'clock at night, which was when our work often began: the ablest, Lionel Birch, was carried off to hospital for an appendicitis operation while actually out working on a story. One night in December 1938 I sat down at ten o'clock to write 118 captions before morning, historical captions, calling for checking of names and dates and places.

Sometimes we were a day late going to press. Sometimes we were two days late. Once when I remonstrated bitterly with Lorant that it was hardly worth going to press now as we were so late, he replied: 'You are quite right, Tom. We take our children to the circus.' So we did. The printers, astonished and delighted to find a print order for a million copies a week two months after the launching, made prodigious efforts. When there was snow and heavy frost in the North, Holding, with his circulation department, organized teams of unemployed men to pass bundles of copies over a snowbound pass to lorries waiting on the further side, and arranged supplies of food and hot coffee to keep them all working through the night. Success carried everything along. Two months after the first issue our print order was a million. After four months it was 1,350,000.

Though I cursed over difficulties which I felt could have been avoided, it was Lorant's sense of timing which made the magazine. He had to feel inside himself just what was wanted. A magazine is quite different from a newspaper. The newspaper comes in over the tape machines; it's largely a matter of choosing and editing whatever news there is. But for a magazine which is sold ten days after it goes to press, the one thing fatal is to follow news. It's better to be capricious – to make a number out of life on Mars, or footballers or mini-skirts – than to construct next week's number out of today's events. Anything *can* be right, provided it sells enough copies and – a point later at times forgotten – provided it does not harm the paper's image, and so destroy its future in order to try to boost its present.

One day in November I found Lorant walking up and down his office, black with thought. When he was angry or concentrated he put on what Raison, the general manager, called his 'rabbit face'. His brow sloped forward, his mouth compressed to a short line, his eyes glared suspiciously at everyone.

'What's the matter, Stefan?'

'This *bloody* Hitler! These *bloody* pogroms! Haven't you seen the papers?'

'Yes, I know. But . . .'

'What do they expect of me? What do the readers want me to do? How am I going to hit back?'

The result of his hours of walking up and down was the story 'Back to the Middle Ages' printed on pages 32 to 38 of this book. Despite all the stories in picture magazines I have since read and studied, this remains for me the finest example of the use of photographs for political effect. The photographs become cartoons. Together they make their point more effectively than thousands of words – a savage and well-earned kick into the vitals of an enemy.

In September 1939 the war began, and from September till April 1940 was the period of the 'phoney war'. During this time Lorant became convinced that the democracies intended to do a deal with Hitler. 'You British citizens will be all right. But what about us bloody foreigners? We shall be handed back.'

At first I did not take him seriously. But when the German break-through came in the spring, I realized he would leave Britain before long. What was I to do? I saw that at the worst I could always find someone else to handle the writing, but if there was no one to plan the picture side of things, the magazine would stop. There was only one way out – I had to learn to handle pictures myself and to make the lay-outs. From that moment I arranged to see every picture story before it went in to Lorant. I would look rapidly through, trying to decide how I would treat it. Later, when the rough lay-outs came pouring out, I saw with what far greater originality and effectiveness Lorant had done the work.

One day in late June he called me into his office. 'Hitler is coming. He caught up with me once. I'm not waiting to be caught again.'

I was still negotiating with people in the Government to try to secure immediate naturalization for him when I learned that he had left on the *Britannic* for New York. At almost the same time our two German photographers were imprisoned in the Isle of Man as enemy aliens, and very soon the only writers I had managed to recruit – Lionel Birch and Richard Bennett – were in the Army.

The Cheerful Start to a Grim Five Years. No one foresaw what the war would really be like. Some expected 1914 all over again. Others thought that all cities would soon be destroyed by the bombers.

Within weeks we were down to five people trying to produce the magazine. Fortunately I was able to persuade Charles Fenby from the *Oxford Mail* to become assistant editor, bringing a much more thorough journalistic background than I had ever acquired, and a wide range of acquaintances in almost every field of life whom he could call on for articles or advice. Honor Balfour, who later stood for parliament as a Liberal, had been recruited already by Lorant. MacDonald Hastings — full of knowledge on everything connected with country life and sport — had written several articles for us and now joined the staff. Before long we were able to add Maurice Edelman — who became a Labour M.P. in the 1945 election and has remained one ever since — and A. L. Lloyd, the expert on folk music, who came to us from the B.B.C. where he was regarded as too left-wing to be handling programmes during a war for democracy. Our first women's editor was Anne Scott-James.

There was plenty to do. The collapse of France had released tremendous vitality in Britain. Men and women gladly worked overtime by day and sat up 'fire-watching'

all night. The greatest source of frustration lay in the Home Guard. This body — originally called 'Local Defence Volunteers' and issued with armbands marked L.D.V. as their sole means of resistance — consisted of young men waiting to get into the Army or working in reserved occupations, older men not yet wanted in the forces, ex-soldiers from the First World War who felt they were never going to get back into action. All had only two wishes — to obtain weapons and secure some training. The authorities had their hands full with the armed forces, or felt they had. For the L.D.V. there was nothing.

At *Picture Post* we knew Tom Wintringham, who had experienced German methods of warfare while fighting for the International Brigade in Spain. He was also an excellent writer with a clear style and a hearteningly vigorous outlook. In a series of articles for us during May and June he established himself, in the eyes of a public utterly disillusioned with generals and field-marshals, as the mouthpiece of new ideas and methods of warfare. One evening Wintringham and I were having dinner at the house of Edward Hulton in Hill Street, and we spoke of the frustration of the L.D.V. over the fact that all they were getting was practice in forming fours when they wanted to learn how to fight. The question came up — why don't we provide the training ourselves?

Between dinner and midnight it was all organized. Hulton had a friend, the Earl of Jersey, who owned Osterley Park, a mansion with huge grounds just outside London. Hulton phoned him, and he came round at once. Yes, of course, we could have the grounds for a training course. He only hoped we wouldn't blow the house up; it was one of the country's showplaces and had been in the family for some time. 'Can we dig weapon pits? Loose off mines? Throw hand grenades? Set fire to old lorries in the grounds?' Wintringham asked. 'Certainly! Anything you think useful,' Jersey told him. I asked Wintringham about staff. Whom could we get? He started noting down the names. Hugh Slater, artist and author, had been in Spain and planned one of the few successful actions on the Government side — the crossing of the Ebro. He was also an expert on destroying tanks. Two Spaniards who had been all through the war could be got hold of too. An expert on camouflage and concealment? Roland Penrose, the surrealist painter. Someone to teach stalking and use of cover? Stanley White, a chief instructor to the Boy Scouts. Explosives? Wilfred Vernon — a former senior technical officer at Felixstowe — just the man to improvise mines, grenades and all forms of destruction. We should need, I jotted down, to rent a couple of small houses near Osterley Park to house our trainees. We should want fifty sleeping-bags

The Man Who Knew. Tom Wintringham had seen modern warfare in Spain. He soon became the mouthpiece of new ideas.

or palliasses to fill with straw; blankets, cutlery, catering arrangements, leaflets printed to send to all units of the L.D.V. offering weekend training . . .

The response was fantastic. The 'school' could have been filled three times over. What it taught was simply 'Do-It-Yourself' War. One afternoon at Osterley I went through the kitchen to get to the lavatory. Vernon was stirring some thick greyish substance in a saucepan. 'What's that you've got there?' I asked.

'Dynamite.'

'God Almighty — just let me finish and get out.'

'Don't worry,' Vernon said, 'Dynamite doesn't go off from being heated, it goes off from being compressed.'

'Yes, but are you sure it understands that?'

In the autumn, when the school had been running some months, Edward Hulton and I were summoned to the War Office. A general, whom Hulton described in *World Review* as the general with the longest cigarette-holder in the British Army, demanded that we show him a licence for running a Military School, and — no licence appearing — instructed us that it must be closed 'forthwith'. In the taxi on the way back Hulton asked me what I thought we should do now.

'Absolutely nothing.'

'Nothing?'

'The general has carried out his orders by giving us *our* orders. Now he can dismiss us from his mind. It's ten to one he'll be replaced in the next fortnight. But if he isn't, let him have the odium of sending troops to close the school, and we'll send photographers to take pictures of them closing it.'

Some month or two later the Army started its own centres for training the Home Guard. It took over Tom Wintringham and the staff, and our school could honourably be given up.

It throws some light on the carefree attitude of those days that we also took steps to collect great quantities of privately-owned weapons through an independent committee in the U.S. A shipload of assorted guns, revolvers and ammunition actually arrived for us in Liverpool, varying from gangsters' tommy-guns to ancient buffalo guns and long rifles from the Louisiana Civil War of 1873. They even included 'Teddy' Roosevelt's favourite hunting rifle. All that could be made serviceable got to the Home Guard. (*Picture Post*, 30 November 1940, told the story.) As for heavier weapons, *Picture Post* produced its own mortar for 38/6, and published instructions for its use and manufacture. 'Powder taken from fireworks is not reliable, so we made our own gunpowder' (*P.P.*, 26 July 1941).

However, with the attack on Russia in June 1941, the immediate danger of invasion had gone by. By

At 'Picture Post's' Home Guard School. The Home Guard had few weapons and no training at this time. The magazine launched its own training school at Osterley.

A Home-Made Mine Goes Up. Home Guards on a training centre at Osterley practise a bit of destruction with a trailer and home-made mines.

degrees the paper could turn from advising its readers how to kill invaders on their doorsteps and destroy tanks in the village streets by ripping off their tracks with pieces of old railway line, to more general criticism of the conduct of the war.

The fact that the experts — with the notable exception of Basil Liddell Hart — had been utterly wrong about the early course of the war, and that leading military figures had played so ignominious a part in the collapse of France, gave amateur critics the confidence to sound off about many aspects of the war effort. They, or perhaps I should say 'we', were sometimes wrong or ill-informed, but our agitation ensured that methods and equipment which would otherwise have got by unnoticed came under sharp scrutiny.

And the fact that *Picture Post* had taken such conspicuous action over the Home Guard meant that a constant flow of critics came or wrote into our offices with ideas for furthering the war effort, saving scarce materials, improving production, clearing bottle-necks in industry, and so on. The paper became involved in criticism of the conditions in shelters — where hundreds of thousands of people spent their nights — and practical plans for their improvement. It also continued to denounce delays and hold-ups in producing war materials, and attacked the poor quality of some weapons — particularly tanks — which were going to the armies in North Africa.

Naturally this criticism caused anger in high places. Ministry officials told us that the paper was 'undermining

'*Make Your Own Mortar for 38/6*'. The Home Guard had got rifles, but they wanted some kind of artillery. *Picture Post* designed this mortar to be made in any garage.

the morale' of troops in North Africa by describing some of their equipment as second-rate. Even if it *was* second-rate — one official told me — that was all they'd got, so hadn't they better be satisfied with it? To this I replied that the man on the spot knows very well if his weapons are as good as the enemy's, or not. What he wants is some sign that people at home realize his position. If the truth is admitted, he can hang on till something better is produced. What makes him sick — as the letters we were getting showed — is the feeling that those at home don't know of his difficulties, and the thought that some of those in authority don't care. Finally the Ministry of Information settled the argument in its own way. It took steps (*P.P.*, 31 January 1942) to make it almost impossible for troops overseas to buy the paper. Many continued to receive it, however, by telling their families to post it to them.

Occasionally it was possible to affect issues *without* publishing the facts. Late in 1942 a distracted young Air Force officer was waiting for me when I came in to work. Shown into my office, he asked me to swear to print the story he was going to tell. Naturally I refused to hand over my editorial judgement to a stranger; I said I would listen sympathetically, but if he wanted a cast-iron promise he must go elsewhere. He then told me about a new type of fighter-bomber lately put into service in North Africa, with which his own squadron had been fitted out. Several had fallen into the sea on the way to Lisbon. On the first bombing raid some never reached the target, others — owing to a too-high landing speed — destroyed themselves on landing. He declared with emotion that he was prepared to be shot for writing the story, which he intended to sign, and that I owed it to him and his dead comrades to make sure it was printed straightaway.

It seemed to me that, if we did what he asked, the issue might never get past the bookstalls, since it obviously involved what would be considered official secrets, and that in any case the matter might be handled by less dramatic means. I asked him to give me a week to deal with it. Through a distinguished scientist who had written for the paper, I had access to the Minister of Aircraft Production, Sir Stafford Cripps, and when the young officer came back a week later, I was able to tell him that the planes he complained about had been grounded, and before long they were all withdrawn from service. No publication had taken place, but it was *Picture Post*'s willingness to publish which had brought the young officer to us, and which perhaps helped also to ensure that investigation and decision followed as quickly as they did.

Important as we felt the work of our paper to be in

supporting and criticizing the war effort, we were also keenly concerned over plans for the new country we hoped would emerge when the war ended. Churchill, as war leader, deprecated all such argument, feeling, no doubt, that the national unity he had so determinedly built up might be split. But letters from the forces showed how intensely concerned they were that post-war Britain should be very different from pre-war, and *Picture Post* had involved itself in the discussion. As early as the first issue for January 1941, at a time when it seemed doubtful whether any independent Britain would survive, we had published a Special Issue entirely devoted to 'A Plan for Britain' which I had asked Julian Huxley to help me in preparing. In it we outlined policies – many of which have since become generally accepted – such as full employment, minimum wages throughout industry, child allowances, all-in social insurance, a state medical service, planned use of all land, and a complete overhaul of education. On the day after publication, I telephoned in to hear what response there had been from readers.

'I can't tell you how many letters there are,' my secretary, Mrs Brosnan, told me. 'They're all still in their sacks. We can't get round to unpacking them till more staff are brought in.'

The response proved to be so impressive that we arranged a conference in London, inviting a number of readers to join in discussions with experts in different fields. This was followed in 1943 by a campaign on behalf of the Beveridge Report on social security, and by financing, or helping to finance, a further study by Beveridge into how full employment could be maintained. It is interesting now to read some of the arguments put forward in the House of Commons by opponents of the Report, which read as if they had been uttered not in nineteen but in eighteen forty-three (see pp.135 and 139), and interesting too that one of the few Tories who spoke up for the Beveridge Report – and for many other issues affecting the quality of life of the ordinary man or woman – was young Captain Quintin Hogg, back from war service in the Middle East.

Those first eleven months between the launching of *Picture Post* and the outbreak of war had been a wild scramble to catch up with the magazine's success. Everything depended on the brilliance of one man – Lorant. No one had ever got around to basic tasks – building up a staff; organizing a methodical way of working; ensuring supplies of pictures through a chain of contacts at home and overseas; creating a really modern photographic library.

Julian Huxley works on 'A Plan for Britain'. For its first issue of 1941, *Picture Post* published a plan for post-war Britain. It seemed visionary. Almost all of it is now accepted as a matter of course.

The war again was a special period. Most of our staff were in the forces. The size and shape of our magazine were dictated by paper rationing. Sales were fixed. Even the contents were to some extent controlled, since our material obviously had to be related to the war, and it was impossible to send staffmen overseas except to war fronts or on stories connected with the war effort. But from late 1945 all this began to loosen up, and during the next few years it was possible to a much larger extent for an editor to make the magazine he wanted. It also became possible to find and blend a talented staff together; to discover a proper method and routine of work; and to get together a picture library which would be unique in this country and of permanent value to publishing in all its forms.

From the policy point of view the main question was what attitude the paper should adopt towards the new Labour Government. I had watched the results of the 1945 election at a party in the Dorchester given by a newspaper magnate and his wife. The party was nineteen twentieths Conservative, and two or three of the guests had said to me with bitterness as Labour successes mounted: 'Your bloody *Picture Post* is responsible for this!' I replied that I thought the bloody *Daily Mirror* deserved a lion's share of the credit.

As editor I had no doubt that a Labour Government would seek to bring about that changed pattern of life in Britain which men and women in the Forces were resolved upon, and would be also better able to yield gracefully to the pressures for freedom and independence building up powerfully in Africa and Asia. Politics, however, made up only a small part of the magazine's coverage, and I believe that one of the services *Picture Post* was able to perform for many readers was to enlarge their field of interest and to demonstrate – before television came to do it better – that a great sculptor can give as much pleasure as a great comedian, and that the ballet is as natural a source of enjoyment as Manchester United.

The picture stories in this book give some idea of the range and variety of subjects covered during these post-war years, but there were others too long to include – like Fyfe Robertson's and Raymond Kleboe's impressive exposure of the disastrous Tanganyika Groundnut Scheme (19 November 1949 and subsequent issues), which raised a storm in the House of Commons and the country which went on for months. Or A. L. Lloyd's and Bert Hardy's vivid and moving reportage on 'Life in the Elephant and Castle' (8 January 1949). The prestige of *Picture Post* and the knowledge that serious subjects would be treated seriously and human stories sympathetically, were now opening doors which had been closed hitherto to newspapers and magazines. Sidney Jacobson and K. Hutton made the first story ever 'Inside Holloway Prison' (13 September 1947). Fyfe Robertson – also with K. Hutton, whose photography was distinguished for sympathy and gentleness of feeling – made an impressive coverage of 'Life in a Mental Hospital' during a long visit (23 November 1946). At the other end of the scale were the first photographs ever taken from inside the Royal Enclosure at Ascot. And at a time when most colour photographs appalled even their creators, Felix Man, after a prolonged study of techniques, began turning out a succession of delicate and accurate colour features.

Thus the years from 1945 to 1950 were years of consolidation. And the fact that sales went up when paper became freer, competition more fierce, and many journals began to suffer, seemed to show that the choice and blend of subjects was right for the audience the magazine was reaching – though, of course, a more skilful blend might have attracted a wider readership still. How was the blend arrived at? How did the magazine function? What principles, if any, were we following?

The starting point for each week's work was a conference on the Tuesday morning. This was attended by the whole editorial staff except for those out on assignments. At this meeting everyone put forward ideas for the coming week: these were argued over, and usually two lists emerged, one for immediate action and another for longer-term planning. I was several times told that this conference and the argument over ideas made Tuesday the most loathsome morning of the week, and one or two senior members disliked having their ideas criticized by juniors. But I was convinced that the paper must represent the thought of as many of us as possible, otherwise it would soon become too narrow.

In the afternoon following the meeting, H. J. Deverson, who had charge of the photographers' assignments, would talk over with me just who should take on each job. Good cameramen are like racehorses; it is essential to know their individual capacities and disabilities. One man will persevere against every obstacle, but has no talent for an emotional subject or situation. Another will be excellent on a story that involves women and children, or the countryside, say, but useless on rough-and-tumble stories involving riot and bloodshed. When we had planned the various photographers' assignments, we allotted the journalists to go with them, and Deverson's assistant would start organizing tickets and supplies of money, checking on passports, visas and health requirements. We always sent out a team of two, photographer and journalist together. To think in pictures is different from thinking in words, and demands, I believe, another type of mind from that of the writer. I have met numbers of 'cameraman-reporters' who claimed to combine both tasks, and when they showed me their work it was usually apparent why they were trying to combine the two – because they lacked any real gift for either.

Our journalists were always instructed to put the photographer's needs before their own and to help him in every way they could. A writer who fails to get the best out of a situation or an interview can usually improve his story afterwards. He can telephone, dig up material in the library of newspaper cuttings, and so on. But if the pictures have been missed, the whole story falls away. In interviewing an important, or a self-important, character a journalist might well get more out of him for his article by a soft approach and polite questioning. But he would probably produce much better pictures by stirring him up with argument and contradiction. If so, he had to stir.

Denzil Bachelor, soon after he joined the paper, exploded to me once: 'You treat the cameramen of this paper like . . . like . . . Royal Children!'

During the middle part of the week the teams were away on their assignments, phoning back from time to time to say how they were getting on – or to ask for another few hundred pounds to be waiting for them in

Delhi or Berlin. Often it was necessary to make sudden decisions based on guesswork. A call at my home at 2 a.m. from Bert Hardy, say, would tell me they were still holding on for an interview with Tito. Should they move to the next job in Greece, or hang on another three days, hoping? Hang on — and we would try to bite the ear of the ambassador!

By Friday we would have the pages in some sort of shape. The production staff would lay them out on the floor, and we would start building them together into a magazine. And now the difficulties would appear. Stories which had sounded utterly different looked surprisingly alike. We had far too many faces! Nothing dramatic. No landscape. Worst of all, no girls. Too many stories were starting on a right hand page. This one can't follow that because they both have a similar make-up, or because both contain too much text. Then we would go through our stand-by pages. Could this story be cut down from four pages to three? Would the theatre-call tomorrow give us some needed glamour? We developed a strange kind of virtuosity about the flow of the magazine from first to last.

'What are we still looking for?' I asked Edgar Ainsworth, the art editor, distractedly.

'A right-hand page with the main picture at the bottom. Should be a child's or baby's face, looking upwards. It has to go opposite the final page of the elephants fighting.'

In the afternoon I took the dummy we had pieced together with such blood and sweat for the proprietor to see. Just occasionally I had nothing to take down. When we looked at the magazine it was obvious it was all no good. No one was going to get worked up over *that* collection of material! There was nothing to do but throw it away and start afresh over the weekend. On Mondays we spent the whole day at Watford with the printers. The revised and completed dummy we would bring back to be criticized at the Tuesday conference — and already a new week had begun.

During the war we had enjoyed on the whole a happy unanimity of staff and management. But with the end of the war differences inevitably started to emerge. In the first place the editorial team split up. Charles Fenby, the assistant editor, became editor of the *Leader*, Ted Castle from the *Daily Mirror* coming in to take his place. MacDonald Hastings went to plan a revival of the *Strand Magazine* of former days, and Felix Man, the photographer, went with him. Anne Scott-James moved first to a fashion magazine and then to a distinguished career in Sunday journalism. She was succeeded by another gifted

journalist, Marjorie Beckett. Maurice Edelman, while reporting the Labour Party's Conference at Blackpool, had been consulted by some young people from Coventry who were looking for a candidate.

'What kind of person are you looking for?'

'Someone like you!'

A few weeks later he had become the candidate, and not long after their M.P.

A new team had to be built up which would include over the next few years names much better known now than they were then — Ken Allsop, Denzil Bachelor, James Cameron, Slim Hewitt (T.V. cameraman), Robert Kee and Fyfe Robertson among them. They were joined by our own staff men coming back from the war, including Lionel Birch and Sidney Jacobson, now editorial director of I.P.C. Newspapers. With the others they made up a powerful team, and one determined to play a part in affecting the future of Britain, of Europe, of our whole human society. It was a talented, individualistic, somewhat hard-boiled group of journalists, distrustful of authority, not apt to accept slogans or to swallow without examination the assumptions of power politics. So far as it had a common political alignment, this would be left, though not very far left, of centre.

Such had also been, during the early 1940s, the attitude of our proprietor, Edward Hulton. Following the Fall of France he had flung himself energetically into helping to organize the Home Guard School, and into the work of various committees concerned with the conduct of the war and the planning of post-war Britain. In 1943 he published a book — *The New Age* — which Tom Clarke, former editor of the *News Chronicle*, described in a review as '. . . a brave, eager book, a refreshing adventure among ideas'. It called for 'a change of heart and a new spiritual and social urge', and the reviewer described the Utopia it envisaged: 'There will be no Stock Exchange . . . no speculations in shares, no genuflexions before an obsolete gold standard, no money "talking" as if it were a commodity. Business will be more controlled, internationally and internally, in an economic system combining nationalization and private enterprise.' This mood continued into August 1945, when Hulton wrote a resounding welcome to Mr Attlee's new Labour Government.

'The great victory of the Labour Party at the General Election was a surprise to everybody, to Labour people almost as much as to anyone else. We now have, for the first time in British history, a Labour Government in power with a large majority. Wise men have long realized that Labour must some day come to power; and it is well that it should do so unfettered. More will be relieved that the form of Conservatism represented by Lord Beaverbrook, and aided and abetted by Mr Churchill in his latest phase, has been flung indignantly overboard . . .

'I am not personally a Socialist . . . still less am I a materialist. Yet I rejoice that latter-day Conservatism has been overthrown. . . . I am more delighted than I can say that Mr Ernest Bevin has gone to the Foreign Office . . .'

However, as time went by, as the war years faded, as the world increasingly split into two halves, West and East, and as the Labour Party ran into the economic troubles of the post-war years, the views of our proprietor moved one way, and the views of the editor and staff either did not move or moved another. I began to receive a shower of notes complaining that the paper was too left-wing; that we were 'soft' in our attitude to the 'People's Democracies' of Eastern Europe; that we were guilty of 'appeasement' in our attitude to the arch-enemy Russia; responsible people now 'looked askance' at the magazine which was 'going rapidly downhill'.

I did not discuss these comments with my fellow-journalists, since I have always considered it an essential part of an editor's job to maintain a peaceful climate in which his staff can do their work unworried. This obviously becomes impossible if he passes on criticisms from above. Nor was it easy to talk these charges over with Hulton himself. A shy and sensitive man, he seemed sometimes – I thought – to agree verbally on articles which later he disapproved of. I am not myself an easy man to work with, and clearly he did not find me so. I certainly made a number of mistakes and errors of judgement, as I can see in turning over these old numbers. But in the year 1950 sales of the magazine were as high as they had ever been. We had a steady sale of over a million and a quarter copies a week, and were making well over two thousand pounds an issue.

In February of that year, with a General Election imminent, Edward Hulton wrote in the paper on why he would this time vote Conservative.

'Nearly everybody is now persuaded that the Soviet Government constitutes a grave menace, not only to Peace, but to our very lives. . . . Although it may very well be true that the Kremlin does not desire war at this particular moment, this is merely because it is waiting, crouching, for a better opportunity to spring upon us. All and every form of appeasement is worse than vain. . . . At this perilous moment, I am, personally speaking, appalled that the conduct of our foreign policy should be in the hands of Mr Ernest Bevin.'

In five years a considerable gap had opened between the proprietor and the editorial staff, personified by myself. Two other events had taken place which would considerably affect the future of the paper. W. J. Dickenson, who had been the mainstay of the firm on the business side, had been persuaded to retire in 1948; and in 1949 the firm had been transformed into a public company. Dickenson had been the only person on the management side with whom I could talk easily and with confidence. Though a businessman through and through, he showed great understanding of editorial problems and tolerance of our eccentricities. Once during the war he had stopped me in the corridor:

'What d'you think it cost sending those two men out on that deep-sea trawler?'

I did a rapid sum: 'About sixty quid.'

'Seven hundred!'

'But how on earth?'

'Well, you insisted they were to be insured for so many thousand each. The rate was sixty pounds a day for the two of them, and they were at sea altogether for ten days.'

'But they *had* to be insured . . .' I began defensively. 'I know they did,' said Dickenson. 'I just thought you'd like to know.'

With his departure new people came in on the management side who had not, as Dickenson had, seen the paper built up from early days, and understood that it had found a readership of its own. Struck by the sales being achieved by magazines of a quite different type, such as *Weekend* and *Reveille*, they argued that if *Picture Post* would only print the same sort of material it could double its sale. I felt, on the contrary, that the paper would lose the readership it had. This attitude was ascribed to my wanting to have things my own way – a failing to which I have certainly always been prone. I was told that it was my personal interest in social questions which was dictating the contents of the magazine, and so standing in the way of the much greater circulation it could easily achieve. The argument raged on, and now, to add to my file of notes complaining about political policy, came others from the management, accusing it of dullness, lack of ideas, failing to keep up with the lively new spirit of the times.

In June 1950 two of our staff, Haywood Magee and Stefan Schimanski, were on their way to Japan to photograph cherry blossom and similar delights. On their way they stopped off in Malaya to record a grim, forgotten war, which might easily have become a British Vietnam. While there, an earlier 'Vietnam' war actually broke out, in Korea. We cabled them to cut the cherry blossom and become War Correspondents. This they did, recording in dramatic picture-stories the retreat of the South Koreans, the Americans and their U.N. Allies, all

Death in Korea. The war in Korea in 1950 was a rehearsal for the horrors of the Vietnam war twenty years later.

down the country into their last toe-hold round Pusan. While they were recuperating in Tokyo, an information officer offered places on a plane going back into the country from which they had so thankfully got away. Schimanski volunteered to go, but never saw Korea. His plane blew up over the sea, and only one survivor, an American who died a few hours later, was picked up.

I was sitting late one evening in my office thinking this over. I had given Schimanski a job only a few months before, believing I was doing him a good turn, but I had done him a very different one. With the advent of heavy American reinforcements, the Korean war was now entering a dramatic phase, and the paper had to be well covered. Our two best men for the job were undoubtedly James Cameron and Bert Hardy, and I was making up my mind to send them, when there was a knock on the door. This surprised me, as I supposed the office long since empty. It was Hardy and Cameron.

'You must be wondering whom to send to Korea. We suggest you send us.'

In Korea they made only three picture-stories. The most dramatic — an overpowering impression of military force and men in mortal danger — was the record of MacArthur's landing at Inchon (*P.P.*, 7 October 1950), which won the Encyclopaedia Britannica Award for the finest picture sequence of the year. The third story they made was concerned with the treatment of prisoners, particularly the treatment of North Koreans by the South Koreans with the connivance of some of their American allies.

Though the story reads mildly enough today, I knew it might cause difficulties, since any criticism of 'our side' could be regarded as anti-Western and therefore — in the climate of that time — pro-Eastern and hence, by another small stretch of meaning, as 'Communist propaganda'. So I waited until James Cameron got home and questioned him. There was no doubt about the facts, nor about the pictures. These 'men' — some all of twelve years old — roped together and with shaven heads, were political prisoners, supposedly opponents of the Synghman Rhee régime. This régime would be abandoned as intolerable by its American supporters in due course. But not for another ten years. And meantime Rhee and his followers were our gallant allies and the defenders of our Christian democratic way of life. As Cameron wrote of the prisoners:

They have been in jail now for indeterminate periods — long enough to have reduced their frames to skeletons, their sinews to strings, their faces to a translucent terrible grey, their spirit to that of cringing dogs. They are roped and manacled. They are compelled to crouch in the classic Oriental attitude of submission in pools of garbage. They clamber, the lowest common denominator of personal degradation, into trucks with the numb

Life at the Elephant and Castle. Most of those who remember *Picture Post* today remember it for its sympathetic photography and true-to-life reporting of such human stories as this.

air of men going to their death. Many of them are. . . . Among the crowds drifting indifferently around, a few bystanders take snapshots, grinning.

Though I felt the story ought to go in right away, I allowed myself a week's further delay while I searched the East European magazines for some picture which would give the opposite side of the case — ill-treatment by the North Koreans of prisoners from the South. To my surprise I actually found such a picture in a Czech magazine. It showed an American soldier dressed up by his captors in false nose and swastika, forced to march in procession trailing the Stars and Stripes in the dust. With Cameron's agreement, we planned the story as an appeal to the U.N. — the nominal authority over the war on the South Korean side — and sent copies to the Secretary General of the U.N. and to the leader of the British delegation, Mr Kenneth Younger. In this form I showed the magazine to Edward Hulton as usual on the Friday afternoon, and on the Monday we went to press in our normal way.

We heard nothing, as was natural, from either the Secretary General of the U.N. or from the leader of the British delegation, but on the Tuesday morning I was rung up by Mr Hulton from his home. He told me the Korean story must on no account appear. It must be taken out of the paper and something else put in its place. I said that since he ordered this I should do it, but added that I should expect him to give me reasons for this instruction, otherwise I should put the pages back for the following week. From that moment I never managed to make direct contact with him either in the office or by telephone. Late in the week I was given an opportunity to speak to the whole board of Hulton Press, following which they wrote that they supported to the full the proprietor's right to put into the paper what he thought fit. I replied that I did not dispute a proprietor's right to employ any editor he pleased, but that as long as I remained editor I must print what I thought ought to be printed. The general manager invited me to resign, showing me a statement to that effect already drawn up for the press. I said I was not resigning: I was being fired, and would only agree to a statement which made this clear. Such a statement was accordingly prepared and sent out to the news agencies.

So ended my twelve-year association with *Picture Post* and Hulton Press; and one of the oddest mementoes of those twelve years I have is a copy of the issue which was never printed, and which today, I suppose, would scarcely raise a glint of anger in any proprietorial, or of approval in any humanitarian, eye.

When the news of this disagreement got around, most of the editorial staff wished to resign. I was against this, considering the paper's future much more important than that of any individual. Finally almost everyone agreed to stay on, provided Mr Hulton would guarantee that the paper's policy would remain unchanged. As earnest of this the staff insisted that Ted Castle, the assistant editor, should take over. Ted, who had intended to resign, finally accepted, since without the assurance of his presence, the rest were not prepared to stay. He was given a guarantee of six months' tenure, during which time he did his utmost to maintain the paper's continuity.

His replacement directly the six months were up inaugurated a succession of short periods of rule, in which a wide variety of talents was called upon. Men from management, advertising, from newspapers and magazines followed each other in rapid sequence, or at times exercised their influence simultaneously. Some, no doubt, had excellent plans for the paper, but none survived long enough to arrest a general decline. The company's net profits, which had been £209,097 in 1949, amounted in 1952 to less than £15,000.

Some extraordinary managerial decisions contributed to this result. Nothing on a magazine requires more delicate handling than a change of price. *Picture Post*, however, was put up in price from 4d. to 5d. in August 1951, and again, only four months later in December,

from 5d. to 6d. 'These increases', the annual report observes, 'had a very adverse effect upon circulation', and in August 1952, the price was put back once more to 4d. In the following year 'considerable improvement' was reported, and in 1955–6 imposing new offices, to be known as Hulton House, were under construction in Fleet Street, though the Chairman foresaw in his report for 1956 that 'the next year or so may prove difficult'.

His forecast was correct. In 1957 the net profit for the year was £11,383, and at the end of the financial year the Chairman reported: 'In May 1957, your directors decided that publication of *Picture Post* must cease, so that the financial position of your company might be fully protected . . .' In 1959 Hulton Press was bought up by Odhams Press, which in due course was taken over by the mammoth International Publishing Corporation.

Why did *Picture Post* fail? In a television interview after its death, the proprietor, Edward Hulton, attributed the collapse to television. Television was certainly bound to affect such a magazine in two ways. It would tend to draw advertising away. And, by showing news events on film, sometimes while they are actually happening, it robs picture magazines of what had been one of their biggest assets – the attraction of a news-story told in a sequence of pictures. Television, however, has not killed *Look Magazine* in America. It has not killed *Life Magazine*. It has not killed *Paris-Match*, nor the string of lively picture magazines with which visitors to Italy, West Germany and elsewhere, are familiar. It has not killed them because these magazines, though modifying their formula from time to time, always maintain their hold on their own body of readers.

Contrary to some opinions, the moving picture does not kill the still picture simply because it moves. Each has its own function. The still picture which made the biggest impact of recent years, that of the Saigon police chief shooting his Vietcong prisoner in the head, would have been lost on television film. It was precisely its 'stillness' – the sense of a moment frozen in time – that made its impact. The many magazines which have successfully weathered the storm roused by the coming of television have all done so by making considerable alterations in their style. They dig deeper into subjects than they used to, going in more for argument and controversy. Pictorially they exploit colour, and they plan and contrive to secure the single dramatic shot – the picture which sums up a story or an issue – instead of relying on the sequence or 'picture series'. But such modifications were made slowly and cautiously, so as not to upset the general balance or give readers the uneasy feeling – so

destructive of all confidence – that the paper doesn't really know what it is trying to do.

With *Picture Post* the opposite was the case. A succession of editors – each anxious to arrest the landslide in sales and advertising but none staying long enough to establish a real character for the magazine – imposed dramatic changes. Stories appeared which were better suited to certain Sunday newspapers and, when these did not draw readers, there would be a serious number or two. But the frivolous or sensational stories had destroyed confidence in the magazine's good faith.

A newspaper sells largely on its handling of news, but a magazine on its personality and the relationship it manages to build up with its readership. Someone who buys, say, the *Listener*, the *New Statesman*, or *Playboy*, buys it because he knows what he will get. He doesn't yet know in detail, but he knows in outline. When he knocks on the door, he knows what voice he is going to hear. No magazine which fails to establish a definite voice ever really establishes itself. And no magazine which keeps changing its voice, sounding one week like the *Listener* and the next like the *International Times*, can hold the attention, still less the affection, of its readers. In my opinion it was vacillation, not television, which killed *Picture Post*.

And it seems to me ironical that the magazine which owed its original success to the intuition of a 'bloody foreigner' that the British were ready for something more serious, and at the same time more lively, than anything they were getting, owed its death to a loss of faith, to the sense that anything will do and the public should be given the sort of commonplace hash it 'really wants'. And it was not bloody foreigners but, in the main, one hundred per cent British citizens who argued like this. In the words of the obituary written by James Cameron:* '*Picture Post* soon painlessly surrendered all the values and purposes that had made it a journal of consideration, before the eyes of its diminishing public it drifted into the market of arch cheesecake and commonplace decoration, and by and by it died, as by then it deserved to do.'

In October 1948, just ten years after the day I had called into Holding's office to hear how the new magazine was selling, I attended a dinner for the staff and everyone connected. It was a happy occasion. I felt surrounded by friends, and I imagined that by our ten years' work we had built up a magazine which would be a permanent feature of British life. I foresaw our successors, and perhaps a dwindling number of ourselves, attending

* *Point of Departure*, by James Cameron, Arthur Barker Limited.

similar dinners in 1958, 1968, 1978. . . . However, hardly two years had gone by before my own connexion with the paper was ended, and by the time 1958 came round there was no magazine left to celebrate.

It is a matter of lasting regret to me that so brilliant and talented a staff should have been split up. It has never again been my good fortune to work with such a group, and while welcoming the success so many of them have achieved as individuals, I often feel that if it had been possible for us all to stay together, a new and potent force in journalism might have been generated. Though my life has been intensely interesting, and varied in a way it could never have been as a magazine editor, it remains a deep disappointment that the paper to which we all gave so much effort should now be only a memory. However, though long life is sought by most human beings and their institutions, there are others who pack much into a short life. By contributing something of special value to their own age and country they make a contribution to the general story of mankind. We honour *The Times* for its dignified march along the centuries, but the *Rambler*, the *North Briton*, the *News Chronicle* and *Horizon* kept alive values which needed to be kept alive.

Perhaps the same may be said of *Picture Post*.

Tom Hopkinson

OUR FIRST AND LAST COVER

The First Cover Which Was Also the Last. This was the cover of the buoyant new magazine launched on 1 October 1938, with 80 pages. The same cover was used for the final issue on 1 June 1957, now only 48 smaller pages.

1938

1938 was Neville Chamberlain's year. Grizzled moustache, prominent teeth, starched wing collar of Victorian respectability, dominated newspaper photographs and newsreels as his exasperating mixture of selfrighteous sentimentality and sharp, if limited, logic dominated British policy.

In February, he virtually forced out of office a popular if weak Foreign Secretary, Anthony Eden, with scarcely more than a ripple on the surface of public opinion. In September, without consulting his Cabinet, or even his War Minister, he ended British isolationism by undertaking to send a British expeditionary force to France in the event of war with Germany. He carried through his appeasement policy in the face of the hostility of almost half the Cabinet. He told them little of what he was doing. They were not, in truth, an impressive lot. Chamberlain knew it, and did not waste much time on them. Some tiresome members were constantly threatening to resign, but only one actually did so, an unsuccessful First Lord of the Admiralty, Duff Cooper, who had distinguished himself as a junior minister at the War Office by proclaiming his belief in the importance of cavalry in modern warfare.

Chamberlain told the British people even less about what was going on. Of two big decisions which would affect their future, they knew nothing at all. The first – the undertaking to France – culminated nearly two years later on the beaches of Dunkirk. And there was an earlier one, to overrule the advice of the Air Staff, and challenge the Luftwaffe over Britain, instead of bombing German aircraft factories. Like many decisions of the Chamberlain Government, it was the right thing done for the wrong reason – fighters were cheaper to build than bombers. It resulted in the Battle of Britain.

The policy which produced the Munich Agreement was like that, too. The Cabinet papers now available have ended once and for all the popular legend of Chamberlain as a trusting old gentleman carrying an umbrella, flying off to see Hitler with, in Harold Nicolson's phrase, the bright faithfulness of a curate entering a pub for the first time. He always saw Germany as the enemy. At the end of 1937, he told the French Prime Minister and Foreign Minister, 'Whatever Germany's ultimate object – and we might assume that this was to gain territory – our policy ought to be to make this more difficult, or even to postpone it until it might become unrealizable.' By extracting concessions from the Czechoslovak Government to its Sudeten German minority, he hoped to deprive Germany of one excuse for going to war.

At the height of the crisis which ended at Munich, the British Government received a number of alarming messages from the conservative German opposition to Hitler, indicating that the Führer was more ready to march into Czechoslovakia than in fact he ever was. Chamberlain's first intention was to fly immediately to see Hitler in the emotional atmosphere of the Nuremberg Rally. Fortunately, he thought better of that, and went three days later, taking Hitler by surprise with his willingness to make concessions. It was not Chamberlain who misjudged Hitler, but Hitler who misjudged Chamberlain. He thought he had frightened the elderly civilian with his sabre-rattling. It was a misjudgement which, as much as anything else, led to the Second World War.

The British people are not on the whole interested in foreign affairs, and they had remained largely indifferent to the long-drawn-out civil war in Spain, the steady erosion of China, the German march into Austria in the spring of 1938. As late as the end of August, a Mass Observation poll found that only a quarter of those asked were showing increasing interest in the mounting crisis over Czechoslovakia. But with September came the smell of fear, the pointed issue by the Government of thirty-eight million gas masks, the digging of air-raid trenches in the London parks. When Chamberlain returned from Munich on the afternoon of 30 September, having bought peace at the price of a dismembered Czechoslovakia, an observer described the Prime Minister's progress as the most shameful sight he had ever seen: the huge crowd seemed ready to roll on the ground like worshippers at the Juggernaut festival to let the saviour Chamberlain ride in glory over them. It was not yet Britain's finest hour.

For many Britons, fear coincided with a belief that war was morally wrong – and that peace was certainly very comfortable. The newer industrial regions of the midlands and the south-east had recovered from the slump of the early thirties, and were enjoying their first taste of what came to be called the Affluent Society. Four hundred thousand cars a year were rolling off the production lines at Oxford, Coventry and Birmingham, and the desecration of the countryside by the motor-car – particularly somebody else's motor-car – was a cause of more immediate concern to the prosperous middle class than quarrels in faraway countries between people of whom they knew nothing. The laureate of middle-class nostalgia, John Betjeman, wrote of segregating 'our lanes and villages' from anything but local traffic, and 'those who ride bicycles or horses or walk'. Some of the villages were the more charming because they were rural slums, from which the young and ambitious fled as soon as they could, to the nearest factory production line.

This was the Year of Optimistic Talk. 1938 was the year of optimism. All men are reasonable, so Hitler must be reasonable too. All conflicts can be resolved by talk, so the clash between Fascism and democracy can be solved that way as well.

There was also another Britain, the Britain of the old heavy industries overtaken by overseas competition and new developments, the Britain of coalmines, shipyards, steelworks and the dole queue. This Britain was more concerned about where the next meal was to come from than about the fate of Czechoslovakia. One worker in three was unemployed — two million of them altogether. A man, his wife and four children existed on 47/6 a week, their food mainly bread and marge and cups of tea. When that marvel of British technology, the luxury liner *Queen Elizabeth*, was launched amid general acclamation, a Clydeside shipyard worker said wistfully, 'Carpenters are lucky. There's work for them even after the launching.'

Sometimes the two Britains met, as at the annual Duke of York's camp for public schoolboys and those described as 'industrial boys'. King George VI had founded the camps before he came to the throne, and was photographed every year performing 'Under the Spreading Chestnut Tree' with his young guests. 'This song', the king's biographer has written, 'may have had as beneficial an influence on the Monarchy as "Lillibullero" had a deleterious effect on James II, when it sang him out of three kingdoms.' The claim is probably not exaggerated. The king was so unlike his flippertygibbet brother, who had run away from his responsibilities and married an American divorcée. In George VI, the middle classes found a mirror of their ideal selves: decent, conscientious, hard-working, rooted in traditional ideas, above all, *safe.*

Laurence Thompson

The Government Candidate at the Oxford by-election
Quintin Hogg, good-looking 31-year-old son of Cabinet Minister Lord Hailsham, asks the girls at a laundry to vote for him and show their confidence in Neville Chamberlain's foreign policy.

The Government Candidate's Wife
Mrs. Quintin Hogg—at right of picture—read all her husband's statements and revised them before they were issued to the electorate.

CRISIS BY-ELECTION

The Oxford by-election, first to be held since the Munich agreement, was of world importance: it gave a verdict on Mr. Chamberlain's foreign policy after a sharp campaign, fought on new party alignments. In this article, Tom Harrisson, organiser of Mass-Observation, sums up the result from the objective reports of his field workers at Oxford.

IN the past few weeks the whole politics of Britain have been shifted by events which seemed at first remote, the business only of a small, unspellable and distant state. For years the ordinary person has been most concerned with home, family, neighbours, street. In the past month foreign affairs have forcibly taken a front-page place for weeks on end. Via the gas mask it has been brought home (literally) to every elector that foreign policy may be as important as street lighting, new housing, or the price of milk.

The Independent Candidate at the Oxford by-election
A. D. Lindsay, academic 59-year-old Master of Balliol (left of picture) came into the by-election at the last moment to provide a united opposition to the foreign policy of the Government.

Dr. Lindsay making one of his many election speeches from a loud-speaker van.

The Independent Candidate's Wife
Mrs. Lindsay—left of picture—helped to organise intensive canvassing after her husband's dramatic entry into the by-election.

Within the next few weeks a long list of by-elections is being fought, on the one main issue of foreign policy. Briefly, was Chamberlain right? And is the present Government to be relied on?

The Government can choose the order in which it will fight these by-elections. It chose to start with Oxford. That was the ideal constituency in which to get a vote of confidence for Mr. Chamberlain's

A By-Election Meeting in Oxford Town Hall °

An interesting feature of the by-election was the intense interest taken by undergraduates, who had no vote, and the comparative apathy of the townsmen, who had. University men crowded to Dr. Lindsay's meetings, although many of the older dons disapproved of his candidature.

What is All the Noise About ?

Children in the street stop playing as a loud-speaker van begins to blare out an election speech.

Socialists Supported Dr. Lindsay

Councillor Frank Pakenham, whose wife, Elizabeth Pakenham, also a Socialist, is a cousin of Neville Chamberlain.

policy. A Conservative stronghold, wi a regular clear majority of over s thousand against all comers. So th Oxford City election became at on a focus of world interest. Rooseve watched it. Mussolini watched Especially, Hitler watched it.

Conservative speakers emphasis Hitler, thus :

"Now suppose you vote again Chamberlain—you can only vote f or against him, because the oth side has no programme. We do n know what it stands for. If you thi you can strike at Hitler by not retur ing Mr. Chamberlain's candida you are mistaken, for Hitler is on waiting to say, 'Look, the count is not behind Chamberlain. T country wants war.' Hitler has alrea said the Opposition want war. F will class Lindsay with Churchill !

The other side, supporting Lindsa Independent Progressive, countered th argument with the poster:

Hitler Says
" Don't You Dare Vote for Lindsay

A fierce straight fight ! The Co servative candidate was the Honourab Quintin Hogg, son of Cabinet Minist Lord Hailsham, Fellow of the worl most exclusive brain-club and colleg All Souls, Oxford. Young, dynami

Their Minds are Not Made Up Yet
The by-election was complicated by the new party alignments, and many
interested electors could not decide for whom to vote.

His Mind was Made Up Long Ago
John Fulton, a Balliol don, was Lindsay's right-hand man during the
election campaign.

n on mountain climbing, he has been
cribed in the Press as "a blue-
d boy with a Cupid's bow of a
uth."

He was actively assisted by attractive
s. Hogg, whose personality so affected
Daily Express reporter, William
kley, that he wrote : " She smiled
merrily with Cupid's lips and bright
e eyes that at once she put 400 votes
his bag."

Hogg is a brilliant scholar. But in this
ction he was opposed by one even
ater, his old teacher, Dr. A. D.
dsay, the Independent Candidate,
cle-riding holder of many distinctions,
ster of Balliol and friend of Gandhi,
ntly Vice-Chancellor of Oxford
nically, Lord Halifax, whose policy
dsay opposes, is the Chancellor.)

Quintin Hogg's main platform plank
: Unity, solid behind Chamberlain. As
said in his election address, " ' Peace
h Honour' is a watchword of the
ty of which I am a member."

Dr. Lindsay's position was more
plicated. He had no ordinary
tion organisation, because he was
y adopted as a candidate ten days
re the election, when the Labour
Liberal candidates withdrew to
ke way for him as an Independent
resenting all points of view other
official Conservative. Suggestion

"He's Talking About the Czechs, but What About Jobs for Us?"
Men in work join men out of work to listen to an election speech outside the Oxford Labour Exchange.

27

Picture Post, November 5, 1938

granted that everyone in the town knew him as well as they did. They were wrong. Over half the Oxford electorate didn't know Lindsay from Adam. And so, with only ten days to go, they wasted three assuming that it wasn't necessary to tackle the vital job of making the candidate mean something to the voters. The very idea of doing that was repugnant to a lot of the dons, who have lived all their lives without speaking Oxford Town English.

Said one—a famous philosopher—"If he can't win on his own merits, without being vulgar, better to lose." By being vulgar he meant talking an uncollege language, putting your stuff across to the many instead of the few.

No wonder a navvy said

"Aye, they're not one of us. Not one of them is if they *hadn't* stood down, so it's not much difference." While another man put it this way, " It's all right, all this, but too much University makes it above the ordinary man like me." A woman, middle-aged, got angry and shouted : " Lindsay's no right opposing Mr. Chamberlain. You could have understood Labour doing it. But he's supposed to be an educated man."

The remoteness of the University from the townsfolk world was not only shown by the professors and teachers. Oxford term was in full swing, and being October term a third of the university's undergraduates had arrived for the first time. They had

Helping Quintin Hogg
Although Proctors, and even candidates, opposed too much activity by them, Oxford undergraduettes took a lively part on both sides.

that this should be done came from the Liberal candidate, Ivor Davies. With less grace, the Labour candidate, another don, agreed. Transport House, bureaucratic Labour headquarters, reluctantly conceded to make no opposition to their candidate's withdrawal, but offered no official help to Lindsay.

In a letter supporting Lindsay, the Liberal ex-candidate predicted : "In this by-election the

issue will be clear-cut." Alas ! the issue was complicated, confused, and the by-election turned out to be both extremely intricate and excessively ill-natured.

Take the confusion about the candidates. One of the reasons for adopting Lindsay to represent a sort of anti-Government Popular Front was that "everyone knew him." Because he was a great University figure, his donnish advisers took it for

Helping A. D. Lindsay
Alan Wood, President of the Union, and himself a Parliamentary candidate, worked for the Independent candidate.

Appeals Were Sent to Every Elector
Addressing envelopes is an important part of a by-election. Undergraduates in St. Michael's Hall send out election statements.

The Socialist Who Retired
Patrick Gordon-Walker, former Labour candidate, withdrew for Dr. Lindsay.

Where Politics Seem Dull
Undergraduettes in the Junior Common Room of a women's college at Oxford far removed from election activities.

no vote or proper part in the affair; they had plenty of fun, though. Just to give a little election atmosphere, here is a report, written on the spot, of one of many incidents in the election:

The Liberal Who Retired
Ivor Davies, Liberal, also made way for the Master of Balliol. Here he is throwing skittles.

Where Politics are Interesting
Undergraduates and undergraduettes working at the Party headquarters of one of the candidates. Members of the University took a big part in the election.

CRISIS BY-ELECTION

Meeting at the Town Hall—700 present. Suddenly Chairman announces that "The Conservative party, with their usual diabolical cunning, I'm sorry, I should say with their usual technique, are outside with a poster display. So you know what to expect."

Immediately many, especially undergraduates, troop out.

Outside the Town Hall steps is a scene of confusion, terrific shouting; police in force, but they cannot keep the crowd from extending on to the centre of the road from both pavements.

The centre of the uproar is eleven undergraduates, each of whom holds over his head a large piece of cardboard with a letter on it. Standing in line, these letters read VOTE FOR HOGG. As the crowd streams out of the meeting, they surround the Hogg supporters. Holding up Lindsay's posters, HITLER SAYS DON'T YOU DARE, they defy the attempts of the police. Within three minutes they have swamped the Conservatives, split them up so that the letters still held up read OT FROG. Then the crowd starts roaring in gathering momentum . . . "HITLER WANTS HOGG."

One of the best brains in the world, a Fellow of the Royal Society, stands on the Town Hall steps and roars out : "A vote for Hogg is a vote for Hitler." And a laboratory assistant starts another slogan, at once taken up amidst tremendous laughter: HITLER WANTS HOGG FOR CHRISTMAS.

Then they grab the remaining Conservatives, pull down their cards, tear them up and form into a procession which goes roaring down Carfax towards Balliol, shouting for Lindsay.

So, what professors lack in pep, students more than make up for. . . .

Then there was the confusion of policy. Both candidates were for : the League of Nations; re-armament; peace; democracy; unity against war. At least, they said so. Underlying everything was a simple unpolitical moral issue, whether or no we had gained peace with honour. But barrister Hogg scored one of the big laughs when he said :

" The issue in this election is going to be very clear. I am standing for a definite policy. Peace by negotiation. Mr. Lindsay is standing for no definite policy that he can name. He stands for national division against national unity. His policy is a policy of two left feet walking backward !"

But Lindsay, lemonade-loving Presbyterian son of a Theology Professor, had a unique line of approach, remote from the usual thumping. In his very first speech, he read part of the lesson for the previous Sunday, to illustrate his argument. It went across—for he was sincere. He got headlines when a man asked him : "Now that our prayers have succeeded in bringing peace from the Munich agreement, is it not ungrateful to doubt and to question that peace ?" Lindsay answered like this :

"Suppose you had a child desperately ill. All night long you pray without ceasing, and in the morning she seems better. You thank God that your prayers have been answered. Then, later on it is discovered that owing to some error in the doctor's treatment, she is going to be disabled for the rest of her life. Would your gratitude to God for saving your daughter's life prevent you from calling in a better doctor who might restore your daughter to health?

That is how I feel about our present very precarious peace. I am sure that Mr. Chamberlain did his best, but I know that it was also he who brought us very near to war. I am sure that it is owing to his policy that we are now in such a very dangerous situation. That is why I oppose him"

Most voters only read the propaganda of the side they supported. They took this point of view :

"There are faults on both sides. But my father and grandfather voted Conservative. So I vote for Hogg."

But a new sort of answer had crept in to Oxford, and was often given :

"I can't say for sure. We've had to alter our views a little lately."

And an oldish man gave his feeling like this :

"I don't know who I'll vote for till I get the pencil in me hand."

No wonder that the canvassers in this election found a record number of persons, nearly a third, who would not "promise" to vote either Lindsay or Hogg. In an ordinary election only one-twentieth refuse a definite answer.

Well, then, what does the result of this election show? I think that the issue was confused by the University atmosphere, and the delay in adopting a single anti-Government candidate with no proper party machine—the machine is two-thirds of the battle. The result shows, the extent to which it is true to say, as has so often been said by press and politicians in recent weeks, that "The country supports Mr. Chamberlain." It shows it under circumstances especially favourable to the National Government.

Hogg, the Conservative candidate left no doubt in the minds of the electorate as to his position in this respect. He stated : "Mr. Chamberlain came back amidst the applause of the entire British Public. And the people of this country will vote for him. It is not enough that we should win. Of course we are going to win. We must win by a vast, an overwhelming majority."

Another thing : Oxford, the first of a whole chain of by-elections, has shown new tensions and tendencies in the party system, new loyalties and disloyalties cutting across the old and rather care-worn traditions. However much the leaders try to squash (as they are doing), the increasing wish for one opposition party, all the indications are that if they persist in that attitude, local parties will revolt, as they did in Oxford. Many Opposition politicians now think that to face the call for "Unity behind Chamberlain," there should be "Unity against Chamberlain."

Hindsight by Quintin Hogg

Looking back at the Oxford by-election after thirty-one years I am astonished at how little my views have changed and how little I have to unsay. The case made against me by my opponents was that Hitler was bluffing and would have backed down had Chamberlain stood up to him in September 1938. This case was false and I denied it, and after thirty-one years my denial still stands up and my opponents' assertions seem sillier than ever.

The choice in 1938 was, as I claimed then, between peace and war, and in November 1938 I made two points, both of which are still valid. The first, made later by Churchill himself on 3 September 1939 when he made that little gem of a speech on the outbreak of war, is that a democracy can only go to war united. In September 1938 the nation was deeply divided. It required one final act of perfidy on the part of the dictators before the nation as a whole was ready to admit that the Second World War, which, in the nature of things we should have to initiate, was inevitable. This involved that Hitler should breach the Munich agreement, which he did in March 1939 when he marched into Prague. On this occasion, I made my own private, and slightly ridiculous, declaration of war on the occasion of the Oxford Railwaymen's dinner, when I rather boyishly predicted that the day would come when the dogs would lick the blood of Hitler in the streets of Berlin as they licked the blood of Ahab when he returned from Jezreel. It was thought at the time this was a somewhat overdramatic remark. In point of fact it was less dramatic than the Götterdämmerung of the Bunker.

My second, and conclusive, reason for rejecting war in 1938 was that we stood to gain by a further, and intensive, period of preparation. In the light of hindsight this appears to me more certain than ever. No one at the time of the by-election foresaw the fall of France. But even then I attached supreme importance to the advent of the eight-gun fighter, which came into full service precisely in the interval between Munich and the Battle of Britain. I could not then know how rotten France was but I guessed then, and know now, that, without the eight-gun Hurricanes and Spitfires, I should not be alive to write these words, nor most of my readers to read them.

I never defended Munich as just. I never defended Mr Chamberlain's rather emotional outburst on his return, which I always recognized as the natural revulsion of an exhausted man who has succeeded beyond his expectations. My interpretation of 'peace with honour' was that Munich represented the last chance of the dictators to prove their good faith, and a final opportunity for the democracies, whilst keeping the agreement, to make preparation for any conflict there might be. I still think that it was only the certain knowledge that we had tried everything before resorting to war that kept us together as a nation in the terrible period after the fall of France.

As a baptism of political fire for a young man, the Oxford by-election was extremely rough stuff. But I won, and I think I deserved to win, since my own case was better argued and more realistic than that of my opponent. By contrast, in the ensuing Bridgwater by-election, Mr Vernon Bartlett defeated his Conservative opponent, who, I fear, adopted a less prescient, and less easily defensible posture, while Mr Vernon Bartlett himself showed a more accurate assessment of the situation than Dr Lindsay.

A Picture of Happiness—The Girl on The Merry-go-Round

Crises forgotten. War scares blown away. Private worries left at the top of the last incline. Only the rush of air. Only the shouts of friends. Only the sudden swooping movement of the caterpillar. Only the fun of the fair. . . .

OCTOBER: MONTH OF FAIRS

LESS than a century ago the list of English Fairs covered 62 pages of small print in Owen's "Book of Fairs." Now there are probably not more than twenty fairs of first importance in the country—each of them a shadow of what it used to be. A fair to-day is not much more than a fun-fair. In olden days it was a great annual market and a meeting—where beasts were sold, wages spent, new labour hired at the earliest of all Labour Exchanges. Fairs that still flourish are at Widecombe, Mitcham, Barnet, Sherborne, Stratford, Nottingham, Oxford. The change from agriculture to industry, and the sensitive ears of genteel residents are the enemies of fairs. Only three years ago Cambridge suppressed the famous Stourbridge Fair—founded by King John in 1211, mentioned by Milton in "Paradise Lost." . . . Whose turn will it be next?

Picture Post, November 26, 1938

The four guardians of German culture today: they

HERMANN GOERING.—*Economic dictator of Germany. Went straight from school to become a fighting pilot in the war. After the war, was inmate of a mental home in Sweden. A Swedish court decided he was not fit to have custody of the children of his first marriage. He once said: "When I hear the word culture, I push back the safety catch of my revolver." First man to think that guns are better than butter.*

JULIUS STREICHER.—*Nazi boss of Franconia, Jew-baiter No. 1. Owner of the notorious "Stuermer." A former schoolmaster who was expelled from his profession. Boasted in a speech: "Accompanied by several other members of the party, I went into Steinruck's cell, and found a miserable object whining and behaving like a schoolboy. I gave him a good thrashing with my whip." Suffers from epileptic fits.*

Anti-Jewish signs on a Jewish clothing-shop in Vienna. One on the left says that the owner is on holiday in Dachau concentration camp.

BACK TO THE

A fortnight ago persecution on a scale unknown even in Germany

It was November 7, on which Herschel Grynsban, 17-year-old Polish Jew, shot Vom Rath, Counsellor at the German Embassy in Paris. Vom Rath died in Paris on the afternoon of November 9. Almost simultaneously the German government in Berlin issued the first of its decrees against the Jews, which must have been prepared before Vom Rath died. These ordered all Jewish newspapers to stop publication. All Jewish cultural and educational associations were to be dissolved.

On the same day, two synagogues were burnt down in different parts of Germany, and there was a small demonstration against the Jews in Berlin.

Early in the morning of November 10, after the beer-halls and cafes had closed, bands of young Nazis, acting simultaneously in towns all over Germany, set fire to synagogues, desecrated Jewish religious vestments and books, smashed the windows of Jewish shops, harried, beat and stoned Jewish people in the

shield its purity from the "contaminated race."

ADOLF HITLER.—*Chancellor and Führer. A former housepainter, his only education an Austrian elementary school, where he was a dull pupil. Speaks no language but German, writes ungrammatical German, declares that he reads only what he knows will please him to read. Two months ago, said the "terrible sufferings" of the Sudeten Germans could no longer be tolerated by Germany, and would be stopped at the cost of war.*

PAUL GOEBBELS.—*Minister for Propaganda and Enlightenment. Entitled to call himself "doctor," he is one of the few Nazi leaders with a University education. Owes his academic distinctions to studies under Dr. Gundolf, a Jewish professor at Heidelberg University. His wife, a Belgian war refugee, was adopted and brought up by a Jewish family in Berlin. He says all Jews must be eliminated from German life.*

MIDDLE AGES

broke out against the Jews.   Here is a brief factual record

streets, and began widespread arrests of Jews.

Later that day began the worst pogrom since the Middle Ages. Looting went on all over Germany and Austria. The houses of Jews were broken into, children were dragged from their beds, women were beaten, men arrested and taken to concentration camps. Foreign journalists were prevented, as far as possible, from gathering details, but it is known that in Berlin several Jews were stoned to death. In the provinces, the number must have been higher.

The police did not interfere. The fire brigades turned their hoses only on non-Jewish buildings. All Jews in the streets or in wrecked shops, who were not manhandled, were arrested. In Munich, 10,000 Jews were rounded up and ordered to leave within 48 hours. This order was later rescinded, but not before hundreds of terrified Jews had run into the forests to hide from the mobs. In Vienna and the Sudetenland, Jews were

Continued on page 37

The damage the Jews were called upon to make good—pillaged shops in a Berlin street. Two of the passers-by smile over their destruction.

These are some of the world-famous Jews for

ALBERT EINSTEIN.—*The greatest physicist since Newton. His theory of relativity marked a new stage in human thought. Formulated also the theory and formulae of Brownian motion, and the law of the photo-electric effect. Awarded the Nobel Prize in 1921. Perhaps the outstanding intellect of our age. Deprived of his nationality and property by the Nazi regime. He lives now in the U.S.A.*

SIGMUND FREUD.—*Founder of Psychoanalysis. The discoverer of the subconscious mind. His work has changed the whole trend of man's thought about himself, and made possible the cure of those nervous ailments which are the scourge of modern civilisation. His clinic in Vienna was world-famous. This 82-year-old professor was forced to leave Vienna when Hitler marched in. Now he lives with his family in London.*

And these are some of the Jews whose work made Germany great:—

HEINRICH HERTZ (1857-1894). —*Among greatest scientists of 19th century. Discovered method of measuring length and velocity of electromagnetic waves, and so established fully the electromagnetic nature of light. This, and other work, prepared way for discovery of X-rays, and laid the foundation also for wireless.*

FRITZ HABER (1868-1934). — *Famous chemist whose research into poison gases and gas masks saved lives of thousands of German soldiers during the war. When shortage of ammonia threatened a German collapse early in the war he discovered, with Bosch, a method of producing ammonia from atmospheric nitrogen.*

PAUL EHRLICH (1854-1915).— *Released the world from bondage to syphilis by discovering salvarsan. In common with Einstein, Haber, and other Jews, he won a Nobel Prize, but his true reward is to have saved humanity untold suffering. Other diseases are now cured by chemotherapy, which he was the first to employ.*

ALBERT BALLIN (1857-1918).— *Built up Germany's modern merchant marine, and reorganised her shipping lines before the war. Head of the Hamburg-Amerika line, whose capital he increased tenfold. A personal friend of the ex-Kaiser, Ballin committed suicide in November, 1918, in despair over his country's defeat.*

whom there is no room in Nazi Germany to-day

LUISE RAINER.—Brilliant stage and film actress. Played in Vienna for three years before going to Hollywood. Her first part, in " Escapade," made her a star overnight. She was awarded the prize for the greatest woman screen-actor for her acting in the part of Anna Held in " The Great Ziegfeld," and for her excellent performance in " The Good Earth." She is married to Clifford Odets, the dramatist.

ELISABETH BERGNER.—Once the most idolised actress in Germany, and one of the great personalities of the stage throughout the world. Unforgettable for every German as Rosalind in " As You Like It." She created the part of St. Joan in Shaw's play in Berlin. Became famous in London for her acting in " Escape Me Never " and " The Boy David." Has played also in many successful films. She now lives in London.

MAX LIEBERMANN (1847-1935). Outstanding modern German painter, former president of the Prussian Academy of Art, who did for German art what the impressionists achieved in France. His paintings broke away from lifeless tradition, were alive with colour and light. They hang in nearly every European gallery.

HEINRICH HEINE (1797-1856).— Poet and journalist, he wrote some of the most exquisite lyrics in the German language. His prose, especially his magnificent writings in the cause of Liberalism, set a new standard of wit and satire. His songs, which can never be discontinued, are now printed in Germany as "anonymous."

FELIX MENDELSSOHN-BART-HOLDY (1809-1847).—Composer of much immortal music. His organ-playing and productions of oratorio established as great an influence on religious music as Handel's. 97 years ago, the King of Prussia made him kapellmeister. To-day, the Nazis forbid his music to be played.

GUSTAV MAHLER (1860-1911). —Austrian composer and conductor, whose work made the Vienna opera the envy of Europe. After conducting in Prague, Hamburg and London, became director of the Vienna opera in 1897. Held the post for ten years. Wrote songs, chamber music and nine symphonies in classical tradition.

Anti-Jewish Signs of a Kind Now Common All Over Germany

On the gates of Francis Joseph's palace just outside Vienna, is a notice forbidding Jews to come inside.

In every park are notices pointing to the only benches where Jews may sit.

A poster advertising Streicher's anti-Semitic newspaper "Der Stuermer." It says "Judism is Criminalism." Streicher and his followers set themselves to foster hatred of the Jews throughout the whole of Germany.

THESE ARE SOME OF THE ARTISTS DRIVEN FROM GERMANY

ERNST TOLLER.—Bavarian proletarian playwright and author, whose play, "Masses and Men" has been produced all over the world. Wrote this play while imprisoned in a fortress for his part in the post-war revolutionary movement in Bavaria.

ERNST LUBITSCH.—One of the world's most brilliant film-directors. His pictures, which include "Forbidden Paradise," "Lady Windermere's Fan," "The Love Parade," and "Design For Living," have given pleasure to millions. He has been deprived of German citizenship.

BRUNO WALTER.—The world-famous conductor, who with Arturo Toscanini helped to found the great Salzburg music festival. A former musical director of Munich and conductor of the New York Philharmonic Orchestra. He was forced to leave Germany as early as 1934.

STEFAN ZWEIG.—Noted biographer and historian, whose lives of Marie Antoinette, Mary Stuart and Magellan (based on a study of psycho-analysis) have been translated into many languages. To-day they are banned in Germany, and Zweig lives in exile in London.

MAX REINHARDT, to whom the modern German theatre owes everything. The father of the Salzburg festival. The greatest German Shakespeare producer. First producer of Richard Strauss. Honoured by Oxford University. Consummate dramatic teacher. Driven to U.S.

THESE ARE SOME OF GERMANY'S JEWISH NOBEL PRIZE WINNERS

KARL LANDSTEINER.—Nobel Prize for medicine in 1930. His research in Vienna on blood groups and nerve tissues of spinal cord established that infantile paralysis is caused by a germ, and opened the way to treatment.

JAMES FRANCK.—Nobel Prize winner for physics in 1925 for work as head of Institute of Experimental Physics in University of Goettingen. At front 1914 to 1918, was awarded the Iron Cross of the first class.

RICHARD WILLSTÄTTER. — World - famous chemist, who won the Nobel Prize in 1915 for his work on chlorophyll and animal pigments. He was awarded the Pour La Merite, highest German decoration.

ALFRED H. FRIED lived in Vienna. He was the creator of the modern peace movement. Founder of the Peace Society, and of the influential paper, "Guardian of Peace." He was awarded the Nobel Peace Prize in 1911.

OTTO WARBURG.—Awarded Nobel Prize for medicine in 1931, for his research on enzymes. His studies of cell physiology were so important that a special institute was built for him in Berlin in 1931.

Humanity at Its Lowest : The Jew-baiter at Work
Young Nazis look on smiling, while elderly Jews are forced to scrub Vienna streets. On the back of this picture the agency circulating it had felt it necessary to print : " Under no circumstances whatsoever may the source from which this picture was obtained, be revealed."

" For Aryans Only." A Sign on a Park Bench
In a Vienna park, where human beings met as equals less than a year ago.

made to crawl the streets.
On the evening of November 10, Goebbels, Reich Minister for Public Enlightenment. said : " The justified and understandable indignation of the German people at the cowardly Jewish assassination has been vented in a wide degree." He ordered violence to cease and promised a " final answer to Jewish assaults " by decrees. Foreign correspondents noted that the pogrom went on all day, and on the next day also.

On November 11, arrests were continued all over Germany. Many Jews, despairing, committed suicide. German

Where the Looters Passed
Clearing up the wreckage of the Kaliski bedding firm in Berlin, after the organised pogrom earlier this month.

One of Many
A synagogue in Berlin fired by Jew-baiters. In this case the caretaker and his family were said to have been burned to death.

BACK TO THE MIDDLE AGES

This Is How It Started

A picture from 1933 after Hitler seized power. Through streets of Nürnberg a young Jew is forced to carry a poster saying, "I seduced a Christian girl."

shops refused to sell food to Jews. Goebbels told foreign correspondents that he sympathised with the people in their desire to protest, denied that there had been looting or that he had organised the pogrom. "Had I done so," he said, "it would have been done more thoroughly." Not a single synagogue, hardly one Jewish shop, remained unwrecked.

On November 12, decrees were announced fining the Jewish community £83,000,000; excluding Jews from all economic activity; banning Jews from all entertainments; ordering Jews to repair and pay for all damage done to their property; declaring that insurance claims from Jews would be confiscated by the State.

On November 14, the collection of fines began. Arrests, it was estimated, totalled 50,000. In the forests round Berlin, picnickers found starving, terrified, Jews. Every foreign consulate was besieged by Jews pleading for visas to emigrate, but there were few who had not had their passports confiscated by the Nazis. Universities were ordered to exclude all Jewish students, and the "Angriff" called for the expulsion of 1,500,000 Jews and half-Jews. On November 15, all Jewish children were expelled from German schools.

Herschel Grynsban had not yet been tried, nor the body of Vom Rath buried.

Hindsight by Tom Hopkinson

On 1 October 1938 Prime Minister Neville Chamberlain arrived back at Heston airport from a meeting with Hitler in Munich. It had been his third visit to the Nazi leader in a fortnight. He carried a sheet of paper which he waved triumphantly to the airport crowds. 'I believe it is peace for our time,' he declared. 'And now I recommend you to go home and sleep quietly in your beds.'

The piece of paper to which such high hopes were pinned was signed by both leaders and affirmed '. . . the desire of our two peoples never to go to war with one another again.

'We are resolved that the method of consultation shall be the method adopted to deal with any other questions that may concern our two countries, and we are determined to continue our efforts to remove possible sources of difference and thus to contribute to assure the peace of Europe.'

To some this document appeared just another trick designed to lull anyone so foolish as to believe it. But to the great majority it implied a willingness on Hitler's part to modify the extremes of Nazi violence and aggression in the interests of European peace. Relief was nation-wide, and the Archbishop of Canterbury described this 'so sudden and unexpected lifting of the burden' as 'an answer to the great volume of prayer which has been rising to God'. The trusting had not to wait long for disillusionment.

One month later, at the beginning of November, 12,000 Polish Jews living in Germany were suddenly arrested and taken by train to the Polish frontier. Poland would not take them in: Germany would not take them back. Among the refugees were the parents of a seventeen-year-old youth living secretly in Paris without a permit. His name was Herschel Grynsban.

On 7 November, in agony and despair, Grynsban went to the German Embassy in Paris and shot an official, Vom Rath, who died two days later. Immediately a gigantic pogrom was unleashed against Jews all over Germany and Austria. Shops and homes were pillaged; synagogues set on fire; 50,000 Jews arrested. So far from condemning the violence, Goebbels – the Nazi Minister for Propaganda and Enlightenment – described it as 'the justified and understandable indignation of the German people'.

Following on the savagery, a flood of anti-Jewish legislation was let loose, which expelled Jews of all ages from the country's economic and social life and placed them in effect outside the protection of the law. Many were murdered. More, it appears, committed suicide.

The effect on thinking people all over Europe was to force them to realize at last that there could be no peace with the Nazi régime, no 'going home and sleeping quietly in our beds', and further that there *ought* to be no peace. But of course not all people are thinking people.

It was in such circumstances that these pages were prepared.

They are propaganda – and propaganda is often taken to be a dirty word. But propaganda is noble or degrading according to the cause it supports, the emotions it appeals to, and the methods it employs. Every organized religion operates through propaganda; it is through propaganda that political and social ideals are spread.

'Back to the Middle Ages' was an attempt to dramatize photographically the monstrous crime which had been – and still was – taking place in the middle of Europe, in the very heart of our Christian civilization. It sought to bring this crime home to readers, and to warn them never to trust to men or to a party which could act like this.

At that time, not two months after the elation of the Munich 'settlement', and ten months yet before war broke out, such a warning was still desperately needed.

THE BOY WHO LOOSED THE STORM

Herschel Grynsban is 17 years old. He is a Polish Jew. His name is funny. It means "Verdigris." It was probably given to his ancestors nearly 200 years ago, when a village official, whose duty it was to allot names to Jews, thought he would have a joke at the expense of a poor Jew. That was Herschel Grynsban's background.

He lived in Paris—in secret, because he had no permit—with an aunt and uncle. At the beginning of November he heard that 12,000 Polish Jews in Germany had suddenly been arrested, marched to trains and taken to the Polish frontier. Poland would not let them in. Germany would not let them back. Diplomatic negotiations began. Meanwhile, four women died of hunger and cold.

Herschel Grynsban's parents were among the refugees. He got a letter from his father describing their suffering.

On November 7th, this 17-year-old boy went to the German Embassy in Paris and shot Vom Rath, the third Counsellor. Vom Rath died. Herschel Grynsban is being held for murder.

He has not yet been tried. Everyone throughout the world condemns his crime. That cannot be excused; and will be punished.

But 50,000 German Jews have been arrested. They have been beaten, tortured, insulted. The Jews have been fined £83,000,000. Their homes, shops, and synagogues have been wrecked; their means of livelihood taken away. Many—it will never be known how many— have been murdered. Some, in terror, have taken their own lives. Many are starving . . . This is Nazi justice in the year 1938.

1939

The tragedy of Munich was a tragedy of miscalculation. Chamberlain hoped — it was never as strong as belief — that he had convinced Hitler of British willingness to accept changes in Europe, as long as they were not brought about by force. Hitler believed that he had bluffed and frightened Chamberlain into surrender. He was under constant pressure from his Foreign Minister, Ribbentrop, who had been convinced by his experiences as ambassador in London that Chamberlain was insincere, and that the British were only waiting to complete their rearmament programme before striking at Germany. Hitler, he urged, must act while Britain was still weak. Ribbentrop was at least partly right.

In March 1939, a sufficient number of dissident Slovaks having been found to furnish the excuse that the rump of the Czechoslovak Republic was breaking up, German troops marched into Prague. Chamberlain had a habit of taking sudden decisions which was described by one of his advisers as like that of a man who huddles under the bedclothes on a frosty morning and counts ten while nerving himself to leap out. In the tense atmosphere following the German invasion of Czechoslovakia, he was persuaded by the *News Chronicle* correspondent in Berlin that an invasion of Poland was imminent. It was as untrue as the information that Hitler was about to invade Czechoslovakia in the previous year; but Chamberlain took one of his desperate leaps out of bed, and on 30 March, with his own hand, wrote an unconditional British guarantee of Poland against any threat to its independence. He also, against his better judgement, agreed to two measures, a limited conscription and an expansion of the Territorial Army, which were militarily useless, since there was insufficient equipment even for the Regular Army, but which convinced Hitler that Ribbentrop was right, and that he had better act quickly while the going was good. He began to put increasing pressure on Poland.

Chamberlain had a profound distrust of Russia, which he believed to be 'stealthily and cunningly pulling all the strings behind the scenes to get us involved in war with Germany'; but he overcame his distrust sufficiently to open negotiations for a joint guarantee by Russia, France and Britain of Poland and other states. The negotiations dragged on throughout the summer, the British and French surrendering point by point to Russian demands, but in the end they were unwilling to pay the price of a free hand for Russia in the Baltic and Eastern Poland. The Germans were more accommodating, and in August a Russo-German pact was signed for which Stalin may have been angling since 1937, and which Hitler believed would call the British bluff over Poland. Instead, three days after the signing of the Russo-

German pact, Britain formally signed the Polish guarantee.

There followed dramatic scurryings behind the scenes, with a Swedish businessman named Dahlerus acting as intermediary in attempts to arrange a visit to Britain by Goering. The German suggestion was that he should land at some deserted aerodrome, be picked up by car and taken directly to see Chamberlain at Chequers, where the staff would have been given leave of absence and the telephone disconnected. There were some raised British eyebrows at this cloak-and-dagger diplomacy, but it was charitably recognized that Nazis could not be expected to behave like English gentlemen, and the suggestion was agreed to. Hitler, however, changed his mind. Mussolini, repeating the tactics of Munich, then stepped in with proposals for a last-minute conference to revise the Treaty of Versailles. The French Foreign Minister, Bonnet, leapt at the idea. Chamberlain was under increasing pressure from the House of Commons,

Low's Comment on the Russo-German Pact. On 23 August 1939, the Russians and the Germans signed a pact to carve up Poland. The famous cartoonist, David Low, rightly foresaw that the partners would before long be at war with one another.

SOMEONE IS TAKING SOMEONE FOR A WALK

his own Cabinet and public opinion, and showed less enthusiasm. In any event the Poles, confident in their British guarantee and the possession of the finest cavalry in Europe, refused to be Munichized. On 1 September, German troops crossed the Polish frontier, the bulk of the Polish air force was destroyed on the ground, and the Polish cavalry picked off from the air like hand-reared pheasants at a Surrey shoot.

After an agonizing delay while the French trembled on the brink, an ultimatum was delivered to Hitler, giving him two hours to announce the unconditional withdrawal of German forces from Poland. The diary of the Foreign Secretary, Lord Halifax, for Sunday morning, 3 September, laconically recorded the last moments of peace: 'I went over to Number 10 at eleven o'clock. Great crowds in Downing Street. At 11.10 still no news. Accordingly the Prime Minister told the Service Departments that they might consider themselves at war.'

The British people had been led to suppose that instant annihilation from the air would follow a declaration of war. In a widely read book published during the Munich crisis, J. B. S. Haldane had forecast that the opening German air attack might kill between fifty and a hundred thousand Londoners. The Committee of Imperial Defence's official estimate was that the opening assault from the air would last for two months, killing 600,000 people and wounding more than a million. Within minutes of Chamberlain's lachrymose broadcast to the nation announcing the declaration of war, air raid sirens sounded, buses and trains stopped, Londoners ran for shelter. It was a false alarm, a fitting prelude to six months of what came to be called the phoney or Great Bore War. Accidents in the blackout, which had been imposed over the entire country, proved more lethal than German bombs.

With the declaration of war there began, sluggishly and clumsily at first, great movements of people which inevitably led to a shake-up in old ideas. By the end of the year, half the families in the country had one or more members on the move. Young men were called up for the Services, workers moved from the depressed areas of Tyneside and South Wales to armament centres like Coventry and Oxford. Above all, there was the evacuation from the big cities of more than a million and a quarter mothers and small children, to preserve them from German bombs.

A tiny proportion of these evacuees came from the slums of London, Liverpool, Glasgow, Birmingham, Manchester, and people who had been intellectually aware for some time of such abstractions as 'problem families' and 'the underprivileged' now found themselves confronted by the reality in their own drawing-rooms.

The Great Evacuation: Three Million Leave the Cities. 31 August 1939. War is imminent. The Ministry of Health orders the evacuation of three million, mostly children, from the cities. They are labelled and given gas-masks in cardboard boxes.

Some of the children were verminous, some had never worn underclothes or eaten a meal from a table. There was a great outcry, at first directed against the evacuees themselves; then a searching of consciences about how such things could be in one of the wealthiest nations in the world. Much of the welcome given by ordinary people of all political parties to welfare legislation during and after the war stemmed from the personal shock of those early evacuation months.

Then in December it began to snow, and went on snowing and freezing for two months. The British people, who had braced themselves to face annihilation from the air, found it almost more difficult to endure the petty miseries of the blackout, verminous evacuees, burst pipes and fireless grates.

Laurence Thompson

Picture Post, January 14, 1939

LESLIE HENSON REVIEWS THE SITUATION, AND

The General Outlook

"The situation as I see it is such that every effort should be made, by all who have any kind of interest at heart or elsewhere, to secure the evolution of those fructifying forces which tend to exercise a beneficent rather than a retrograde influence on the progress of events."

Foreign Affairs

"Casting our eyes abroad, what do we see, if indeed we can be said to see anything at all, and not rather to be gazing with horrifying uncertainty at a maelstrom of conflicting impulses tending towards an ever-more-possible—if not absolutely inevitable—dissolution."

Finance

"I foresee a difficult time for financial experts. There is little money in the money-market, and people tend more and more to take out what little there is."

Sport

"In sport, 1939 will be a remarkable year, filled with a number of spectacular successes. It is hard to foresee at this early date exactly by whom the successes will be won."

Love

"I am happy to be able to report a most beneficent confluence of congenialities for those in love. They will remain in love—not, in all cases, with the same partners."

FORECASTS THE COURSE OF EVENTS IN 1939

Home Affairs

"Turn rather to events at home. Here we are fortunate in the possession of a multitude of prophets, able to forecast from the increasing number of bicycle sprockets employed by the crofters of the Western Isles, an ever-growing demand for more of everything, everywhere."

Personal Affairs

"And so in a cloud of uncertainty the year goes out. Fortunately, in our private lives we are on firmer ground. We can be sure that we shall be genial, large-hearted and progressive—and that everyone with whom we come in contact will be mean, narrow-minded and depraved."

The Open Air

"Open the air of Britain has always been. Open it will remain during the ensuing twelve months. In some quarters it will be, if anything, more open than before."

Disarmament

"It will be illegal to carry a revolver or a life-preserver. But to carry a rifle may at any time become compulsory, particularly in the civilised countries."

. . . For The Future

"1939 will be succeeded at a rapidly-decreasing interval by 1940, the first year of a new decade—which in turn will give way to a further twelve-month period, 1941."

Hindsight by Tom Driberg

People new to politics, and not old enough to remember the pre-war years, sometimes wonder why many older people still seem obsessed by the memory of those years. Sidney Jacobson's harrowing article supplies the answer. Harking back can become boring: it would be much more boring if, by some mischance or miscalculation, anything like the conditions in which Alfred Smith and his family existed were to occur again.

Mass unemployment was the greatest domestic disaster and disgrace of those shabby years — as shameful a blot on the record of a rich nation and its Conservative governments (one of them miscalled 'National') as the betrayal of Czechoslovakia and the appeasement of Hitler were on their record in international affairs.

All who are now more than forty or fifty years old must have some painful memories of the impact of those conditions on decent individuals like Alfred Smith. The worst distress that I encountered was in South Wales. In March 1939, visiting that deeply depressed mining area as a newspaper columnist, I called at a house in a drab terrace in Porth. It was 2 p.m. – after dinner-time – but neither Dai Davies nor his wife Gwyneth had eaten any dinner that day. 'You've come on the hardest day,' she said. On the following day he would draw his weekly 45s. from the Public Assistance. (But she had managed a dish of faggots and peas for their seven children: this had contained two faggots – 5½ oz. of diluted mincemeat; it had cost 6d.)

Mrs Davies was house-proud: the larder's empty shelves were clean. She was proud, too, of the eldest child, a boy of fourteen doing well at the County School. But he wasn't going there just then: his mother was 'trying to patch him together'. She said: 'They dress so nice up there. It do break your heart when you can't buy them those expensive clothes. . .'

Dai Davies was thirty-nine. He had once been a strong young boxer. Now he was nearly finished — out of work for seven years on end, coughing his lungs out with silicosis. ('Take it easy . . .' the doctor had said. 'Plenty of good food.') When he lost his job down the pit, in 1932, his silicosis had only been 'suspected'. An Act passed in 1934 made it impossible for him to claim compensation more than three years after ceasing work.

Yet the coal-owners were trying to negotiate a cut in miners' pay – the lowest pay then being 50s. 6d. for a six-day week, with no guarantee of regular work.

The tragedy of the Smith and Davies families was repeated nearly two million times in the Britain of 1939. It is unlikely, but not impossible, that the tragedy should be repeated. Unemployment is still too high in the north-east, in Lancashire, in Ulster. An apprehensive harking back is not unnatural.

But such families were, by a terrible irony, lucky a few months later: the Second World War broke out and, as Professor Asa Briggs has said, 'Warfare necessitated welfare.' War meant full employment, more care for the potentially useful disabled, fairer distribution of food through rationing (plus cheap meals in British Restaurants); then Beveridge and the development of social security (drastically amended and improved since 1964).

Even if unemployment were to grow again, there are now far better provisions for cushioning its effects on family life. If we assume that Alfred Smith would, in September 1969, have been earning £20 a week when in work, he would now, if unemployed, be receiving something like £16 16s. 4d. a week in benefits.

This figure is made up as follows:

Basic benefit for husband: £4 10s.
Basic benefit for wife: £2 16s.
Basic benefits for his four children: £1 8s., 10s., 8s., and 8s.
Family allowances: £2 8s.
Earnings-related benefit: £3 13s. 4d.
Rent (the maximum allowed as supplementary benefit for this purpose): 15s.

Alfred Smith would also nowadays have a set of N.H.S. teeth; and, despite the charges imposed, since these are recoverable, they would have cost him nothing.

Of course there has been a steep change in the value of money – the cost of living – in thirty years: but this still represents a big improvement, in real terms, on the 1939 situation.

Is it *too* big, as is alleged by some – often by people who have always enjoyed a different, more private, and much more comfortable kind of social security? As they, rightly, also say: 'It's all got to be paid for.' It *is* paid for, in varying proportions – through taxation, through contributions – by all of us, *including those who now and then have to draw benefits*.

It seems, therefore, an appropriate way of showing that, in a civilized society, we are all members one of another.

PICTURE POST

Vol. 2. No. 3.   **January 21, 1939**

Before the Labour Exchange : One of 1,830,000 Workless
There are over 1,830,000 Unemployed in Great Britain. From a group outside Peckham Labour Exchange we picked out one, Alfred Smith (X)
and followed him with the camera.   On the following pages is the story of his daily routine.

UNEMPLOYED!

**Britain is a rich country.   But at the beginning of this year, it had 1,831,372 registered unemployed, and
many more not registered.   This was 3,269 more than in November, 1938, 165,965 more than a year ago.
In two years, the figures have risen by 207,770.   Is this volume of unemployment necessary?**

ALFRED SMITH lives at 52, Leo Street, Peckham.   He is a little man, thin, but wiry, with the pale face and bright eyes of a real Londoner. He wears a cloth cap and white muffler, old brown jacket and corduroy trousers. He talks animatedly, likes a joke, walks with his hands in his pockets, shoulders bent, head slightly forward.   And he looks down as he walks—the typical walk of an unemployed man.

His face is lined, and his cheeks are sunken, because he has no teeth. He is only 35 years old.

He has a wife and four children.

He has not had a regular job for three years.

When Alfred Smith married 12 years ago, he was a skilled workman, a spray enamel maker, earning good wages. Things went well with him for nine years. But then the chemicals used in this work made his teeth rot, so that they had to be

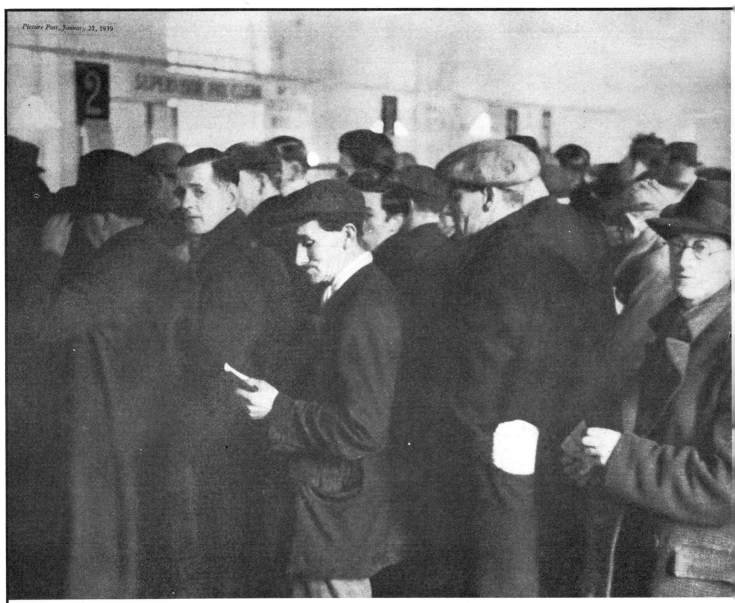

THE LINE MOVES FORWARD SLOWLY AT THE LABOUR EXCHANGE
There has been a frost, and many more men have been thrown out of work. The unemployed have to wait about half an hour before they draw their pay. While they wait, they chat quietly about jobs—jobs they have held, jobs they have missed, jobs they hope to get. They all want work, but many of them have been " out " for years.

2 *Inside : The Husband Queues Up*
Alfred Smith, an unemployed man, is standing in the queue to draw his unemployment pay. He has stood there nearly 150 times since he last had regular work.

extracted. He fell ill, was away from work for five weeks, and lost his job. He has not had a regular job since.

Before he lost his job, Smith had ordered artificial teeth and paid 15s. towards their cost. He has never been able to get them finished. That is why his cheeks are sunken.

In the days when he was doing well, Smith and his wife believed in large families. They have had seven children. Three died. Those living are Frances, aged 9; Edna 8; Peter 4½ and John, 3½. So, with the parents, there are six in the family.

Smith gets altogether £2 7s. 6d. a week, and is thus better off than many. That is because the doctor has granted him relief of 4s. a week because of his children. Frances, aged 9, suffers severely from rheumatism because her home is damp. Peter and John are ailing; and Smith gets 4s. a week extra for them.

His unemployment pay is made up of :

	£	s.	d.
Standard benefit	1	19	0
Supplementary grant		4	6
Doctors' relief		4	0

Every 156 days, he has to go before the Unemployment Assistance Board, where his benefit and grant is reviewed.

Smith goes to the local Employment Exchange three times a week, Monday, Wednesday and Friday. Friday is the big day, when he draws his pay. Then Mrs. Smith

4 *Outside: Wife and Children Wait*
On the other side of the road, holding the shopping basket, wait his wife and children. They must wait for him. All last week's money was spent two days ago.

goes with him, and he hands over the money to her, keeping a shilling or so for fares, cigarettes, newspapers for a week.

The rest of the money, roughly, goes on:

			s.	d.
Rent	..	..	14	6
Clothes Clubs	..	..	6	0
Insurance	..	..	1	8
Coal Club	..	..	2	0
Coke	..	..	1	0
Lighting and fittings	..	3	0
Bread	..	..	6	0
Other Food	..	..	16	0
			50	2

This leaves a debit of about 4s. a week. The Smiths say they can only live by getting into debt. When some unbudgeted expenditure—shoes, blankets, etc.—arises, it can only be met by cutting down on food, or heat, or light.

The children get some milk free—two pints a day for the youngest children, half a pint each for the elder under the London County Council's scheme.

Smith, his wife and the four children, spend much of their lives in the basement of a tenement house in Leo Street, Peckham. Their home, on paper, consists of three rooms and a kitchen; in fact, two rooms on the ground floor are one medium-sized room, about 12 yards long by 5 yards wide, divided into two by a

5 **ALFRED SMITH TELLS THE CLERK: "NO WORK"**
He has had no regular work for three years and he comes to the Labour Exchange three times a week. He signs on, gets two tickets signed, draws his unemployment benefit. Before he leaves the Exchange, he carefully studies the list of vacant posts in the hall. Will there be a chance for him to-day? Will his luck change?

6 *The Exchange Has Given Him His Money: He Hands It Over to His Wife . . .*
Alfred Smith draws £2 7s. 6d. a week. 4s. a week is extra, which he gets because his two youngest children are ailing. He gives all the money
to his wife to pay rent, clothes club, insurance, housekeeping. She gives him back a shilling for cigarettes, newspapers, fares.

8 *Where the Unemployed Can Afford to Buy*
At the street stall, Alfred Smith's wife looks for cheap oddments—a pair of stockings for Frances,
some shoes for Peter, a scarf for Edna.

partition. One part is entirely filled by a bed. The other is bare: the furniture has been sold.

In the basement, there is a small kitchen, largely filled by stove and sink. The living room, about five yards wide by five long, has one window, of which more than half is below ground level. Only a little light filters in. That is why the Smiths' pay so much for lighting; in winter, they need artificial light all day. Here they eat, sit, talk and some of them sleep, because it is the warmest room. At the back of the house, there is a small, unspeakably grim yard. Not a blade of grass grows there. That is their "garden."

For this accommodation, Smith pays 14s. 6d. a week rent, about 30 per cent. of his total income. He has frequently applied to the Council for a house, but under the law these six people living in two rooms are not overcrowded until one girl and one boy reach the age of ten. Until then, they must carry on in their present home. And, so far as hard work and kindness and scrupulous cleanliness can make it, it *is* home. Like tens of thousands of other wives, Mrs. Smith has kept it so.

She is a good "manager," she buys carefully in the cheapest market and she makes the money go a long way. This is a typical day's food in the family of a man without work:

Breakfast: Tea, bread and margarine. A bit of bacon on Sundays is a rare luxury.

Dinner: Stew, or boiled fish, potatoes, bread, tea. Sunday dinner, cheap broken meat, potatoes.

Afternoon: Tea.

Night: Cocoa, bread and margarine.

Very occasionally, they have fresh fruit or greens. The doctor ordered the youngest children to have

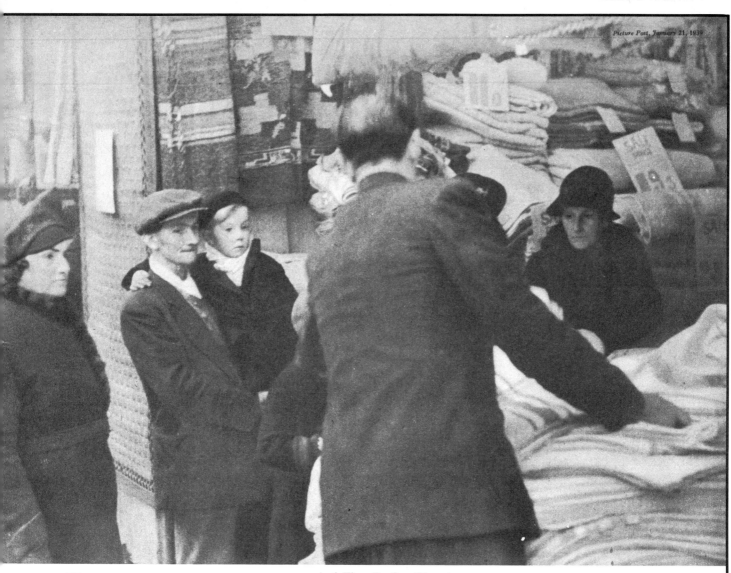

7 . . . *And They Go Out Shopping*
It is a nice blanket and they need one for the children's bed now that it has turned so cold again. But they can't afford to buy it here. They must do their shopping round the corner, at street stalls, where things are cheaper.

"plenty of fruit and vegetables." But fruit and vegetables, however healthy, appease hunger less than bread and margarine or stew. Malnutrition, rather than actual under-feeding, is the biggest danger to the children of the unemployed.

How does a man, with time to spare and no money to spend, pass his days?

"The waiting about is the worst part of being out of work," says Smith. "I begin by waiting outside the Labour Exchange, then I wait to apply for jobs, I wait to speak to foremen, I'm waiting all the time. Waiting for something to happen, something to do, somebody to talk to."

He does not get up particularly early on a Friday, because until he has been to the Employment Exchange there is nothing much he can do. It is warmer in bed, and he takes up less space. When he does get up, he has breakfast, helps with the children, then goes to the local Employment Exchange.

There, outside a low, grey building, groups of men, nearly all wearing cloth caps and mufflers, are waiting for the doors to open. They know one another—they meet three times a week. Some of the unlucky ones have been coming here for years.

All the talk is of work—jobs heard of, jobs applied for, jobs not secured. "Walked all the way to Houndsditch, but, when I got there the foreman said there was some mistake, there wasn't a job going at all." . . . "So I said to 'im, you can't call 'elping to put the kids to bed domestic service, can yer?" . . . "Going to take me on as 'is assistant, 'e was, but the super, says no, I only 'ad a general labourer's ticket, that wasn't good enough for 'im." . . . "Blooming 'itler,' e was."

The doors open at 9.15, and the men queue up

9 *But This Doesn't Cost Anything At All*
Schools are closed for Christmas holidays, so the Smith children come out too. They are on the left of the picture—Edna, Frances, Peter and John.

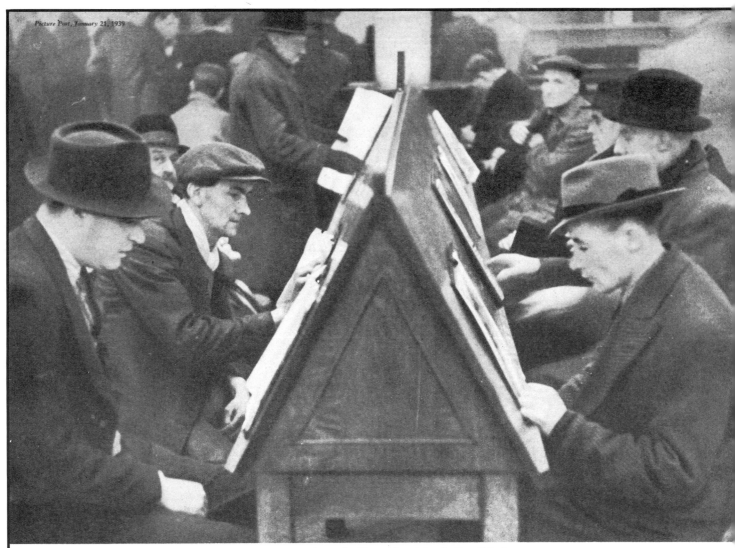

10   *Where the Unemployed Look For Work*

While his wife finishes the shopping, Alfred Smith sets out again to look for a job. He stops at the Public Library, where he reads through the columns of small advertisements in the newspapers, notes the addresses of possible openings.

quietly and file into the large, dim hall. They make very little noise, most of them are used to the routine. But a frost has brought out many more than usual, especially in the building trade. The hall is full and the clerks look a little rushed and harassed.

They are brusque but not at all un-friendly to the unemployed.

When Smith reaches the grille, he says: "No work" to the clerk. The clerk knows Smith has had no work and Smith knows the clerk knows, but he has to say it. If he forgets,

the clerk tells him : "Say 'no work'." That is the regulation, and the unemployed are ruled by regulations. But the clerk likes Smith because he says "Good morning, no work," quite brightly.

Smith signs on, signs two tickets

for his benefit, takes them to two entering clerks, then goes to the pay clerk and draws his money. All this, from the time the doors open, takes about half an hour.

Next, he studies the classified list of vacancies on the notice-board.

11   HE TURNS OVER ONE PAPER AFTER ANOTHER
Once he was a skilled workman, earning good pay. His last temporary job was digging trenches during the crisis

12   HE MUST BE SURE NOT TO MISS A CHANCE
He is classified as a painter's labourer. But he is ready to do anything, to go anywhere—for work.

16

13 *The Picture Of Our Time: Alone, Walking for Miles, Trying to Find a Job*
He is 35. He has strength, intelligence, humour. He has a wife and children whom he loves. He should be in the prime of his life. But he is unemployed. He lives on the charity of the State, which cannot find him work. But he wants to work, to be a man, not a number on a Ministry of Labour card. He is one of nearly 2,000,000.

Outside, Mrs. Smith is waiting; if it is holiday time, she must bring the four children with her, because they are not old enough yet to be left at home by themselves.

Mrs. Smith goes shopping. Smith goes to try for jobs he has heard of, or read of at the Exchange. He stops on the way at the Public Library to look through the newspapers. He reads the news as well as the advertisements, but it is surprising, he says, the number of men out of work who only go to the library to look at the illustrated society weeklies.

Like all other able-bodied unemployed, Smith covers big distances looking for work. Once he walked from his home in Peckham to Edmonton, in North London, because he heard there was a job going there. It took him from early morning to midnight; there was no job.

If he is not too far off by then, Smith goes home for his midday meal, then goes out again looking for work. When he has tried at all the places advertised, he drops in at factories, warehouses, workshops, on the chance of picking up a job. But when these

close, he knows another day's quest is over. He goes home to help his wife—who has been ill, and is not strong—does some cleaning up, potters about, goes into the street to talk to friends, plays with his children. And so his days pass, slowly.

Smith does not whine: but he feels he has some just complaints. Long ago, he gave up the exclusiveness of a skilled worker. Now, he is classified as a painter's labourer. He has lost, too, the mute feeling of bewilderment and helplessness that came on him when he first lost his job, saw his

14 **HE ASKS FOR A JOB**
The foreman is sympathetic, but there is nothing doing. He does not need any more men.

15 *After a Whole Day Looking for a Job, Alfred Smith Comes Home*
From their basement room, his wife asks the inevitable question. For three years, he has had to answer "No." Quietly, she tells him dinner is ready, hands him the front-door key.

DOES IT SURPRISE YOU THAT UNEMPLOYED DO THIS IN DESPERATION?

THEY AGITATE FOR WINTER RELIEF

18 Unemployed chain themselves to railings of house of Mr. Ernest Brown, Minister for Labour. Later they brought a coffin to Mr. Chamberlain's home.

Out-of-work demonstrators stop traffic by lying down in Oxford Circus, covering themselves with posters. Another day they went into the Ritz. Asked for tea.

16 This Is His Home

*They sit down to the chief meal of the day—
boiled fish, dry bread, tea. This is their
largest room. Besides this, they have two half-
rooms, and a kitchen. They pay 14s. 6d. a week rent.*

savings melt away, became dependent on the dole
and the kindness of officials. He has become interested in politics, and has learned to express himself.

There were, he says 1,831,372 insured persons
out of work in December. There are many more
who are not included in this figure because they
are not registered. Yet this is said to be a
wealthy country, and there is no trade depression.
He feels that, even admitting some unemployment
is unavoidable under present conditions, there are
far too many being kept out of work by red
tape, lack of vision and apathy.

One of the strongest complaints he has to make
is over-classification. He, himself, is now classified
as painter's labourer, and this has prevented him
from getting jobs as a general labourer.

"My last bit of work," says Smith, "was digging
A.R.P. trenches during the crisis. But when
there isn't a crisis on, I can't get a job digging."

He is strong and alert. He has kept his spirit
through three long years of disappointment. But
he is beginning to feel that perhaps there is no
longer a place for him in our scheme of things,
that he must change it or perish. He wants work,
he cannot find it. And Alfred Smith is only one
of two million.   SIDNEY JACOBSON

*This is the story of unemployment from the
point of view of the man without a job. In
one of our next issues, we shall show what
the Government does to help the unemployed.*

17 His Relaxation: Digging the Yard Where Nothing Grows

*The day is nearly over. It is too late to go out again to look for a job. He can only wait for to-morrow,
try to make the time pass a little less slowly by digging up his back yard.*

SCOTLAND
AND HOME RULE
by
COMPTON MACKENZIE

Ever since the Union there have been Scots who wanted self-government. To-day the Scottish Nationalists command increasing support, and have already achieved some success. Final test of the party will probably come next September, when the nation-wide Scottish Convention gathers in Glasgow.

LET nobody suppose that self-government for Scotland is a novelty of political hopes. As long ago as 1745, thirty-two years after the Union, it was the most powerful Jacobite argument used. It was again to the fore at the close of the 18th century, when it was linked up with Irish aspirations. It was to the fore when Chartism was prevalent, and at the beginning of the 19th century self-government for Scotland was as much linked up with Left tendencies as to-day, to so many people in Scotland, it again seems linked up with Left tendencies.

In 1894 Lord Rosebery, a Scots Prime Minister in favour of Home Rule, told an Edinburgh audience that he, as a Minister, would not be standing to oppose Scotland in the breach, and that, if he was not a Minister, as a man he should hope to be in the storming party. Brave words, but nothing came of them. Some years ago

Scotland Lifts up her Voice
Few Englishmen have heard much of the discussion on Home Rule for Scotland—but a plea for it covers almost every bridge on the Edinburgh-Glasgow road.

the late Lord Strathcarron was chaffing me about Scottish Nationalism and telling me that he had been in favour of Home Rule when I was an infant in arms. "That is just what we Nationalists complain of," I retorted. "We are tired of sentimental resolutions in the House of Commons over a period of forty years."

Prior to the Great War, Home Rule was fostered by the Young Liberals, but with the collapse of the Liberal Party after the War the movement for Home Rule was dispersed among diverse comparatively small associations.

Cunninghame Graham, Ruairidh Erskine of Marr, C. M. Grieve, Lewis Spence, T. Gibson, Angus Clark, and last but by no means least that single-hearted patriot, R. E. Muirhead—these are some of the names which one day a self-governing Scotland will cherish.

In 1927 John MacCormick, a student of Glasgow University, resigned from the Labour Club and formed, with the help

Where Scotland's Own Parliament May One Day Meet
Donaldson's School, Edinburgh, is suggested by many Scottish Nationalists as a possible Parliament House for a future Scottish Parliament. The building—"Scotland's Escorial"—was built in 1841 by James Donaldson of the "Edinburgh Advertiser" as a school for deaf and dumb children. It took nine years to build and its walls are ten feet thick. Queen Victoria is said to have coveted the school as a residence.

Leaders of the Scottish Nationalists in Conference: "Government from London is Unworkable"

A meeting in Glasgow of leading members of the Scottish Nationalist Party to plan the big convention from all over Scotland which takes place in September. The present campaign is for "a reasonable measure of independence," including the re-establishment of Scotland's Parliament in Edinburgh. Left to right are Robert MacLaurin, W. J. Clark, Glasgow University; John McCrindle; Sandy Milne and Robert Brittain of the youth movement; J. Alasdair Clark, finance convenor of the Scottish National Party; Rev. T. M. Murchison; J. L. Kinloch. Back to camera is Robert Gray, chairman of the Committee.

of one or two other ardent spirits, the Glasgow University Scottish Nationalist Association. Soon afterwards, on his initiative, all the various small bodies advocating Home Rule accepted, some a little more, others a little less than what they severally stood for, in order to merge themselves in the National Party of Scotland.

Whether compromise is a sound basis on .which to build a drastic reform was doubted by many at the time and is doubted by many to-day. It is significant that since the demise of *The Scots Independent* no paper of even faintly comparable merit and force has been inspired by the series of compromises which has marked Scottish Nationalism during the last decade.

Nevertheless, there *was* a grand spirit of enthusiasm abroad, and an opportunity was given to test the new Party when Cunninghame Graham was nominated as Scottish Nationalist candidate for the Glasgow University Rectorial Election of 1928.

I shall never forget the amazement of the country when Mr. Stanley Baldwin puffed home only 66 votes ahead of Cunninghame Graham, who had knocked down Mr. Herbert Samuel and Mr. Arthur Henderson in his pursuit of Mr. Baldwin.

I was with the old warrior in the Caledonian Hotel in Edinburgh when the result came through. "Thank God, I shan't have to compose a Rectorial Address," he said. "And this is as good as a victory."

62-year-old James McCrindle States the Case

" God knows we need Home Rule! It couldna be done worse here than it is being done frae London. We don't want to separate ourselves from the English people, but we want a true federation. After all, Westminster is already overburdened with business. Why can't we be allowed to look after our own affairs? It would help England too."

SCOTTISH NATIONALIST LEADERS : *Robert Gray*
Chairman of the Committee which met recently to outline a comprehensive plan for the reconstruction of Scotland, and one of the leading members of the Scottish National Party, through which, during the past six months, the Nationalist movement has gained much ground in Scotland.

J. M. MacCormick, Party Secretary
"I first became interested in Scottish Nationalism when my mother told me how, as a schoolgirl, she was forced to wear a wooden board round her neck for not learning English fast enough." As a 22-year-old student, Mr. MacCormick founded the University Nationalist Association in 1928.

Three years later I was nominated as the Scottish Nationalist candidate for the next Rectorial, and elected over the heads of Sir Robert Horne, Professor Gilbert Murray, Mr. Tom Johnston and Sir Oswald Mosley.

Meanwhile, various constituencies had been fought with a steady increase in the Nationalist polling, the most successful being Oliver Brown in East Renfrewshire, and John MacCormick in Inverness-shire.

Yet, though deposits were being saved, seats were not being won, and in 1932 the Duke of Montrose, Sir Alexander MacEwen and Professor

Ewen G. Traill
Former president and one of the leaders of the Nationalist Association in Glasgow University, recently ordained as a Minister in the Church of Scotland.

Miss Pearl Cook
One of the earliest members of the Scottish National Party; a fluent speaker and able propagandist. Secretary to the organiser of the Glasgow Juvenile Instruction Centres.

Dr. John Macdonald
One of the most active members of the party, and for several years its South-Western area organiser. An eloquent speaker and hard-working organiser.

James Miller, of the Party Youth Movement
"Government from London condemns Scotland to economic dislocation. We want the establishment of a Scottish Parliament elected by the Scottish people. After all, only 14 hours are devoted to purely Scottish affairs in the English Parliament each year."

Robert MacLaurin, Scientist
A famous Scottish inventor of low-temperature carbonisation processes for the manufacture of smokeless fuel, oil and gas. "Scotland should reap the benefit," the Party claims, "of Scottish intellect and ability." At present most of it is drained away to the South.

Dewar Gibb formed a new Home Rule Party, somewhat timorous perhaps in its policy, which was presumably designed to calm the nerves of those who wanted some form of local Home Rule, but were afraid of some of the extremists of the National Party.

In the end, by another compromise, the two parties were merged in the present Scottish National Party, which aims in effect at the same kind of Home Rule for Scotland as obtains in Northern Ireland.

During the last seven years the Scottish National Party has worked hard to create an opinion in favour

Aitken Ferguson
A well-known Scottish Communist. The Nationalist movement in Scotland is linked to a considerable extent with left-wing politics, as it was a hundred years ago

John McCrindle
A Clyde fisherman who left school at 11, he has become a well-known scientist and author, and a much-quoted authority on ornithology, horticulture and archaeology.

J. L. Kinloch
Leader of the Clan Scotland Youth Movement, which he founded five years ago. It is non-party; aims at the political education of Scottish youth.

The Scotland the Nationalists Dream Of
The River Doon in Alloway. Here natural beauty and history meet. One of the most beautiful spots in Ayrshire, it is not far from the cottage in which Robert Burns was born, and the famous Brig o' Doon, scene of his poem "Tam o' Shanter," is only a few yards away.

of Home Rule, and undoubtedly the fact that to-day all the Scottish Departments function from Edinburgh instead of from London is due to their influence and devoted work.

At this point let me affirm as emphatically as I can that if Scotland is without Home Rule to-day the Scots themselves are to be blamed for it, *not* the English.

It is our own fault if basic industries like coal, iron and steel, ship-building, and textiles have steadily declined ever since the war.

It is our own fault if unemployment is relatively much higher in Scotland than in England.

It is our own fault if the population of the Highlands is decreasing so fast that, at the present rate, within a century the Highlands will be literally a desert.

The Robert Burns Cottage in Alloway
For his love of country and his strong democratic opinions, fearlessly expressed, Burns is the idol of Scottish Nationalists. He was a fervent and open supporter of the French Revolution.

Inside the Boyhood Home of Burns
A reverent pilgrimage is made every year by thousands to see this cottage and its simple furniture.

The Scotland the Nationalists Have to Deal With
Knightswood, largest housing scheme in the country, alongside which runs the Forth and Clyde Canal. One of the Nationalists' demands is for a Mid-Scotland ship canal to allow vessels from the Baltic and North Sea a through passage to Glasgow. This, they claim, would be of incalculable value to Scottish trade.

It is our own fault that we have allowed our fishing to be practically destroyed. It is our own fault, because we are content with the Parliament at Westminster, in which—if every one of the seventy-four Scottish Members voted as one—they could make no impression on the overwhelming majority of non-Scottish Members.

So long as that state of affairs continues, so long must Scotland gradually decline.

The final test of what the Scottish National Party can accomplish may come next September, when a nation-wide Scottish Convention will be held in Glasgow to adopt a comprehensive programme of reconstruction. In the words of Mr. MacCormick, the Hon. Secretary of the Party, here are some of the reforms which will be

Scotland's Heavy Industry
Colville's famous Clydebridge works, from which came all the plates for the "Queen Mary" and "Queen Elizabeth."

Where the Largest Liner in the World is Being Built
The "Queen Elizabeth" being completed at Clydebank. Scotland is one of the most highly-developed industrial countries in the world. In many parts, however, it is one of the poorest.

SCOTLAND'S PAST : *On the Walls of Stirling Castle*

Stirling shares with Ayr the honour of being a pilgrimage centre for the Scottish people. In 1296 Edward I of England led his army into Scotland, took the town of Berwick, and massacred many of the citizens. After a triumphal march he returned home. Within a year a popular rising under Sir William Wallace regained the independence of Scotland for the time being, by winning the battle of Stirling Bridge.

The Wallace Memorial in Stirling

For a short period Wallace governed Scotland, but in 1298, deserted by some of the nobles who had supported him, he was defeated by Edward I at Falkirk. In 1305 Wallace was captured, taken to Westminster, and condemned to death. His head was displayed in London, and the four quarters of his body at different points in Scotland. His example, however, inspired the victory of Robert the Bruce who, in 1314, defeated the English at Bannockburn.

Scotland's Most Famous Street
Princes Street, Edinburgh. On right is the Scott Memorial.

put before the Convention :

"New bridges and piers; a revival of the coastal shipping fleet; a new fishing fleet; towns entirely rebuilt; thousands upon thousands of new houses; the development of light industries; nationalisation of railways on a Scottish basis; national responsibility for all main roads; nationalisation of essential steamer services; introduction of uniform freight rates; a large scheme of railway electrification; the construction of Forth and Tay Road bridges; and a mid-Scotland ship canal."

To these, one supposes, will be added an intelligent and really vigorous effort to solve the problems of the Highlands and Islands.

If such a Convention can offer a programme which will at once capture the imagination and appeal to the common sense of the Scottish people, the Scottish people will vote themselves a Parliament to put that programme into operation.

Two years ago I made a vow not to speak or write again about Scottish Nationalism until the soul of a resolute nation was visible through a fog of committees. I break that silence now, because once again I fancy I hear the wind stirring in the pines and the birches and the heather.

Let us pray that war will not be the instrument to restore to Scotland what little is left of her national life at the end of such a catastrophe.

May the National Convention not only speak ! May it act before it is too late !

Looking Out Over Scotland's Capital
Edinburgh from the King's Bastion of the Castle. The gun is what citizens used to call "the great iron murderer, Muckle Meg," reputed to be the second most ancient cannon in Europe.

These Once Were Scotland's Own Crown Jewels
In the Crown Room of Edinburgh Castle, the Scottish Crown Jewels and the crown worn by Robert the Bruce, the James's, and Mary Queen of Scots were discovered by Sir Walter Scott after they had been lost for 100 years.

Hindsight by Fyfe Robertson

If Compton Mackenzie could have looked ten years ahead I doubt if he would have broken his vow of silence about Scottish nationalism. The Convention he looked forward to – with, it now seems, incredible naïvety – as 'the final test of what the Scottish National Party can do' never met; war intervened. And already, six years before he wrote, the twin Scots curses of caution and schism had begun again to erode the passion of the ardent and alienate the poets and writers whose dream of a cultural renaissance had inspired and popularized nationalism.

The man who started the compromising process of base-widening that ended with the political fatuity of the National Covenant of 1949 was the man who as a student had founded the old National Party – Glasgow lawyer John MacCormick, a stubborn gradualist who in 1933 purged his independence extremists so that he could form – in alliance with the Tory-born Scottish Party – the new Scottish National Party, with the aim not of independence but Home Rule within the Commonwealth – and no truck with the poets.

The new party did worse at the 1935 General Election, and three years after Compton Mackenzie wrote with – surely – forced optimism, the party split again. Douglas Young, poet, writer, and Greek scholar, was elected chairman, and MacCormick and his followers broke away to form the Scottish Union, later renamed the Scottish Convention. The biggest unit in the nationalist movement had split roughly on the issue that still divides nationalist sympathizers – independence v. Home Rule.

MacCormick and his Home Ruling Convention enjoyed a last blaze of popularity. Two million people signed the 1949 Covenant. In terms of practical politics it was a useless demonstration, but it was a propaganda headline-maker. Home Rule was at last widely popular.

But it was the party of independence, the S.N.P., a very different party now, that made the real running and emerged in the fifties as a political force significant enough to shake the three traditional parties. The new leader, Dr Robert McIntyre, who in 1945 became – briefly – the first Nationalist M.P., remoulded the party. Culture got not a back seat, as in the Convention, but no seat at all, and the general policies were aimed at the little man – economic freedom, a property-owning democracy, protection against the State and the big combines, land reform, education to be geared to economic needs. McIntyre denies the reality of the struggle between Socialism and private enterprise. His emphasis is on disciplined, organized work at the grass roots, among the uncommitted and in particular in local government.

It would be naïve to suppose that the steady and latterly rapid success of the S.N.P. is due to its policies. Widespread anxiety about the future, with unemployment at twice the national average, emigration rising, and new industries lagging behind the rapid contraction of the old, political frustration at the unwillingness or inability of Westminster to legislate in time or at all for special Scottish needs and problems, rosy Tory and Labour promises but little performance, a basic and wide disillusion with the old parties – these are the realities behind the surge of popular support for the S.N.P.

Even the Home Ruling Liberals have lost support, but the chief sufferer has been Labour. In England, disillusion with Mr Wilson's Government has benefited the Tories; in Scotland the S.N.P. And Mrs Ewing's spectacular Hamilton by-election victory in 1967, a huge surprise south of the Border, was not so surprising to Scots who had studied the steady growth in the S.N.P. poll in successive general elections. Labour's biggest defeat was in the municipal elections in May 1968, when S.N.P. candidates gained 103 seats and lost two. Labour gained four and lost 88.

This, and Hamilton, shook Liberals and Tories into new approaches. But neither the piecemeal devolution proposed by Liberal M.P. David Steel, nor Mr Heath's suggestion of an experimental Scottish Legislative Assembly and more devolution, cut much ice with S.N.P. sympathizers dreaming of independence and still bathed in Hamilton euphoria. Only Labour, sure that an independent Scotland would lose economically, and that coming prosperity would end 'the absurdity' of nationalism, remained officially unmoved.

S.N.P. support is from the middle, which explains why Tories call it Left (it is in fact gently so) and Labour sneers at 'tartan Tories'. It is widely based, and it is – dismayingly for Labour – strong among younger voters and among skilled trade unionists.

A 1968 survey in Dundee, where no S.N.P. candidate stood at the General Election, showed among voters between 21 and 44 that 21·5 per cent intended to vote Labour, 29 per cent Tory, and 34 per cent S.N.P. The same survey showed that though the S.N.P. had weak support among professional and managerial voters (17 per cent against the Tories' 67·5) it had more than Labour at 8 per cent. And more significantly, remembering the proportions in the electorate, the S.N.P. with 29·5 per cent got more support among skilled manual workers than Labour (27.5 per cent). The Scottish T.U.C. and the Scottish Labour Party have veered historically from outright support for nationalism to outright opposition. Today only the hard-hit Scottish Miners want self-government, but the S.N.P. is clearly strong among trade unionists generally.

The party's emphasis on economic nationalism is a welcome change from the backward-looking nostalgia of earlier days. However, unsolvable economic argument is a poor substitute for fire in the belly, and present ills make a less certain emotional base than a genuine belief that only independence can generate a national dynamic that could halt emigration, revive the Highlands, canalize native skills and enterprise and idealism, and build a truly balanced economy.

There is much of that genuine belief, and this year's General Election should show if there is enough of it to off-set Scottish caution, and change sufficiently the traditional class-based voting pattern. If world conditions and Wilsonian belt-tightening bring economic revival in time, I would not bet on a landslide to the S.N.P. But if national economic stagnation continues, with no easing of taxation and still more State control, Labour could meet Scottish disaster.

Compton Mackenzie fancied he 'heard the wind stirring in the pines and the birches and the heather'. Today's Nationalist wind whistles in the mines and the factories and the housing estates of industrial Scotland. And they can hear it, now, in Westminster.

The Man Who Loosed The Storm on Europe

At ten o'clock on the morning of Friday, September 1, 1939, Hitler addresses the Reichstag. In the President's chair sits Goering. "Since a quarter to six this morning," Hitler declares, "We are fighting back. From now on, bomb will be answered by bomb." This statement is the nearest thing to a declaration of war that the Poles are to receive.

In February 1939 *Picture Post* asked Wickham Steed, a former editor of *The Times*, to go down with cameraman Felix H. Man to Chartwell and interview Winston Churchill. Churchill – the man the Tory Party did not trust – was no more than a backbencher under the Chamberlain administration. He had held no office since being Chancellor of the Exchequer under Stanley Baldwin ten years earlier. Steed completed his profile with the words: 'His abiding care is the safety of Britain, the Empire and the Commonwealth. Should some great emergency arise . . . his qualities and experience might then be national assets; and the true greatness, which he has often seemed to miss by a hair's breadth, might, by common consent, be his.' In a brief introduction *Picture Post* added its own prophetic comment: 'At 64 the greatest moment of his life has still to come.' Called to the Admiralty in September 1939, Churchill's speeches already marked him out as destined to become the war leader of his country before long.

T.H.

The New First Lord Arrives at the Admiralty

For months a large body of Government supporters, sections of the two Oppositions, and millions of private people, backed by powerful newspapers, have been demanding the inclusion in the Government of Winston Churchill—the man who long ago warned Britain of Germany's secret rearmament and of Hitler's secret intentions. For months his inclusion has been delayed. At last, on Sunday, September 3, a few hours after Britain has declared war, it is announced that Churchill has been appointed to the War Cabinet as First Lord of the Admiralty—the post he was occupying when war broke out a quarter of a century ago.

1940

The most eventful year in recent British history began with the dismissal of a popular War Minister, Hore-Belisha, and ended with the second Great Fire of London, as German incendiary bombs rained down on the City. In the months between, British armies had been chased out of Norway and France, and British airmen had established a superiority they were never wholly to lose. Britain had also acquired a new Prime Minister and, as some would say, recovered its soul.

The Hore-Belisha affair had important consequences, and was a characteristic example of the hysterical atmosphere of the phoney war. The popular newspapers attributed his dismissal to anti-semitism, a plot by British generals to set up a military dictatorship, and secret Government sympathy for the Nazis. The truth was both simpler and more complicated. Before Chamberlain became Prime Minister, he had been dismayed by the War Office's inefficiency in equipping the Army for modern war. He put Hore-Belisha there with a brief to dynamite obstacles, and get the job done. But although the War Office was inefficient, the fundamental cause of the hold-up was a disagreement about the role the Army was to play. The War Office said an expeditionary force would have to be sent to the Continent. Chamberlain, basing himself on Liddell Hart's doctrines, said this was unnecessary. When he changed his mind in September 1938, it was too late, and the Army went to France with only too apparent deficiencies. Hore-Belisha, a tactless man, had made many enemies and failed – not entirely through his own fault – to equip the Army. Given their opportunity, his enemies struck, the final dagger-thrust coming from Churchill, First Lord of the Admiralty, who wanted the War Office for the more pliable Eden. Churchill did not achieve that until later, but he did get rid of Chatfield, the Minister for the Co-ordination of Defence, and so emerged as the War Cabinet's dominating voice.

In April the Germans anticipated a Churchillian plan to invade Norway by doing so themselves, and Churchill's handling of the ensuing campaign proved so disastrous that Chamberlain had to resign. The Labour Party had refused to enter a coalition Government under Chamberlain, but were willing to do so under another Prime Minister. The Labour leaders distrusted Churchill's judgement, and favoured Halifax, but Halifax wisely declined the succession. On Whit Monday, 13 May, Churchill, as coalition Prime Minister, faced a predominantly pro-Chamberlain House of Commons made more hostile by the Conservative belief that Chamberlain had been sacrificed for Churchill's defects. In a speech that subsequently became famous, Churchill said he had nothing to offer but blood, toil, tears and sweat; that his only policy was to wage war, his only aim victory.

As Churchill spoke, the first German tanks had crossed the river Meuse, and within a few days had torn such a gap in the supposedly impregnable Allied line that they threatened to cut off the British and French armies in northern France. The British commander, Lord Gort, was no great general, but he had enough sense to ignore Churchillian exhortations to stand and fight, and retreated on the small Channel port of Dunkirk, from the mole and open beaches of which some three hundred thousand British and French troops were evacuated through the inspired improvisation of the Royal Navy.

On 22 June French emissaries accepted German armistice terms. The news was received with a fervent 'Thank God!' by the British Air Staff. Churchill's attempts to commit British fighter strength to the defence of France had been frustrated only by the dour, covenanting commander-in-chief of Fighter Command, Sir Hugh Dowding, who told a friend, 'God put me into this job because I alone could stand up to Churchill.' Cautiously husbanding his limited resources, given a decisive advantage by the radar net which pinpointed German lines of attack, Dowding proceeded to win the air battle over Britain and, like Gort, was promptly sacked for his pains.

After what was generally described as the miracle of Dunkirk, an ill-equipped Britain prepared for a German invasion which, it was said, was likely at any moment. There is no very strong evidence on the German side that invasion was regarded as a serious possibility. The Army High Command, anxious to avoid a war on two fronts, wanted to eliminate Britain, but were discouraged by the German Navy's patent inability to land the necessary troops. Hitler himself took only a sporadic interest in the plans for Operation Sealion, which he regarded mainly as camouflage for his intention of attacking Russia.

Of this, the British remained wholly ignorant. They engaged in a great deal of misdirected activity, building concrete pillboxes often sited the wrong way round, engaging in midnight forays against non-existent German parachutists, imprisoning inoffensive German refugees under conditions which at least one of them described as worse than German pre-war concentration camps. But they never doubted their ability to beat the Germans.

When German bombing of British cities began in September, there was momentary panic. But the knock-out blow from the air proved to be a myth, like the invincibility of the Royal Navy and the impregnability of the Maginot Line. At the year's end, the country was saved from the threat of bankruptcy only by the promise of American Lease-Lend, but it was still fighting, and because it was, Hitler could no longer win the war.

Laurence Thompson

1940 *The 'Miracle' of Dunkirk:* 300,000 men are rescued by inspired improvisation.

Picture Post,
June 8, 1940

WE DEDICATE THIS PICTURE . . .

We dedicate this picture to the Fuhrer.   We dedicate this picture to the "moderate" Goering.   We dedicate this picture to those of our own politicians who promised us that Germany would never be allowed to attain air-parity with Britain; that they had secured peace for our time; that they were abundantly confident of victory. . . . It shows a Dutch father wounded all over, but forgetful of what he is suffering.   The dead girl on the corner is his daughter.

WHAT WAR MEANS TO-DAY : *Soldier and Civilian Shelter Side-by-side*

They are all soldiers now. Even the old. Even the women and the children. Only some are armed and can hit back. Others are not. The machine-gunning of refugees is a regular part of the Nazi blitzkrieg. It was so in Poland. It was so in Holland and Belgium. It is so in France.

DIARY OF THE WAR—No. 39   **THE THIRTY-SEVENTH WEEK**

BLITZKRIEG

The lightning war smites Europe. It blisters its way between the Allied Armies, cleaving them in two. It carves out a charred road to the English Channel. It scorches the Belgian Army and stuns the Belgian King into surrender.

May 21, 1940

The darkest day of the war.

Arras and Amiens fall to the German mechanised forces. Through the corridor between these two towns, large motor-cycle detachments roar on to Abbeville and seize it. The Germans claim that the fall of Le Touquet can be expected at any minute. The enemy, moving at incredible speed, has reached the Channel. The Allied Armies have been bitten in two. The Corridor between them, now thirty miles wide, is a charred thoroughfare for tanks and motorised divisions, patrolled by clouds of low-flying planes. The Germans, streaking on north up towards Boulogne and Calais, are making a bid for the total encirclement of the Northern Allied Army. Can that fatal corridor between Arras and Amiens be closed? The world waits for the answer on which so much depends.

In France, the weight of German planes is loading the scales against civilisation. At home, Lord Beaverbrook, the new Minister for Aircraft Production, asks aircraft factories to work seven days a week, 24 hours a day. At last it is being realised that minutes saved mean planes gained. And that only planes mean survival.

May 22, 1940

Arras is recaptured by the French. The British counter-attack between Arras and Douai. The Belgians are holding the line. But the German thrust towards the coast continues, spreading terror and destruction behind the Allied lines.

The answer comes. In a little under three hours, Parliament passes the most revolutionary measure in its history. The Government is given complete control of all persons and all property in the country. Banking, munitions firms, wages, profits, hours and conditions of service are all brought at once under Government control.

Herbert Morrison, the new Minister of Supply, subsequently announces that the Government is taking over full control of all armament works. For these concerns the Excess Profits Tax is raised to 100 per cent.

C. R. Attlee, the Labour Leader, who introduces the Bill for the Cabinet, declares that the Government will now have sufficient powers, even if the

AMID ROLLING SMOKE-CLOUDS WITH TERRIFIC DIN FRENCH HEAVY TANKS RUSH INTO ACTION

Sights never seen since primeval monsters wrestled in the swamps cover the plains of Flanders and Northern France. French, British and German tanks crash into action. They fight in lines, in columns, in masses. Single tanks on each side fight it out in hundreds of separate engagements.

French Tanks Hold up a German Column . . .
There are Germans down the street. Those lorries are German lorries. Held up by the barricade and the tanks behind.

. . . The Same Scene from the Tank's Trapdoor
The enemy have left their lorries. For the moment there is quiet. Soon firing will burst out from a near quarter.

Picture Post, June 8, 1940

THE BATTLE OF TANKS

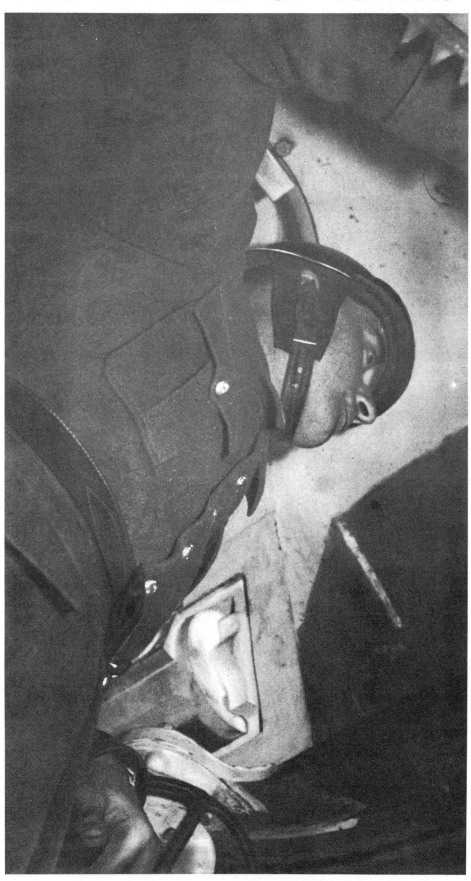

country is invaded and Parliament is unable to meet. In its scope, the new Act is totalitarian. But it passes through Parliament without opposition, and the people of the country freely approve it.

Other measures include the Treachery Bill, and changes to the Emergency Powers Act which enable the Government to detain leaders of political organisations likely to be made use of by the enemy. Sir John Anderson, the Home Secretary, does not wait long to use his new powers. The same night, orders are issued for the arrest of leaders of the British Union of Fascists, the Right Club, and the British People's Party. Next day, Sir Oswald Mosley and many of his closest associates, past and present, are arrested and taken to prison. Among those detained are A. Raven Thompson, N. Francis Hawkins, John Beckett, and Capt. A. M. Ramsay, M.P.

May 23, 1940

German armoured troops enter Boulogne, and there is fierce fighting in and around the town. London claims that the British forces have been successfully withdrawn, and that, at most, only a handful of men have fallen into the enemy's hands. British warships lying off Boulogne see at dawn the vanguard of German tanks crawling along the coastal road to the port. They open fire, inflicting heavy casualties, but also blasting parts of the town to ruins. It still seems

INSIDE A TANK : *The Commanding Officer in His Turret*
He is the captain on the bridge. From his turret he steers the tank, decides when to fire, and at what target. An immense pride in their machines distinguishes the men of the Tank Corps.

THE GERMANS TEACH THE WORLD A NEW WORD, "BLITZKRIEG": *This Was a Church*

The beautiful churches of Northern France know what "blitzkrieg" means. In many parts it has worked more havoc in a few days than the World War in several years. German tanks and armoured vehicles had orders to wreak the greatest possible destruction upon everything.

This Was a Street . . .

French boys search the ruins of what was once a street of peaceful homes. A scene repeated a hundred times over in the towns of Northern France during the past weeks.

that no infantry have come up with the tanks to consolidate the Nazi gains. A German claim to have taken Calais is denied by the Allies.

Elsewhere on the battlefront, there are signs that some big Allied counter-offensive is impending. British troops, in a thrust towards Cambrai, are advancing between the rivers Scarpe and Scheldt, fighting for every yard they take. They are to the north of the gap made in the Allied front by the German offensive to the south. The French counter-attack and their advance troops reach the outskirts of Amiens, held for two days by the Germans. At its narrowest point, the gap between the Allies is still about 30 miles.

The R.A.F. has further successes in the war in the air. It claims in one day to have shot down 40 enemy aircraft for the loss of only 6 fighters. It intensifies its bombing of German communications and convoys, road and rail bridges and ammunition works. One of our bombers penetrates to Leipzig, where a power station is bombed. German warplanes are seen off the East Coast of Kent, but are driven off by anti-aircraft fire and fighters. It is estimated that Germany has now lost 1,500 planes in two weeks.

Evidence accumulates—even when propagandist "atrocity stories" are discounted—of the brutality of German warfare in Belgium and France. From neutral observers, as well as British and French correspondents, come authenticated accounts of bombing and machine-gunning of civilian refugees, of bombs deliberately dropped on hospitals and hospital ships, of a reign of terror in the occupied parts of

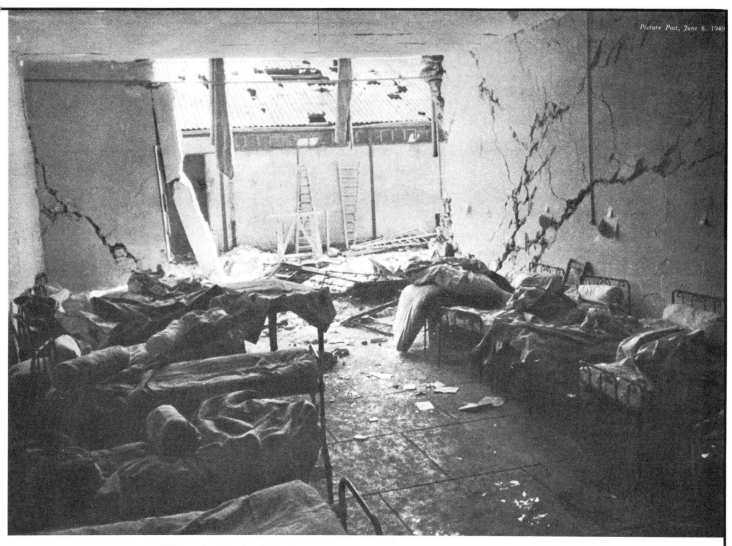

Where the Work of Healing Was Carried On: A Hospital After Bombardment

It was a hospital.   It had all the markings of a hospital.   It was bombed by Nazi airmen.   In a number of cases hospitals marked with the Red Cross have been not only bombed—but singled out for special bombing.

Belgium and Holland.

These horrors, as well as the successes of the German armies, are profoundly influencing American opinion. It has not yet reached the stage where the U.S.A. will be prepared to abandon its neutrality, but there is growing support for the move to help the Allies with war materials by relaxing the 'cash and carry provisions' of the Neutrality Act. Almost anything is possible, in fact, "short of war."

Another important political development which has followed the fall of Mr. Chamberlain is a change in the attitude towards Russia. As Italy becomes more and more menacing, the London press begins to present Russia as the champion of the Balkans against Mussolini's designs. The *Evening Standard*, long bitterly anti-Soviet, calls for immediate resumption of normal diplomatic relations, and declares that Russia's attack on Finland was only part of her plan to keep out of the major war. A day later, it is learned that Sir Stafford Cripps, the Socialist whom the Labour Party expelled some time ago for his Popular Front activities, may go to Russia as an official envoy to discuss trade relations. Sir Samuel Hoare, until recently Lord Privy Seal, is to be our new Ambassador to Spain.

May 24, 1940

The battle to squeeze the gap between the Allied armies rages without a decision. The French advance further on Amiens, and in the Sedan sector they repulse a German attack and later successfully counter-attack. The B.E.F. has to face

French Tanks Roll Up to the Attack

Men look twice when they see a tank come up the street.   It may be French.   It probably is.   But it may be German disguised as French.

Picture Post, June 8, 1940

THE STORY OF A BELGIAN CHURCH TOWER: *At Twenty Minutes Past Seven the Tower is Still Standing*

Picture Post, June 8, 1940

FIVE MINUTES LATER: *German Bombs Have Struck the Tower. It Falls Amid Clouds of Smoke*

Picture Post, June 8, 1940

THE END OF HIS WAR

He was a German motor-cyclist. His job was to ride at the head of a motorised column. Behind him came cars of high-up officers, tanks, lorries crammed with petrol and supplies. R.A.F. bombers came over. French artillery knew their distance to a yard. The column was knocked out.

THE PRICE THE NAZIS PAID: *One of Hundreds of Shattered German Planes*

A couple of hundred planes in Norway. Five hundred in Holland. Five hundred more in Belgium. Up to a thousand more in France. So, week by week, the toll of German planes shot down has mounted. They are being used up faster than they are being made. So are their crews.

The Remains of a German Petrol Store After a Raid by the R.A.F.

the hardest fighting of the day on the Cambrai-Valenciennes road.

In Boulogne, the position is still obscure. The Germans do not claim its capture, but the French admit its fall. Calais is heavily bombed, and the Nazis say they have captured Ghent, 18 miles east of Brussels.

Day by day the war becomes more ruthless. The French allege that the Germans bombed Metz, an open town, and in reprisal a German town behind the lines has been bombed.

May 25, 1940

The most critical week-end of the war opens with the news that 15 French generals have been dismissed from their commands, which include Army and Army Corps.

For the first time since the invasion of Holland and Belgium, German and Allied war communiques are in sharp contradiction. The Germans claim that the ring around the Allied armies has been closed, and that the Belgian Army, parts of the First, Ninth and Seventh French Armies and the bulk of the B.E.F. are cut off. Courtrai, as well as Ghent, they say, has fallen and Vimy Ridge is also in Nazi hands. Here thousands of men, whose sons are fighting over the same ground, fell in the battles of the last war. The French, however, declare that the Allied armies in the north are not encircled, that Calais is strongly held, and that the great battle in Flanders is only just beginning.

Both in Britain and France there are indications that in future military news will be sparse. Silence about the movements of troops and the phases of the battle, is now imperative. In London, the public

A German Prisoner is Questioned by Officers in a French Prison Camp

The value of a prisoner is small. He is only one man who will take no more part in the struggle. As against that, he has to be fed and housed, watched, guarded, medically cared for. The real value of a prisoner is the value of the information he can give.

is officially told through the newspapers that "the situation is very grave, but it should be remembered that the form of warfare employed by the Germans has its weaknesses as well as its strength."

There is a freshening spirit in the Government and the people of Britain. The first German bombs have fallen on English soil—the first drops of the shower of steel that Hitler has threatened. German troops are only 25 miles from the coast of Kent. German parachutists must be expected at any moment from now on. Britain faces the most formidable trial in her history without despondency or alarm.

May 26, 1940

To-day the German onslaught is concentrated against the Allied forces in the north. Striving to grind away the Allied left flank, the enemy delivers a series of determined and costly attacks against the Belgian troops. Immediately the British go to the assistance of their Allies. The German losses are colossal. Entire platoons are mown down by the fire of automatic weapons. The number of German divisions operating in this northern sector is believed to be six times as great as the number of those who have infiltrated through the corridor.

But without regard to the losses of their men, who die like cattle, the German commanders maintain their pressure. Near Oudenarde, enemy troops force their way across the Scheldt. At Courtrai they make a violent mechanised assault against the Belgians. The Belgians do not budge.

But, higher up, in the Oudenarde sector, the Allies are forced to withdraw from the line of the Scheldt to prepared positions behind the River

The Nazis Behind the Wire

THE R.A.F. HITS BACK: *Bombs Falling on a Column of German Transport*

A hundred and fifty German lorries, tanks and armoured cars are passing through a town.   They are travelling from east to west.   They form a support column for the invader.   And they form a target for the R.A.F.   Part of the main road is obscured by smoke.   Bombs are bursting to the south-west of the town, and a salvo of a dozen bombs is falling towards the railway line.

Vol. 8   No. 12.

PICTURE POST

September 21, 1940

TRAINING AT OSTERLEY PARK SCHOOL : *The First Phase in the Making of the Home Guard*
Soon after the Home Guard was founded the demand for a real training became overwhelming. To meet this demand PICTURE POST and its proprietor stepped in. A school was founded at Osterley Park, near London. The aim of the school has been to teach members of the Home Guard to become "first-class irregulars." The school's work has now been recognised by the War Office.

THE HOME GUARD CAN
FIGHT

by TOM WINTRINGHAM

An immense problem now faces the Home Guard. Is it to go forward or hang fire? Properly trained, it can—by the end of the coming winter—become the chief defensive force of the British Isles.

AS I was watching yesterday 250 men of the Home Guard take their places for a lecture at the Osterley Park Training School an air-raid siren sounded, and a dozen men with rifles moved to their prearranged positions as a defence unit against low-flying aircraft. The lecturer began to talk of scouting, stalking and patrolling. And as I watched and listened I realised that I was taking part in something so

new and strange as to be almost revolutionary—the growth of an "army of the people" in Britain —and, at the same time, something that is older than Britain, almost as old as England—a gathering of the "men of the counties able to bear arms."

The men at Osterley were being taught confidence and cunning, the use of shadow and of cover, by a man who learned field-craft from

Baden-Powell, the most original irregular soldier in modern history (with the possible exception of Lawrence of Arabia). And in an hour or two they would be hearing of the experience, hard bought with lives and wounds, won by an army very like their own, the army that for year after year held up Fascism's flood-tide towards world power, in that Spanish fighting which was the prelude and the signal for the present struggle. I could not

THE MODERN SOLDIER LEARNS BY LECTURES : *A Demonstration at the Home Guards' School*

The Home Guardsmen, in the course of two days at the Osterley Training School, learn how to make and use explosives; how to destroy tanks and parachutists; how to defend streets and cities; and how to wage guerilla warfare.

help thinking how like these two armies were : the Home Guard of Britain and the Militia of Republican Spain. Superficially alike in mixture of uniforms and half-uniforms, in shortage of weapons and ammunition, in hasty and incomplete organisation and in lack of modern training, they seemed to me more fundamentally alike in their serious eagerness to learn, their resolve to meet and defeat all the difficulties in their way, their certainty that despite shortage of time and gear they could fight and fight effectively.

How the Home Guard School was Started

The school that they were attending had in a way been made by themselves. Two or three months ago, when this newest army in the world was first proposed, I wrote two articles in PICTURE POST on ways to meet invasion, on the experiences of Spain, and on the first rough steps to be taken for the training of a new force. So many queries piled into the offices of PICTURE POST, so many requests for more teaching and more detail, that it was natural for Mr. Edward Hulton to think of the idea of a school for the Home Guard—or, as they were then, the L.D.V. Osterley was a PICTURE POST idea, and Osterley has given free training to over 3,000 of the Home Guard at Edward Hulton's expense. The same evening that he decided to go ahead with the idea, he got in touch with Lord Jersey, who permitted

us to use the grounds of his famous park at Osterley.

On July 10 the first course was given at the school. Our aim was then to give 60 members of the Home Guard two days' training three times a week. By the end of July over 100 men were attending each course, 300 a week. The numbers rose sharply in August; during the week when this was written one of the courses included 270 men. Those attending the school in July were nearly a thousand; those attending in August over 2,000; the September figures will probably be around 3,000. We could not keep them away with bayonets—if we had any.

Attempt To Close Down the School

But all was not plain sailing; there were prejudices to be broken down. Soon after the school was founded an officer high up in the command of the L.D.V. requested Mr. Hulton and myself to close the school down, because the sort of training we were giving was "not needed." This officer explained to us with engaging frankness that the Home Guard did not have to do "any of this crawling round; all they have to do is to sit in a pill-box and shoot straight." The "sit in a pill-box" idea, a remnant of the Maginot Line folly not yet rooted out of the British Army, met us on other occasions. We fought it in every way we could. We could not accept the instruc-

tion to close the school down, and received support from high quarters of the War Office for our decision to continue. And when the officer who considered Osterley unnecessary sent a circular round to units in his area, pointing out that Osterley had not been approved, we found an increase in the numbers coming to us from that area.

Home Guard units not hitherto aware of our existence learned of it through this circular.

The Teaching at Osterley

We left out of our teaching things necessary to the Home Guard that we believed could be better taught to them elsewhere : drill, signalling, much of musketry. Our lectures and demonstrations included :—

Modern tactics in general, and German tactics present and future. The use and improvisation of hand-grenades, land mines and anti-tank grenades. The use of various types of rifles, shot-guns, pistols, etc. Camouflage, field-craft, scouting, stalking and patrolling. Guerilla warfare in territory occupied by the enemy. Street tactics and defence of cities; the use of smoke-screens. Troop-carrying aircraft, parachutists, and defensive measures against them. Field works, road-blocks, and anti-tank methods. Observation and reporting.

The aim of the school was to teach members of

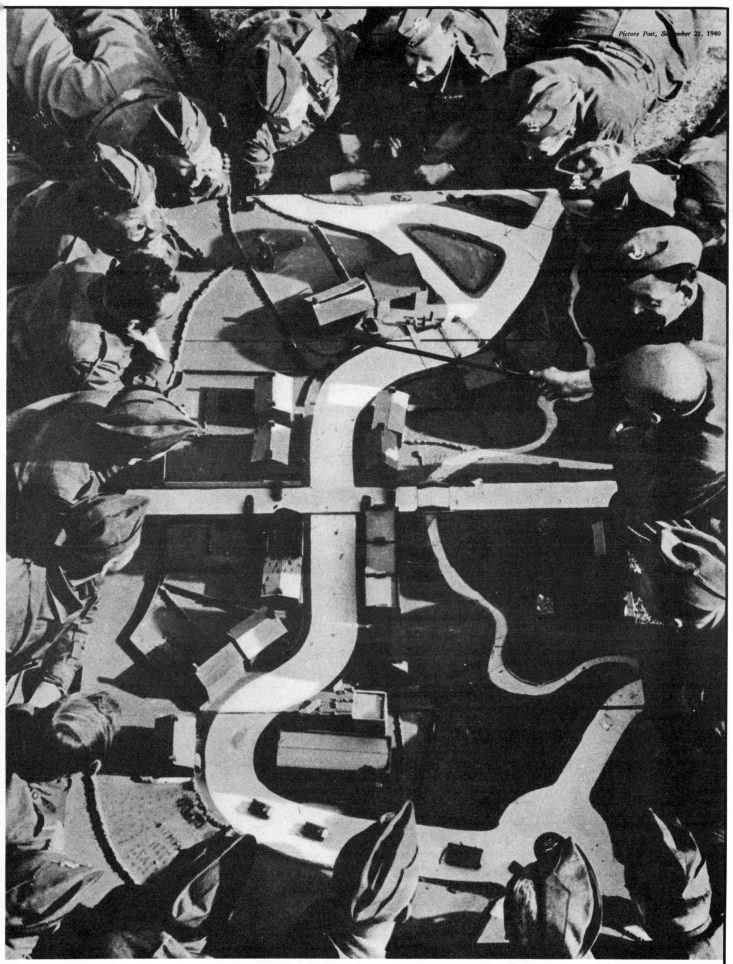

HOW TO SMASH THE BLITZKRIEG: *A Lesson in Village Defence*

The instructors are men with practical experience of modern methods of warfare. The learners are Home Guardsmen who, in time of invasion, would be called upon to defend a typical village such as this. With the aid of the panorama, they are shown their job.

Picture Post, September 21, 1940

THE MODERN SOLDIER LEARNS FROM GAMES : *How First-class Irregulars are Trained*

Games are not despised—particularly those that teach quickness of thought and action, and train the different senses. Here the game is to creep up soundlessly on the blindfolded man and snatch an object from his hand, without being discovered. In war the object might be a sentry's rifle in the darkness.

the Home Guard to become "first-class irregulars." But we were at all times careful to point out that irregular soldiers, though necessarily organised and trained on somewhat different lines from Regulars, need discipline and obedience.

Our view of the future of the Home Guard, which governed and shaped all our teaching, is that stated in the title of this article—the Home Guard can fight—which is also the title of a summary of the lectures given at Osterley, which I hope will soon be published by the Hulton Press as a sixpenny pamphlet.

NEW DEVICES AND TECHNIQUES ARE TRIED : *The Revolver That Fires Through the Holster*

A type of holster, developed in Mexico and South Africa, for quick shooting.

The revolver can either be drawn from the holster in the ordinary way . . .

. . . Or, for snap-shooting, it can be fired from the hip through a hole in the holster.

82

Our work at Osterley received official approval early in September, when we were thanked by the Army Council, and the War Office decided to take over the school.

Home Guards Can Defend Britain

The Home Guard is at present a reinforcement to the Regular Army, and the latter still carries almost all the weight of the defence of these islands against invasion. If we are to have any chance of victory the Home Guard must be, as soon as possible, a force so organised and trained and equipped that it can say to the bulk of the Regular Army. "Go and see the world, brothers; we, with the help of a few of your divisions, can safely be left to look after Britain."

In Napoleonic times battles were fought on a few square miles of ground, and any troops who could not reach these few square miles were unlikely to have decisive effect. Much later, in 1914, battles stretched over very many miles of front; but it was still almost essential for troops to be present, among the thin lines of men who were the fronts, if they were to be valuable. The whole development of modern war has added more and more value to those troops who are placed behind, sometimes very far behind, the outpost lines of an army.

The Germans have greatly developed the tactics of attack in depth, by the use of armoured divisions, of troops landed from the air and of Fifth Columnists. These tactics can best be resisted by a force which is naturally disposed by the conditions of its formation across the whole depth of the country. We can possess an army that is so thick a line that it fills the whole map. The Home Guard can be such an army.

Plan Of Training

To perform the task, it must have at least a considerable amount of training in the following operations:

Defence against low-flying aircraft. Defence against deep penetration by armoured units; also counter-attack against isolated armoured vehicles. Defence of towns, street by street, and counter-attack to regain villages and towns. Limited operations in aid of Regular forces counter-attacking in the open field. Defence and counter-attack against troops landed from the air. Guerilla warfare in areas temporarily occupied by the enemy.

The training necessary for these duties, which are limited as compared with the duties of Regular soldiers, should not be the same in all respects as that of the Regular Army. In the time available, it cannot be the same. Regular Army instructors do not always find it easy to train irregulars; and the Army is expanding so rapidly that almost all capable instructors within it are needed by the Regular units. There is, however, enough military experience within the Home Guard to make it possible for the members of this course to train themselves to become "first-rate irregulars."

Home Guard Must Be Mobile

Even if the bulk of the Regular Army goes abroad, as it must do if we are to take the offensive, Regular troops will remain in Britain to stiffen the outposts on the beaches, and to be the principal shock troops for counter-attack against any foothold won by the Germans. The Home Guard will be mainly holding forces, providing part of our outposts, and most of our defence in depth. They will be strategically static in most cases. Even in the event of invasion, most of the Home Guard must stay close to where they are raised. But if they are to take over from the Regulars some part of their duties, strategical mobility for a certain proportion of the Home Guard will become necessary. And even those units which do not move far from their home quarters must be tactically mobile. Tactical immobility is to-day suicide. It is the Maginot Line. Those who "sit in a pill-box" seldom get a chance to shoot, either straight or crooked; they find the enemy floods round them, and they become isolated.

MODELS PLAY THEIR PART IN TRAINING: *The Dive Bomber in Action*
The dive bomber is vulnerable—if you know how to tackle it. The Home Guards at Osterley School are trained with a model that behaves very much like the real thing.

A Central Instructors' School

For the development of the necessary training we suggest a central instructors' school for the Home Guard. It should give a fuller training than can be given in two days. And as the Home Guard is passing from the stage of improvisation to that of organisation as an army, this training may well need to be more "official" and more standardised than that which we gave.

But it should be noted that we did not teach only "guerilla war." We have had a great deal of help from the Press, both British and American; but just in a few papers aspects of our training, that were of very small importance, received exaggeration to such a point that it became distortion. We were represented as teaching murder rather than teaching war; our insistence that any weapon is good enough to kill Germans with, if you know its values and limitations, was misconstrued into an advocacy of knives and home-made grenades as compared with more modern and more standardised weapons. At this central instructors' school should be taught the use of all the standard weapons at present available

to or likely to become available to the Home Guard. But there should also be some teaching in improvisation, because in modern war standard supplies all too often run out, and you have to make do with what you can "organise."

A Home Guard Army Council

There is a second step we believe to be necessary if the Home Guard is to get the training necessary for its share in victory. That is the establishment of some form of Home Guard Council, responsible for formulating the task of the Home Guard, controlling its training and developing its organisation. The departments of the War Office are working desperately hard at the training of a Regular Army, its equipment and its organisation. This Regular Army grows very rapidly indeed. It is natural and inevitable that the Home Guard should only get a little of the attention of these War Office Departments. Men who are thinking for ten hours a day about the needs of a Regular Army do not find it easy to adjust their minds, during their extra overtime work, to the different needs of this very different force. I am

A LESSON IN DEALING WITH A TANK

An old car towing an "armoured" trailer serves as tank. Home Guards practise blowing u
up with miniature mines of black powder.

Exploding the Anti-Tank Mine
Concealed in a pit, one of the Spanish War anti-tank
experts explodes the "mine" with a small battery.

not proposing a new commanding body for the Home Guard, but a new organising body. And I believe that it should consist of four officers from the War Office in high positions; three Members of Parliament who are also Home Guards, probably one from each party; and two or four members of the Home Guard who as "citizen soldiers" may have more time for Home Guard duties than a Member of Parliament can spare.

Such a body could straighten out the present natural defects of organisation in the Home Guard. And such a body could undertake the larger job of transforming the present undifferentiated "all in one piece" Home Guard into the skeleton of a real army. The Home Guard needs sub-units of younger men and older men with appropriate duties. It needs sub-units differentiated technically for movement, signalling, and other technical jobs. It needs a supply service and a medical service : it would be wise to entrust a very large amount of the work of these services to women. It needs despatch riders, wireless operators, men who can copy maps or repair machines and weapons—there are a thousand other similar categories. The skill and the technical knowledge to meet these demands exist within the Home Guard itself. Only organisation is needed to make them available. Such organisation can come slowly and indirectly from the War Office, which is not accustomed to the organisation of part-time volunteers. It can come much more efficiently and rapidly from a Home Guard Council

that thinks mainly in terms of part-time volunteers. And such a council would also realise to what extent there is need for an increase in the number of full-time officers and men controlling and organising the Home Guard.

Increase Home Guard to 4,000,000 Men

The Home Guard as a whole will need to increase in numbers if it is to shoulder the duties we have outlined. Recruiting should be reopened, and if necessary a recruiting campaign should be launched. (I myself doubt if it will be necessary.) The aim should be to increase the Home Guard during the autumn to a strength of 2½ million men, during the winter to 3 million, and during the coming year towards its probable maximum of 4 million.

After that maximum is reached the numbers of the Home Guard are likely to decrease, as further age groups are called up for the Regular Army.

It may be stated that the numbers I mention above are larger than those likely to be suitably armed at the times stated. I repeat the arguments I have already used on this point. The Home Guard needs strengthening, and needs to become a combatant force. More recruits means more time for training and less strain on the individual member who is sometimes called on for more hours of guard duty than he can efficiently do. The rate of supply of arms need not be an obstacle to the increase in the number of the Home Guards, because the manufacture of simple hand-grenades

A LESSON IN THE USE OF SMOKE: *The Defenders Await the Assault*

Around the imaginary fort there is no cover to assist the attacking force in making an assault. The defence has a clear line of fire over the whole area. As a simple exercise, the attacking force is taught to conceal its advance behind smoke.

is an extremely easy business and should be a relatively rapid one. And efficient units can be produced in which only one-third of the men serving carry rifles or automatic weapons; the remainder carry hand-grenades and anti-tank grenades.

Home Guard to Relieve Regular Troops

As the Home Guard increases in numbers and improves in technique and organisation, it should progressively take over certain defensive duties now carried out by others. In one large area where German air attack has been heavy, units of the Home Guard have been providing reliefs for sub-units of the Regular Army. The process works in this way : a platoon of the Regular Army is holding a number of posts where constant vigilance is essential. At convenient times sections of the Home Guard are moved to these posts, where they replace a proportion (not greater than half) of the Regular troops employed. A small number of the Home Guard take it in turns to remain at the posts during the night; others perhaps are detailed to reinforce the posts at "stand-to" before dawn.

On another part of the coast, defence is assured during daylight by posts held by the Regular Army which are fairly far apart. During the night it is considered useful to fill the gaps between these posts by other posts, held by the Home Guard, who take it in turns to man their unit's positions. These systems by which the Home

How the Attackers Creep Up Under the Cover of Smoke Bombs
Throwing smoke bombs in front of them, the attackers move up to their objective. The defence is blinded. The attack has a chance to develop behind a protecting screen.

Picture Post, September 21, 1940

A LESSON IN CAMOUFLAGE: *A Rifleman in Hiding*

The fallen tree-trunk gives him complete protection on one side. On the other, it gives him protective colouration by breaking up the sunlight with shadow. The sniper himself wears a camouflaged overall and helmet. His rifle is swathed with material. Even his face is dyed.

When France fell in June 1940 there was a tremendous uprush of determination throughout Britain. The Germans would invade, it was believed, before the autumn. Almost every man, able-bodied or otherwise, wanted to be ready to fight them when they came. Popular pressure had forced the Government to set up the Local Defence Volunteers, later to become the Home Guard. But they lacked either training or weapons. Borrowing Osterley Park from the Earl of Jersey and appointing Tom Wintringham as Director, *Picture Post* set up its own highly successful school of 'Do-It-Yourself' war. It also organized the shipment of arms from private sources in the United States.

T.H.

Guard is "sandwiched in" to Regular formations can be extended. In other cases where men of the Regular Forces guard points of military importance during the day, the Home Guard relieve them at night.

Defence Against Low-Flying Aircraft

I believe that the Home Guard should progressively take over part of our defence against low-flying aircraft, including control of part of the balloon barrage. Many of the men operating this barrage must be full-time workers, but there is no reason why they should not come under the organisation of the Home Guard, who might next tackle control of the machine-guns used against low-flying attacks. Finally they might well be made responsible for what I believe to be an important but neglected aspect of our defence against the bomber; the creation of smoke screens on a wide front that will make it impossible for raiding aircraft to spot the targets of importance, and particularly the factories in which work is continued during raids.

To hand over functions such as these, partly or completely, to the Home Guard will make the work of the latter more interesting and better training, and will bring in recruits. It will prevent men resigning during the winter owing to the boredom of long hours of apparently useless sentry-go.

Besides this programme of training and of gradually extending tasks, the Home Guard Council that I propose can settle various problems now agitating the members of that force—

problems almost always raised in that last hour at Osterley, when we discussed the application of our ideas within the units from which our students came. One smaller problem is that of responsibility for arms; a larger one is that of leadership.

Home Guards Must Take Arms Home

I am in favour of men carrying their arms, and taking them home. Arms are not well looked after unless men are personally responsible for their care. The swiftness of German attack makes it unlikely that the Home Guards, in areas first attacked, will have the time to return from their work to depots near their homes and receive their arms from the depots. This is a question in urgent need of settlement.

And the question of leadership is even more urgent. For real discipline, which is a fundamental need in any army, there must be respect for the leadership. In many units of the Home Guard there is this respect, and the leaders deserve it. In some there is not; and in these units—which I hope are fewer than appears—there is only one thing to be done. The resignation of all officers in these units should be secured; some should be re-appointed, not necessarily in the same positions, and new officers should be added from amongst those who combine military experience with the ability to learn and teach modern warfare.

Trained to new methods, equipped, organised and led, the Home Guard can fight—can be the "line" that cannot be pierced by any German invading force whenever it cares to come.

SOME OF THE MEN WHO TEACH AT THE HOME GUARD SCHOOL

Tom Wintringham

Director of Training. From 1916-18 he fought in France. He went to the Spanish War as a journalist. He stayed there to become the first commander of the British Battalion of the International Brigade. In this war, Wintringham's articles in PICTURE POST and elsewhere have established him as one of our best-known military writers. The taking over of the school by the Government gives official approval to the campaign to give proper training to the Home Guard.

Peter Wyatt-Foulger

Commanding officer. In the last war he was a captain in France and the Near East, commanding infantry, armoured vehicles and machine-guns. Now he lectures on anti-aircraft musketry. When Home Guard members report at the school for a course, he forms them into platoons and appoints temporary officers. He disposes the rifle unit and anti-aircraft sentries in readiness for low-flying aircraft. If German aircraft fly overhead, he directs ground fire against them.

Hugh Slater

Expert in the tactics of modern warfare. Learnt street fighting in the International Brigade in Spain. Found out how to destroy tanks in command of the British Anti-Tank Battery later in the same war. In 1938 he was appointed Chief of Operations XV Brigade Staff and was engaged in the planning of the successful crossing of the Ebro in 1938. When not fighting wars, is a painter and journalist.

Stanley White

One of the chief instructors of the Boy Scouts' Association. He learnt scouting from Baden-Powell himself. Now he passes on his knowledge of scouting, stalking, patrolling to the Home Guard. By Boy Scout training games he teaches them to be "first-class irregulars." Besides instructing at Osterley, he is also in charge of the headquarters of the Boy Scouts at Gillwell Park, Essex.

Wilfred Vernon

The mixer of Molotoff Cocktails and dispenser of improvised explosives. During the last war he was senior technical officer at the Felixstowe Air Station (R.N.A.S.). Later he became aircraft designer. Now instructs in how to tackle parachutists and aircraft, how to improvise mines and grenades, how to identify enemy 'planes and put them out of action. Wilfred Vernon is the ideas man who stages the mock warfare devices, and invents new ways of making bombs.

Roland Penrose

Lecturer and practitioner in camouflage. By profession he is a member of an organisation carrying out camouflage schemes for factories and Government departments. By leaning, he is a surrealist painter. He has exhibited his modern paintings all over the world. In his spare time he teaches the principles of successful camouflage to the members of the Home Guard

1941

In May, 1941, Lord Hankey, secretary to the War Cabinet in the First World War, and now a member of the Government, wrote a long private letter of complaint about the Prime Minister. The war, he said, was being run as a dictatorship. Orders went out from Churchill in person, not from the Service departments. The Chiefs of Staff were worn out by incessant late night meetings. 'No less than four high officers in the service Staff organization separately and independently sought me out and poured their hearts out to me. . . . Then came a very able Civil Servant with deep misgivings at Churchill's complacency. . . . Finally I learned that Menzies, who had at first completely fallen for Churchill, had become alarmed at the position.'

Menzies, the Australian Prime Minister, in London to attend War Cabinet meetings, told Hankey he would insist that Churchill must take proper advice from his political and military advisers. It was in vain. Churchill went on being Churchill, making mistakes on a gigantic scale, but embodying in his siren-suited person the national will to win.

The continuing distrust of the Prime Minister in high places was never reflected in public opinion. Churchill's popularity, as shown by the Gallup Poll, fell below seventy-eight per cent only in the blackest days of 1942. Most of the British people had a single simple war aim. They were sick of being mucked about by an Austrian housepainter with the comic name of Schickelgruber, to whom they felt themselves immeasurably superior. They wanted him eliminated so that they could get back to their own affairs. Vera Lynn's 'We'll Meet Again' said more to them than Churchill's sham-Augustan rhetoric; but Churchill was the one politician who seemed eager to get on with the job, and they gave him their confidence until it was done.

Under this last flamboyant flowering of the Whig aristocracy, Britain became more genuinely egalitarian than ever before or perhaps since. Two able and formidable Labour ministers, Bevin and Morrison, looked after the home front between them, and saw that there was no repetition of the industrial turmoil of the First World War. Unemployment vanished. Wages rose faster than prices. Food and clothes rationing ensured that everybody ate and dressed in much the same way. The middle classes accepted with patriotic stoicism the conscription of their sons and — something Lloyd George had never dared attempt — their daughters. The German U-boat campaign, reaching new heights in 1941, ensured a concern for the welfare of British farmers they had never known between the wars, and led to an agricultural revolution which became one of the productivity wonders of the world.

And in 1941, the British for the first time had a land victory to celebrate. A small Commonwealth and British force under General Sir Richard O'Connor chased a much larger Italian army back from inside the Egyptian frontier to beyond Benghazi, capturing almost twice its own number of prisoners on the way. It did not last. Hitler came to the rescue of his junior partner, who had hastily entered the war in expectation of easy pickings from the French defeat. Greece, which Mussolini had unsuccessfully invaded, was overwhelmed, and a British force unwisely committed to help the Greeks was bundled out, as from Norway and France. Crete fell to airborne invasion. Rommel appeared in Libya, and forced O'Connor's weakened army to retreat into Egypt. For the next two years, British and Germans chased each other up and down the Libyan coastal belt, victory and defeat being more often due to problems of supply than to superiority in arms or valour. Both sides regarded the Italians, who had started the desert war, as an extraneous nuisance.

None of this was the real war. That began on 22 June, when German armies crossed the Russian frontier. Churchill pledged immediate solidarity, remarking privately that 'if Hitler invaded Hell I would make at least a favourable reference to the Devil in the House of Commons'. By December the Germans had reached the outskirts of Moscow, thrust deep towards the Caucasus, and were besieging Leningrad. The Russian Government tottered, but the attempted German knock-out failed narrowly through a combination of Hitler's amateur generalship and the Russian weather.

On 6 December the Japanese sank most of the American Pacific fleet in a surprise attack on Pearl Harbor, and began an invasion of the British Empire in the Far East. The battleships *Prince of Wales* and *Repulse*, the main British naval strength in the area, were caught without air cover off the coast of Malaya, and sunk. Singapore was threatened.

But on the night of Pearl Harbor, Churchill recorded, he went to bed saturated and satiated with emotion and sensation, and slept the sleep of the saved and thankful. America was in the war and Britain, he believed, was saved.

Laurence Thompson

Picture Post, May 3, 1941

The Man the Nazis Are Trying to Rattle: A British Citizen of 1941

*He is the English city dweller. His home is the Nazi bombers' target. His few poor possessions, bought with the savings of years, are their military
objective. And when a bomb falls, and makes of his home a shapeless heap of bricks, he calmly salvages what he can and starts afresh.*

 caption: Picture Post, January 4, 1941

'Two Nations'

Disraeli accused Britain of being 'two nations', and in 1939, when the Second World War began, Britain was still two nations. There were nearly two million unemployed, many of whom had had no work for years. The story of one such, Alfred Smith, was told by *Picture Post* during January 1939. With a wife and four children, he received altogether £2 7s. 6d. a week. Smith had been a spray enamel worker and the chemicals he used rotted his teeth. Before losing his job, he had ordered artificial ones and paid 15s. deposit. But he could never find the money to complete payment, and the State took no interest in such matters. So Smith's cheeks caved in. The family's breakfast was tea, bread and margarine. Their supper was cocoa, bread and margarine. They had a bit of a stew with potatoes at midday.

No wonder that at this time, four people out of every ten in Britain, and seven children out of every ten, were undernourished.

Early in the war a dispute arose; it was fought out in the papers and on the air. The dispute was between those who said Britain should have 'War Aims', and those who said 'Get on with the fighting and think about all that afterwards'. Churchill as war leader was against

talk about 'War Aims', fearing the argument might breach national unity. But papers such as *Picture Post*, which was receiving hundreds of letters from men and women in the armed forces, knew what they were thinking. They were ready to fight, but wanted to know what they were fighting for. One of the things they were *not* fighting for was two million unemployed living on £2 a week or less.

For 4 January 1941 we decided to prepare a Special Issue summing up what we believed our country's 'War Aims' should be. We called it 'A Plan For Britain'. The plan — for its day — was revolutionary. A job for every able-bodied man. Minimum wages. Child allowances. An all-in contributory scheme of social insurance. A positive health service. A bold building plan — to start immediately war ended — in order to root out slums. The same kind of education for all up to 13, with the public schools brought into the general system. Holidays for all . . . and much more which today we all take for granted. But this was 1941, and our Special Issue unleashed the biggest flood of letters we had ever had. They were still being read and sorted a month later.

T.H.

Vol. 10 No. 1

PICTURE POST

January 4, 1941

B. L. COOMBES AND HIS SON: *Two Generations Look Out Over Their Native Land*
They climb the mountain above their Welsh home. They look down the valley scarred by colliery refuse. They look on the mines, idle in the midst of war. In their hearts lives faith that we are moving towards better things.

THIS IS THE PROBLEM

by B. L. Coombes

A Welsh coalminer wrote in to us. He said: "I have written something about life to-day, as it looks to me and my mates. Is it any good to you?" We have taken his article to begin our special number.

I AM in the middle forties—old enough to have seen many things and formed a few opinions. All my working days have been passed in two of the great industries—agriculture and mining. So my living has come off the land, or from under it.

I thought agriculture should be important, because the beginning of all industry is in the land. We worked hard—all the hours of daylight. Yet we couldn't get a decent living. Heavy rents, tithes, and market conditions beat us. It came to the point where the price for swedes wouldn't cover cartage to the station. So, one day in late autumn, when the unwanted apples were killing the grass in the orchard. I went eighty miles away to work in the mines. It was the beginning of a new life.

That night, in my new home, I found that

"**NEAR HERE IS A DISUSED MINE** *and some of my mates are busy trying to find bits of coal in the rubbish. For there is no coal to be bought and, even as I write, we have no coal in this house. Yet from this window I can see the mountain so full of coal that the seams crop out to the daylight.*"

"**I AM NOT WORKING MYSELF,** *hundreds of my mates are idle, and the inside of the great mountain of coal towering over my home is at rest.*"

THIS IS THE PROBLEM—*Continued*

apples were dear and scarce; so were swedes. The people would hardly believe that I had seen them left to rot. Yet I found straight away that the coal we had valued so highly—in the country —was of no account here. It was left behind in the workings, thrown over tips and buried— wasted just as badly as the crops.

Now, for more than twenty years, I have seen this black mineral torn from the heart of the earth and used as if it was of no value. Even in the middle of the war, at this very moment, it seems that no one wants it. For here I am, not working myself, hundreds of my mates are idle, and the inside of the great mountain of coal towering over my home is at rest. We are not allowed to go under the earth. And we must be very careful where we walk on the surface. It seems that the palsied hand which made our farming derelict has stretched over the mountains into the coalfield and made that derelict too.

I ask myself how can it be that no one needs coal? Near here is a disused mine and some of my mates are busy trying to find bits of coal in the rubbish. For there is no coal to be bought, and even as I write, we have no coal in this home. Yet from this window I can see the mountain so full of coal that the seams crop out to the daylight.

There are collieries close to this spot equipped and able to bring out more than six thousand tons of coal a day between them. Yet their engines are not moving and the workers are waiting, shivering before their empty grates.

As I look out of the window, I think of my own life. I married young, and our only daughter did likewise. So now, out in the backyard, I can hear the voices of our little grandsons. They come to visit us often because we have a little space out back and, after all, children must play sometimes.

Our only son, aged 15, is out there too. He is a natural mechanic, and now, so it seems, he is trying to make an aeroplane out of two old bicycles. For he is "idle", too; the country doesn't want his skill or his labour.

This sounds very gloomy, I know. This country, at war, seems to have no need of my strong and mature middle-age, no encouragement for my boy's inventive youth. So will there be any place for the grandsons, the youngest generations? I'm sure there will be. But to get a better world, somebody must go pretty deep into the evil things of the old world—see just which way we have been going and which way we ought to be going.

I have no war aims except to win it in such a way that real peace terms are possible and to banish the shadow of war for ever from our lives. Before we can do that we must look into the origins of this war. It seems to me something like this.

We claim to be a nation that plays the game, and "that's not playing cricket" is a national reproach. But have you ever seen a cricket team win when its batsmen crouched over the wicket and refused to use the bat no matter what was sent along? That is the sort of game we've seen our leaders playing

"I MARRIED YOUNG, and our only daughter did likewise. So now . . . I can hear the voices of our little grandsons."

"OUR ONLY SON . . . is a natural mechanic . . . he is idle, too; the country doesn't want his skill or his labour."

in the past, and what is the result? We are left alone on the field and in a war that we must now fight and win.

We of the working class play cricket too, but our hands are hard and our leisure time is short. Therefore we develop more hitters and those are the men to deal with crooked stuff, such as a dictator sends along. We want more sledge-hammer users in our Government and fewer umbrella carriers. More than half of my mates saw what was coming when Spain was sacrificed, and we collected from our small earnings to help what we knew was the first line of the defence; then Czechoslovakia was betrayed and a moan of sorrow went through the mines. Since then, we have always wondered whether they who governed us were wilfully blind or incredibly stupid.

Those blunders have finished for ever the tradition of a class that was born to govern; and educated to believe that only the best was good enough for them. Almost alone amongst the great nations we still worship the idea of the family crest—the idea that we should look up to a man on account of his birth. For my own part, I feel I can say I have never sought easy work or shrunk from soiling my hands. There are thousands—no, millions !—like me, who are willing to do hard and dangerous work as long as they get a fair reward for it. But this one thing angers us—the idea that a man is a dolt if he does work which dirties his hands or his clothes ! The fact is that men like us have got to be efficient at our jobs—because we can't get promoted for muddling things !

I feel there must be great changes in the men and women who run this country. There must be new ideas and new methods. Then when our own land is shaped we can invite the spectators from all over the world and tell them "Now, we are really playing the game. Do you like it?" They might find something worth copying.

Hallo ! There is a commotion out the back. It reminds me that my thoughts have been running away with me.

The coalman has arrived and the boys—the sons and grandsons of unemployed miners—are clapping because there are hopes of being warm.

"Only a hundredweight," the coalman tells us, "and it was a job to get it. Poor stuff it is, too, but I've got to charge two and sevenpence."

A month ago we were cutting much better coal for two shillings a ton. Between the dear coal and the cheap cutting, the scarce apples and those that rot, I think I can see the peace aim I would like to achieve. It is security—security against war and exploitation, by man or country. And what I ask for ourselves should be granted to the whole world.

From across the valley, that great grey mountain seems to be frowning at me.

"SO WILL THERE BE ANY PLACE FOR THE GRANDSONS?"
Picture Post has asked a number of experts to answer the miner's question. He has faith that the answer will be 'Yes'. In the following pages they show how the answer can be made 'Yes'.

THE FIRST NECESSITY IN THE NEW BRITAIN

WORK FOR ALL

by Thomas Balogh

Author is an expert on finance and economic problems. Used to work in the League of Nations Secretariat. Now a Tutor at Balliol College, Oxford, and works in the Oxford University Institute of Statistics.

The Man Who Asks for Work
B. L. Coombes, the Welsh miner, with his grandson. He asks work for himself, and a future for the new generation.

YOU have probably come to believe—through hearing it often repeated—that it will take a long time to pay for this war, and that we shall be very poor as a nation, long after it is finished. If you stop to think for a moment you will realise how distorted this is. Just think what makes up the wealth of a country. It is the country's natural resources, its factories, its labour or skill. Realising that this is so, ask yourself why we should be faced with poverty. To be sure, we are forced to use our natural resources now by turning them into guns, and all kinds of means of destruction. But we are having to pay for this wasteful kind of production at this very moment by the sacrifices we have to make—increased taxation, rationing, etc. Indeed, there is good reason to think that we ought to be paying a more drastic price at the moment for our essential immediate duty of winning the war.

Once the war is over, once we have completed our immediate task, there is most certainly the danger that many of our factories may have been destroyed. But we are building new ones, and it will be mainly a matter of turning them over from the production of destructive weapons to the manufacture of goods for use. Moreover, the amount of skill available to us ought to have increased enormously as the result of the war. Before we have gone much further, it will be essential to train millions of workers now unemployed, or engaged on non-essential industries, in the production of war materials. All these will be added to the ranks of those who can turn out in peace time the kind of goods which will be of use or enjoyment to mankind. Therefore, our ability to produce need not have been greatly diminished, and could have even increased. If our foreign assets will have decreased, again there will be in our hands the means to replenish them.

A Warning from the Last War

This is all very well, you say, but there will be far too *much* labour available. We shall have to demobilise an army of three, four or five million men; and how can they all find jobs? Won't it be just the same as last time? Yes, we can answer quite clearly, it will be exactly the same as last time—if we allow it to be so. The fact is that we must not allow it. At the end of the last war, most of the warring countries possessed the main "controls" that were necessary for a planned economic development, the best utilisation of the national wealth, and the steady employment for which the workers have since been looking. But these "controls" were thrown away. In this way we lost by unemployment more national output than the whole of our national capital, if you exclude the value of land and of our natural resources. In other words, we could have built

as many houses again as we did and increased productive capacity very considerably. Of course if, after this war, we have to replace many of our factories, it will be more difficult to do what we ought to have done last time. But international co-operation will greatly reduce this difficulty.

Now let us consider what a "control" is. You have heard of "price control" and perhaps of "exchange control." But the most closely related to our present point—the point of providing employment for everybody—are the control of labour, or what is now called "man-power," and the control over demand. The first of these controls depends on an estimate of the number of workers required in factories producing materials

---

WHAT WE WANT

- *A job for every able-bodied man.*

- *State control of the banks and individual investment.*

- *A State-managed company to make Community investment.*

- *Lower income-tax, but a tax on property.*

- *The national plan related to an international plan.*

---

of war; when the estimate is made, steps are supposed to be taken to see that this number of workers is made available by training the unemployed or withdrawing workers from non-essential industries. This is an operation which should work quite scientifically, and it is the only kind of operation by which man-power can be used to its greatest advantage in wartime. The alternative is to have one employer offering higher wages than another, workers leaving their own trade for others, the unemployed remaining untrained, and so on; in fact, sheer chaos, or what is called a "free labour market." There are two alternatives then when war ends—the chaos of a free labour market (or "every man for himself"), and a planned scheme releasing labour from the services as it can be absorbed in industry, and so controlling and stimulating the demand for it as to ensure stability of employment.

Take another example of control—from the manufacturer's point of view. Control of essential materials gives "priority" to manufacturers who are producing goods urgently required by the fighting Services. It would be shocking if the Services had to bid against each other, for instance, for the amount of steel available. That would result in fabulous prices; perhaps the Services would never get their steel at all because somebody else would outbid them. You couldn't conduct a war in that fashion. Yet that is exactly how we tried to conduct the peace. We made no

attempt to control man-power according to the real requirements of the country; we made no attempt to control commodity markets and production. These things were dependent on the uncertainties of a badly managed monetary system aggravated by the speculator. When peace comes again, our chance of providing stable employment and social security for the masses of the people will depend on whether we leave everything to chance, or whether we control the supply of essential labour and materials according to the requirements of a country which will be faced by the task of reconstruction.

How NOT to Provide Work

I have tried to indicate what a control is. And I have said that the necessary controls existed in 1918. Why then were we faced in a comparatively short space of time after 1918 by a vast unemployment problem? The fact is that in 1918 the sufferings of four years of war produced an urgent desire to be rid of everything that war meant, and led to a demand for an instant abolition of all State controls, however well they had functioned. Officialdom had made plenty of blunders and became even more unpopular than usual. The reactionaries, the "liberals" who were in favour of instant economy—you remember the Geddes Axe?—knew what they wanted—freedom from control. The economists, who saw deeper, were divided among themselves and had no contact with the masses. The masses were deceived by the cry of "A Land Fit for Heroes" into thinking that there would be permanent work and social security for all, and that these things merely had to be looked for. Hence the cry for "decontrol" went hand in hand with the cry for demobilisation.

It was every man for himself, whether he wanted to find a job, or whether he wanted to invest money in the work of reconstruction which caused the post-war boom. Nobody could bother to plan the supply of labour for this work. Nobody could bother to plan the work itself on a national scale, and it was left to speculators who wanted quick profits and cared nothing for the future. Hence, when everybody was bidding against everybody else, there occurred an artificial rise in prices and wages. And afterwards, when the frenzy of speculation had exhausted itself, came the crash. In fact, to return to an example which I gave previously—it was just as if the fighting Services had been in violent competition for a limited amount of material and, after a violent bout of bidding on the Stock Exchange, had fallen back exhausted. Only now, in peace time, the competing services were those which should have been fighting for the nation's victory in housing, in health, in enjoyment, and everything that makes life worth living. They fell back exhausted because the speculators were exhausted and the monetary mechanism could and would not further sustain them.

To complete our rather gloomy picture of what happened when "decontrol" took place too quickly, we should note that the crisis which showed itself in the permanent body of unemployed, was further deepened by the return to financial "normalcy" as Mr. Baldwin's American colleagues called it, or what is popularly called "being on the

Work Can be Made Universal, Pleasant, Secure, by Proper Planning of the National Resources
Men and women pour out of the factory gates. There will be plenty of reconstruction work after this war—more than we can cope with. After the last war speculation ran riot and the boom was artificial. This time we must have a national plan to make the best use of our resources.

Gold Standard." This meant that our capital was being reckoned as worth far more than we could afford in terms of resources and labour—which was very nice for the owners of the capital, but not so nice for those who had to pay the price in ever-rising unemployment.

We should be thankful that we escaped so lightly as we did. In other countries, unrelieved despair drove the masses into the arms of fanatics such as Hitler, so that the doom of orderly progress was sealed until another war could be fought.

The Temptation of a Boom

Now, we must learn the lesson of what happened last time and decide firmly that it shall not happen again. Make no mistake about it, there will be plenty of temptation. We are never free from a certain distrust of the bureaucracy, which seems slow and incapable of grappling with wartime problems. And this tendency to abuse the civil servant becomes even more tempting in peace time because, in this country, the civil servants always seem to be so anxious to be rid of their responsibilities. Hence it may again be a popular cry — fomented by the men who want freedom to speculate and get quick profits—that we should rid ourselves of Government control and get back as quickly as possible to that state of "freedom" which was supposed to exist before the last war.

The temptation will be the greater because we shall be offered the prospect of a post-war boom, with the chance of big profits for a few, and high wages for a minority of the workers. How is such a boom likely to arise? Obviously, there will be the urgent work of rebuilding what has been des-

Work For All Means Pay For All
Steel-workers collect their wages after the week's work. A planned economic system can offer properly-paid work to every worker.

THE TRAGIC TALE THAT MUST NOT BE REPEATED:

Work on Munitions in 1918
On Armistice Day, November 11, 1918, our factories are turning out shells at full speed. Stopping of munitions at once will mean chaos. So, even in peace, munitions are produced until contracts are completed.

The Building Boom After the War
Heavy Government expenditure, high wages and profits cause a boom. Building houses has been practically stopped during the war. Now there is a sharp revival.

The General Strike of 1926
Depression still reigns in the coal-mining industry, and the striking of miners is supported by organised labour in other industries. Through lack of a planned Government policy, 162 million working days are lost.

Sweeping Up After the Wall Street Crash
In October, 1929, the boom collapses on Wall Street, New York's Stock Exchange, and panic follows. Fortunes melt like ice under the sun. The crash ushers in the greatest business depression in the United States.

WORK FOR ALL—*Continued*

troyed by bombs and shells. There will be a tremendous demand from all the territories which have been the scene of active hostilities, and they will make desperate efforts to obtain supplies at home and abroad. Now, it is true that the world ought to be in a better position to meet such demands than after the last war, because the productive capacity of the overseas world is ever increasing. All the same, the intensity of the demand will cause a shortage in some materials, the speculator will step in, and prices will soar. That is what we call a "boom." And it is probable that this boom will be concentrated in the economically strongest countries—the U.S.A. and Britain—which are best able to meet the demand for goods. But what would be the results? Capital would be attracted from the territories which needed it most—that is, the devastated areas—to those which needed it least. And the history of the U.S.A., which developed its unemployment at the very time when it was drawing gold from other lands, showed how the strong country suffers when that happens. In such circumstances, we should soon find ourselves engaged in the same old scramble for foreign

markets. We should then discover that, while we seemed to be hard at work at providing materials for the rebuilding of Europe, we were being paid only on paper—for the weak countries would be denied the chance to pay with anything else. Paper payment would soon fail to satisfy the speculator, who would try to realise the profits on which he could lay his hands, and close down the business, leaving the workers to fend for themselves at the labour exchange. At the end would come the same old unemployment problem, which we know so well.

We must decide now that we will stop this from happening. It can be done.

The Plan We Must Have
The most important thing is to realise that the end of the war will not be the time to return to what used to be called "normal"—that is, complete freedom for the speculator to make high profits out of the world's need of reconstruction. On the contrary, the reconstruction must be planned exactly as war production ought to be planned. Just as Government controls are needed at present to enable the nation to throw its whole

strength into the war-effort, so a system of Government controls—reformed both in character and personnel—is needed to enable us to throw our whole strength into the peace effort. Man-power must be controlled so that it can be directed where it is most needed, and demobilisation must take place not as it did last time—when millions of men were thrown on the labour market—but according to the work which can be provided. The supply of materials must be adjusted according to the task. In fact, we must have a national plan of reconstruction. Now the word "plan" is somewhat unpopular, especially because it denotes a certain amount of compulsion or direction which is not favoured by a freedom-loving people. But we have surely reached the stage of overcoming this prejudice, which has been fostered by the people who want freedom to profit at the expense of the majority.

Control of Investments
Our national plan makes it necessary to take certain preliminary steps.

We must be able to control investment. This must be extended not merely to investment in

Picture Post January 4 1941

The Era of Strikes: 1921 Volunteers Sign Up
By the middle of 1920 the boom has cracked. Government expenditure is drastically cut. There is no national plan. Unemployment is rife, short-time general, stock markets demoralised, wages falling.

Strike-breaking at Its Worst
In the United States, strike-breaking takes its worst form. There, too, boom has been followed by business depression. America lacks conciliation machinery between labour and employers. Strikes become "little wars."

The National Government Comes In
With the autumn of 1929 begins the severe depression. Our production falls steeply, unemployment rises. Blame falls on the Labour Government, which is succeeded by MacDonald's National Government.

The Flight of Gold to the U.S.
Owners of capital take fright at the state of Europe. They send their capital to the United States. Till by the present day, the United States holds nearly three-quarters of the world's gold stock.

Continued overleaf

houses or fixed plant, but also in working capital. At the same time, it will be necessary for the community as a whole to undertake investment should individual initiative fail.

This means control over the issue market and banks (as well as dividends and reserves of companies) on the one hand, and, on the other, the establishment of a huge State-managed investment company which would provide capital at appropriate rates and conditions, or undertake direct investment (housing schemes, etc.) itself.

It also means a co-ordinated price and wage policy, with tribunals to enforce equity and prevent hardships. It means the continuation of the system by which manufacturers are now given "priority" in the supply of their materials. It means a real control of man-power. Every person must be able to find a job at appropriate wages. Unemployment benefit, except perhaps as a short transition pay, must not play any part in our economic system. And in so far as the minimum standard of social and health services cannot be secured by an appropriate management of investment and prices and wages—and in many instances it cannot—direct subsidies will be necessary.

The Need to Lower Income Tax

The chief danger is that individual initiative and enterprise will disappear under the weight of Government control. The task is to find the correct compromise between planning and individualism, and it is surely within the genius of the British people to reach that happy goal. There is one step which should be taken as soon as possible — to change the basis of taxation.

The truth is that if we continue to tax enterprise we cannot hope to revive individual initiative. The only solution which offers itself—if we do not want to have a violent change in the whole social structure—is the lowering of income tax and the establishment of a tax which hits property, whether gainfully invested or not. Such a property tax does not prevent the accumulation of capital, but it prevents its misuse, and reduces inequality that is due to inheritance not to ability. If we had such a tax now, and if at the same time rationing would enforce saving on everybody, the post-war outlook would be brighter.

If we are to make a success of such a system it would have to be based on practical international understanding in planning. Otherwise the national plans are likely to lead to friction and clashes. It is obvious that such planning is not possible whilst maintaining the traditional concepts of sovereignty. They will have to go. Whether as federations, or otherwise, the Continents will have to be unified and themselves brought into co-ordinated relations.

Much can be said against this advocacy of ordered progress. It will be difficult to administer. Admittedly. We must educate the administrators. It will mean much red-tape and waste. Certainly. But it cannot cause the waste that resulted from the deflation and economic nationalism of the inter-war period.

If we are not going to secure a working compromise between individualism, collective planning, and social equality, individualism will perish and in its ruin will smash those who resisted change and retard the progress of the remainder.

Continuing THE TRAGIC TALE THAT MUST NOT BE REPEATED :

The World Economic Conference Opens
Ramsay MacDonald opens the conference, called in 1933, to consider the world's economic ailments. But nobody is willing to co-operate or make temporary sacrifices. Short-sighted nationalism reigns supreme.

Financial Scandals Reveal a Rotten System
Stavisky, in France, has raised about £3 millions by issuing fraudulent municipal bonds. He commits suicide, others are put on trial, crowds riot in Paris. The whole world is horrified by what is brought to light.

Merchant Ships Are Laid Up
The world depression leads to a headlong fall in world trade. As a result, Britain, the world's "sea carrier," has to lay up hundreds of her merchant ships. Thousands of her seamen, too.

The Luxury Liner is Built
The Cunard Line wants to recapture the "blue-ribband" of the Atlantic. But the construction of the "Queen Mary" has to be suspended during the depression. Then the Government provides part of the cost.

SOCIAL SECURITY *by* A. D. K. Owen

Author is Stevenson Lecturer in Citizenship at University of Glasgow. Now acting secretary of Political and Economic Planning, engaged on studies of social and economic reconstruction.

IF there is one reform which would mean more than any other to each one of us it would be a drastic overhaul of the British social security services. We have every reason to be proud of these services. They have been a great boon to us all. But they are full of gaps and deficiencies, and the time is ripe to bring them into line with present-day needs.

The basis of any future arrangements should be a National Minimum—a standard below which no one should be allowed to fall, in employment or out, in sickness or in health, during widowhood or in old age.

This would mean that everyone would be guaranteed enough of the right kind of food to keep them fit and healthy. And, in addition, an allowance would be made to cover a moderate rent, clothing, general household expenses, and some conventional luxuries. The money value for these things would vary from time to time according to changes in the cost of the various items, and, as our economic life recovers after the war, we

might increase the allowance to include a few more conventional luxuries. It is to be hoped that the great majority of people would enjoy a much higher standard than this minimum, and, if we are

---

WHAT WE WANT

- *A minimum wage for all able-bodied adults.*
- *Allowances for the children.*
- *An all-in Contributory Scheme of social insurance.*
- *Special forms of help from public assistance.*

---

prepared to make the necessary changes in our economic arrangements, there is no reason why this should not be so. Think, however, of what it would mean to you and me to know that there

was a guaranteed minimum, even though we hoped never to have to rely on it.

To establish this National Minimum, we should have to work to this sort of plan :

(1) fix a minimum wage for able-bodied adults that will cover the minimum standard needs of a married man and his wife, and introduce a system of children's allowances, financed by taxation, to cover the minimum standard needs of their children;

(2) reorganise the contributory insurance services to provide an "All-in" social security policy, covering unemployment, sickness, invalidism, workmen's compensation, widows', orphans' and old-age pensions, and a fixed sum at death to meet burial and other expenses;

(3) expand the work of the existing Assistance Service, to provide *extra* help and *special forms* of help to people whose needs are not satisfied by standardised social insurance benefits, and to meet the needs of people (such as workers on their own account) who cannot be conveniently included in the contributory insurance scheme.

The most revolutionary thing in this plan would be the introduction of children's allowances.

The Unemployed Vainly Search for Work . . . .
The unemployed look for jobs in the public reading room. They tramp for miles, buoyed up by a vain hope. The Government has no plans to prevent this waste of productive power.

. . . . While the Rich Can Forget the World's Troubles
The rich get away from the world at a French resort. The profits of many fall during the depression, others thrive on the general collapse. Many go away to forget what is happening.

Our Workless March to London . . . .
Hunger-marchers take the road for the capital to state their grievances. They come from the distressed areas. These came from Jarrow, one of the hardest hit towns.

. . . . Germany's March to Hitler
Hitler promises Germany steady work and a golden future. He uses Germany's misery and despair to grab power for himself. So depression turns into preparation for a new war.

These allowances might be paid either in cash or in the form of coupons which could be exchanged for milk and other foods essential for children, and for children's footwear and clothing. No longer would the wife of a man earning £2 a week have to wonder how she could find 5s. 11d. for boots for her little boy. No longer would the mother of a large family wonder where the next day's dinner was coming from. The State would ensure that her family was at least warm and fed. Any who were temporarily unemployed would be decently provided for without discouraging men with low earning capacity, but large family responsibilities, from seeking new employment.

The payment of children's allowances would simplify the "All-in" social security policy. It would not be necessary to provide for dependent children out of insurance funds, but provision should be made for the wives of insured men, and other adult dependents. Men who fall out of work on account of slack trade, sickness, or industrial accidents, would all receive weekly benefit in the form of incomes covering their needs (including their wives' needs) at the National Minimum standard. Where a man was only partially disabled—and therefore able to earn a little—his allowance could be adjusted accordingly.

As a great deal of the premium income of the friendly societies and commercial insurance companies would become available to finance the "All-in" State scheme, the weekly contributions which would be necessary need not be heavier than hundreds of thousands of working-class families are now paying for insurance stamps and in small premiums of various kinds. Everyone earning less than £500 a year should be included in this scheme, and those who wished to have more "protection" than the National Minimum provided should be quite free to make supplementary arrangements on their own account.

The administration of these services should be in the hands of a Ministry of Social Welfare, which should absorb the Assistance Board, and some sections of the Ministries of Labour and Health. The Ministry would be directly responsible for the distribution of children's allowances. They would also handle any cases where an additional allowance might be necessary for any reason. But they would not determine this allowance by a "Means Test." That would be a thing of the past. A "Needs Test" would be the only ground on which they would work.

There is no reason why we should wait until the end of the war for this Ministry. It should be established now to implement the policy which has been outlined above, not in the distant future, but in 1941.

The Unwanted Worker
The picture of the unemployed man which we published in "Picture Post," summing up the problem.

Picture Post, June 14, 1941

THE GIRL NEW YORK CROWDS TO SEE: Nineteen-year-old Carmen Amaya Does Her Spanish Gipsy Dance

To the Beachcomber Night Club in New York flock the bored, the indolent, the tired, the idle. They come to see the most amazing exhibition of vibrant agility New York has to offer—the spectacular gipsy dancing of a nineteen-year-old Spanish girl.

23

Vol. 10 No. 5   **PICTURE POST**   February 1, 1941

THE NIGHT OF THE BLITZ: *Roof Spotters Are the First to See the Fire*

The night is dark. The city is silent. On the roofs of high buildings stand the spotters. Overhead the pulsing drone of enemy bombers. Suddenly a bomb falls, then another. Somewhere, a burning building starts to light up the sky. Immediately the warning is given.

FIRE-FIGHTERS!

For a fortnight one of our photographers slept every night at a fire station. Nothing happened. The Nazis were laying off London. Then came the storm. Out all night, in one blazing building after another, he lost a £50 camera, a tripod, a pair of trousers. In return, he got a burned leg—and these pictures.

THE next morning, nobody seemed quite to know what had happened. The air was full of smoke. Vast buildings stood blind and eyeless in street after street. On the corners little groups of clerks and typists gathered among the ashes, wondering what to do next now that their offices were smouldering ruins, now that their jobs had disappeared. A haggard fireman, stooping over a length of hose, eyed them for a moment and straightened his back. "Why don't they run along home?" he said. "We ain't the Zoo."

It was Monday morning. The previous night the raiders had roared over London leaving a wake of fire and wreckage right across the centre of the city. Buses lay on their sides, buildings burst into flames, stray passers-by fled down the streets keeping close in to the doorways until they reached a shelter. And in the watchroom of a fire-station the ticker-tape began to tap (the watch-room tapes were tapping all over the city), 66—8.15 . . . 66—8.15 . . . 66—8.15. The brisk A.F.S. girl at the desk knew that 66 meant the number of the alarm, 8.15 meant the time the alarm was given. And as the ticker stopped, astonishing things happened. All the bells in the station began to trill until it sounded like a giant aviary. Illuminated panels in the Appliance Room —where what laymen call the "engines" are kept— had lit up the number of the alarm and the name of the street as: "66 Stamboul Lane." From floor to floor down the electro-plated poles slid half a dozen men. Technical ingenuity has never yet devised a quicker way of getting from the fourth floor to the ground than by these poles, beloved of old-time Keystone comedies. But this was no comedy. The men buttoned their shirts as they ran. Their tunics, belts, axes, hammers, gasmasks, all their gear was on the machine in the Appliance Room. And on to this machine they now jumped. Someone shoved the sliding doors apart, the light trailer-pump drawn by a one-time taxi roared out into the night full of bombs, flames and falling wreckage.

Before they had turned the corner of Stamboul Lane, E.C. at 8.19 p.m., Sub-Officer Dunn, in charge of the pump, knew by the way the sky was lit like day, knew by the way the scorch of the fire took his breath, that more help and plenty of it would be needed. The pump pulled up, the men sized up the situation, and Sub-Officer Dunn slipped into the telephone booth, pushed the "Emergency" button, and called his station. "Message from Stamboul Lane fire. Make the pumps up to ten. It's pretty hot." It was then 8.22.

In the next few minutes, more pumps arrived.

INSIDE THE CENTRAL CONTROL ROOM ALL IS QUIET
This is the Central Control for all the six districts and 60-odd sub-districts of the London Fire Region. When the alarm comes through, the telephone seated by the map. Nobody rushes. Nobody shouts. But in a

The district officer came, with a Dual-Purpose appliance and a Water Unit, complete with collapsible dam and 6,000 feet of hose to relay water from the distant river.

The Superintendent followed in his high-powered fire car.

The Water Unit men lay their hose at a 20-mile-an-hour speed. They rigged their 5,000-gallon dam of tubular steel and canvas, as close to the fire as possible. Under the Superintendent's orders the men tried to surround the fire. They clambered on sloping roofs, they rushed into cavernous ware-

An A.F.S. Girl Takes a Call
More pumps are needed. An A.F.S. girl passes the call to District Control.

Details of the Call Are Charted Up
On the Mobilising Board at District Control, a girl moves a pin. Each pin means a pump. Each move means another engine at the fire.

AND ORDERLY : *A Fire to Them is Just an "Incident"*

girl transfers the message to a vacant booth in the centre of the room. An A.F.S. girl takes down the message. Another hands it to the mobilising officer flash the necessary pumps are called for, the firemen are on the way.

houses smouldering already, and in the midst of a great blaze which dwarfed them and their appliances they fought the fire from the tops of slender ladders. They fought as their comrades were fighting all over the city that night. "These days," said the Superintendent, "our lads have got to be good and they've got to be brave." They are.

It costs over five million pounds each year to keep the city's fire fighting forces going. The money is spent on maintenance of a wartime fire force of some 18,500 men (as against 1,900 firemen in peacetime). In return for this outlay, citizens are

given the colossal and tangible reward of thousands of buildings safeguarded against spread of fire.

The force, A.F.S. and L.F.B. combined, is on duty over 120 square miles of city territory. Administratively, all are controlled from the

Firemen Rush Down to Man the Engines
The bells ring. The indicators light up. In a few-seconds the firemen are in the Appliance Room and manning their engines.

Off They Go
The big D.P. (dual-purpose) pump flies out into the night, to face the fire and the blitz.

Picture Post,
February 1, 1941

THE FIGHT IS ON

sprawling and impressive headquarters on Thames side, near Lambeth Bridge. The simple facts of life for the fireman are that ordinary firemen get £3 12s. a week, plus 10s. rent money, and A.F.S. receive £3 5s. plus an allowance for meals, and that the lower ranks of both must normally work 48 hours on and 24 off (for officers it's worse, they may work more than 72 hours continuously with one day off).

Now let us speed up the review. Watch a batch of Heavy Unit and D.P. appliances streak over the bridges that lead to the city's centre to cover an urgent call to a big 30-pump fire. Or ride with one of the fast fireboats from Lambeth downstream to the dockside to deal with a stick of incendiaries on a reeking fur warehouse. Look at the men as they fit together the 50-foot lengths of hose, couple it to a hydrant and have a jet of water playing on the fire at the rate of 900 gallons a minute before you can wink an eye. Watch the men on the "branch" (branch means nozzle) crawl under an arch, climb up a rickety roof, manœuvre for position, and fight full in the face of a fire that roars like a waterfall and withers steel girders as if they were feathers. Duck your head and quake as the night raiders come back, guided by the glare, and drop their clutches of iron eggs all around, while the firemen and auxiliaries get on with their job without a blink. Go through the night and the next day with them and end up at the station when it's all over—it may be an evacuated school or a garage under the arches—and watch them, greyfaced and haggard-eyed trying to dry their drenched clothes, and nearly dropping with exhaustion while the station radio plays "Keep Your Thumbs Up and Say It's Ticketty Boo," and finally go to bed yourself. And if "he" is over and dropping incendiaries, it may be that in the few minutes between the time you close your exhausted eyes—though you've only been watching, not working—and the time you go to sleep, there will be fifty telephone calls and alarms in the London area, with someone shouting "I want the fire brigade!"

THEY FIGHT FROM ABOVE
Whole strategy of fire-fighting is to surround the fire. These men climb on a rickety roof to attack the fire from above.

THEY FIGHT FROM BELOW
Burning wreckage falls in the street. The gutters are flooded. The firemen pour 900 gallons of water on the fire in a single minute.

THEY FIGHT FROM THE INSIDE
His stock-in-trade is his courage. His armament is the hose. He fights within the smouldering ruin.

12

FROM A DOZEN POINTS, WATER IS PUMPED ON THE RAGING FIRE

They have occupied all the vantage points. They have surrounded the fire. Now they give it all they've got. And all they've got is water. If water is scarce, then they must call for a water unit. That means two lorries, a mile of hose, and a steel and canvas dam to hold 5,000 gallons of river water.

THEY CONCENTRATE THEIR FORCES . . .

The fire turns night into day, winter into summer. In the heat and the glare, the firemen attack.

. . . BUT STILL THE FIRE GAINS GROUND

They have worked for hours. But the blaze still grows. Now they must try a new tack.

13

THE HEIGHT OF THE BLAZE : *Eighty Feet up in the Air a Fireman Strikes at the Heart of the Fire*

Stark and grim is the climax of the fire fight. Blazing walls are crumbling. The fire is bursting through. Overhead, guided by the flames, the German bombers are circling. One after another they release their load of death. Unmoved, unflinching, the firemen run out their ladder. One man mounts, higher and higher, till he is alone above the flames. There, eighty feet up, he strikes at the very source of the fire.

THE MAN ON THE LADDER: *In Clouds of Smoke and Steam He Faces the Fire Alone*

All night long they have fought the fire. They have fought it in the streets streaming with water. They have fought it within buildings blazing like a furnace. On to the flames they have poured a hundred thousand gallons of water, concentrated at colossal pressure. And still the fight goes on. From our rule of anonymity we except these pictures. They were taken by A. Hardy, one of our own cameramen.

SIDNEY WEBB *With his beard, his pince-nez, his quiet voice, he might be some retired schoolmaster. Instead, he is the spiritual and literary father of the British Labour movement. For over fifty years, he and his wife have investigated, compared, analysed, summed up all that has to be known of labour conditions, labour aspirations. Though a Labour Government made him a Peer in 1929, he prefers not to use the title. He is known throughout the world as Sidney Webb, and under this name he will be remembered.*

Two Friends of the Soviet Union

by G. BERNARD SHAW

This is the first full-length article G. B. S. has written for PICTURE POST. He writes it about two octogenarians who, for over fifty years, have been his friends and allies. He writes it as a tribute to two wonderful lives.

THE WEBBS, Sidney and Beatrice, officially The Right Honourable the Baron and Lady Passfield, are a superextraordinary pair. I have never met anyone like them, either separately or in their most fortunate conjunction. Each of them is an English force; and their marriage was an irresistible reinforcement. Only England could have produced them. It is true that France produced the Curies, a pair equally happily matched; but in physics they found and established science and left it so, enriched as it was by their labors; but the Webbs found British Constitutional politics something which nobody had yet dreamt of calling a science or thinking of as such.

When they began, they were face to face with Capitalism and Marxism. Marxism, though it claims to be scientific, and has proved itself a mighty force in the modern world, was then a philosophy propounded by a foreigner without administrative experience, who gathered his facts in the Reading Room of the British Museum, and generalized the human race under the two heads of *bourgeoisie* and proletariat apparently without having ever come into business contact with a living human being.

The Quarrel with Capitalism

Capitalism was and is a paper Utopia, the most unreal product of wishful thinking of all the Utopias. By pure logic, without a moment's reference to the facts, it demonstrated that you had only to enforce private contracts and let everybody buy in the cheapest market and sell in the dearest to produce automatically a condition in which there would be no unemployment, and every honest and industrious person would enjoy a sufficient wage to maintain himself and his wife and reproduce his kind, whilst an enriched superior class would have leisure and means to preserve and develop the nation's culture and civilization, and, by receiving more of the national income than they could possibly consume, save all the capital needed to make prosperity increase by leaps and bounds.

What Karl Marx Did

Karl Marx's philosophy had no effect on public opinion here or elsewhere; but when he published the facts as to the condition to which Capitalism had reduced the masses, it was like lifting the lid off hell. Capitalism has not yet recovered from the shock of that revelation, and never will.

Sixty years ago, the Marxian shock was only beginning to operate in England. I had to read Das Kapital in a French translation, there being no English version as yet. A new champion of the people, Henry Mayers Hyndman, had met and talked with Karl Marx. They quarrelled, as their habit was, but not before Hyndman had been completely converted by Marx; so his Democratic

BEATRICE WEBB *As a financial magnate's daughter she knew luxury. As a social investigator working in an East End sweat shop she knew hardship, poverty, misery. When she married Sidney Webb in 1892, the famous partnership began, described by a friend as "two typewriters that click as one." She investigated social conditions under Capitalism, also under Communism in the U.S.S.R. in 1932. Now, at 83, she is still hard at work, has just finished a new introduction to "Soviet Communism: a New Civilisation."*

Federation presently became a Social-Democratic Federation. Socialism, in abeyance since the slaughter of the Paris Commune in 1871, suddenly revived; but Marx, its leader and prophet, died at that moment and left the movement to what leadership it could get.•

Socialism was not a new thing peculiar to Marx. John Stuart Mill, himself a convert, had converted others, among them one very remarkable young man and an already famous elderly one. The elderly one was the great poet and craftsman William Morris, who, on reading Mill's early somewhat halfhearted condemnation of communism, at once declared that Mill's verdict was against the evidence, and that people who lived on unearned incomes were plainly " damned thieves." He joined Hyndman, and when the inevitable quarrel ensued, founded The Socialist League.

Sidney Webb, the Prodigy

The younger disciple had followed Mill's conversion and shared it. His name was Sidney Webb. He was an entirely unassuming young Londoner of no extraordinary stature, guiltless of any sort of swank, and so naïvely convinced that he was an ordinary mortal and everybody else as gifted as himself that he did not suffer fools gladly, and was occasionally ungracious to the poor things.

The unassuming young cockney was in fact a prodigy. He could read a book as fast as he could turn the leaves, and remember everything worth remembering in it. Whatever country he was in, he spoke the language with perfect facility, though always in the English manner. He had gone through his teens gathering scholarships and exhibitions as a child gathers daisies, and had landed at last in the upper division of the civil service as resident clerk in the Colonial Office. He had acquired both scholarship and administrative experience, and knew not only why reforms were desirable but how they were put into practice under our queer political system. Hyndman and his Democratic Federation were no use to him, Morris and his Socialist League only an infant school. There was no organization fit for him except the Liberal Party, already moribund, but still holding a front bench position under the leadership of Gladstone. All Webb could do was something that he was forbidden to do as a civil servant : that is, issue pamphlets warning the Liberal Party that they were falling behind the times and even behind the Conservatives. Nevertheless he issued the pamphlets calmly. Nobody dared to remonstrate.

G. B. S. Meets the Man He Sought

This was the situation when I picked him up at a debating society which I had joined to qualify myself as a public speaker. It was the year 1879, when I was 23 and he a year or two younger. I at once recognized and appreciated in him all the qualifications in which I was myself pitiably deficient. He was clearly the man for me to work

Under Lenin's Portrait, Mrs. Webb Reads Lenin translated their work into Russian. His portrait was a present from the Captain of the Soviet ship that took them to the Soviet Union.

More Than 80 Years Old, They Are Still Working On: The Webbs at Home

*Theirs is the most famous partnership in modern English politics. It has been responsible for the greatest series of books in modern social literature.
In 1935 it was crowned by their monumental work on Soviet Communism. Now they are launching a new edition of this famous work.*

with. I forced my acquaintance on him; and it soon ripened into an enduring friendship. This was by far the wisest step I ever took. The combination worked perfectly.

We were both in the same predicament in having no organization with which we could work. Our job was to get Socialism into some sort of working shape; and we knew that this brainwork must be done by groups of Socialists whose minds operated at the same speed on a foundation of the same culture and habits. We were not snobs; but neither were we mere reactionists against snobbery to such an extent as to believe that we could work in double harness with the working men of the Federation and the League, who deeply and wisely mistrusted us as "bourgeois," and who would inevitably waste our time in trying to clear up hopeless misunderstandings. Morris was soon completely beaten by his proletarian comrades : he had to drop the League, which immediately perished. The agony of the Social-Democratic Federation was longer drawn out; but it contributed nothing to the theory or practice of Socialism, and hardly even pretended to survive the death of Hyndman.

The Fabian Society's Rise to Power

One day I came upon a tract entitled Why Are The Many Poor? issued by a body of whom I had never heard, entitled The Fabian Society. The name struck me as an inspiration. I looked the

Society up, and found a little group of educated middle class persons who, having come together to study philosophy, had finally resolved to take to active politics as Socialists. It was just what we needed. When I had sized it up, Webb joined, and with him Sydney Olivier, his fellow resident clerk at the Colonial Office. Webb swept everything before him; and the history of the Fabian Society began as the public knows it to-day.

Their Simple Hampshire Home
Passfield Corner, Liphook, is the home of two great students. Books are the chief furniture, and it is a home of quiet simplicity.

Barricades manned by Anarchists, and Utopian colonies, vanished from the Socialist program; and Socialism became constitutional, respectable, and practical. This was the work of Webb far more than of any other single person.

Marriage to Beatrice Webb

He was still a single person in another sense when the Fabian job was done. He was young enough to be unmarried when a young lady as rarely qualified as himself decided that he was old enough to be married. She had arrived at Socialism not by way of Karl Marx or John Stuart Mill, but by her own reasoning and observation. She was not a British Museum theoriser and bookworm : she was a born firsthand investigator. She had left the West End, where she was a society lady of the political plutocracy, for the East End, where she disguised herself to work in sweaters' dens and investigate the condition of the submerged tenth just discovered by Charles Booth and the Salvation Army. The sweaters found her an indifferent needlewoman, but chose her as an ideal bride for Ikey Mo: a generic name for their rising sons. They were so pressing that she had to bring her investigation to a hasty end, and seek the comparatively aristocratic society of the trade union secretaries, with whom she hobnobbed as comfortably as if she had been born in their houses. She had written descriptions of the dens for Booth's first famous Enquiry, and a

history of Co-operation which helped powerfully to shift its vogue from producer's co-operation to consumers' co-operation. Before her lay the whole world of proletarian organization to investigate.

It was too big a job for one worker. She resolved to take a partner. She took a glance at the Fabian Society, now two thousand strong, and at once dismissed nineteen hundred and ninetysix of them as negligible sheep; but it was evident that they were not sheep without a shepherd. There were in fact some half dozen shepherds. She investigated them personally one after the other, and with unerring judgment selected Sidney Webb, and gathered him without the least difficulty, as he had left himself defenceless by falling in love with her head over ears.

Their Literary Partnership

And so the famous partnership began. He took to her investigation business like a duck to water. They started with a history of trade unionism so complete and intimate in its information that it reduced all previous books on the subject to waste paper, and made organized labor in England class conscious for the first time. It travelled beyond England and was translated by Lenin. Then came the volume on Industrial Democracy which took trade unionism out of its groove and made it politically conscious of its destiny. There followed a monumental history of Local Government which ran into many volumes, and involved such a program of investigations on the spot all over the country, and reading through local archives, as had never before been attempted. Under such handling not only Socialism but political sociology in general became scientific, leaving Marx and Lassalle almost as far behind in that respect as they had left Robert Owen. The labor of it was prodigious; but it was necessary. And it left the Webbs no time for argybargy as between Marx's Hegelian metaphysics and Max Eastman's Cartesian materialism. The question whether Socialism is a soulless Conditioned Reflex à la Pavlov or the latest phase of The Light of the World announced by St. John, did not delay them : they kept to the facts and the methods suggested by the facts.

The Face of a Thinker
Born Beatrice Potter, daughter of a G.W.R. Chairman, her formal title since 1929 has been Lady Passfield, but she hates the title, prefers to be Beatrice Webb

Two Allies of Soviet Russia Walk in their Garden
In their Hampshire home they are far from the noisy tormented world. But for them the struggle of Soviet Russia is a matter of life or death.

Finally came the work in which those who believe in Divine Providence may like to see its finger. The depth and genuineness of our Socialism found its crucial test in the Russian revolution which changed crude Tsarism into Red Communism. After the treaty of Brest Litovsk Hyndman, our arch Marxist, denounced it more fiercely than Winston Churchill. The history of Communist Russia for the past twenty years in the British and American Press is a record in recklessly prejudiced mendacity. The Webbs waited until the wreckage and ruin of the change was ended, its mistakes remedied, and the Communist State fairly launched. Then they went and investigated it. In their last two volumes they give us the first really scientific analysis of the Soviet State, and of its developments of our political and social experiments and institutions, including trade unionism and co-operation, which we thought they had abolished. No Russian could have done this all-important job for us. The Webbs knew England, and knew what they were talking about. No one else did.

They unhesitatingly gave the Soviet system their support, and announced it definitely as a New Civilization.

It has been a wonderful life's work. Its mere incidental by-blows included Webb's chairmanship of the London County Council's Technical Education Committee, which abolished the old Schoolboard, the creation of the London School of Economics, the Minority Report which dealt a death blow to the iniquitous Poor Law, and such comparative trifles as the conversion of bigoted Conservative constituencies into safe Labor seats, and a few years spent by Webb in the two Houses of parliament. They were the only years he ever wasted. He was actually compelled by the Labor Government to accept a peerage; but nothing could induce Beatrice to change the name she had made renowned throughout Europe for the title of Lady Passfield, who might be any nobody.

For the private life of the Webbs, look at the pictures. I know all about it, and can assure you that it is utterly void of those scandalous adventures which make private lives readable. Mr. Webb and Miss Potter are now Darby and Joan: that is all.

1942

On 1 January 1942 the twenty-six members of what President Roosevelt had optimistically termed the United Nations joined in a solemn declaration that they would wage war together and not make a separate peace.

The declaration was intended primarily as a gesture to Russia, believed to be still suspicious that the capitalist powers would seize any chance to join Germany in an anti-Communist crusade. The Soviet leaders, however, also harboured the suspicion that the Western allies would be happy to stand back and watch Russia and Germany exhaust each other in a bitter struggle. They showed themselves less interested in gestures than in the reality behind the slogan which began to appear chalked and painted on British walls and pavements: 'Start the Second Front – Now.'

Although the British granted to the most ruthless of dictators the secular canonization of calling him Uncle Joe, Russian secrecy and their own parish-pump preoccupations kept them from grasping the scale of warfare in Russia, where thousands of tanks were manoeuvring in vast battles across hundreds of miles of country. Six hundred thousand Russian prisoners were captured in one operation alone. Four million Russian prisoners died in German hands. There were a million deserters from the Red Army, and Stalin's government might well have been overthrown if the German conquerors had not been ordered to behave with an insane brutality towards people who, particularly in the Ukraine, welcomed them originally as liberators.

On this scale of events, there was not a great deal the British could do to help Russia, and in any case the long and lamentable tale of British retreat continued well into 1942. In February, General Perceval, an intelligent and able staff officer, but inexperienced in field command and left almost without air cover, surrendered Singapore and 60,000 men who had scarcely fired a shot. In March, the Japanese won a naval victory over a scratch Allied fleet, which opened the wealth of the Dutch East Indies to them. In June, Fortress Tobruk, which had remained in Commonwealth hands since O'Connor's early victories, was taken by Rommel, and Mussolini hopefully arrived in Libya ready to enter Cairo in triumph on a white charger.

Criticism of Churchill's conduct of the war, once confined to the inner circles of Westminster and Whitehall, became more overt. Independent parliamentary candidates broke the electoral truce by contesting and winning four by-elections. One of them, Tom Driberg, whose constituency voted a few days after the surrender in Libya, won temporary fame as the Member for Tobruk. In July, the critics plucked up courage to challenge the Prime Minister in a vote of confidence, but the proposer of the motion, an earnest and worthy supporter of Chamberlain,

Sir John Wardlaw-Milne, dissolved discontent in ridicule by suggesting that the Duke of Gloucester should be appointed commander-in-chief of the British Army.

In fact, though even the Prime Minister in his most exuberant moments would scarcely have chanced his arm in saying so, the tide had turned. In June, in a great though almost unpublicized carrier battle off Midway Island, in the north Pacific, the Americans set a limit to Japanese expansion. Rommel could get no further into Egypt than Alamein, and Mussolini returned disconsolate to Italy. Most important of all, the German drive in Russia was brought to a halt at Stalingrad, where casualties on both sides reached figures almost, but not quite, comparable with those achieved by the most successful generals of the First World War.

Despite continuing Russian pressure, however, there was no sign of a Second Front, only a muddled Canadian raid on Dieppe, which was beaten off with the loss of more than half the men engaged. Churchill put off Stalin's importunities with the promise of 'a deadly attack upon Hitler' in 1943. He then persuaded a reluctant Roosevelt to join in an Anglo-American landing in French North Africa which effectively ended any prospect of a cross-Channel invasion in the next year. The invasion was put under the command of the unknown but diplomatic General Eisenhower, whose diplomacy, it was thought, would be useful not only in reconciling Anglo-American differences, but also in soothing the susceptibilities of a number of French prima donnas of varying political opinions. The British General Anderson would attend adequately to the fighting part of the assignment. Thus, for a few more months, the British were able to cherish the illusion that they remained the senior partners in the Anglo-American alliance.

In the event, Anderson became bogged down in difficult hill country in Tunisia, and although Montgomery forced Rommel to retreat from Alamein, the intention of sandwiching the Germans and Italians between the First and Eighth Armies was frustrated until the following year.

Towards the end of 1942, a harassed Chief of the Imperial General Staff confided to his diary that 'we are going to have great difficulties in getting out of Winston's promise to Stalin, namely, the establishment of a Western Front in 1943. Stalin seems to be banking on it, and Clark Kerr [British Ambassador in Moscow] fears a possible peace between Hitler and Stalin if we disappoint the latter.' The C.I.G.S. had, however, a happy compromise up his sleeve – an Anglo-American invasion of Italy which would be *almost* as good as a Second Front, and which Churchill, never able to resist a phrase, was shortly describing as a blow at 'the soft underbelly of the Axis'.
Laurence Thompson

The Scowling Duce. Benito Mussolini, Italian dictator, sees his hopes of easy pickings from the war frustrated. British success in North Africa paves the way for an invasion of Italy.

ONLY A FEW OF THE MANY CRITICISMS WE HAVE MADE IN PICTURE

NOV. 1939: LACK OF WAR NEWS

JUNE 1940: THE NEED TO ARM THE PEOPLE

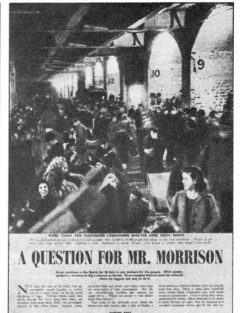

NOV. 1940: SHELTERS

SHOULD WE STOP CRITICISING?

A new practice comes into being. Papers that criticise are dropped from the list of those subsidised for export by the Government. There are some in high places who would like the voices of criticism to be stilled. In Singapore and London they have taken their first steps.

THIS may be the last copy of *Picture Post* which will be seen by our forces in the Middle East. If your husband or brother or your friend has been in the habit of buying *Picture Post* to get a glimpse of home when he came back from the lines, he may get no more such glimpses. The troops from the Dominions—Australians, South Africans and New Zealanders—may see no more of *Picture Post* either. Here is the reason.

The copies which go out to the Middle East—in the case of *Picture Post* some 10,000 in all—are sent out under a subsidy scheme. This subsidy is arranged by the Ministry of Information. It is not paid to the publishers of the paper, but to the big wholesale export houses through whom the various publications are distributed. It is two-fold; a subsidy of so much a copy, and a guarantee by the Ministry of Information to buy back from the wholesalers any copies which are sent out and not sold. It is what is known in the trade as the "sale-or-return" system. This subsidy and the guarantee make it possible for the retailers to handle business which would otherwise be too costly for them, and to put a number of British publications on sale in the Middle East at reasonable prices. *Picture Post*, for instance, was on sale at about the equivalent of fourpence.

Two or three weeks ago the big wholesale export houses received instructions that the official subsidy scheme would no longer apply to *Picture Post*. It would still, however, apply to *The Illustrated London News*, *Vogue*, *The Sphere*, to *Illustrated*, and to *Punch*. In the case of *Picture Post* alone it would be discontinued.

Now between *Punch* or *Vogue*, and *Picture Post*, there is clearly no comparison. With *Illustrated* or *The Illustrated London News* there clearly is. Our paper and theirs are papers of a similar type, relying on the treatment of events in photographs. Why is the subsidy being discontinued in the case of our paper, and being maintained in the case of the other two?

That is not a difficult question to answer, for there is one thing above all which distinguishes *Picture Post* from either of the other two. *Picture Post* is a paper which not only reports, but criticises. It is a paper of opinion—on politics, on social questions, above all on the conduct of the war. If there are people interested in stopping *Picture Post* from going to the Middle East, it is an easy guess that they are interested in stopping it because of the critical articles which we publish from time to time.

But in working this out we are not dependent entirely on guesswork. There is evidence. Back in November an issue of *Picture Post* was officially prevented from going out to the Middle East. It was banned. This was the issue dated November 22. It was stopped on account of an article by Edward Hulton which reprinted criticisms from the American magazines *Life* and

> " A FREE PRESS IS THE MOST WATCHFUL SENTRY OF THE STATE, A 'YES' PRESS IS FATAL TO GOOD GOVERNMENT "
>
> BRENDAN BRACKEN at the FOREIGN PRESS ASSOCIATION LUNCHEON, SEPT. 1941.

Look about the quantity and quality of American aid. The article in *Life* had been headed by the Americans themselves—"Ships Carry a Trickle of Arms to Britain." Because we considered it important for British people—living in a democracy—to know what the Americans thought of their own war effort at that time, and of the extent of the supplies on which we were depending, we reprinted those American comments. What happened? The American magazines which originally voiced the criticisms had not been prevented from circulating in the Middle East.

Picture Post which reprinted them was.

Those criticisms appeared in this country at a time when our army in Libya was being publicised as the finest equipped force that had ever been put into the field. Its speedy victory was proclaimed in resounding phrases, even before it had moved to the attack. Yet in little more than a month almost every paper in the country was publishing despatches stating that the tanks we were using in Libya—to a large extent American—required heavier gun-power in order to stand up to the German ones, and that our airmen were badly in need of a genuine "tank-buster," or dive-bomber. As I write this article I am faced by a heading in the *Daily Express:* "U.S. War Production Condemned: Jealousy, Waste, Inefficiency." Reading through the article which follows, I see our criticisms repeated one by one by the Senate Defence Investigating Committee.

Again, a month later, in our issue of December 20, we published another article which met small welcome in high places, though in this case there was no ban. It was an article by Tom Wintringham, "What Has Happened in Libya." It ended:

"We have an army that is very good. As Churchill has told us, it began this job with equality on the ground and superiority in the air. Can Mr. Churchill find leaders for it who will understand what Rommel was being taught from 1935? Can we find a staff worthy of the fighting men and commanders? That is the key question raised by the fighting in Libya, and what we know as yet of how that important battle has gone."

When that article was written General Cunningham was being widely written-up as a master of desert warfare. When it appeared it was already known that he had been replaced by General Ritchie. The fact that Wintringham's words had substance did not make them any the more palatable to authority. No doubt his criticisms played their part in bringing about the decision to stop *Picture Post* from going to the Middle East. And this time it was not to be a ban on a single issue. The subsidy was to be cut off altogether.

POST SINCE WAR BEGAN : OUGHT WE TO HAVE KEPT QUIET ?

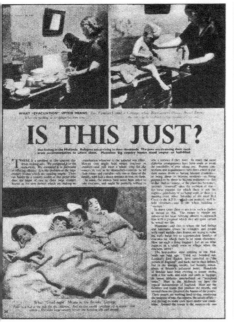

NOV. 1940: THE COUNTRY HOUSE SCANDAL

JUNE 1941: CRETE

SEPT. 1941: NEED FOR ARMS SPEED-UP

This decision was rapidly made known. Within a short time of the wholesalers receiving notice that their subsidy was to be ended, the British Council — supposed propagandist body — had written to us to cancel the one copy a week they posted to Transjordan, the 162 copies they sent to Turkey, and the 332 copies they sent to Iran.

NO QUESTION OF PROFIT INVOLVED

Now there is, fortunately, no question of private interest in this case. The 10,000 odd copies which formerly went to the Middle East can be disposed of very easily in this country. We could dispose of them very easily if there were fifty times as many. The subsidy was not paid to us in any case, but to the exporters. Our only personal concern is that we do not like being cut off from many good friends—and some members of our own staff—in the armies of the Middle East. Our much larger concern is for the much larger question—is authority to be allowed to stifle criticism?

If it can't stifle it completely at the source, is it to be allowed to cut it off here, and dam it up there—to bar Cecil Brown, the American broadcaster (who was turned out of Italy for being pro-British) from the radio at Singapore because he told the truth about British unpreparedness, and to stop *Picture Post* from going to the Middle East because it said that even in that garden not everything smelt sweet?

And here comes up an important question. When the Ministry of Information decided to stop our paper from going to Libya and Egypt, to Palestine, Iraq and Iran—who is it that is being protected from the dangerous thoughts which we disseminate? Is it, perhaps, the Arabs and Egyptians?

A good case could certainly be made out for saying that in these countries the one over-mastering need is to present the picture of a strong united Britain. That the peoples of those countries are not used to our habits of criticism, and that differences of opinion to them spell weakness. "Let us quarrel at home and link arms abroad." The answer to that is easily found if the Ministry wants to find it. How many Arabs and Egyptians are in the habit of buying *Picture Post* at 4d. a copy? How many of us would buy a paper in Arabic costing us about a third of an average day's earnings? Not many, you imagine. Our information is that not many did. Still fewer, probably, were in the habit of reading *Punch* or *Vogue*, exported under the same scheme. Our information is that by far the larger number of copies of *Picture Post*, "almost all" would probably

not be too strong, were bought by the people you would expect to buy them—the British and Dominion troops fighting in those countries.

On the opposite page to this are some very fine words by the Minister of Information, words for which every journalist who cares about his calling must be grateful. The question is—Do those words apply to British and Dominion troops? Or are these men of ours the exception— do *we* need a Free press, and must they be protected from hearing the voice of criticism raised?

There is not the least doubt that there are many in high places who think in just that way. They cannot stop papers from publishing their views in Britain, but wherever they can stop them, they will. They are already doing so.

That raises one question for the newspapers of this country. It raises one also for the people of this country. The people should consider now and make up their minds what kind of a Press they want—for that, in the end and after many battles, is the kind of Press they will get.

Censorship in the war was voluntary. Criticism was free. But the government had means to try and damp down critics. When *Picture Post* – despite Ministry warnings – continued to criticize, particularly the quality of military material in North Africa, the Ministry cracked down. Its aim was to stop *Picture Post* being read by troops in North Africa and the Middle East. Its method was to cut off the subsidy paid – not to the paper, but to the export firms handling distribution. *Picture Post* alone was so excluded. The fighting men could still buy *Vogue*.

T.H.

Liberty of the Press, like every other kind of liberty, is not something which happens. It is not something we are allowed to enjoy by favour of a benign government. It is a condition of a free people, and, like other freedoms, it is only maintained by fighting. It is kept alive by being exercised, and it depends for its existence on the courage with which journalists use their freedom, and the determination with which ordinary people support them when they use it.

WHAT LIBERTY OF THE PRESS MEANS

To those, if there are any in Britain, who think it does not very much matter whether the Press is free to criticise what happens in Singapore, or here in Whitehall, there is one question to be put: has this war been fought in such a way as to place our commanders and our holders of high office above criticism's reach? Can they fairly come to us and say, don't question, *trust*? Or does there come clanking behind them a whole chain of ugly names—from Norway to Penang, from Ironside to Brooke-Popham—the men who knew, the places that were safe?

When I was asked to become editor of *Picture Post* in July, 1940, I decided that it was not going to be my practice to sign articles in this paper. Editors should work to make the reputations of their papers, not themselves. I put my name to this one because it is an article of criticism, and those who criticise should give their names. I have written it because I think that what has happened is not just a matter of office routine—10,000 copies to be sold in Britain instead of in the streets of Cairo or the canteens of Libya and Palestine. It is a matter which concerns the freedom of British citizens to read the things they want to read, even if those things are distasteful to men of power and influence. I have written it also because I want friends of this paper in the Middle East to know why they may not be seeing *Picture Post* in future. Whether this copy will get to them or not is another question. We shall see, and we shall let you know.

Meantime we intend to continue our policy exactly as before, to criticise when there is need for it, to applaud when it is deserved. Criticism is no pleasure—for one thing it involves four times the work of bland approval or a simple record. We think that that is the course we ought to follow, the one most likely to help in winning a war we are all determined must be won.

What do you think? We should like to know.

TOM HOPKINSON.

PORTRAIT OF A NAZI GRENADIER

DOWN in a hole in the ground crouches a man. He is a soldier, a German, a panzer grenadier. By his side are his grenades. At his back is the waterproof sheet which he pulls over his head as camouflage, and for protection against weather. Somewhere to the rear are his food supplies and reserves of ammunition. Behind that is the remains of the mechanised transport that brought him here. Behind that again is his much-bombed Fatherland. And behind that the coast on which the Second Front will one day open. That, he knows, is what lies behind. What is there in front? The Russians. The advancing, victorious Russians. They are in front, and for all he knows, they are on both sides of him as well. He is manning what Goebbels calls "The Tartar Wall." But he knows better. It is not a wall at all. There is no longer any wall, and there is no longer any hope. He has come a long way since the Hitler Youth rallies of his boyhood, but he is not likely to go much further—and he knows it.

The B.B.C.'s Other Brains Trust : "Answering You" on the N. American Service
Every week, experts meet to broadcast answers to leading questions, sent in by U.S. listeners, on Britain's war effort. Left to right : Two members of the U.S. Forces, Geoffrey Crowther (Editor of "The Economist"), Tom Wintringham, Tom Harrisson (of "Mass Observation"), Gèorge Strauss, M.P.

THE B.B.C. TALKS TO N. AMERICA

It's one of the B.B.C.'s most ambitious programmes. Starting at 11.15 p.m. each night, 7½ hours non-stop service of news, talks, features, and variety goes out to America. What's it like?

IT'S hard to believe that you're talking to America at all. When it's too late to get a bus and the last taxis on the streets are hustling the last of the restaurant goers home to bed, you stumble through the black-out to a building that was once a West End store. The main hall of the shop is now partitioned off into nests of offices like an egg box. The bare walls are roughly painted, and the marble staircase—which used to lead to the basement—now looks as ludicrous as if it were furnishing a hay loft.

The studios are underground. On your way to

them, you are guided through narrow passages lined with compartments like a railway coach. But, at this time of night, most of them are empty. Through half open doors, you occasionally get a glimpse of a shirt-sleeved figure behind a battery of telephones; a tousled-haired body—probably belonging to a producer with an early morning programme to see to—dossing down on a camp bed; a trousered secretary dividing her attention between a typewriter and beef tea. The night duty staff.

Down below, on the studio floor, you see

Three of Britain's Spokesmen On The War
Left to right : Major Lewis Hastings (Land), Peter Masefield (Air), H. C. Ferraby (Sea).

engineers—men and girls—bending over turntables cutting discs. You go into a room labelled Red Network, where two more girls are in charge of a formidable control board. Finally, you're shown into a little cell heavily-lined with some sound-absorbent material. Your guide retires, to watch you through a glass-panelled window. And you are alone with the microphone and the clock.

A few minutes before your zero hour, an announcer joins you in the studio. Together, you watch the clock. As the second hand climbs the last quarter-minute before you give your talk, the announcer says " Quiet, please," in a mechanical voice. You gulp at a glass of water and, as the second hand licks on to the hour, a red light flashes a warning. The announcer starts :

" This is the North American Service of the British Broadcasting Corporation . . ."

Ten minutes later you leave the studio. As you pass the disc room on the way out, you hear your own voice—like an echo—repeating the talk all over again. The engineers are checking the recording they've made of your talk for transmission later in the night.

Back in the outside world again, nobody ever says to you—as they do after you've spoken in the

Where the Recordings for Talks to N. America Are Made
Many of the speakers give their talks during the night—"live." But recordings are also made so that the talks can be transmitted again. Most North American programmes are broadcast twice.

The Tommy Handley Programme You Never Hear

In an underground theatre, Tommy Handley broadcasts to overseas listeners in a special half-hour programme. The show goes out in the North American Service at 4 a.m. on Saturday mornings. The announcer at the mike is Roy Rich. The audience in the studio is there by special invitation.

Home Service—" I heard your broadcast last night." If you tell people about it, they listen half-doubtfully. And soon, in your own mind, the thing grows unconvincing too. Talking to America in the small hours of the morning from the basement of a disused draper's shop in wartime London . . .

It is difficult to believe.

Then, weeks (perhaps months) later, a letter arrives for you with a foreign stamp; from someone who heard your talk " as clearly as if they were in the room with you "—they always say that—in Florida, or New York, or San Francisco, or, surprisingly, from somewhere on the east coast of Africa. And then the astonishing power that was yours for ten minutes begins to dawn on you. Then, in a way that mere figures can never convey, you realise what a mighty instrument has come into being.

The world service of the B.B.C. has developed so rapidly that most of us still think of the letters as if they spelt only a couple of programmes on the Home wavelengths. If we've heard of the existence

This Is London . . .

Betty McLoughlin, one of the B.B.C.'s fifty-four wartime announcers, introduces a N. American programme.

of other services, we're disposed to discount them. They can't be picked up on an ordinary medium-wave set, and, even if we've got the right sort of set to listen, we've got a shrewd suspicion that they're just "propaganda"; not worth listening to, anyhow.

That's largely the fault of the B.B.C., which could put the matter right—quite simply—by broadcasting on the Home Services regular extracts of the programmes—translations when necessary—which are being transmitted overseas. And, indeed, in a democratic country we are entitled to hear how our voice is being represented abroad. But that's by the way.

The fact is that, now, the Home programmes

"Freedom Forum" : A Programme Which Represents Every Shade of Political Opinion

Left to right : Sir Frederick Whyte, K.C.S.I., Professor Harold Laski, Lanham Titchener (B.B.C. producer), G. M. Young, Ed. Murrow (European Director of Columbia Broadcasting).

An Outdoor Broadcast: America Meets "John Londoner"

Every week, an outdoor recording van goes out into the London streets to collect unrehearsed interviews with ordinary Londoners. Here's Stewart Macpherson, a Canadian on the B.B.C. staff, talking with an ex-serviceman.

Canadians Working With the B.B.C.
Jack Peach, Radio Liaison Officer of the Canadian Air Force, and H. Rooney Pelletier, C.B.C.

represent only a part—and a fractional part at that—of the B.B.C.'s transmissions. Since the war started, four complete networks—carrying regular programmes simultaneously to the four corners of the globe—have been instituted. The B.B.C.'s peace-time staff of 3,000 has swelled to over 10,000. The organisation has spilled over and spread to temporary offices and studios—some of them as big as the original Broadcasting House itself—all over the country. Not even the people in the B.B.C. can trace the beginnings and the endings of it. But here's the picture of a single ser-

vice, the week's programmes to North America. If you multiply the impression by forty—in broadcast time—you'll have a good idea what the B.B.C.'s war-time transmissions entail.

The service is called the North American, but that simply means that it's primarily intended for listeners in the United States, Canada, Newfoundland, and the West Indies. But it's also listened to —and sometimes re-broadcast by local stations—in West Africa, Central and South America, Australia, and other parts of the world.

It goes out for seven and a half hours every night,

Radio News Reel Goes On The Air
A sound picture of the day's news. This nightly programme is an important overseas feature.

beginning at 11.15 p.m. (double summer time). So, in America, it's picked up on the East Coast about 5.15 p.m., and on the Pacific coast at 1.15 p.m.

The technique of the programmes is quite different from the conventional B.B.C. style of the Home Services. The whole tempo is slicked up on American radio lines. The programmes are spotted in fifteen minute sessions (at most, half an hour) with not more than a twenty-second interval between. The big features are "trailed" at intervals during the night with talk about the personalities who are coming on the air. The accents of American and Canadian announcers and commentators mingle with the voices of the English speakers.

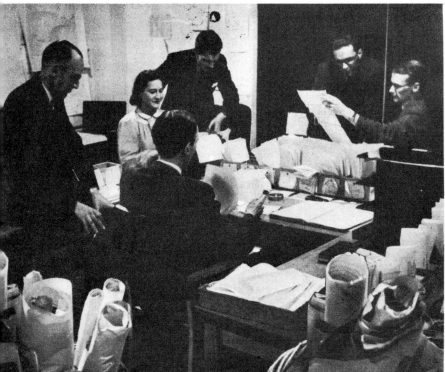

In the News Room, Ten Minutes Before a Bulletin Goes Out
B.B.C. news to America is shorter and snappier than the news on the Home Service Programmes. Five quarter-hour bulletins are sent out each night—the first at 11.45 p.m., the last at 6.30 a.m.— as well as Radio News Reel, a "sound dramatisation" of the day's news.

The Man Who Rings Up America
Maurice Gorham, Director of the B.B.C.'s North American Service, talks to New York.

The policy of the service is to give America a true picture of what people are doing and thinking in Britain. If that gets across, the B.B.C. believes—quite rightly—that the propaganda will look after itself.

What kind of programmes are sent out? Well, you'd enjoy hearing a lot of them yourself. Every night, Radio News Reel presents a dramatised sound picture of the day's news with last minute commentaries. Five days a week, there's a serial—radio serials are very popular in America—called "Front Line Family," which records the day by day adventures of a typical family in wartime London.

Every week, a panel of experts—a sort of overseas Brains Trust—answers questions on the war sent in by American listeners. It's called "Answering You." Every week, there's a radio exchange called "Hello, Children," between parents in London and children in the U.S. Tommy Handley broadcasts a

OVERSEAS WORLD SERVICE SHORTWAVE BANDS TO—EUROPE, U.S.A., CANADA, SOUTH AND CENTRAL AMERICA, THE WHOLE OF AFRICA, MIDDLE EAST, FAR EAST, AUSTRALIA, NEW ZEALAND, THE MEDITERRANEAN, THE NORTH, SOUTH AND CENTRAL ATLANTIC AND PACIFIC OCEANS, FORM A CONTINUOUS WORLD SERVICE THROUGHOUT THE 24 HOURS.

1	2	3	4	5	6	7	8	9
				ENGLISH & NORWEGIAN 18½ hours	ENGLISH & FINNISH 18½ hours	ENGLISH & SWEDISH 18½ hours	ENGLISH & ICELANDIC 17½ hours	ENG & F 16

THE B.B.C. NETWOR
*The B.B.C. broadcasts day and night, in ⟨
by the Corporation.   Broadcasting*

half-hour show. Bebe Daniels and Ben Lyon interview members of the U.S. forces over here in a programme called "Stars and Stripes." Bands li Geraldo's are relayed from the American Eag Club. Priestley, Wickham Steed, Vernon Bartlett broadcasting under such titles as "Democra Marches," "Britain Speaks," "Democracy Hel Itself"—are regular speakers. And regular w commentaries are given every night by a brillia team of speakers who (in striking comparison most of the people on the Home Services) real do comment on the strategy and tactics of th war.

Outdoor broadcasts, giving a sound picture life in this country and unrehearsed interviews wi typical Londoners, are a permanent feature. An

DAILY TRANSMISSIONS TO EUROPEAN COUNTRIES

A ICELAND 17½ hours in ENGLISH & ICELANDIC

B NORWAY 18½ hours in NORWEGIAN & ENGLISH

C SWEDEN 18½ hours in SWEDISH & ENGLISH

D FINLAND 18½ hours in FINNISH & ENGLISH

E DENMARK ½ hour in DANISH

F HOLLAND 1½ hours in DUTCH

G GERMANY 4 hours 10 mins. in GERMAN 30 mins. News in MORSE

H POLAND 1½ hours in POLISH

Y MALTA 30 mins. weekly in MALTESE

X CYPRUS 1 hour weekly in GREEK

W TURKEY 1 hour in TURKISH

V GREECE 1 hour in GREEK

U ALBANIA 5 mins. in ALBANIAN

T BULGARIA 40 mins. in BULGARIAN

S YUGOSLAVIA 50 mins. in SERBO-CROAT 15 mins. in SLOVENE

R ITALY 2½ hours in ITALIAN

Q CORSICA & SARDINIA receive B.B.C. FRENCH and ITALIAN services

P SPAIN & PORTUGAL 3 hours special services

I BELGIUM	J FRANCE	K L SWITZERLAND	L AUSTRIA	M CZECHO-SLOVAKIA	N HUNGARY	O RUMANIA
4½ hours in FRENCH 15 mins. in FLEMISH	4½ hours in FRENCH 30 mins. News in MORSE	receives FRENCH, ITALIAN and GERMAN services from B.B.C.	4 hours 10 mins. in GERMAN 30 mins. News in MORSE	1½ hours in CZECH	25 mins. in HUNGARIAN	40 mins. in RUMANIAN

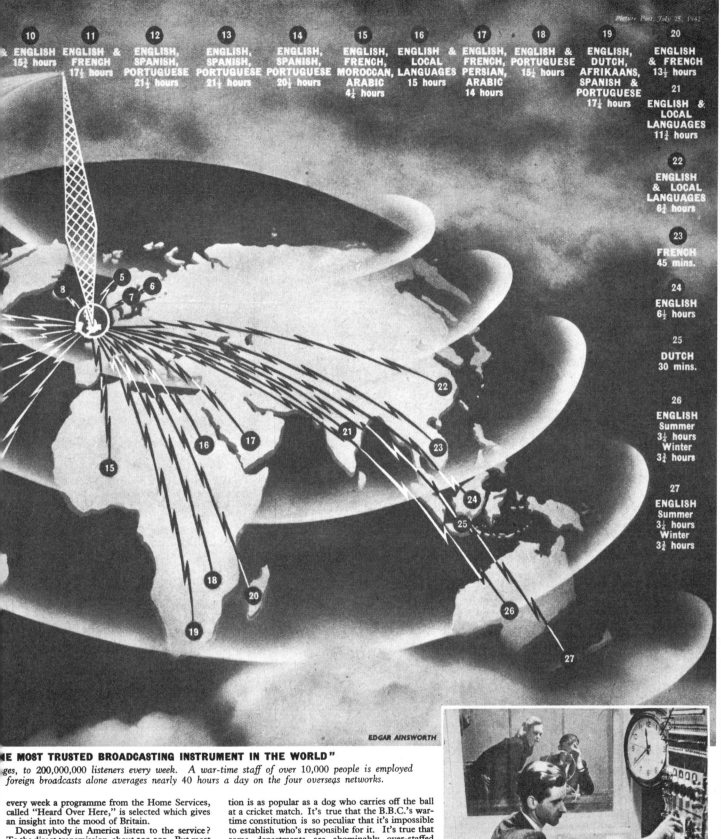

10	11	12	13	14	15	16	17	18	19	20
& ENGLISH 15½ hours	ENGLISH & FRENCH 17½ hours	ENGLISH, SPANISH, PORTUGUESE 21½ hours	ENGLISH, SPANISH, PORTUGUESE 21½ hours	ENGLISH, SPANISH, PORTUGUESE 20½ hours	ENGLISH, FRENCH MOROCCAN ARABIC 4¼ hours	ENGLISH & LOCAL LANGUAGES 15 hours	ENGLISH & FRENCH PERSIAN, ARABIC 14 hours	ENGLISH & PORTUGUESE 15½ hours	ENGLISH, DUTCH, AFRIKAANS, SPANISH & PORTUGUESE 17½ hours	ENGLISH & FRENCH 13½ hours

21
ENGLISH & LOCAL LANGUAGES 11¼ hours

22
ENGLISH & LOCAL LANGUAGES 6½ hours

23
FRENCH 45 mins.

24
ENGLISH 6½ hours

25
DUTCH 30 mins.

26
ENGLISH Summer 3¼ hours Winter 3¾ hours

27
ENGLISH Summer 3¼ hours Winter 3¾ hours

EDGAR AINSWORTH

...E MOST TRUSTED BROADCASTING INSTRUMENT IN THE WORLD"

...ges, to 200,000,000 listeners every week. A war-time staff of over 10,000 people is employed ... foreign broadcasts alone averages nearly 40 hours a day on the four overseas networks.

every week a programme from the Home Services, called "Heard Over Here," is selected which gives an insight into the mood of Britain.

Does anybody in America listen to the service? To the direct transmission, about 300,000. But most of the features, especially the very popular ones, such as "Answering You," "Stars and Stripes," "Radio News Reel," the news bulletins and so on, are rebroadcast by American radio stations to their own listeners (which is the best advertisement the B.B.C. service could have). Every word sent out from London is carefully monitored in the United States, and extracts from the war commentaries, especially, are widely reprinted in the U.S. press.

Throwing brickbats at the B.B.C. is a national pastime. And anybody who defends the institu-

tion is as popular as a dog who carries off the ball at a cricket match. It's true that the B.B.C.'s war-time constitution is so peculiar that it's impossible to establish who's responsible for it. It's true that some departments are abominably over-staffed and others abominably under-staffed. It's true that there are plenty of tom-fools inside the B.B.C. and quite a number of able men who are shut out. But if you admit nothing—if you think every programme put out by the B.B.C. stinks—it's still a tremendous achievement that, in less than three years, the B.B.C. has grown from a largely domestic organisation into an instrument of world importance; that, if you turn the knob of a radio set anywhere in the four corners of the earth, you'll pick up the proud words: "This is London . . ."

The Night's Programmes Begin
Macdonald Hastings (behind panel), author of this article, broadcasts a London Letter.

121

THE PRESIDENT: *Head of the First Officer Selection Board*
Colonel J. V. Delahaye, D.S.O., M.C., who pioneered the new system of
choosing officers in the Scottish Command. A system which is already
completely displacing the old "interviewing" method throughout the Army.

THE CANDIDATE: *He Is To Be Tested For a Commission*
Instead of being judged on a fifteen-minute interview, the candidate is
invited to attend a three days' test. The men who decide his appointment
live with him, observe his behaviour under all conditions.

A NEW WAY TO CHOOSE OUR ARMY OFFICERS

**An entirely new system for the appointment of our Army Officers is being tried out. It is one of the most progressive moves that have
been made since war began. If successful it will put an end to all talk of "class-favouritism", and should lead to a high increase of efficiency.**

The First Step: A Testing Officer Meets the Candidates
*While they're up before the Board, the men are treated as officers. The Testing Officers treat the
candidates as equals, get to know them all personally before forming an opinion.*

PUT your head into the brass hat of the Adjutant-
General. Imagine that you've got his job; the
job of organising and making the best use of the
army's man-power. Out of the raw material presented to you by the Ministry of Labour, you've got
to assemble the pieces for manufacture into a
fighting force.

On one side, you know precisely what sort of
army you want. On the other, you can only surmise
what sort of material you're going to get to make it
with. Unlike the navy or air force or industry
you're given no choice as to whether you'll accept
a man or not. You've got to take what comes to you.
Somehow, you've got to fit every piece into the
machinery. And you've got to find one potential
officer for every twenty men.

How will you set about it?

The first step—the rough break-up of the
material to determine its immediate employment—
will be relatively easy. By comparing each recruit's
age, medical category and civil record with the army's
needs, you should have no difficulty, in the great
majority of cases, in making up your mind what's
to be done with him.

Deciding which arm a man is best suited for is a
concrete problem. He's got to go somewhere and
the jobs to which he can be put are limited. But,
having distributed your material, your real troubles
are only just beginning. You've now got to pick
it over to find your potential officers. How do you
intend to tackle the job?

Be warned—before you begin—that you're
stepping on very dangerous ground. There's
nothing concrete to work on now. You're looking
for abstract qualities; character, leadership,
initiative, personality, dash. And you're not
attacking a purely military problem. The selection
of officers is a social problem too.

If there's the slightest hint that you're giving preference to any one class or section, you'll be embroiled in a controversy. But, if you allow sentiment to warp your judgment, you may lose the war. So, somehow, you've got to make sure that the right men are given the King's commission, and, at the same time, satisfy the public—and the army—that the system of selection is fair. If you think that public opinion doesn't matter, you'll soon find out how wrong you are. Because if the word gets round that there's a wangle, you'll discover that there's a check in the flow of potential officers putting their names forward for commission.

The Job of Finding Officers is Not Easy

What's the solution? Until a few months ago, the army took the view that the only possible way of selecting potential officers was by the interviewing system (imperfect as that system had proved itself to be).

A man who showed promise in his unit was recommended by the C.O. for an interview. On the strength of the interviewer's impression in a fifteen-minute talk, the candidate was either rejected or sent on a course at an O.C.T.U. Stories got round that it was no use putting up for a commission unless you'd won your colours at cricket and rode to hounds. And, though the stories were largely untrue, there was a growing hesitance to apply for commissions. In its favour, all that could be said for the interviewing system was that civil employers had never been able to better it. Against it was the fact that more than half the candidates recommended for commission proved unsuitable to become officers when they were tested in actual training.

The alternative to the interviewing system was suggested at the end of last year, when Lt.-General Sir Andrew Thorne (C.-in-C., Scottish Command) agreed to try out a daring experiment. It was known that, for a long time, the Germans had been employing elaborate tests to select potential officers for the Reichwehr. For instance, they'd been subjecting men to electric shocks with a view to studying their facial expressions as they underwent the experience. The German system—aided as it was by the precise records of every citizen kept under the Nazi regime—was thought unsuitable for this country. But a modified and, in many ways, a sounder system was proposed as an alternative.

How the New System Works

A series of tests was devised and, at the beginning of the year, a number of officers and cadets whose qualities were already accurately known, volunteered as guinea-pigs. They were put through the course as numbers. And the conclusions of the testing

One of the most valuable techniques to come out of the war was a more practical and efficient method of choosing men for positions of responsibility. The old method had been by interview. A group of officers — largely ex-public school-boys — interviewed candidates for what they considered to be qualities of 'leadership', discovering them as a rule in people very like themselves. Under conditions of test, more than half those recommended for commissions proved unsuitable, and soon many who were highly suitable were not troubling to apply. Colonel Delahaye — a professional soldier with a lively, pioneering mind — worked out a different system. It took not fifteen minutes but three days. And it worked. Modified and adapted, his system is today made use of throughout much of industry and civilian life.

T.H.

TESTS AND INTERVIEWS: *An Officer Candidate Addresses His Men*
The tests in the various Selection Boards vary. But the purpose is the same. To give each candidate a chance to show his mettle. This one speaks on "Is Saluting a Waste of Time?"

The Psychiatrist Interviews a Candidate in His Office
The psychiatrist—a medical man with a special mental training—forms his own independent opinion of the candidate's personality. Later, he compares notes with the other officers of the board.

The Sort of Problem an Officer Might Have Sprung on Him
"Supposing you're walking along, with a girl on each arm, like this" says the S.M., "and a private tries to pull one of the girls away from you. What would you do?" The candidates try to answer.

board tallied exactly with the known facts about the men.

Soon after, actual candidates for commissions in the Scottish Command were invited to go before the Selection Board for a two-day test. The candidates were as delighted with the new system as the examiners. Before long, the number of men putting their names forward for commissions increased from an average of fifty a week to more than double that number.

The Adjutant-General (Sir Ronald Adam) decided to adopt the new tests throughout all the army commands. A few months ago, the old interviewing system finally died and the Officer Selection Boards succeeded them.

Candidates, instead of a fifteen minute interview, are now invited to attend a two or three-day test. While with the Board, they are treated as officers, and live in an officers' mess with the officers of the staff. Rigid military discipline is studiously avoided. Every effort is made to put the men at their ease.

Differences of Education Are No Bar

One of the basic principles of the new system is that it operates entirely independently of inequalities in education, upbringing or social background. The men are tested, not under their own names, but as numbers. What the tests seek to discover is

THIS IS HOW ONE OF THE OFFICER CANDIDATES TACKLED THE JOB OF

not what a man knows, but his native ability to learn; and not what he's done, but what he will do if he's given the opportunity.

The character of the tests varies considerably. From week to week modifications are being introduced and new ideas tried out. The programme is deliberately fluid because it is quite clear already that the possibilities of development are unlimited. But the form is clearly defined.

First of all, the candidate is asked to do a series of written intelligence tests. These are nothing new. They are psychological tests which have been tried out and proved valid over a number of years both here and in America. They give a good guide to a man's native ability to learn. Verbal tests are also being used experimentally as a guide to character, but no weight is being given to the results until they are proved by experience to be of value.

The next step—usually on the second day—is to study the men's performance under stress. The reason is that, in battle, most actions are fought under conditions of at least partial fatigue.

The candidates are given a cross country run or a period of physical training. While they're still exhausted from the effort, they are each asked to solve a problem of organisation, such as any subaltern might be called upon to deal with. Finally,

A Test for Leadership: A Candidate Is Called Upon to Deal With Parachutists
The situation is imaginary. To deal with it requires no specialised military knowledge. All the testing officer wants to see is whether the candidate can make some sort of a plan and see that his men carry it out.

Exhausted, He Must Remember Right
He's been round the obstacle course. Still panting, he must remember: "At 06.50 hrs. 23 enemy tanks and about 65 M.F.V.s were moving N.N.W. from map reference sheet 106/426154."

CROSSING THE DIZZY GAP BETWEEN A SCAFFOLD AND A NARROW PLANK

HOW ANOTHER MAN TACKLED IT

Neither of the two men had seen the obstacle before. How they approached it told the Testing Officers something important about their characters. Can you guess what it was?

whether he's a cautious man or a dashing one, whether he's got physical and moral courage.

Follows a series of tests to discover whether the candidate has a natural gift of leadership. He's put in charge of six or seven others, and given a problem designed to show whether he can appreciate a situation, make a reasonably quick and sensible plan, give clear and practical orders, and see them put into action. The essential feature of these tests is that no special military knowledge is necessary.

Apart from the practical tests, each candidate is given several interviews. The most important is with the Board's psychiatrist, a medical man who makes an assessment of the candidate's inner character. The psychiatrist fulfils the reverse function to the Military Testing Officers, who form their

The Candidates Hunt Down a Spy
The candidates are told there is a spy in the vicinity. By organising a search, picking up clues, they have to hunt the man down. Once again what matters is the way they set about the job.

they are taken to a specially designed obstacle course which, while within the power of any fit man, calls for the use of intelligence and ingenuity.

Each man tackles the course separately under the eyes of the testing officers. The obstacle may be something quite simple, such as a barbed wire fence which the candidate is called upon to cross with the aid of a few forked branches broken off a tree. Or it may be a more elaborate device such as a narrow plank rigged on a scaffold. The candidate has to climb a ladder, get across a dizzy gap, walk the plank and swing to the ground hanging on a rope.

Little Things That Show a Lot

The behaviour of different candidates as they come up against the various obstacles is extraordinarily illuminating. The last thing on earth the testing officers are interested in is whether a candidate is a good gymnast or not. What they're watching to see is how he deals with an unexpected situation, what ingenuity he shows in overcoming it,

Which of These Men Shows The Greatest Dash?
One takes care to reach the stile first and climbs over. Another waits his turn to follow. A third scrambles through the wire at the side.

After an Exhausting Work-out Candidates are Tested in the Noise of Battle
Much of an officer's work has to be done when he's tired, and often when he's under fire. So candidates
are given a hard work-out and immediately presented with a problem in organisation. Meanwhile, the
drill instructor makes it even more difficult to think by introducing battle effects.

opinion purely from the outward behaviour of the candidates during the tests. Apart from the psychiatrist, a candidate may also be interviewed by the visiting member—a commanding officer of a typical unit—who forms his opinion without any special knowledge of the tests, but from his own practical experience of men and, finally, every candidate is interviewed by the President.

At the end of the tests, the Selection Board—President, visiting member, psychiatrist, Military Testing Officers—meet to discuss which candidates should be recommended to go to O.C.T.U. The

feature of this Board Meeting is that each member has formed an independent opinion of each candidate's qualities. And none—with the exception of the President—knows what the others think.

Put together, their combined judgment is as unprejudiced a character study as it would be possible to have. And it's significant that, in the majority of cases, there is complete agreement in the conclusions of each member of the Board.

What are the results from the new system? The Selection Boards have not been running long enough yet to see. But this is already proved. The

The Test in Silence
Besides tests out of doors under difficult conditions
there are tests in a quiet classroom. Men are shown
these boards, told to write down their thoughts.

percentage of candidates turned down by the Board tallies exactly with the percentage of candidates, passed under the old interviewing system, who were afterwards failed in their O.C.T.U. course. The conclusion is that, in O.C.T.U., candidates approved by the Board will, in nearly 100 per cent. of cases, be passed for commissions.

The Selection Boards have already won the complete confidence of the candidates who've come before them. There is every indication that, in the selection of the right men as officers, they will prove a triumphant success. But there's more in the system than that.

This is a brand new idea; an idea which, if it's properly nurtured and developed, has possibilities which transcend the immediate needs of the war. It shows a way of measuring natural ability which must become increasingly accurate. And I believe that the Selection Boards have in them a potent germ which, in the future, may well revolutionise methods of promotion in industry, and, more important still, solve the problem as to which members of our community should be given the benefit of advanced education.

To the Adjutant-General, Sir Ronald Adam, to the anonymous group of men who've devised and are now working on the Officer Selection Boards may a writer (who has often kicked the Army about the place) be permitted humbly to raise his hat?
MACDONALD HASTINGS.

AFTER THREE DAYS: *Selection Board Meets to Choose Men for Officer Training*
Every officer on the Board now knows every candidate personally. With all the facts before them
the members of the board compare notes and decide which men they will recommend for officer training.

Vol. 17. No. 8

PICTURE POST

November 21, 1942

A Picture That Sums Up the Whole Campaign : The Conquerors Advance Over a Battlefield Strewn With German Dead
In an endless stream the armoured infantry and the guns pass over the desert. Ahead the remnants of Rommel's scattered and defeated army are fleeing for whatever refuge they can find. Behind they leave their dead. The victors have had no time to bury them. They drive on in pursuit.

VICTORY IN AFRICA

Out of Africa comes something new for the British people. A smashing victory over Rommel and his forces. The story of it is told in magnificent pictures taken by our army cameramen.

WE fight for a sea, the Mediterranean, and it is because of our superiority on other seas that we were able to fight in this theatre of war. Never before in these three and half years has the superior Allied strength in this element exerted itself with such telling effect. We are apt to overlook this strategic lesson because tactically the Navy played the least spectacular role in the opening round of the war for the Mediterranean. Yet consider what command of the sea has meant to us. In spite of the immense length of our supply lines from Britain and America round the Cape to Egypt, we were able to build up a stronger force to the east of El Alamein positions than Hitler was able to build at the end of his far shorter lines from Genoa and other Italian ports. The Germans have complained that their much publicised Afrika Corps was called upon to fight an enemy stronger in men and materials : if this complaint has any substance it implies a deadly criticism of their own powers of organisation, for all the advantages, geographically, were in their favour.

One of their military theorists, quoted recently by a French paper, long before the beginning of this war voiced the opinion : "England can only be properly attacked and mortally wounded at one

The Victor
General Montgomery, Commander of the Eighth Army, stands up in his tank to watch the battle.

point—Egypt." For our part, we provided striking evidence of our belief in this theory by taking away some of our best troops from the defence of these islands in the hard and anxious summer of 1940 and sending them to Egypt. But Hitler failed to follow the advice of his own military theorist, declined to follow through after his invasion of Jugoslavia, Greece, and Crete, and preferred to turn aside to the attack on Russia. His under-estimation of the importance of Egypt persisted until October, 1942, with disastrous effects on his own fortune.

We might reverse the German theorist's judgment and say : "England can only properly launch an offensive with real hope of success at one point—Egypt." This theory was brought to the test on October 23rd when the R.A.F. launched its offensive on Rommel's airfields and troop concentrations in Egypt, and the artillery barrage followed before the infantry went in to clear a way for the armoured offensive. Within two days, 1,400 prisoners were taken, and the Australians in their northward thrust had reached Tel el Eisa. On the following day, the Axis had gathered together its main strength in the north in preparation for a full-blooded counter-offensive, but were frustrated

(Continued on page 130)

FOR THE FIRST TIME OUR CAMERAMEN GET PICTURES TO MATCH THE STORY

The opening of the battle. Against Rommel's airfields and troop concentrations an air bombardment of ferocious intensity is launched. When Rommel begins to withdraw, the R.A.F. press home their advantage, disorganise his transport, block the roads, demoralise his troops.

The Battle That Opened

By the second day after the battle was joined gaps
Tanks and armoured cars pass through in face
concentrating all his armour in the no

The Men Who Made the Whole Plan Feasible : The Infantry Go Forward Under a Smoke Screen to Take a Strongpoint

In every infantry struggle the Eighth Army is victorious, every enemy counter-attack is driven back and every strongpoint taken. One of the outstanding
reasons for the success of the plan of attack is the accurate dove-tailing of all branches of the Army and the perfect timing of operations.

eatest Allied Offensive
made in Rommel's minefields.
vy shell-fire. Now, the enemy is
oaring to counter-attack.

The Fate That Overtook Most of Rommel's Armour
A German Mark IV has been knocked out on the battlefield, and now British sappers have completed the destruction. For the first time in this war Allied tanks have been equal to German. The skill with which they are directed decides the issue in the main battle of armour.

The Men Who Consolidate Victory After the Tanks Have Gone Forward : British Infantry in the Heart of the Furious Battle
The tanks have fought it out, and now our infantry use a knocked-out enemy tank as cover during an enemy rearguard action. Rommel uses up his best infantry in futile counter-attacks. Ours consolidate the break-through, and widen the gap through which our whole strength is hurled at the enemy.

AFTER THE BATTLE : *The Scene the Desert Sand Will Obliterate*
Wreckage and ruin, mile after mile, the pathetic fragmentary ruin of a retreating army. Here an overturned gun, there a meal that was never eaten. Four greatcoats in a ditch, and a handful of love-letters blowing across the road.

A Corner of the Battlefield
Two Italians who were fighting on when their anti-tank gun took a direct hit.

by another violent artillery bombardment. On October 27th, Rommel launched his counter-attacks. They were repulsed, and on the following day, important units under his command were pocketed by an Australian thrust to the sea. By November 1st a substantial corridor had been formed west of Tel el Eisa, our armoured formations passed through it, and the major battle followed. Such, in brief, was the outline of that victory in Africa which made possible the whole Mediterranean offensive. Within two days, Rommel's retreat had begun. For a week afterwards the remnants of the Axis forces were chased over the frontier of Egypt and beyond, pounded at every point by the R.A.F., which had wielded from the beginning complete superiority over its opponents. When the Americans were announced on November 6th to have landed in French North Africa, the whole picture of the world war changed from an aggressive Hitler to a defensive Hitler, from an alliance of nations, apparently passive and planless, to an alliance inspired by a practical detailed plan to win the war.

We have seen that this plan is based on the belief that Egypt must be the starting point. Will it succeed? We can answer this question only by outlining the reasons why this was the only plan open to the United Nations. If we were in Hitler's shoes, with his military record behind us, we might

A Wounded Man is Lifted Tenderly Out of a Tank
There came a signal from the tank. They had a badly-wounded man aboard. The ambulance raced up, and soon the wounded man was on his way back.

Prisoners: A Weary Procession of Despondent Men
They moved into battle as soldiers, they shamble despondently out as prisoners. Men of the Afrika Korps who, a few weeks back, were hammering on the gates of Egypt. Now prisoners of the Highland Division.

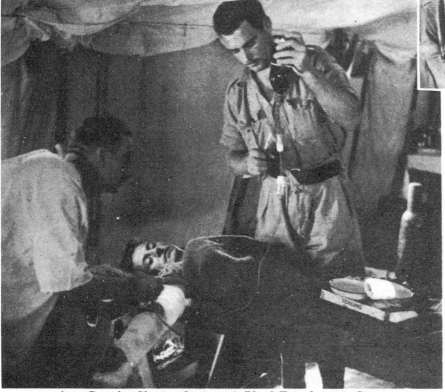

Captured Officers Give Their Names
Among the thousands of prisoners are German and Italian officers. All are passed on back.

argue, "What are Churchill and Roosevelt likely to do? Every nation wants to fight on interior lines if it can: that is, it fights along the shortest possible supply routes. Their shortest routes are from England to France. Therefore, they'll build up until they're strong enough to launch a second front in France. I shall see that they're too late when they do launch the Second Front."

The Allies might argue in a different way: "Hitler is afraid of a second front in Europe, we know. So he's prepared against it, as well as he can. And once we're in Europe he can concentrate against us. Supposing we concentrate our strength not at the nearest front, but the farthest? That means North Africa. Does Hitler's weakness there make up for the time it takes our ships to cross the sea?"

Apparently the answer was 'yes'. And this decision has proved entirely correct.

And what of the advantages of the Allied plan to concentrate on the Mediterranean? Just as we chose, wisely, to fight Hitler where he was weakest, so our initial success leads us towards another theatre of war where we have the best chance of success—Italy. But whether or not we are able to concentrate all our forces against Mussolini, one primary objective of the war is within our sight, the freeing of the Mediterranean and the opening-up of Germany's southern flank.

At a Casualty Clearing Station: A Blood Transfusion is Given
In the first days of the 8th Army's drive forward many pints of blood from the "blood banks" were used, and many lives saved by transfusions, which give wounded men strength to face operations.

1943

Sir William Beveridge

Britain began to fill with Americans. At first they were welcome, if not always for the right reasons. But they were better paid than their British counterparts, as the British had been better paid than the French at the beginning of the war, and so were attractive to the girls. It became desirable for an esteemed American broadcaster to explain frankly to both peoples that there were going to be stresses and strains in their personal relationships which could not be resolved by politicians' bromides about 'our common heritage'.

There was so little to spare from the war effort that only the most rudimentary repairs had been made in the bombed cities, where on a windy day dust and grit from skeleton buildings stung the skin, and in high summer the hosts of rosebay willow-herb advanced upon the bomb-sites of central London like harbingers of the returning forest. The British, who had gone so confidently to war singing 'We're gonna hang out our washing on the Siegfried Line', seemed as far from the Siegfried Line as ever.

The war news was better, but remote. Sinkings of Allied shipping in the Atlantic dropped at last to manageable proportions. Field-Marshal Paulus surrendered with 91,000 men at Stalingrad, and King George VI, wishing to mark the victory by some courtly gesture, sent the Russian people a Sword of Honour which Stalin is said to have received with deep emotion. There was still no Second Front, but instead, after the Germans and Italians had surrendered in North Africa, British and American armies invaded Sicily and began a long, slow slog up the Italian peninsula. Stalin is said to have received this news, too, with deep emotion.

Mussolini fell, and was whisked away by a German paratroop rescue squad to preside forlornly over a shadow government in northern Italy. Marshal Badoglio sued for an armistice, and the Italian fleet sailed under the white flag of surrender between the bomb-scarred walls of the Grand Harbour at Valletta. But the British had never taken the Italians seriously, and victory over Mussolini was regarded as a poor substitute for the long-delayed victory over the real enemy.

A wave of strikes gave forceful expression to war-weariness and disillusionment. Clearly some new stimulus had to be found, and found it was by turning men's eyes to the good life they could expect after the war, when Hitler had at last been beaten.

In 1941, Arthur Greenwood, then a Labour member of the Government, had commissioned Sir William Beveridge to produce a plan for universal social security. Greenwood and Beveridge had served together in the secretariats that produced ambitious reconstruction plans to follow the First World War, and had bitter experience of what happened to even the best-laid plans when a Government was uninterested in implementing them. When Beveridge's report was published in the last days of 1942, Greenwood, though out of office, had taken steps to ensure that it received the maximum publicity. The B.B.C. trumpeted abroad its virtues in twenty-two languages – it was, after all, a powerful piece of propaganda that Britain was already behaving as if the war were won. The Government pronounced only a cool blessing on Beveridge, and 121 M.P.s voted in favour of a motion demanding stronger Government approval, in spite of threats by Ernest Bevin to resign if they pressed the motion to a division. Churchill had never made any secret of his belief that there could be no question of looking forward to a better world until the war was won; but under the prodding of Greenwood and the Labour cohorts, and in the prevailing climate of discontent, he appointed a Minister of Reconstruction who, if he did not reconstruct very much, was at least a visible sign of good intentions.

And Beveridge went marching on. He himself was a Liberal of a Fabian turn of mind, and his report, which would have been revolutionary if implemented in 1906, was by now some way behind the times. That mattered little, however, in comparison with its symbolic importance. In thousands of Army camps from Shetland to the frontiers of India, where tedium was relieved and a certain amount of enlightenment spread by the weekly Army Bureau of Current Affairs lecture, Beveridge was a required subject of discussion. In factories, too, and even in pubs, people talked – perhaps sceptically but with interest – about this conception of a Britain without unemployment and without poverty. Perhaps it was all window-dressing; but in the doldrums of 1943 it meant a great deal to be reminded that there could be a world better than Woolton pie, the overcrowded bus, and the dim spiritual erosion of the blackout.

There were, however, less benevolent planners of the future at work than Sir William Beveridge. At Tehran at the end of November, Stalin, Roosevelt and Churchill held their first summit meeting to decide the shape of the post-war world. They rearranged the frontiers of Poland, for the integrity of which Britain had gone to war. Churchill outlined plans for using the Mediterranean as a springboard into the Balkans which caused Stalin to berate him until Churchill became red in the face. Stalin demanded the promised invasion of France. Roosevelt supported Stalin. His decision settled the matter; and, though he may not have been aware of it, settled the division of Europe between east and west for a generation.

Laurence Thompson

1943 *In the wintry air of Russia the Germans begin to smell defeat.* The Russian tanks are rolling, and now for the first time they are rolling westward. The Germans are forced to yield up Russian territory which Hitler had said would be theirs 'for eternity'.

AN OPEN LETTER TO THE TORY PARTY

The letter is written by Captain the Hon. Quintin Hogg, M.P. He spoke strongly for the Beveridge Plan. It is only a few months since he returned from the Middle East but already he is moved to protest against the mischievous tactics of reactionaries who would lead the nation to political chaos and the Conservative Party to suicide.

Fellow members of the Conservative Party —

I WRITE you this letter as a Conservative, whose loyalty to the principles and policy of our party has never been questioned. I do so with some diffidence because I have but lately returned to this country, with some regret because it will cause controversy between friends, and such controversies are often bitter and seldom profitable.

But I want to ask you—each one of you—a few straight questions. Are you quite satisfied with the part which we are playing at the present time? Are you content with the impression we are making on the country? Are you sure that we are being quite true to our best traditions? Are we decisive enough in our answers to current problems? Are we being progressive enough in our attitude to reform? Do we justify our claims to merge our individual interests in our devotion to the common good? Do we deserve the confidence of the country—and, if we do, are we going the right way to get it? Disraeli wrote in 1835—"The Conservative Party is the National Party, the really democratic party in England." Are we living up to this?

"National or Nothing"

The Conservative Party is either a national party or it is nothing. It is to this fact and to no other that it owes its continued survival after the disappearance of so many of its historical rivals. Once the suspicion is allowed to grow that it is a class party, that it is abandoning the high ideal for which it has stood literally for hundreds of years and is serving the interests of individuals, or of a section of the community instead of the nation at large, the Conservative Party is not only dead but damned. No electoral truce, no Parliamentary majority, and no skilful tactics will save it. Nor, you will agree with me, would we deserve in such circumstances to be saved.

Our destruction would, even in the eyes of the best of our opponents, be a disaster. British politics are built up on the assumption of at least two political parties. Each competes with the other for popular support; each has its characteristic contribution to make to the common good. In such circumstances, the defeat of one or other of the parties may be a good thing or a bad, but the virtual elimination of either is a national catastrophe because it upsets the natural balance upon which the working of our Parliamentary system depends. Yet the responsibility for preserving the lives of parties depends upon the parties themselves: if either the policy of the Reformers becomes too revolutionary, or that of the Conservatives becomes insufficiently progressive, a great electoral defeat is the absolutely inevitable consequence.

In time of war our great political parties do not merge—they simply co-operate. Each retains its own separate organisation and party discipline, but each must make sacrifices in order to retain the confidence and goodwill of the others. In such circumstances a heavier responsibility naturally rests upon the party with a majority of the House of Commons. The minority party has something to gain, and little to lose, by an appeal to the electorate: yet they are asked to refrain out of respect for the principal of national unity. The majority party has the power, but it is under a grave responsibility as to how it uses it. The blame for a rift in the system of co-operation will in the first place inevitably be laid at its door.

So far, all three political parties have an honourable record of support for the Prime Minister since he took office in 1940. I have no word of complaint against the handful of independent members who add, as it seems to me, a useful note of criticism

in the general chorus of approval. Nevertheless, it would be absurd to pretend that the Prime Minister could have remained in office for nearly three years without the steady support afforded by the three political parties and their party discipline.

Perhaps you will agree with me that the need for a continuation of this state of affairs is not less now than it was in the summer of 1940. We are about to face a great and costly campaign which, we hope, will achieve decisive victories. But even victories are not won without reverses. And

Conservatives Should Support the Beveridge Report
Capt. Quintin Hogg, left, and Viscount Hinchingbrooke discuss their amendment before the Parliamentary debate. They were two of forty Conservatives who pressed for legislation on the Report.

battles are not fought without casualties. Reverses and casualties call for calm heads and united action.

And when the war with Germany is over, do you think that the need for unity will disappear? We shall still be at war with Japan. We shall have to carry through a peace settlement which, we hope, will avoid the mistakes made last time. We shall have to demobilise a national army, navy, and air force. We shall have to settle the principles on which we want to reconstruct our national, and our international life.

Do you suppose that the Conservative Party can bear this burden alone? Do you think that we can carry on without Liberal and Labour help, any more than the Liberals or Socialists can carry on without help from us? Let any Conservative who doubts what I say pause for a moment and consider the effects on our chances of recovery from a series of industrial strikes, or an outbreak of party warfare on the lines of pre-war political divisions.

And if you agree with me, agree with me, too, where our real duty lies. We must give to Labour Ministers the same loyal support and enthusiasm which we demand for our own leaders. Mr. Churchill has gathered round him a pretty useful team—Eden, Bevin, Morrison, Sinclair, Woolton, Cripps. The team is working smoothly and loyally together. Let anyone presume to interfere with it and to discriminate between different members, and the whole structure of Mr. Churchill's carefully balanced edifice of national unity will fall to the ground.

On the whole, the Labour Party is playing pretty well. Consider Mr Arthur Greenwood's resolution on the Beveridge Report. No attempt was made to force the pace or make party capital. Indeed so innocuous did the resolution appear that some of

us younger Tories felt constrained to move an amendment to put a little ginger in it.

But what about our own attitude on the Catering Bill? Was it as generous? The other day I went down to support the Government candidate at the Bristol by-election. I found Miss Jennie Lee's ablest ally was none other than Sir Douglas Hacking, former chairman of the Conservative party. When I appealed for national unity behind Mr. Churchill's Ministry I was met by cries of: "What about the two hundred Tory M.P.s who put down a resolution against the Catering Bill?" Sir Douglas Hacking was blissfully cooking the Conservative goose in a sauce which just suited Independent Socialist propaganda. And when Mr. Jimmie Maxton accused the Tory party of a vicious attack on the lives of little waitresses in teashops and lodging houses, the party had only Sir Douglas Hacking to thank for the taunt.

Thank goodness the Second Reading was passed with more than a hundred Tory votes backing Mr. Bevin's measure.

And what do you make of this, ladies and gentlemen? Only a day after the passing of the Catering Bill Second Reading a Conservative back bencher started cross-examining Sir Stafford Cripps about his speeches in the country. They were not, of course, Conservative speeches. But Sir Stafford Cripps is not a Conservative, although, writing as a Conservative, I found nothing whatever to quarrel with in what he said.

But still, that is not the point. The point is, would the question have been asked if Sir Stafford Cripps had been a member of the Conservative Party? Did the back bencher object to Cripps calling the workers "comrades"? Aren't they? And must we all say, "Ladies and gentlemen"? And isn't Cripps himself the best judge of what time he can spare for his speaking engagements?

The fact is that there are shortsighted people on both sides of the political fence who are jeopardising, for party reasons, the whole structure of our national unity now, and our chances of recovery after the war. The Catering Bill was neither a Conservative nor a Socialist measure. It was a Bill whose principles had the unanimous support of an all-party Cabinet. It provided simply that the catering trade should come into line with most other industries in the matter of hours and wages, and that, in return for Government assistance, the Government should have some say in the reconstruction which is designed to put the industry on its feet after the war. Cripps is, as a matter of fact, neither a Conservative nor a Labour Minister. He is an Independent Socialist whose sincerity and abilities are not in doubt, if most of us have had to differ from him pretty considerably in time of peace.

"Heading for Political Chaos"

If matters like the Catering Bill and Cripps' speeches are to be the subjects of party warfare in the middle of a war, where exactly are we going? I will tell you. As a nation we are heading for political chaos. As a party we are heading for political suicide.

Fellow members of the Conservative Party, I appeal to you to put a stop to the tactics of a short-sighted and reactionary rump. Tell them that they are ruining the party. Tell them to take a long view. Tell them to stick to the principles of Disraeli, and to leave clever party politics alone for the time being.

I am, Ladies and Gentlemen,
Your obedient servant,

Quintin Hogg

PICTURE POST

The Man Who Wrote the Report Comes to the House of Commons to Hear What is to Happen to It.
Sir William Beveridge, author of the most famous Report in British social history, comes to the House of Commons by taxi-cab. He sits in the gallery and hears the House, after three days of discussion, decide on a mangled version of his work—and that still subject to financial approval—by 335 votes to 119.

BEVERIDGE: THE FIGHT IS ON

The Government has filleted the Beveridge Report. As far as Parliament is concerned, the battle is over and the Report defeated. But once before, over the Hoare-Laval Pact, this country spoke its mind, and the Government had to follow. Shall we hear, during the next few months, this country speak again?

THE House of Commons has said its say. It has not precisely rejected the Beveridge Report—indeed, so far as words go, it gave it a kind of welcome. It has not even quite killed the Report. It has done something different. It has filleted it. It has taken out the backbone and the bony structure. It has added up the portions that are left—and assures us that they amount to 70 per cent. Sixteen portions out of twenty-three by the Herbert Morrison reckoning—and the only proviso attached is that none of those portions is quite definitely and finally guaranteed. The Treasury, Sir Kingsley Wood, the Chancellor of the Exchequer, beaming blandly and chuckling above their spectacles, may still find the whole business too expensive and decide against it.

How was the work of filleting done? Why was it done? And what steps can the British people still take—if they want to take any?

First, it is doubtful if, in the whole history of our country, there has been a document which aroused hopes so deep and widespread as were aroused by the Beveridge Report. Though they went deep, and though they were felt by the overwhelming majority of the nation, they were perhaps never at any time very strong. It seemed all too good to be true. Not the report itself, of course. That is the merest common-sense. But the idea that the Government would pass it into law, and get to work straightway to carry out its recommendations. We know our Governments better than that. But there did seem one chance, the hovering possibility that the Prime Minister—who in the conduct of the war has so often gauged the spirit of the people—would understand it now; and that some high proportion, not thirty or forty, but an effective number of Tory members would be enough in touch with their own supporters to know what the Report has come to mean.

Matters turned out differently. The voting—but, above all, the speeches—show that the people are ahead of Parliament in their appreciation of this issue, as they have been ahead over every other great issue since the beginning of the Spanish War.

The opponents of the Report—from Sir John Anderson all the way down to Sir Herbert Williams—spoke as though the basis of the Report were an attempt to cadge money off the rich on behalf of the not entirely deserving poor.

Yes. They might be willing to give something. They recognised the justice of the claim. But not all that was asked. And certainly not now. And, above all, they could not make promises for the future. Sir Arnold Gridley wondered "how want is to be defined. Can it necessarily be met by any specific monetary sum? The family of a hard-working and thrifty man can live without want, perhaps on £3 a week, whereas the family of a man who misuses his money or spends it on drink or gambling may be very hard put to it if his wages are £5 or £6 a week."

The fear that small children or old age pensioners may take to drink or gambling is a very real one to a large section of the Conservative Party.

Sir Ian Fraser congratulated the Chancellor on having "done a most difficult thing." He had called the House back "from the fancy fairyland in which

Two of the Signs of Want With Which We Were All Too Familiar in the Years Between the Wars

A "Hunger-march" arrives in Hyde Park to protest against the Means Test—the penalisation of thrift which the Beveridge Report proposes to abolish.

Mealtime in a family where want was not a word, but a constant companion in the struggle to keep going.

BEVERIDGE : *continued*

it loves to indulge, to reality, and thereby rendered a great service to us all." Have you, reader, ever seen your own Member? Did he look the kind of person who loves to "indulge in fancy fairyland"? My own wears a rather different aspect.

Further in his speech Sir Ian carried misrepresentation to the pitch of mania. Objecting to Sir William's plan to make insurance compulsory and national, so as to cut the cost of collection to a fraction, he declared that Sir William's object in doing this was "to steal a capital asset so as to get some revenue for his scheme."

Finally, Sir Herbert Williams let out of his own private bag the largest cat released on the floor of the House of Commons since Baldwin explained why he had to fight the 1935 election on a lie. He did it with the words "If the scheme is postponed until six months after the termination of hostilities the then House of Commons will reject it by a very large majority." Exactly. If we don't get the foundations of a new Britain laid while the war is on, we shall never get them laid at all. Sir Herbert Williams and others of the same kind—or nearly the same kind—will see to that. For so huge an indiscretion the Conservative Party should un-knight Sir Herbert instantly.

The Only Definite Promise

These snivelling objections are quoted for one purpose only : to show the low level at which the opponents of the Report chose to conduct the battle. They fought it on the Poor Law level, the three-ha'penny, ninepence-for-fourpence, Kingsley Wood and Means Test level. The common people of this country were asking for more than their directors and controllers chose to give them. They could get back where they belonged, and say thank-you the mercies were no smaller.

The only unequivocal, unmistakable assurance given during the debate was handed to the insurance companies. They had conducted a considerable campaign against the Report, involving a moderate sum of money. "Death-watch beetles disintegrating the fabric of the whole scheme" was the phrase Mr. Mack, M.P., himself an insurance worker, used of them. The effort was wasted. There was never the least danger of these immense private interests being interfered with. Sir John Anderson dismissed the mere idea with the most significant short sentence spoken during the debate : " the view of the Government is that with the other proposals of the Report they have quite enough on hand."

But if the Report appeared to our representatives in this cadging light, how did it appear to the people of this country? And how did it appear to the peoples of the world, to whom the Government took

care that its *existence* should be made known? It appeared first as a mighty weapon of war, more powerful than thousands of Churchill tanks, having greater destructive force than hundreds of the dive-bombers we do not make.

What the Germans Thought of the Report

The Germans thought the same. When the B.B.C., back in December, began to make the Beveridge Report and its meaning known to an oppressed Europe, the Nazis were beside themselves. What became of their promised New Order if Britain should decide upon a real one? The very day the Report came out, Dr. Schmidt of the Nazi Propaganda Service was put up to try to answer it. All the leading Axis papers followed suit. The Report—designed to cast out fear from the people of Britain—brought terror to the rulers of Germany, Italy, Japan. They attacked it for reasons as confused and contradictory as any produced by its opponents in the Commons. It was belated. It was incomplete. It wouldn't work. All the best bits were copied from National Socialist measures.

The Axis shook at the thought that Britain would grasp the leadership in social reform which they claimed as the basis of their own New Order. They were terrified that the millions of Europe—German and Italian millions among them—would lose heart for a war against a country which was building a better future now. Hitler realised, the people of this country realise, a fact which was scarcely mentioned during the Parliamentary debate.

The Report is not a mere local affair, a financial re-arrangement amongst the inhabitants of the British Isles. It offers hope in a new social order to people all over the world. Beveridge, describing his plan on the B.B.C., was listened to in Europe as a man stating a major British war aim. Hitler has written in "Mein Kampf" that Germany lost the last war, among other reasons, because she lacked war aims. Here, coming over the air in the evening, was an idea which could make real the nebulous aspirations of the Atlantic Charter. That they could deride as meaningless—and did. But the Beveridge Report made Goebbels tremble. He did not have to tremble long. On February 17, after the first day's debate in the House of Commons, the German News Service was able to declare: "The Beveridge Plan was given so much publicity for the sole purpose of demonstrating to the world Great Britain's claim to leadership in the social sphere. In Europe . . . there has been nothing but laughter at this attempt. . . . It now transpires that the whole Beveridge humbug has feet of clay. . . . The wine of enthusiasm of the British Leftists has been watered down by insurance experts, doctors, pensioned officers, and big

business men. . . . Nothing will remain of the comprehensive social scheme but the ensuring of a State grant for the veterinary treatment of cats and dogs."

But the Beveridge Report was much more even than a great war-time weapon. It was a means of developing and extending British influence in peace.

What the Report Means to British Prestige

Consider : when the war ends, the paramount influences in the world will be three : Britain, the U.S.S.R., and the United States. In population and national resources Britain is by far the smallest of the three. If we intend our country to remain a mighty influence, we can only do it in one way, by leading in the world of ideas. By setting the pace in progress towards a juster, fuller, and more generous life. By making our country, in fact, what we have always claimed it to be—"the envy of the world." If we lead the way in social progress, other countries will model their social life and organisation on the British in the twentieth century, just as they modelled their constitutions and political life upon the British in the nineteenth.

If anyone—Sir Herbert Williams, for example—thinks we can lead the world and become the envy of mankind by following orthodox Conservative policy, let him think back. Not far. Only three years. Under Baldwin and Chamberlain those policies had a long run—or rather a good crawl. If they had been allowed to creep on for only another three months, the possibility of having a policy at all would have been taken from us. Three more months of Chamberlain and the Conservatives, perhaps even three weeks, would have meant defeat. There is no leadership of the world to be found that way. Europe knows it. And we know it too.

What else did the Beveridge Report mean to the British people besides a weapon of war and a means of post-war leadership?

The Beveridge Report stood as a symbol and a test. It was a symbol of our determination to build a better country. It was a test of the present Government's willingness to undertake that task. Every one of us who has lived and worked in this country for the past three and a half years is aware of a new spirit in the land. Dangers shared, the more equal division of necessities, new chances of promotion and distinction to the ordinary man and woman, have given the poorest the feeling that he has a real stake in the land. They have removed from the conscience of the well-to-do some of the burden which comes from enjoying privileges that have not been earned. Our society has been juster; and we—in spite of separations and hardships—have, on the whole, been happier because of it.

Can this new spirit survive when the danger which brought it into being is removed? Or is it to

WANT : *The First of the Five Giant Evils, and the One the Beveridge Report Would Have Banished from the Land of Britain*
Back in 1938 one of our cameramen was walking through a great city of the north—a proud and wealthy city. He had his camera with him. He saw this scene and snapped it. "There was nothing special about the picture" he told us. "Such scenes were quite common in those days." During the war the extremes of want have largely vanished. It was the intention of the Beveridge Report that they should not return.

THE FIRST OF MANY FACTORY MEETINGS: *A Resolution to Support Beveridge*
The workers of a tool factory near London meet in their lunch hour. They pass a resolution demanding that the main basis of the Beveridge Plan be put into operation without delay. They declare that this will strengthen the bond of national unity in the war against Fascism.

Moving the Resolution
Ron Dunton, tool maker, chairman of the Shop Stewards Committee, moves the resolution. His mates raise their hands in answer.

be devil-take-the-hindmost once again? So far as this Government is concerned, we have our answer. In the Britain of to-morrow there is still to be a 'We' and 'They.'

The Sole Argument Against : Finance

What were the arguments on which a hope so full of promise was rejected? It is not too much to say that the argument—not the feeling or the instinct behind the argument—but the actual argument on which the Report was turned down was just this single one. It can be put into a phrase : "Can we afford it?" "The only argument of substance against any part of Sir William Beveridge's latest Report is expense," declared Mr. J. R. Clynes, M.P. The argument had a sub-division : "If we guarantee a decent standard of life to our own people, shall we be able to sell our goods in competition with other countries?"

Can we afford it? No : say the Conservatives, we cannot. "The Beveridge Report proposed to fasten on the people a burden of taxation which will render inevitable a catastrophe even worse than that of 1931" said Sir Herbert Williams. Many would not go so far. Their argument was not that we definitely cannot afford the proposals—but that

we cannot know whether we shall be able to or not. An excellent idea—that of eliminating want, but who can say whether this country can afford to have want eliminated? Maybe it will need to have a certain amount of want in order to keep going.

Let us bring this question down to earth with a small parable. A certain man had a large family. He had three sons and two daughters. He had an aged mother, and his wife had an old uncle without means of support. They lived in a small house in a suburb. There was no garden, no fresh air, no change of exercise. The old lady sat by the fireside all day. The uncle lived and hoped for an occasional shilling to buy cigarettes and a newspaper to himself.

One day the man's wife said to him : "Look here, we cannot go on living like this any longer. The children are always ill; my life is going by without my living it; the old people would be better off if they were dead. Let us move farther out into a larger house with a garden. The children will be able to run about. I shall have room to hang up the washing. The old uncle will be able to work in the garden. He will grow a certain amount of greenstuff, and recover his self-respect; and on fine days the old lady can sit out-of-doors. Of course it's a risk, because it will cost more. But it means so much to

our happiness, let's back ourselves and chance it !"

"No," said the husband. "Not until I know how much I shall be earning in ten years' time. We may be able to afford it now—but who knows where we shall be then?"

The Export Trade Red Herring

And what of the export trade? Well, what of it? To me, and to those who think as I do, the idea that after this war we are all going straight back to cutting one another's throats in the effort to export more and import less—for the sake of enjoying a lower standard of living and seeing a balance on the right side in the Bank of England's account book—is delirium. There could only be one answer to that—a general refusal. A *World Strike*. The only account book that ought to matter after the war should be the world account book—by which raw materials are directed to where they can be manufactured, and products of industry sent to where they can be used. We reject altogether the idea that the British people must force down their standard of life for the sake of trying to undersell the Japanese.

But even if we accept this farcical idea. Granted that pre-war conditions are to return, the scramble for markets—with the wars that will certainly follow

WHAT THE BEVERIDGE REPORT MEANS TO WOMEN

WHY should women work to bring the full Beveridge Report into operation? Because here for the first time they are offered the full status to which they are entitled.

The war has exploded the old idea that a married woman is a mere "adult dependant." Sir William Beveridge dismisses this idea as "indefensible," says that most married women are occupied on work which is vital though unpaid. Without their help, their husbands could not do their paid work, and without it the nation could not continue. A married couple are a team, and each of the partners is equally essential. Hence, the Beveridge Report recognises the housewife. That is the salient point.

How would this recognition affect the housewife on the practical question of insurance? Married women would be taken as a separate insurance class—they are No. 3 of the six classes into which the whole population is divided. On marriage, a woman would begin a new insurance life. She would acquire at once a right to a Housewife's Policy, with numerous grants and benefits attached to it. Women should note here that special provision is made for a woman who continues to work after marriage. She has a choice of insurance : either she can be exempt from it, paying no contributions of her own—just as though she were not working. Or she can contribute, and qualify for benefits, though these will be on a smaller scale than the benefits for unmarried women.

The grants and benefits to which the housewife would be entitled are most important—and humane. They give a married woman help at just those times when she is likely to need it. But they do not allow her to become a useless burden. She has a responsibility to the community.

Now, as to marriage, the Report proposes a grant of £1 for every 40 contributions made before marriage, with a maximum of £10. It points out that this is desirable as a sort of compensation, since, on marrying, a woman gives up all her previous qualifications for benefits; but it regards this grant as optional.

At the present time the expense of having a baby is a serious worry to a woman at a time when she should be as free from anxiety as possible. The Report recognises this fully. It proposes that every married woman should have a maternity grant of £4; that she should, of course, have proper medical attention and nursing; and that every woman who earns money at a job should have maternity benefit of 36s. a week for 13 weeks, provided she gives up her job for this period.

And then, on the question of widowhood, the Beveridge Report takes an entirely new line. To-day, every widow has a small pension automatically. This, says the Report, is inadequate during the difficult time immediately following a husband's death, and superfluous later on for women who could perfectly well work.

So the Report purposes to give every widow a benefit of 36s. a week for 13 weeks after husband's death—to cover the time when she has many difficult adjustments in her life, such as moving, perhaps, into a smaller home. But, for widows of working age, there would be no permanent pension. (Naturally, a woman with children would get the normal guardian's benefit and children's allowances.) In other words, a married woman is to have new responsibilities as well as new benefits. She is expected to do some kind of work all her life—either running a home or doing a job—until she reaches the retiring age of 60.

The recognition of the housewife, and the help for married women on marriage, in maternity, and at widowhood, are the proposals which particularly affect women. But nearly every section of the Report affects them in some way. They already know the Government's attitude on the children's allowances. It is proposed not to pay 8s. a week for every child after the first, as Beveridge suggested, but 5s. This is a setback. But any children's allowance is a victory of principle, and it will encourage more women to work for the full provisions of the Report which has become the Housewives' Charter.

WHAT A MINISTRY OF SOCIAL SECURITY WOULD MEAN TO THE ORDINARY CITIZEN

What happens to-day to an individual who meets with misfortune : an extreme case to illustrate the maze through which Beveridge has pointed out a clear, simple way.

1 John Jones, a man of 64, finds that he has fallen out of work through no fault of his own.

2 He draws unemployment pay : at this point his case is dealt with by the Ministry of Labour.

3 After 26 weeks he is no longer entitled to the dole and is turned away to go elsewhere.

4 He has now to go to the Assistance Board. Here he applies for the unemployment help he needs.

5 The first of many investigators arrives at his home—this time from the Assistance Board.

6 He falls ill. Unable to work, he is no longer able to get help from the Assistance Board.

7 A new investigator arrives—from the Approved Society, which now deals with his case.

8 Still another investigator —from the local Public Assistance Committee, to which he has had to apply.

9 His 65th birthday present: a visit from a fourth investigator — to look into his pension claim

Wife Falls Ill

Child is Ill

All Mean More Investigators

Son Steals

MEANWHILE

A MINISTRY OF SOCIAL SECURITY WOULD COMBINE ALL THESE FUNCTIONS

John Jones when he falls out of work has plenty of trouble besides the gnawing anxiety about his family's welfare. He is passed from one set of officials to another until he feels like an official form worn out by constant stamping. How absurd that a fresh investigation has to worry him whenever he suffers a new misfortune, that there is no single set of papers about him and his family for everybody to consult ! When he comes to the end of his road—an old age pension—

he reaches the crowning absurdity: at this point his case actually comes under Customs and Excise! It is this state of affairs which a Ministry of Social Security would cure. John Jones would go to one local office for all his claims; there would be one set of papers about him and one investigator to help and advise. And the people working in this office would not treat him as a wrong-doer, but as a man fallen on evil times who must be lifted up again.

—then what is the industrialist's first need? Obviously, a labour-force, well-fed and well-cared-for physically, free from haunting anxieties, able to devote itself solely to the business of production. Big industrialists should have seized the Beveridge Report with both hands. They should have forced it through against every opposition. It would have meant the establishment of their fighting force—and at a cost given by a Conservative member as an addition of a mere 2% to the total wage charge of the export industries. Instead, they looked at the size of their own contributions under the scheme, and did sums on little bits of paper to show that the unemployed—who used to assemble in thousands on the off-chance of a casual job—would not consider it worth their while to work.

Well, they have won their battle. Or have they, perhaps, not won it? Have they won only the first round? Have they made certain, not that the British people will not get the Beveridge Report—only that this Parliament will not freely give it them? And what can the British people do, if it feels its representatives have on this occasion not represented it at all?

Once before, in the past few years, the long-suffering British people got up and spoke its mind. The occasion was the agreement between Sir Samuel Hoare and Pierre Laval to divide up Abyssinia for the benefit of Mussolini. The result almost made Mr. Stanley Baldwin jump out of his skin. He had no idea we felt so strongly. He never imagined that we were capable of speech. When he found we were, he sacked Sir Samuel and put Mr. Eden in his place.

How can we once more make our voice heard in high places? Only by speaking. The nation has other voices than the voice of Parliament. Separately those voices may be only squeaks, but enough squeaks make a roar. Every factory, workshop and office has a voice. Clubs have voices. So have trade union branches. Political societies and groups have voices. Universities, colleges and schools have voices. Every kind of woman's organisation

has the power of speech. Now, if they are interested, let them speak. And let the ordinary individuals who compose these groups take the trouble to attend their meetings. There cannot be the smallest doubt that, if the country wants the Beveridge Report it can have it. It can have it unfilleted, in the way Sir William Beveridge left it. But it will have to say so. And, in saying so, it should make two things clear : First, it wants the report as a war-aim, not as a war-distraction.

Second, there is no question in the country's

minds of the Government resigning. Such an issue has not arisen. There is not the slightest reason why it ever should. The Government cannot desert its war-time post over a social disagreement, any more than the rest of us can. The Government is conducting the war with considerable success. Let it, as Mr. Eden said, get on with that. Meantime, let it appoint a Minister of Social Security, and let him get busy on making the report into a fact. And let him get busy now.

TOM HOPKINSON.

THEIR PAPERS WERE TWO OF THE REPORT'S CHIEF OPPONENTS

Lord Camrose : "Daily Telegraph"

Lord Kemsley : "Daily Sketch"

Most persistent of all critics of the Beveridge Report were the papers owned by the Berry brothers—now Lords Kemsley and Camrose. Both, after giving the scheme an apparent welcome, ran leading articles, feature articles and letters attacking the scheme day after day.

Hindsight by Kenneth Clark

The chief motive behind the War Artists' scheme was a belief that it was better for artists to go on painting than to join the forces and probably be killed. The first war had shown that some artists can do good work when commissioned to paint scenes of warfare; Stanley Spencer's war scenes in the memorial chapel at Burghclere are probably his finest works. In the second war the War Artists' Committee had to choose the artists and give them appropriate commissions. Paul Nash surpassed the work he had done in the 1914–18 war with his *Dead Sea of German Aeroplanes* and his great picture of the Battle of Britain, which really expresses the sense of glory of those months. We had less luck with some of the other veterans. Wyndham Lewis wouldn't play, Roberts was sunk in aggressive gloom, Kennington had turned into a social realist who should really have been dropped by parachute into Germany. The bombing of London was a new and moving experience, and we had the good fortune to find three artists who could convey it to posterity in remarkable works of art. John Piper had already made a reputation as a painter of ruins, and was a natural choice; there was in the work of Graham Sutherland a love of strangeness and a hint of menace which made us feel that the visual tragedies of war damage would appeal to him; perhaps our greatest piece of luck was persuading Henry Moore to draw in the tube shelters. In 1939 he was known purely as an 'abstract' artist, but I had fortunately seen one or two groups of draped figures that he had done in 1938 which suggested that the problem of representing huddled, sleeping forms would appeal to him technically; while the human qualities of courage and stoicism would appeal to his warmth of heart.

Of course many of our commissions were straight-forward records, and often these could have been better done by the camera. But every now and then a realist like Charles Cundell produced a synthesis of experience that a camera could not give. Much the best portraits we obtained were the bronze heads by Epstein; some of them, like those of Bevin and Portal, are among his master-pieces. Did we discover any young, unknown painters? The answer is no, but this was not for lack of trying. The reason, I think, is that art obeys its own laws, and at this time the artistic impulse was moving away from illustration. The work produced by middle-aged artists now out of fashion is not worthless. I believe that Edward Ardizzone's drawings will be used as marginalia by historians of the war; and Barnett Freedman's 'polyphoto' portraits of a submarine crew and an aircraft factory will give a more vivid idea of what we all felt like than any series of photographs.

When it was all over we found that we had about 15,000 works of art to distribute. We sent them to galleries all over the country and the Commonwealth and I hope that some of them may still give pleasure to a budding artist in some remote New Zealand township.

It remains to say a word about Stanley Spencer, whose record of Clydeside ship-building is the pretext of this note. Posterity may well decide that he was the most remarkable painter of all those who recorded their feelings about the first war. By 1939 he was in an uneasy frame of mind. The value of his early work had been a kind of visionary intensity which had made his descriptive realism strange and memorable. But as with all visionary artists, his power of transforming the commonplace came and went, and was not at his command. He had been deeply moved by the first war; by 1939 he was wrapped up in his personal problems. However, we thought that the sight of men on girders with blowlamps was so strange, and so far from his ordinary experience in the village of Cookham, that it might arouse in him the necessary excitement. On the whole we were proved right. The long, frieze-like paintings of ship-building haven't the intensity of his Resurrection, but they are superior to most of his later work, and will remain one of the best things to come out of the War Artists' scheme.

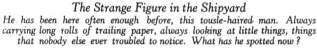

The Strange Figure in the Shipyard
He has been here often enough before, this tousle-haired man. Always carrying long rolls of trailing paper, always looking at little things, things that nobody else ever troubled to notice. What has he spotted now?

What is it He Has Drawn on the Paper?
He has put something down on the paper, but you can't really make out what it is. He hasn't finished yet. He's looking over there again, as if he's seen something new, something that nobody's ever seen before.

A WAR ARTIST ON THE CLYDE

"Advance!"—"Retreat!"—"Surrender!"—"Victory!" The war words grow bigger and bigger in the headlines. Some people have the feeling sometimes that they don't know what to make of it all. The man who makes something permanent of it—something for posterity—is the artist. Here is an artist, Stanley Spencer, at work in a great centre of war industry.

A SMALL, tousle-haired, spectacled man in pyjamas stands below the giant stanchions, the steel girders and the sheets of metal swaying from the menacing arm of the crane. All around him there is noise: the noise of the hammering, the burning, the riveting. The air is filled with mist and the stench of burning metal. Just beyond him there is a great shape, the looming hull of a ship over which men swarm and toil as they fit the new sections. Still further away, you can see the reason for all this violence: the ships are moving through the murky water towards the war which has called them into being.

The tousle-haired man in pyjamas peers over the shapes that surround him, reaches for a notebook and writes in it: "Don't forget the finished shipping." It is a reminder to himself not to get lost in the details, but to take a look, before he ends, at the purpose of it all. But, the next moment, he is screwing up his eyes at one of the detailed contrivances which help to create the "finished shipping"; he is staring at the tool in the hand of

the man who is riveting a steel plate. And, as he stares, he twists a length of the great roll of paper which trails from his hands. On the paper, he has made a sketch of what he sees, but then he looked at it and it wouldn't do. He begins to sketch again. Around him stand a few silent workmen, and they bend their heads to see what was on the paper.

The man in the pyjamas is Stanley Spencer. It is true that he has kept his pyjamas on, but he has put some other clothes over them—a suit and a pullover. The presence of the pyjamas, however, is a sign that their wearer has no time to waste on personal details or sophistication, but is determined to give all his time to the great task of putting down on paper a scene that may be lost for ever if he misses a moment. He is as urgent as the figures with which he is filling the great mural of shipyard work which he has been painting for most of the war, and sections of which have been on view at various times in the National Gallery—"Bending the Keel Plate," "First Instalment

to the *Pridella*," "Welders," and so on.

When he has finished he will have done something more than sketch a continuous episode of wartime life, he will have created something that will endure when the mood of the moment is forgotten. The skeleton of a hull, the steel plates, the punching machines—to us they are all parts of a modern process which must be completed faster and faster so that we can win the war. But, in the artist's picture they are something more. The machinery may be modern, but the human figures are timeless: they might be building the Ark for Noah. Spencer's mural, in fact, is a chapter in the unending labour of man. He is inspired not only by what he sees—"The variety, tremendous!" he exclaims, but by the spiritual life that is within him. "Mine is a Wesleyan, Non-Conformist atmosphere," he exclaims. He carries a pocket Bible with him, and remarks in astonishment that "It's quite hard to get these nowadays." And his speech is salted with Biblical phraseology. "Seek and the technicalities shall be added unto

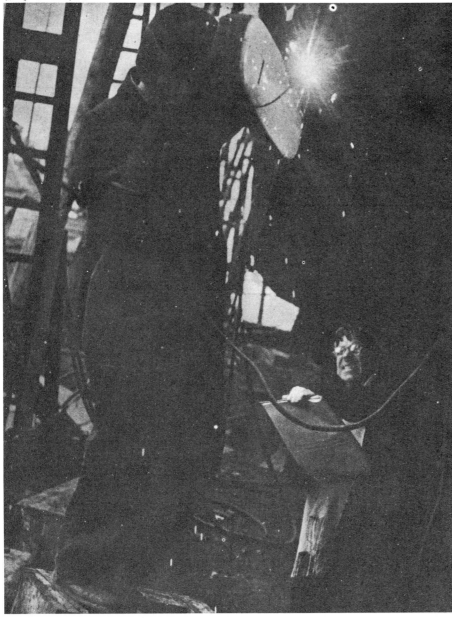

you," he says, as his eyes seek amid the steel girders.

Stanley Spencer was born at Cookham in Surrey 51 years ago. His father, a professor of music and the village organist, used to read the Bible aloud to his eleven children, choosing the passages, not for their meaning, but for their music. More than one of the boys shared the father's musical talent, and Stanley's early life was lived in an atmosphere of music by the great composers. There was another long-remembered pleasure. On winter mornings he and at least one of his brothers used to run naked down to the icy river, swim to an island, and dry in the warming sun, returning filled with an exaltation which inspired his earliest paintings after he had become a pupil at the Slade. So Spencer is distorting himself when he makes himself out to be puritanical in outlook : his best work owes a great deal to appreciation of the sensuous world. But, of the religious inspiration there is no doubt. He has painted the Bible's great events—the journey to Calvary and the Resurrection—as if they belonged to his own life-time.

His best-known work up to now has had its roots in the soil out of which he grew himself--the village of Cookham where he was born. On Clydeside he has discovered a new world, a world of metal. He is excited about it. He stops to pick up a handful of shavings. "Isn't this mysterious," he says. "What's it all about?" He stops in front of a twisted length of wood and murmurs, "Very true !" He writes down notes to himself, such as "Don't for the Lord's sake forget that. riveter eating bread."

"It gives me an anchorage," he explains, "to which I can toddle back if I get too involved." And it is a fact, that he is always in danger of getting too deeply buried in detail : but we shall know the larger purpose when the whole work is finished.

The last war, he went to Macedonia for two and a half years, hated army life and sat in front-line trenches within a quarter of a mile of the enemy, forming an image of the Bulgar as a sinister spirit hovering over the Balkan landscape. This war he has spent mostly on Clydeside, forming an image of modern machinery as the spirit which broods over those fat moon-faced human beings who work as if they are harnessed to a divine purpose.

His discovery of this new world may lead him to fresh heights as an artist. And the Clydeside workers with whom he lives have discovered a new world, too, for they are conscious of the artist among them, and they feel a true respect for him. They will never see their work again—but the picture will remain.

The Clydeside workers will not be the only people to see an artist at work. Two Cities film company are producing a film called *Out of Chaos*, written by its director, Jill Craigie, about how an artist creates a picture, and Stanley Spencer is one of the artists appearing in it. How does he feel about acting in a film ? "Well," he says, "I never do anything arty; at least, I hope not. I am a worm wriggling about among the legs of men."

And how does he come out as an actor in this promising film ? These pictures should show.

WHAT THE ARTIST IS SKETCHING : *A Burner Prepares for Welding*
With the oxy-acetylene apparatus, the burner works on the plates before the electrical welding. Below him, the artist draws what he sees.

The Great Scene of the Clydeside Shipping : The Artist Leaves the Details for a Moment and Looks Out on the World
His eye is for details. They are the details he needs for the vast mural he has been painting for years. But to-day he writes himself a little note "Don't, for the Lord's sake, forget the finished shipping." Then he goes back to the human details he loves best, "The variety," he exclaims, "is tremendous !"

"I Just Wriggle About Among Men's Legs": He Talks to Jill Craigie About the Film She is Making—About Him

Jill Craigie is directing a film for Two Cities—"Out of Chaos"—about the creation of pictures by artists. Stanley Spencer is one of the stars in it. "But I never do anything arty," he exclaims. "At least I hope not!" They discuss the scenes in which he appears.

Details He Still Requires: The Riveter

Amid the din and stench of the yards, the artist sketches, unconcerned. He sees a mystical liaison between the men and their work, is fascinated, and absorbed.

He Stands on the Crane

From the cabin of the giant crane he can get a different view of the pattern he has been drawing.

A WAR ARTIST

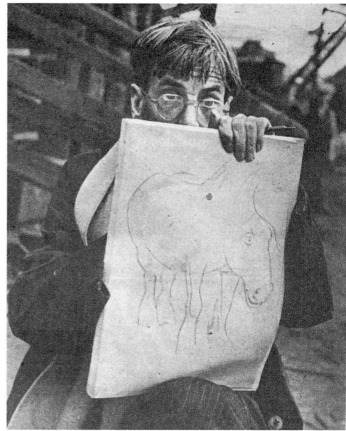

ON THE JOB

ON THE CLYDE

OBLIVIOUS OF NOISE,

STANLEY SPENCER

MAKES SKETCHES

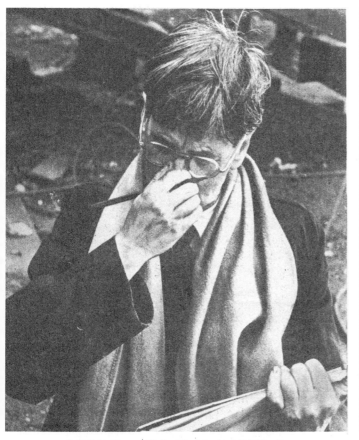

WAR, ONLOOKERS

AND CAMERAMAN

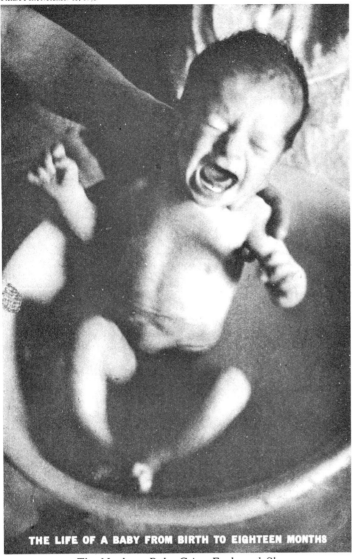

THE LIFE OF A BABY FROM BIRTH TO EIGHTEEN MONTHS

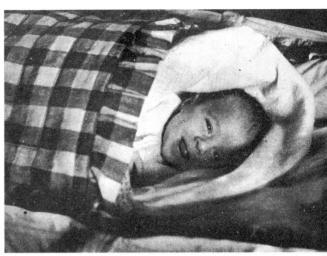

6 WEEKS *Her First Real Smile*
She gives her first genuine smile, with pleasure behind it. Her eyes smile as well as her lips. She has become a person.

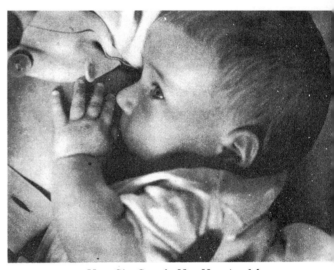

3 WEEKS *The Newborn Baby Cries, Feeds and Sleeps*
These photographs, taken by its mother, show the progress of a particular baby during its first eighteen months. Naturally children vary. Don't be surprised if your own develops more quickly in some ways, more slowly in others.

3 MONTHS *How She Spends Her Happiest Moments*
A "good baby" takes a quiet satisfaction in feeding. If a baby is difficult, probably the mother is not managing it well. All doctors stress the importance of the mother feeding her baby herself.

WHY WOMEN DON'T HAVE BABIES

an enquiry ; by Anne Scott-James

In spite of a wartime boom in babies, our birth rate declines alarmingly. Why are women reluctant to have children? Why is the big family dying out? After talking to well-known doctors, economists, feminists and social workers, we suggest some of the changes which would help to make babies more popular.

EVER since the last war, there have been lone voices crying in the wilderness about our falling birth rate. But the prophets of disaster—who usually talked in terms of the most complicated statistics—were regarded as cranks or scaremongers by the world at large. It isn't easy to get worked up because "the net reproduction rate in England and Wales has dropped from 1.33 to 0.78 since 1850."

But this war has given us a shaking. It has made it clear to ordinary men and women that increasing manpower ought to mean—not unemployment—but prosperity. At last, not only the statisticians, but business men, social workers, doctors, ordinary taxpayers, ordinary parents of young children—anyone, in fact, who has a stake in the future—are beginning to feel that the facts are alarming, and the problem urgent. You can't ignore the experts when they confront you with simple, human facts such as these :

We have already 2,000,000 less children under 14 than we had in the last war.

By 1950—only seven years from now—there will be more voters over 45 than under 45. Post-war Britain will be dominated by middle-aged and elderly people.

By 1971, there will be twice as many people eligible for old age pensions as there are now.

By the same date, there will be threequarters of the present number of people under 45 to work, earn, and, if necessary, fight.

There will be a declining demand for goods, with all the possibilities of poverty and unemployment. Industry will be revolutionised. Hair-restorers and backache cures may become bigger industries than chocolate and cosmetics.

No ; the problem can hardly be dismissed as academic. On the contrary, the shortage of babies is of real importance to everyone with ten years or more to live, and—following one of the best House of Commons debates of the year—the Government has now promised a full enquiry. Because we thought the subject so important, we have been collating some ideas and opinions. We have talked it over with doctors, economists, feminists and social workers who have studied the problem, and have remedies to offer.

How It Has Happened

Many stupid things were said about the falling birthrate in the 1930's. "Good-time girls won't have babies" was a typical headline. "Selfish wives prefer cocktail bars to nurseries" was another. There was a hardy joke about Baby Austins and babies.

Of course, these wholesale condemnations were absurd. Most people who have put thought and work into the subject agree that the decline in population is not a sign of degeneracy, but is a problem that has come with progress. It is the most advanced races which are feeling it most; and many parents are having small families, not because

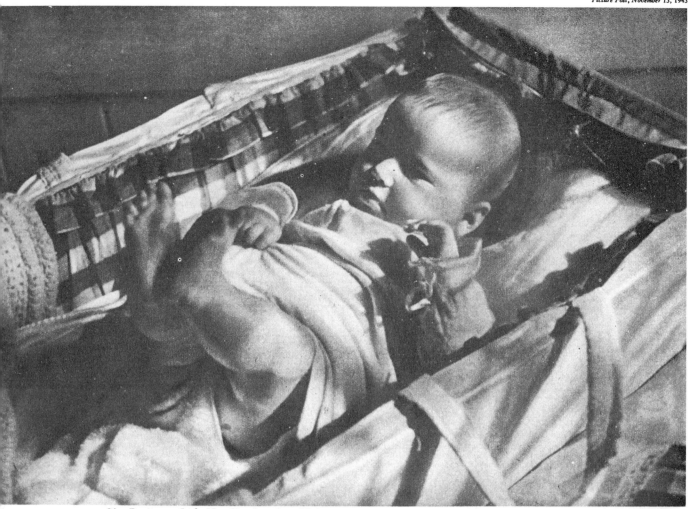

4 MONTHS   *She Begins to Lift Her Head and to Kick*
Now she can make plenty of movements. She has discovered how to use her hands. She goes on to explore her feet. She can lift her head, but—mercifully—cannot yet turn herself right over.

they are good-time gals or want Baby Austins (why shouldn't they?), but because they have a greater sense of responsibility than before. They want higher standards of living and education for their children. (Children are dependents in this century; they were wage-earners in the last.) And women want higher standards for themselves. They want less drudgery in the home, and a fuller life outside it.

So any policy that is framed must be a forward-looking policy. The reactionary methods tried out by Germany and Italy have been not only revolting but unsuccessful. They have tried making an obscene religion of motherhood. They have encouraged promiscuity; forbidden contraceptives;

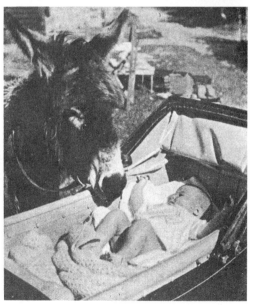

5 MONTHS   *She Is Not Afraid*
No one has suggested to her that strange things are frightening. So fear does not occur to her.

barred women from professions. But none of these methods—not even the joyous prospect of getting a medal from Mussolini—has succeeded in keeping up the population.

It is no good our shutting women up at home; banning contraceptives; smugly praising Victorian

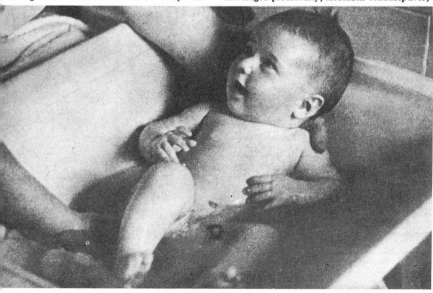

3-4 MONTHS   *She Enjoys Her Bath*
At this age, bathing is not just a hygienic routine. It is a daily treat. She loves being swished about in the water. She loves the kind of toys that float in the bath.

5-6 MONTHS *Her Mother's View of Her*
She is now immensely active. In her pram or
on a rug, she spends most of her time kicking.

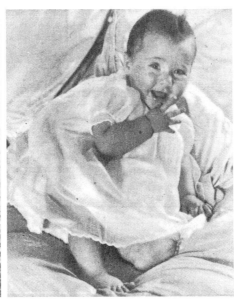

6 MONTHS *She Sits Up Alone*
She sits up gingerly at first, very soon gains
confidence. She likes looking around.

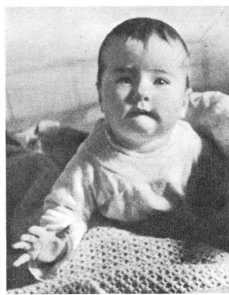

6-7 MONTHS *She Starts to Wriggle*
She doesn't crawl, but she can propel herself
for a short distance on all fours.

fecundity. If we need more babies, we must work
out a modern way of getting them.

1: Social Reform the First Step

The country cannot expect women to have larger
families until we can offer them a much higher
standard of social services. After the war, there must
be a real drive to relieve the drudgery of women.

We all know that after the war there will have
to be a great housing scheme. But we shall want
not only more houses, but better planned, *family*
houses. Houses of good size with plenty of room
for children, with labour-saving equipment to save
housework and washing-up, and with space for the
laundry and the pram. R. F. Harrod, an economist
who has made a special study of the birthrate, thinks
that local authorities should be directed to see that
there are enough modern houses for the 4-5 children
family in each district, and that these should have
priority over other building.

Then there will have to be some system of home
helps that every mother can afford—perhaps Mr.
Bevin's expected Domestic Charter will recognise
the claims of families. Not everyone will want a
full-time domestic or nanny; but if there were
domestic exchanges working on a rota basis (some
authorities have started them already), women could
get part-time help for at least a few hours a day.

If we want bigger families, we must certainly open
more nursery Schools. Only a superhuman woman
can cook, shop, run a house and look after three or
four children all at once. There are always some
diehards who tell you that " the working classes
have done it for generations." But it is just this sort
of slavery which makes working class women look
middle-aged at thirty, and old at forty.

Nursery schools save a great deal of anxiety. If
a mother can take her youngest children to a
nursery school where they will be safe, and get
good food and training, she can do her shopping
and housework in half the time, and be fresh when
it is time to take the children home again.

These social services obviously give direct help
to the mother of a family. But every step towards
better living — from town planning to communal
kitchens—is going to make family life easier.

2: Financial Help for Families

Ever since the 1850's, children have been
becoming more and more expensive. Children were
once wage-earners at six or seven, are now
dependents up to fourteen, and will be dependents
up to fifteen with the raising of the school leaving
age. In abolishing the barbarities of child labour
and illiteracy, the country has never done anything
to help parents cope with their new responsibilities.

The Beveridge scale of family allowances—not yet
accepted by the Government—would be a substantial help to working class families; 8s. a week
for each child after the first is a real contribution.

But this rate of allowance is never going to
produce more babies in the middle classes, where
they are just as badly wanted. The amount is
simply too small to help. It is to meet this difficulty
that R. F. Harrod has worked out a new and
brilliant scheme of *graded* family allowances.

Under this scheme, in addition to the universal
8s. per child, there would be benefits for children,
rising in value with the parents' income. The
general taxpayer would not, of course, pay for these
larger allowances. It would be a scheme of compulsory graded insurance, each man contributing—
and benefiting—according to his income.

Mr. Harrod has worked out a tentative table
showing what the contributions and allowances
would be at various income levels. For instance, a
man earning £500 a year would pay £25 a year,
whether he has children or not. The man without
children would get nothing back. A man with two
children would get back less than his contribution;
a man with three children would get back a little
more; and a man with four or more children would
get back very much more than he paid in. Thus,
all the childless men with £500 a year would be

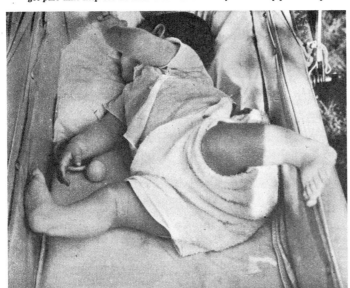

6-7 MONTHS *She Curls Into Fantastic Attitudes*
Most mothers are convinced their children are going to be dancers. They
find them curled up like rag-dolls when they are asleep.

6-7 MONTHS *She Begins to Use Her Hands*
Now she can really use her hands. She pinches things that don't belong to
her. She pokes and bangs them. She likes to suck them, too.

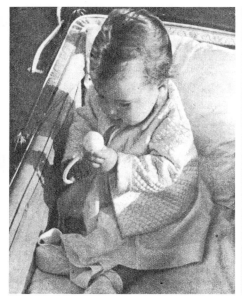

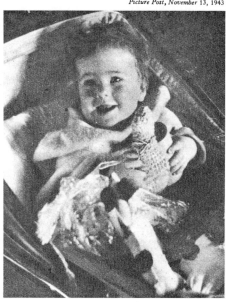

8-9 MONTHS *She Uses Her Toys*
Things to rattle, things to drop, things to throw out of the pram, have become a joy to her.

11 MONTHS *Almost a Biped*
Clinging to her play-pen, she begins to pull herself up. She uses chairs and table-legs too.

12 MONTHS *The First Conversation*
She knows a few words. She knows her name. She knows when people are talking to her.

helping to pay for the children of other £500-a-year men; and the same would apply at all income levels.

R. F. Harrod has some other financial proposals to help the family. There should be fresh legislation, he says, to cover hire purchase. Hire purchase is the basis on which thousands of couples set up house.

There should be low rates of interest fixed by law, relief from payments during illness or unemployment, and strong safeguards against fraud.

3 : The Psychological Aspect

But the problem is not wholly economic. Lord

Horder, who, as a great doctor and progressive thinker, should be a skilful judge of the country's moods and feelings, believes that the psychological side of it has been under-estimated. He thinks that some married couples are indifferent to whether

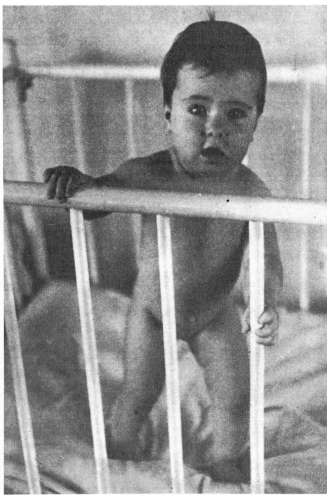

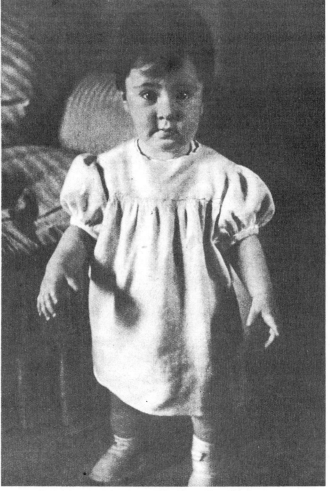

11 MONTHS *For the First Time She Stands Alone*
She passes the first big landmark in her life. She can stand by herself. It is a triumph—and she knows it.

12 MONTHS *She Takes Her First Few Steps*
Concentrating hard, she takes a few uncertain steps. By now, she can convey her feelings. She has favourite toys, favourite clothes.

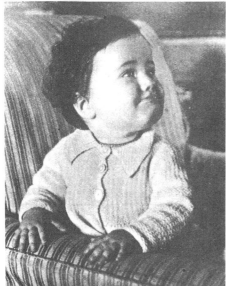

13 MONTHS *She Can Clown*
She makes jokes. She mimics. She strikes attitudes. She's always attracting attention.

14 MONTHS *She Makes Things Work*
She finds your watch, your torch, your fountain pen irresistible. She tries out the piano.

16 MONTHS *She Builds Things Up*
She builds up blocks. She bangs about with constructional toys. She feels effective.

they have children or not, and that women are "more tender-minded" than they used to be. Many women are hesitant, even positively nervous, of having children; and there is a greatly increasing number of caesareans—often suggested in advance—which means a full anæsthetic and freedom from the troubles of childbirth.

Because the problem of the falling birth-rate is so varied and subtle, Lord Horder thinks it is vital to enquire thoroughly into the causes. He believes that we can take no positive action to check the decline until after the war, when we know what the social fabric of the country is going to be—but that in the meantime we can complete our researches into causes. What we can work on, too, is the whole eugenic side. War, says Lord Horder, is naturally

15-18 MONTHS *She Makes Friends*
She knows not only her parents, but other people as well. She has very positive likes and dislikes.

dysgenic—it "takes the flower and leaves the weed" —and there is a greater need than ever to work to improve the quality of the children that *are* born.

4: The Woman's Case

In the long run, it is wives who decide on the size of their families. That is why Dr. Summerskill, M.P.—always the stalwart champion of women— says that if the country needs more babies, we must "examine the conditions of the producers."

Wives, says Dr. Summerskill, are still treated officially as unpaid domestic helps. They are being asked to produce babies as a kind of unpaid junior partner. Their share in the running of a home is in fact as important as the husband's; yet, financially, they are entirely dependent, and in many households have to ask for money as a favour. We must emancipate women inside the home as well as outside it, says Dr. Summerskill; for this decline in families is a great Women's Revolt. We must give the non-earning wife a legal right to a share of her husband's income, and so a real status in her own home. Then, family life will have prestige again.

16-17 MONTHS *The Instinctive Interest That Children Seem to Find in Books*
She likes the books that belong to her—and the books that don't. She recognises pictures, enjoys going through picture-books with a grown-up. And she raids the shelves for books to play with.

Another side of the woman's problem is that women who want an all-round life can only find it outside home. There ought to be more and more opportunities for women to combine a home and outside life. Better social services will help them at home. More provision for part-time jobs, more encouragement for married women in the professions, in social work, and in industry, will help them outside. When you have this sort of attitude, then many women who have a real talent for professional work, and do not now marry, will be able to use that talent, and to marry as well—and so be in the running for having children.

5: A Better Medical Service

Probably no woman who ever *positively* wanted a baby was put off having one by the physical difficulties of the job. The war has brought plenty of evidence of feminine courage, for more babies are being born now than for a decade past, although conditions are bad, and the difficulties of looking after and equipping a baby are scandalous.

At the same time, an improvement in our maternity services—still barbarous in some respects—would give us many more children by increasing the survival rate.

"Go for the survival rate, and for the highest possible standard of babies" is what Seymour Leslie is urging, who has been for many years Secretary and Organiser of Queen Charlotte's Maternity Hospital. He showed us all the special equipment and services at Queen Charlotte's—and they are superb. Unfortunately, the standard of maternity services in England is patchy, and conditions in many districts are prehistoric.

First, this hospital gives an analgesic, or pain deadener, to every mother—the Minnitt's gas-and-air method which is agreed by all doctors to be absolutely safe. Now, this analgesic can be used with complete safety by midwives provided they are given some training for out-patients. Queen Charlotte's have a mobile squad of midwives who have the apparatus fitted to their motor-bikes. Yet, in the country as a whole, only a tiny proportion of midwives are trained to use Minnitt's apparatus, and it is customary to use no analgesic at all.

"My mother never heard of anæsthetics, and she had thirteen children," is the sort of comment you hear from people—chiefly men—who think there is no limit to what women will put up with. To which there is only one answer: "My great-grandfather had

18 MONTHS   *The Complete Little Human Being*
*She is a person with a circle of friends and belongings. She can play happily for hours by
herself—or provide very good company for the people who know her well.*

a leg off at twenty without an anæsthetic, and lived to be ninety. But would you do the same ?"

Infant care is another important branch of Queen Charlotte's. The pædiatrician—the specialist in the prevention of child diseases—is becoming more and more important in the field of medicine. Standards of obstetrics and pre-natal care in England are high, but our infant care is still backward. The lives of many babies will be saved as this science develops.

Another new advance in infant welfare at Queen Charlotte's is the Human Milk Bureau, copied from a famous American hospital—a store of frozen human milk. It is the only one in England, though there were many on the Continent before the war.

Most important step of all—if we want more babies we must plan for more maternity accommodation. And we must plan not for present, but for future needs, *or we shall always be behindhand.* We talked to a gynæcologist with many years' experience on the Continent, who is now practising in England. He told us he was appalled when he first came over by our shortage of accommodation. "Why should any woman have to beg for a hospital bed?" he says. "Surely she has a right to one?"

6: The Attitude Matters Most of All

But there is something more that has got to happen if the larger family is to come into fashion. We have got to get rid of the "no children, no dogs," attitude. People have got to feel *that children are a good thing.*

Social reconstruction, financial help, family

allowances, a better status for women, a revised medical service, are all essential. But something more intangible has got to be created as well. There is one country which has attempted nearly every enlightened measure to increase her birthrate—Sweden—and even Sweden has so far failed.

It would be foolish at this stage to try to draw up a black-and-white schedule suggesting means of making nineteenth-century families seem desirable to twentieth-century parents. Probably, social improvements will in time make large families more popular. When a father no longer worries himself to death with "How shall I ever educate them?" and when a mother no longer asks herself ten times a day. "How shall I ever get through in time?" much will have been done.

But probably the most constructive thing we could do now is through education—we could encourage people to think about family life at a much younger age than they do at present. There are very few schools in Britain where any sort of domesticity is taught at all. At the best girls' schools, where academic teaching may be very high indeed, there is often no cooking, dressmaking, or domestic science—let alone mothercraft—in the curriculum. It seems lopsided that many girls should read Greek and Latin, but have no notion how to fry an egg.

If a bigger proportion of school time were given over to teaching the home-making subjects, wouldn't girls—and boys too—grow up with a wish to use their knowledge in making a real family life?

Into the Future
*And now—looking for new worlds to conquer
she can climb upstairs, though not yet down.*

1944

Nineteen-forty-four was the year of Overlord, rockets, and the Butler Education Act. At the time it was Overlord which filled men's minds, but the Butler Act, with its system of selective higher education, was to create a meritocracy which by the nineteen-fifties was beginning to emerge as a new ruling class; and Wernher von Braun's rockets, designed to wipe out London, have – among other things – carried man to the moon.

The British general Sir Frederick Morgan was responsible for planning the invasion of Normandy, code-named Overlord, and the British C.I.G.S., Sir Alan Brooke, who as a corps commander had been chased out of France in 1940, had been promised command of the operation by Churchill. In the event, command went to the American Eisenhower, with an American in Morgan's place as Chief of Staff. It was recognition of the hard fact that, in point of numbers and weight of equipment, America was now the senior partner. The condescension which had been a feature of the British attitude towards America in the early days of the alliance began to turn slowly to exasperation, exemplified by the prickly Montgomery's well-publicized rows with even more prickly American generals.

In Asia, the 'forgotten' Fourteenth Army, under perhaps the most able British commander of the war, General Slim, first halted the Japanese at Imphal and Kohima, and then began the long slog forward through the Burmese jungle towards the river Chindwin. In Russia, Marshal Zhukov reconquered the Ukraine. In Britain, south coast harbours filled with landing craft, Hampshire lanes harboured fleets of camouflaged tanks and lorries, and the air was heavy with the roar of bombers on their way to pound the German Atlantic Wall.

D-Day was scheduled for dawn on 5 June, but a storm was blowing up in the Channel, and Eisenhower postponed the invasion for twenty-four hours. At 4 a.m. on 5 June, at the end of a fifteen-minute conference, he gave the order for next day, 'Okay, let's go.' The enormous machine began to roll – 600 warships, 4,300 landing craft, 10,000 planes, one type of which, the Mosquito, was a war-winner. At 6.30 a.m. on 6 June the assault went in, and by midnight 75,000 British and 57,000 Americans were ashore in Normandy. Those who remembered the travail of landing three British divisions in a friendly port in 1939 were wont to declare, no doubt with exaggeration, that Overlord was easier. By the end of July, thirty-six divisions, more than one and a half million men, were in Normandy, and for the first time since the invasion of Russia, the Germans were forced to divert substantial forces from the Russian front.

A week after D-Day, the first flying bomb fell on London, and a new evacuation began, on a scale comparable with the worst days of the blitz. The bomb – a pilotless plane – had an effect on morale comparable with that of the German dive-bomber in the early days of the war. It was less the damage it did than the unnerving effect of hearing the approaching drone, then waiting tensely for the cut-out that presaged its fall. Nine thousand flying bombs launched between June and September killed just over six thousand people – a great diversion of effort with small result. But the British people were tired, and felt that, with their armies hitting the Germans in France, they should be safe from such dangers. There was worse to come. In September the rockets began to fall. They gave no warning of their approach, and whereas more than a third of the flying bombs had been destroyed by fighters or A.A. fire, no defence was found against the rockets. If the invasion had been delayed – if the Germans had not driven out some of their best scientists because they were Jews – rockets with atomic warheads might have achieved in 1944 the knock-out blow of pre-war imaginings and post-war reality.

The German people, too, were weary and disillusioned. In July Colonel von Stauffenberg and a number of high-minded associates failed narrowly in an attempt to kill

PICTURE POST

FRONT LINE PADRE
Round the corner is the war : the Padre encourages the men who are going in.

HULTON'S NATIONAL WEEKLY
SEPTEMBER 9, 1944

In this issue :
THE ROAD TO VICTORY 4ᴰ

Vol. 24. No. 11

1944 *The breakthrough: after ten weeks of bitter fighting in Normandy, British troops are on the move.*

Hitler and make peace. A purge of dissident German generals and civilians followed, some of them hanged by piano-wire from meat-hooks, their death-agonies filmed for Hitler's edification.

In December the Führer scraped together twenty-eight divisions for a desperate counter-offensive in the West. He chose the hilly, wooded country of the Ardennes, where the French had been decisively broken in 1940. The Americans in the sector were caught off balance, driven back forty-five miles, and had to be rescued by Montgomery, which did little for Anglo-American relations.

It was the gambler's last throw. One of Hitler's generals described the mental and physical wreck to which the conqueror of Europe had now been reduced: stooped, pale, hands trembling, left arm uncontrollably twitching. He spent much of his time under drugs, in an underground bunker, raving at his commanders that they must not give an inch of ground, moving armies which no longer existed across maps of territory already lost.

Laurence Thompson

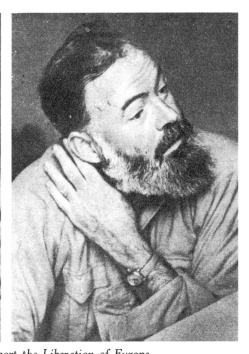

The Author of " For Whom the Bell Tolls" Comes to Britain to Report the Liberation of Europe

"I'm only a reporter now—doing articles and covering the war for Collier's Magazine. I cable 6,000 words a day."

"Of course it was different in the Spanish war. I wasn't there to watch—but to fight. I liked that a lot better."

"These stitches? There are 52 of them, but there's no romantic history, I'm afraid. Just a crash in the black-out."

HEMINGWAY LOOKS AT THE WAR IN EUROPE

"**G**OOD morning, gentlemen. Have you had breakfast?"
The author of *For Whom the Bell Tolls* squats on his bed in white pyjamas and a khaki shirt. His hotel room is littered with books and military kit.

He throws a timorous glance at the camera.

"Well, what do you want me to do? I'm not an actor you know. I'm a writer."

We look at the man as he reclines massively against the headboard, one hand plucking at the patriarchal beard which encroaches on his ruddy, boyish cheeks. He looks like a mixture of prophet and mountain shepherd, prepared to do a little fighting in the intervals. He watches carefully as the

"Back Home I Start Work at Five"
"I've been working since five. I like to start things early. It comes of living in the country."

cameraman gets ready.

"Is that a Leica? I always use a Rolleiflex; used it a lot in the Spanish Civil War. I don't now, of course. I just write war reports for Collier's Magazine. Someone else takes the pictures. And now the others are doing the fighting too."

"Will you be writing war reports for long, do you think?"

Hemingway's large face spreads into a quick smile.

"I don't know, and I wouldn't tell you if I did. There are some things about it I like, and some I don't. I like going out with the men and watching the action. But I hate the writing part of it. I'd rather write books. You see," he continues warming up and raising himself on his pillow, "when I work on a book, I only write about 350 words at a time. Now I have to cable them 6,000 words a day. As a matter of fact I have rather a tough time with this punctuation for cables," and before I can stop him he has slid off the bed, stalked to a corner cupboard, and handed me one of his typescripts, in which every question-mark is written out in its full dozen letters.

The typescript tells part of the story of D-Day, with

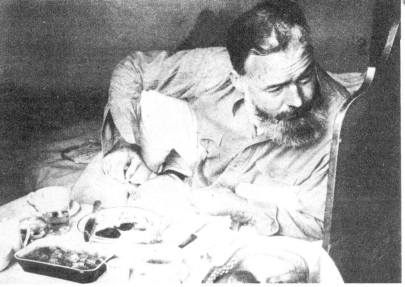

"What? Sure You've Had Enough? I Hate Eating Alone"
A large, genial, impressive figure—surprisingly gentle and extremely friendly—makes his unusual breakfast: bacon, mushroom, rhubarb, toast and whisky.

American assault boats carrying men from transports to the most bitterly contested beach in Normandy.

"Were you in one of these?"

"From three in the morning until late in the afternoon. It was the longest battle I'd ever been through without a drink. That's why I'm not likely to forget it."

"Did you get that there?" nodding at the gash across the dome of his forehead.

"No, I got that when my car ran against a static water tank. Fifty-two stitches but very unromantic, I'm afraid."

There's a knock at the door and a waiter comes in, wheeling the breakfast. With a puzzled look Hemingway gazes at his bacon, mushroom, toast and rhubarb, but does not stir. He seems not to realise what it's all doing here, or who can have ordered it.

"You're quite sure you've had your breakfast?"

"Positive."

So the breakfast must be his. He takes a roll and breaks it reluctantly. Still not quite certain. But as he looks his face lightens. "This is a typical good hotel breakfast," he says. "Always the same, but excellent. Much better than at home. But I do feel a perfect pig eating like this, with you fellows just sitting round working."

The howl of a siren interrupts him. He points his fork at the door and says: "Some people don't seem to mind these things, and others don't care for them at all. It seems to worry the women most."

The meal over, he sits down at the typewriter, reads over yesterday's script and sets about removing commas that should have been spelled out. Then he turns to us once more.

"You don't suppose I could have some of those photographs, do you? I should like to send some to my boys. I've got one in Italy, you know. The other two are at school back home. Normally I'd be with them now."

We promise to send them, and say good-bye. Before we are out of the door Hemingway is back at his work. He is still wearing a khaki shirt and pyjama trousers, and he's got another 3,000 words to do for Collier's before the next knock at the door brings another equally unexpected meal.

"Isn't That One of Those Flying Bombs Just Going Over?"

In his bedroom in "Southern England," Ernest Hemingway hears the flying bomb—latest weapon in the war between humanity and Fascism. That war, so far as he's concerned, has been going on since the Spanish fighting began in 1936.

"Clothes? I Wear What's Around"

A khaki shirt and white pyjama trousers are Hemingway's outfit for this morning's writing.

The War Correspondent Goes Back to His Typewriter

He works for Collier's, an American weekly magazine. Since being over here he has flown over Normandy, and landed there by landing-craft.

The President of the B.M.A.
Lord Dawson of Penn is President of
the Association. He says, "The White
Paper is statesmanlike."

The Chairman of the Council
Dr. Guy Dain is Chairman of the
Executive Council. He expresses con-
cern about the voluntary hospitals.

DO WE WANT A STATE MEDICAL SERVICE?

**A Survey is made by the British Institute of Public Opinion to find out what
people think of the idea of a National Health Service. It shows 55 per cent. in
favour of it. 60 per cent of doctors interviewed supported this basic proposal of the
Government's White Paper on Health. How the Institute gathers its information
and the background to the inquiry are discussed in this article.**

Chairman, Insurance Acts Committee
Dr. E. A. Gregg is concerned with the effect
of the White Paper on National Health
Insurance and the Panel System.

THIS is a long and complex article. The subject
it has to cover is a complicated one. The future
of the Medical Service in this country is obviously
of the greatest importance to each one of us. Our
health and happiness, the length of our life, the
health and happiness of our children will depend
upon it. It would seem that no one could possibly
have a greater concern in the future of the Medical
Service than each one of us has. But there are two
bodies of men who have all this, and something else,
at stake. The something else is their livelihood.
The bodies of men are the doctors, and the medical
students—the doctors of the future.

Now the position to-day is that the Government
has produced a plan for the future of the Medical
Service—the plan is in the form of a "White
Paper" of proposals. It is generally referred to, in
the discussion going on, as "the Government White
Paper." We all have the right to make our voices
heard, and to give our opinion on a matter that
concerns us so closely. And the medical profession
have a right, and are clearly also under an obligation,
to find out the wishes of their members.

The British Medical Association, as the controlling body of the medical profession, invited the
British Institute of Public Opinion to conduct an
inquiry among doctors and to find out their views.
A carefully-compiled questionnaire has been sent
out to every doctor—including, of course, those
in the Services. At the same time, the *News-
Chronicle*, who have been making regular use of the
B.I.P.O. to investigate the attitude of the public to
the public on the questions of the day, asked the
B.I.P.O. to investigate the attitude of the public to
the Government's White Paper, and the questions
it brought up.

The case for a State Medical Service is older than
the Beveridge Report, though Beveridge's "Assumption B" caused as much excitement among the
doctors as his other assumptions had caused among
the insurers. He supposes a comprehensive health
service, ensuring "that for every citizen there is
available whatever medical treatment he requires, in
whatever form he requires it," and that this service
should be "without an economic barrier at any point
to delay recourse to it." Poverty must be no bar to
a man's right to life. There were doctors whom

THE PICTURE THAT

*The Government's proposals for a State
where it has met to discuss the White Paper on
doctors are*

Beveridge's Assumption frightened. They remembered that in 1922 the Labour Party had called for
a Public Health Service which should be "free and
open to all, irrespective of their financial or social
status." It seemed to them that a National Health
Service, involving a centralised control of doctors
and hospitals, would convert the doctors into State
servants, submit them to the incompetent administration of bureaucrats, reduce their earning capacity,
and destroy the voluntary doctor-patient relationship, traditional in British medicine.

The Treasurer
Dr. J. W. Bone sits at the right hand of
Lord Dawson. His job is to look after the
B.M.A.'s finances.

AS NEVER BEFORE BEEN TAKEN: THE COUNCIL OF THE BRITISH MEDICAL ASSOCIATION IN SESSION

edical Service are of vital interest to the 47,000 members of the B.M.A. Its Council is seen in session at B.M.A. House, Tavistock Square, London, ational Health. It has asked the British Institute of Public Opinion to find out the views of the medical profession. The survey shows that 69 per cent. of favour of complete hospital and specialist services being available to everyone in a general ward free of charge.

In February of this year, Henry Willink, Minister of Health, and Tom Johnston, Secretary of State for Scotland, published, as a White Paper, the Government's proposals for a National Health Service. The plan for a comprehensive service, open to all and free of charge, was a bold compromise—bold because it recognised, for the first time, that the people's health is the State's responsibility; but it was a compromise, because the status of the voluntary hospitals was to remain unchanged, except that they could "contract-in" to the scheme, and there would still be private practice. The original critics of the Beveridge scheme weren't pleased by the Government's concessions to the supporters of State medicine, or appeased by the compromise on the voluntary hospitals and private practice. What will the doctors in the Forces say when they find that, during their absence, their practices have been restricted or dissolved? What will happen to the independence of science, expressed in the teaching and healing at the voluntary hospitals, if they are submitted, even in part, to Whitehall control?

What scope will there be for the noble, charitable impulses of the public and the consultants, if they can't find a place in the voluntary hospitals? The White Paper, they said, was the first instalment of State-controlled medicine. And anyhow, they added, as though this settled the matter, the public doesn't want a National Health Service with State control.

If the public is called in as witness that Britain doesn't want a National Health Service, it is worth testing the public's real opinion. Is there, then, any

The Secretary
Dr. Charles Hill, the B.M.A.'s Secretary. He provides the main contact between the B.M.A. and the public.

Some of the Medical Men Affected by the Government's Plan
From left to right, Dr. G. MacFeat, Dr. I. D. Grant, and Mr. N. Dougal Callander, members of the Council, listen to the chairman's report. The Council is an elected body which represents the profession in matters concerning public health and medical organisation.

PLANNING A SURVEY OF OPINION

Gerald Barry (in shirt sleeves, centre), "News Chronicle" editor, discusses the questions with H. Durant on his left, director of the B.I.P.O. The "News Chronicle" has first rights of publishing answers.

TABULATING THE ANSWERS:

The official questionnaire with the answers marked on it are sent to an independent statistical firm to be tabulated.

CARD-INDEXING THE ANSWERS:

The answers are recorded on a special card-index system for future reference.

CALCULATING THE RESULTS:

When all the forms have been sorted, the percentages of opinion are worked out.

THE SURVEY BEGINS : *A Woman Interviewer Samples the People's Views*

Miss Renee Gill who has been helping with the surveys of the British Institute of Public Opinions for six years, asks the opinion of a London flower-seller. He has never been ill or used a hospital, but he's in favour of a National Health Service.

way of deciding what the "public" is thinking at a given period on any subject?

Dr. George Gallup, an American professor of journalism, invented a system of testing opinion which, he considered, could quote the "public" authoritatively. Gallup decided that the way to assess opinion was to sample it, in the same way that a peasant will test a field of wheat by examining a few ears taken from different parts of the field. By interviewing a small proportion of the adult population, scientifically selected as representing the whole, he considered that adult opinion—public opinion—could be assessed. From opinion to forecasts: from his surveys, Gallup forecast the result of elections, political trends, even changes in taste. His interviewers asked their questions on the street and in people's homes, and his forecasts were accurate. The British Institute of Public Opinion uses his method.

Their Question No. 9 : "On the whole, would you like the idea on a publicly-run National Health Service, or would you prefer Hospitals and doctors to be left as they are?" is the key to the general questionnaire. "Should the National Health Service include everyone?" is the key to the doctors' questionnaire.

In conducting a questionnaire as to people's views on the organisation of the medical profession, the B.I.P.O. was not inquiring into something remote and incomprehensible to ordinary men and women.

Most citizens, the "Consumers" of the medical service, have had experience of hospitals and doctors as they are, and are therefore in a position to answer whether they want things to be changed.

At present, Britain's health services are not centrally controlled. Though the Ministry of Health has jurisdiction over some hospitals, such as those for infectious diseases, and Poor Law infirmaries, the voluntary hospitals are self-governing, while the School Medical Service is under the Board of Education. The doctor in private practice and the insurance companies also remain outside the Ministry's control. The prospective patient—who is all of us—is affected consciously or unconsciously by the Ministry of Health's inadequate powers of supervision over his health. The Ministry can't make a national plan for the use of our hospital service, because the voluntary hospitals are outside its control. It can't provide a service of specialists for poor patients. The worker and middle-class person who has attended the out-patient departments of the great voluntary hospitals knows how, despite the devotion and even self-sacrifice of doctors and nurses, they feel as they wait on the benches that institutions which depend on charity

THE HOUSEWIFE:

She would like the present medical system to stay—particularly the voluntary hospitals.

THE MEDICAL STUDENT:

He thinks doctors should have more say in organising public health schemes.

THE AMERICAN VISITOR:
She has been in a British Hospital, but she's strongly in favour of hospitals belonging to the State and not depending on philanthropy.

THE RETIRED GENTLEMAN:
He's opposed to any State interference in medicine. Thinks that the doctor should be at the patient's service, not the State's.

ALL OVER THE COUNTRY THE SURVEY CONTINUES: *In the North*
A labourer tells Miss Joan Beardsley that he's in favour of a free public health service. When he was ill, he needed an expensive medicine which the Panel wouldn't pay for. His doctor had to pay for it out of his own pocket.

THE WORKER:
He would like medical treatment to be free for all. But it should be a right, not charity.

for their existence cast the shadow of charity on those who benefit from them.

Many middle-class people are reluctant to attend public hospitals for that reason, preferring their illness to the imaginary stigma of the method of cure. Many workers enter hospitals with an unjustified humility, forgetting that the State has a moral obligation to safeguard the health of its citizens. According to the B.I.P.O. Survey, 9 per cent. of the public is dissatisfied with the way in which it is treated in the out-patients' department of hospitals.

While the Ministry of Health can't plan the campaign against disease, the doctors—the general practitioners—are expected to fight its local battles. The family doctor, overworked even in peace-time, can't waste his working day keeping people healthy. He has to rush about, curing them when they're sick. Preventive medicine by the private doctor scarcely exists. Nor is he trained to give the comprehensive service to patients which modern scientific knowledge can offer. The general practitioner, by definition, does not specialise; but refers cases to specialists for diagnosis and treatment. Those who can afford to pay a private doctor often can't afford the fees of a specialist. At the present day, millions of people are cut off from prompt attention by specialists, merely because they can't afford the cost.

Does the National Health Insurance scheme help the general public? It applies to employees whose salary is less than £420 and who are entitled by it to free treatment by a doctor "on the panel." The doctor gets a head-tax for each person registered on his panel. Apart from its exclusiveness, which withdraws its benefits from half of the population, the panel system has the other great defect of encouraging the doctor to swell his practice to a degree which affects his efficiency, for the sake of getting more patients, and more fees, on his list. What worker is unfamiliar with the consulting room of the, possibly well-intentioned but harassed, doctor who seems to grudge the time needed to take his temperature? The panel system has the merit of giving medical care to people who once were denied it; but approaching the second half of the twentieth century, the public wants its benefits to be extended and its working improved.

Sixty-eight per cent. of the public, according to B.I.P.O., don't "want to get rid of the panel, leaving only private doctors." They want "to make some such system as the panel work satisfactorily."

The Government White paper makes proposals which are a stride forward from the old system of the benevolent bed-side manner general practitioner and the perfunctory panel doctor. And although

THE COMPANY DIRECTOR:
He thinks that the old system needs bringing up to date, without absolute State Control.

THE SHIPBUILDER:
The Government ought to take over, and let us have a service to keep people well.

Picture Post, August 12. 1944

HOW AN INTERVIEWER WORKS: *A B.I.P.O. Representative on Tour*
T. N. Latham, 70-year-old interviewer, finds a case. The little girl has fallen and cut her ankle. Does the mother want a free Health Service for all. She says that she definitely does. The Clinic is looking after her daughter very well.

He Makes a Cycling Reconnaissance
Over the gate, he picks up the opinion of a housewife. She thinks the old system's all right.

He Buttonholes Two Shoppers
They don't want to talk. They're on the way to catch a bus. So Mr. Latham moves on.

some of the benevolent G.P.s have bared their teeth at the idea that their total fees might be diminished, 68 per cent. have welcomed the idea of "grouped practice." The White Paper suggests something which has already been developed by voluntary pioneers in Britain, and as part of the State Medical System in Russia—the grouping of doctors, and perhaps specialists, in Health Centres which will devote themselves to preventive as well as curative medicine. There will be airy waiting rooms where the patients won't spit and hawk all over each other, private consulting rooms, nurses and equipment for minor surgery. And it will be free—a public service paid for out of taxation. The doctors in group practice would be paid by salary. Would there also be private practice? The Government. says "Yes." You can go to your doctor under the National Health Scheme, and get treated free of charge; or you can go to him as a private patient, and pay. Which is absurd, unless you envisage two classes of patients—one being treated for rheumatism under the National Health scheme for five minutes without a smile, and the other being treated for rheumatism privately for ten minutes with a smile and conversation. The White Paper also proposes the creation of a Central Health Service Council, a technical and expert body to advise the fortified Ministry of Health—a reform long advocated by medical critics of lay bureaucracy who are not necessarily extreme individualists.

Does the public want a National Health Service? Do the doctors want it? The comparative answers to the British Institute of Public Opinion's questionnaire show where the opinion of the public and the doctors coincide and differ.

Fifty-five per cent. of the public, and 60 per cent. of the doctors, want a free National Health Service. 49 per cent. of medical students questioned were in favour of the Government's proposals, while 36 per cent. thought the country's medical service would suffer by their introduction. But 72 per cent. of the students were in favour of a free medical service. 69 per cent. of the public wants Health Centres for better treatment. 89 per cent. of the students are in favour of Health Centres. 68 per cent. of the doctors want them.

What can we conclude from the Survey? It is certain that the old organisation for the medical care of the public is due for change; and that opposition to change comes not only from a small section of doctors, who fear it on grounds which have little to do with the public's health, but also from an inadequate appreciation by the public of the benefits which the change to a planned system can offer.   MAURICE EDELMAN.

Hindsight by Maurice Edelman

A quarter of a century ago, fifty-five per cent of the public wanted a State Medical Service. I imagine that a poll today would show that more like eighty per cent, having experienced it, now want it. The Tories have become converted to the general idea of a National Health Service, although they talk of 'selectivity' as a means of establishing degrees of priority between patients. The Labour Government has reintroduced pre-scription charges, and thus diluted its 1922 plan for a Public Health Service which should be 'free and open to all, irrespective of their financial or social status'. Nevertheless, the free Health Service has arrived as a national institution. The age of the private doctor for the public is over.

What the National Health Service has forfeited has been the intimacy (and the limited resources) of the family practitioner. What it has gained has been the access by millions to clinical and therapeutic services which in the past they could ill afford, if at all. The new patients of the Welfare Age have been demanding – often over-demanding. The National Health Service has been imposed on by unscrupulous clients, tired doctors, and gold-digging drug companies. Over-prescribing and over-charging are giant evils which the Service has still to tackle. Above all, post-war Ministers of Health have failed to provide an adequate infrastructure of training and accommodation to service the colossal scheme of free medical care.

Yet the N.H.S. remains a solid and perfectible achievement of the 1945 Labour Government. In the balance sheet of its credits and debits, I have no doubt that it has brought vast benefits to the nation's health which outweigh the inconveniences of long queues, doctor and nurse shortages and inadequate hospital services. Much that is now taken for granted as a public entitlement would have been a dream before the war. Much that is freely available to the poorest in Britain is the envy of the affluent American middle classes, crushed by medical charges. I'm glad to have belonged to the Parliamentary Labour Party that brought the N.H.S. into being.

Vol. 24. No. 11

PICTURE POST

September 9, 1944

ON TO THE KILL : *The British Second Army Starts the Pursuit*
After ten grim weeks of fighting in Normandy, the German Seventh Army collapses. Along roads littered with German graves and German dead, in a choking cloud of dust, the British columns ride forward to victory.

THE ROAD TO VICTORY

Two members of our staff, Macdonald Hastings, writer, and Leonard McCombe, cameraman, come back from the British forward areas in Normandy, bringing pictures and story which will rank among the most vivid and moving documents of the war.

ASK a British soldier, ten years hence, what he remembers best of that famous victory of 1944 in Northern France, and, if he still cares to talk about it, he'll tell you it was the bouquet of smells : the sickly smell in the intestines of a landing craft, the sweaty whiff of damp battledress, the stomach-retching stench of dead cattle, the sour air of a blasted village, the peculiar unforgettable odour of a German prisoner.

Ask a German what he remembers best, and, for a Teutonic certainty, he'll say it was the horrific orchestra of the allied instruments of war : the nightmare drumming of the artillery, the wasplike persistence of the aircraft, the whine of shells, the poop of mortars, the crump of bombs, the unspeakable quavering note of a Typhoon rocket.

Ask a Frenchman, one who belonged to that war-torn countryside, what he remembers best, and he'll tell you of the wounded horse that dragged him and what was left of his possessions in an over-loaded cart to safety; of the crops that were never harvested; of the cows that died for lack of milking; of the litter of tree stumps that was an apple orchard; of the tank track that was a garden; of the graveyard that was a farm.

Ten years hence—if, by that time, you're not too bored with war-time reminiscences to listen, or too young to care—ask me what I remember best of the collapse of the German Seventh Army, and, being middle-aged and sentimental about the past as I shall be then, I'll probably tell you that, for me, the most magic moment was the beginning of the pursuit, the

The Race to Get After Them
A stray of the battlefield, adopted by a British soldier, makes sure that he's coming too.

The Dust That Chokes
The dust clouds stirred up by the convoys make it difficult to breathe, even to see.

THE TRAIL OF DEVASTATION BEHIND THE RETREATING ENEMY

For sixteen weeks, the British army had to blast its way forward, kilometre by kilometre. The line of our advance is a blackened waste, terrible evidence of the desperate struggle we had before, at last, we broke them.

But, when you're sharing the same map square with the enemy, it's a wonderful check on your enthusiasm. A mortar barrage is just as unpleasant whether you're winning or losing. And, way out there, in the tip of a British salient, with the Jerries holding out on our two flanks and our immediate objective a village which was stiff with them a few thousand yards in front, the end of the campaign on our tiny sector of the front seemed as far off as ever.

Why should our fellows think otherwise? Ever since D-Day, they'd had nothing for nothing. All

sight of the columns of the British Second Army riding the road to victory like gods on a cloud of dust. And, ten years hence, lots of other people will be writing and saying much the same sort of thing. You needn't believe it. War is only romantic in retrospect. The ridiculous truth—and it's as well to admit it while the memory is still warm—is that what I personally remember best is that up in the forward infantry areas, where we happened to be, we didn't know the battle was won until we heard a rumour that Monty had said so and we didn't believe it until we picked up the news on the wireless.

Even then, we didn't feel sure enough not to dig in good and deep; not to curse the tanks who advertised themselves, and us, to the enemy gunners by raising a flag of dust on the edge of our camp.

We Didn't Know We Were Winning

True, the picture on the maps looked good. The Americans were pushing through, with the slightest of opposition, to only Army Corps knew where. Judging by the disposition of everybody in our sector, the enemy-held area round Falaise was narrowing fast. The newspapers, two days old when we devoured them, were cock-a-hoop.

the way, from Caen to Falaise, they'd had to fight for it, feature by feature, village by village, against the best troops that Germany could put into the field; bloody good troops, too, who fought like cats. And the blackened, blasted line along every kilometre of the British advance was the proof of it. Ypres in the last war wasn't bashed flatter than Caen or Aunay or Villers Bocages.

Of course, we knew we were on top of them. We'd got the air, we'd got the guns, and we'd got the measure of their tactics. But, up till then, there was no sign that they were cracking. As we went

The Horses the Germans Used in a Desperate Attempt to Save Their Skins
The inventors of the blitzkrieg are forced to fall back on horse transport. But the R.A.F. blast the escape routes and our gunners stonk their convoys off the roads.

Picture Post, September 9, 1944

forward, the ambulances still rolled back. The Jerries hung on to every village until our guns stonked them out of it. And then it wasn't over. Every pig-sty was good for a sniper. Everything you trod on or touched was liable to go bang.

The familiar Hun wasn't pulling out in such a hurry that he couldn't find time to pepper the roads with pressure mines, smash up what remained of the French peasants' poor store of possessions, and play all his usual dirty little games with booby traps.

Booby Traps Everywhere

Booby traps. All France seemed to be a booby trap. And our fellows never seemed to learn. Or they didn't want to. I saw three of them killed because they turned the tap of a cider cask without having a shufty first. And, time and again, we were warned to beware of corpses. It was a German joke to booby-trap the bodies of the fallen so that the people who came to bury them were wiped out too.

As we advanced, we were picking up the usual trickle of prisoners; but they were only the rubbish which the S.S. Divisions leave behind them, rather like mines, to delay our advance and cover their own retreat. They had no officers, no fight in them, and most of them weren't even Germans. As far as we were concerned, the real Jerries were still making an orderly withdrawal.

The whole world was getting excited about the triumphant climax of the campaign and, somehow, the enemy on our sector didn't seem to have heard anything about it. And then the buzz went round

The Dust That Draws Enemy Gunfire

The Forward Surge of an Army: The Work of Road Control On Which Everything Depends
Right up the lines of communications to the forward areas, the shell-pocked battered roads are stiff with transport. The columns must go through.
In every ruined town, at every crossing, military police signpost the axis of the advance, tell the convoys where they are, wave them to victory.

WE DRIVE INTO A TOWN: *The Man Who Rushed In to Get a Sniper*
The Germans have pulled out of another little town. But there are prisoners to be rounded up, snipers to be accounted for. Watched by the few remaining inhabitants, one of our patrols runs in to search out the last enemy.

The Dog that Lived Through It
Half dead with terror, its owners gone, a dog crawls out of a ruin to watch our troops enter.

that, somewhere in the forward areas, Monty had turned up on the road and shouted to one of the brigadiers :

"The Battle is Won ! On to the Kill !"

It sounded genuine. It was just the sort of thing that Monty would say. And, that night, as we stewed our tea—desert rat style—over petrol fires in old tins, we talked till the fields of corn went red in the sunset.

During that night, we noticed that our guns were easing up; those guns which, when you got near them, literally pulled at your clothes with the force of firing. Next morning, we heard that our division, which was infantry, was out of contact with the enemy for the first time since D-Day. And then we got the hard griff. The enemy was on the run. The chase had started. Already, the corps commander had moved his own headquarters

"MA BELLE MAISON . . ." *The Familiar Tragedy is Played Once Again in the Smoking Ruins of Argentan*
She is watching her house, her beautiful home, on the other side of the street. What she sees you can see among the smoke and flame in the picture on the opposite page. Her husband tries to comfort her, tells her how lucky they should feel that they themselves have lived through the bombardment to make another home. But the woman is disconsolate, broken with suffering.

Picture Post, September 9, 1944

The Sight that Awaited Us When We Went Into Argentan

The fifteenth-century Gothic church of St. Germain is badly damaged. Part of the town is burning.
The Germans have pillaged the shops, persecuted the inhabitants, booby-trapped the houses. But
this is one of their last nests of resistance in the Falaise area.

so far forward that it was in front of division, even brigade. Everybody was on the move. The roads were packed. And, before long, our orders to join in the leap-frogging race of an army pursuit came too.

Troops are Like Schoolboys

When you've been fighting for every foot of territory, it's a marvellous, exhilarating feeling to get a clear run. There's no change of air which does a man so much good as a change of battlefield. There's no greater relief than to get away from the old smells, to slip off the edge of the old dog-eared map squares, to escape from the unpleasant memories which every battle-scarred piece of ground holds for every soldier who fought for it.

When the order comes to move, troops, who are very like schoolboys, pack up as excitedly as if they were going for a holiday. They throw things at each other, wage mock fights, and work out noisy practical jokes. The browned-off feeling, which is the worst epidemic that a fighting unit can get, clears like the air after rain. There's a picnic atmosphere.

To an army commander, a pursuit is a complicated manœuvre, a game of chess, in which there are never enough squares to move all the pieces.

" Triste ! Triste ! Triste !"

His head bandaged, his hands wounded, tears rolling down his cheeks, the 74-years-old cure of Argentan stands in the ruins of his church.

A FEW HUNDRED YARDS FROM THE ENEMY : *As a British Soldier Goes Into Action, the Padre Wishes Him Good Luck*
Under shellfire, in the thick of the battle which decided the fate of the German Seventh Army, a Roman Catholic padre cheers the troops of as they go forward to the attack. A few hundred yards more and they'll be in open sight of the enemy.

But to the fighting units, to the ordinary soldier, the move is a routine as circumscribed as the moves of any individual chess piece. Everybody knows what to do, when to go, and where. And the whole business happens as unhurriedly and efficiently as the tour of a travelling circus.

It's rather like moving a circus, too. A camp in the field, like a circus, is all canvas and caravans. And, wherever the British army goes, a circus of animals—the strays of the battlefield—collect about it. There's scarcely a unit in France without a camp following of dogs, cats, poultry, rabbits, pigeons, even cows. The dogs have usually been picked up—battle-shocked, starving—out of the ruins of some farmhouse. The cats have wandered into the camps in search of food and warmth, and, finding both, have attached themselves to a truck. The poultry, the cows and the tame rabbits are the

The Price of Victory
As the battle rages round them, the Methodist and R.C. padres carry out the last rites for the fallen.

The Germans Who Are Taken Prisoner Think They're Lucky . . .
As the battle swings onward, little groups of prisoners, smiling to be alive, are routed out of their foxholes. The white tape is an indication that the road isn't cleared of mines.

refugees who pay their way in milk, food and eggs. And it's astonishing how they settle down to a mobile life. Hens actually scratch and roost and lay eggs on the floor of a Bren carrier. And I saw rabbits nibbling contentedly under ammunition boxes among a battery of medium guns. The cows are the only impermanent camp followers. They're usually brought in in the first place half dead for lack of milking. And it's worth recording that, right through the Normandy campaign, the British soldiers have milked thousands of cows into the ground just to keep them going until their owners returned to the areas.

A Pursuit is Like Any Other Move

I'd like to be able to tell you that, when the pursuit began, it was a triumphant and exciting race. But, in reality, things don't work out that way; not for the ordinary footslogger anyhow. For us, it was like any other move, a tiresome business of packing everything on to trucks, groping along through a fog of dust over shell-pocked roads, and, finally, landing up in an apple orchard, just like the one we'd left, with the same sour apples and the same dead cattle for company.

We heard what was happening on the radio. We didn't see the hard evidence of victory for ourselves until we'd moved forward not once but several days in succession. And then we picked up their trail.

In the infantry, you're not like the Recce and armoured people who go swanning about all over the countryside. In the infantry, you usually only see what's happening in your own area. And so we didn't get mixed up in the fun again until we started mopping-up enemy pockets that the armour had left behind. Mopping-up sounds like a piece of cake. But, when you're dealing with S.S. men with an occasional Panther hull-down in the middle of them, it isn't funny. Still, there's no job quite as satisfactory as rounding-up prisoners. And, soon, our cages were filling up nicely.

The Jerries had their tails down all right. They told us, most of them, that they'd had nothing to eat or drink for three days. And they looked it.

In Support of the Infantry, the Armour Probes Forward
Our artillery stonks the objective until it's a mass of rubble. Even then, some of the enemy hold out. Then it's the turn of the armour. Finally, the infantry mops up the position.

. . . This Is The Fate of the Rest of Them
He fell, not fighting, but fleeing. His pall is the mud spattered over him by our advancing columns.

When Trouble Waits Round the Corner
Crawling cautiously up the ditch, guns at the ready, one of our patrols, looking for the retreating enemy, finds a blazing vehicle. The enemy isn't far behind it.

THESE ARE THE FACES OF MEN IN ACTION:

He is one of the foremost men in the foremost platoon of the British Army. His unit has just driven the Germans out of a position. Now he looks out, from under cover, at a little village across a valley to which the enemy have retreated.

Under Shell-Fire, With Mortar-Fire Just Ahead

One of a line of men of a British infantry division. They are pushing forward under shell-fire up a dusty road. They are approaching a cross-roads round which mortar-fire—particularly detested by most fighting men—is concentrated. As the camera snaps them, they push on into range.

The Tank Driver Who Sees the Mortar Shells Come Down

He's driven through shell-fire, and now he's going to drive through mortar-fire. This is the day he's been training for, and he's ready for it : but don't ask him to pretend that it's a picnic.

Their uniforms were ragged. They were crawling with vermin, and they looked fearful every time one of our aircraft went overhead.

We could see why they were so windy as we rumbled forward along the line of the German retreat. They had good reason. Every fifty yards, over miles of country, there was the wreckage of a German tank, gun or vehicle, blasted as if it had been hit by lightning. The Typhoons had been doing their stuff with the rockets.

The smell of dead horses which the Jerries had used to try and get their stuff away was pretty fearful. But the sight of all that wreckage and the columns of grey-uniformed, grey-faced men being marched back to the cages made up for a lot.

The French Were Really Glad to See Us

The French people were tops. You got pretty bored shaking hands and having flowers thrown at you, but there was no doubt the French were pleased to see us; although we had had to blow their homes to pieces to get there. We gave them cigarettes and boiled sweets. They gave us their home-brewed cider and what they call Calvados and what our fellows call fire-water. They stuck "V" matchboxes in their lapels and rang the church bells incessantly wherever we went.

The Resistance people, who all seemed to have a Cross of Lorraine armlet, guided us to the places where little groups of the enemy were still holding out. And they also roped in their own collaborators at all hours of the day and night. The collaborators were nothing to do with us; but we kept an eye on them and handed them over to the Civil Affairs people.

The Sergeant Gives the Word to Open Up

*He is a sergeant in charge of a machine-gun section. He and his men—
dusty and sweating with battle—are under cover by the corner of a farm.
As the enemy break away along the hedges, he gives the word to open fire.
His face is the face of a man at war.*

The Man at the Gun Replies

*Spent cartridge-cases heap up in the gap of the hedge where he is stationed.
They mount round the legs of the tripod. His own knees slip on them,
and his fingers on the gun handles are slippery with sweat. He catches
the Sergeant's order, grunts and gets on with the job.*

Fighting was still going on. Our guns were stonking them out of the last bolt-holes. Round about—behind, in front and on our flanks—patrols were winkling out the remnants from where they were skulking in the woods. The sappers were bull-dozing the wreckage of their material off the roads to let ours go through. The pioneers were filling up the shell holes. You had to look out for mines if you got on a quiet road in a jeep or a motor-bike. But, as a battle, it was all over. The German Seventh Army had had it. And Normandy too. . .

Perhaps, when all's said and done, the memory of what happened to that lovely Norman landscape and its people is, for an Englishman, the most poignant memory of all. You see, fighting in Normandy wasn't like fighting in a foreign land. You remarked on it at every twist of the road, on every hill crest, in every river valley, in every farmstead, copse and pasture. The dust, the devastation, and the dead couldn't blight it. The Norman countryside is like Southern England.

There are the same flowers and trees in the woods, the same creatures in the hedgerows, the same sleepy streams, the same luscious grass, the same civilized order in the landscape. Even now, from a distant view, you might easily mistake the Normandy countryside for West Sussex or the Weald of Kent. But not in close-up.

Very soon now, there'll come a time when nobody wants to hear about the war again. Certainly, I don't want to write about it. But I pray that, deep down inside us, we remember the rape of Normandy because what happened there is what, by a hairs-breadth, this other Normandy was spared.

The Barn That is On Fire Behind Us

*The Germans know the machine-guns are around here, but they can't pick up the exact spot.
They shell the farmhouse, and set fire to the barn. But the machine-guns go on firing.*

1945

Only one hope remained to Hitler, a split between his enemies; but unity held, if only just long enough.

Early in February, the three puissant old gentlemen, as Evelyn Waugh called them, continued at Yalta their planning for the future. One of them had up his sleeve a weapon of such magnitude that it immediately moved the world into a new dimension; but their planning continued to be in the old terms of territory and spheres of influence. Once again Roosevelt sided with Stalin against Churchill, and Stalin openly voiced his suspicions of the West. After the conference, Goebbels made his prophecy of the iron curtain which would fall on a Europe divided between East and West following the defeat of Germany.

One by one the war leaders began to make their exits. Roosevelt went first, on 12 April. Mussolini followed a fortnight later, executed by Italian partisans, his body with the face kicked in hung up by·the heels in the public square of Milan. On 30 April Hitler shot himself in his Berlin bunker. Goebbels immediately tried to make a separate peace with Russia, Admiral Dönitz with the West. Both were rebuffed. On 7 May Germany surrendered unconditionally to the still United Nations.

In Britain, the coalition Government began to break up. Attlee and Bevin favoured its continuation until after the defeat of Japan, but Morrison — who cherished hopes of replacing Attlee — pressed for an early Election. The Election took place on 5 July, although the result, because of votes from servicemen overseas, was not known until three weeks later. Labour fought largely on a programme of nationalizing the Bank of England, fuel, transport, civil aviation and steel. Conservative tactics were dictated by Churchill and his evil genius Beaverbrook. They purported to detect in the mild commuter from Stanmore who led the Labour Party a man likely to introduce the Gestapo and concentration camps into Britain. When this failed to carry conviction, they discovered that behind Attlee stood the sinister figure of Professor Harold Laski, that year's chairman of the Labour Party. Like many before and since, Laski had tried to establish control by the party conference and executive over the parliamentary Labour Party, in which attempt he got small change out of Attlee. He had also written, some years before, a book which laid him open to the accusation that he advocated violent revolution. The *Daily Express* and a number of hecklers at Laski's meetings had an enjoyable time, and Laski brought a libel action, which he lost.

Neither nationalization nor Professor Laski cut much ice with the voters, particularly those in the Services. They voted for Beveridge and the better life, and gave their votes to the party they thought more likely to provide it. To Attlee's surprise, and Churchill's bitter disappointment, Labour was returned to power with a majority of nearly 150 — the first majority Labour Government in British history. It had fought the election under the banner, 'Let Us Face the Future', and faced it with a Government consisting mainly of stalwarts from the wartime coalition, with an average age of over sixty. One of the newcomers, Emanuel Shinwell, Minister of Fuel and Power, was driven to complain that the party had been talking about nationalizing the mines for over fifty years, but had omitted to prepare any plans for actually doing it.

Chamberlain had sacrificed abstractions like honour and morality for the sake of peace, and when war came, had tried to fight it so economically that he laid himself open to the jeer of seeming primarily concerned to ensure that Britain could pay the indemnity after losing. Churchill — with the tacit consent of the British people — had thrown everything in: overseas investments, export trade, merchant navy, borrowings of nearly £3,000 million. Soon after the new Government took office, the economist Lord Keynes warned that Britain faced 'a financial Dunkirk' without substantial American aid. Lease-Lend was cut off with the defeat of Japan, and Keynes went to Washington to negotiate a substantial loan. There was a strong isolationist current flowing in the United States, and many Americans were less than anxious to help a potential business competitor, particularly a Socialist one, but a loan of 3,750 million dollars was eventually granted, on condition that sterling would be made convertible. When the Commons debated the loan, 71 Conservative and 23 Labour M.P.s were prepared to face the consequences of doing without it. The rest voted for the loan, and many were thereafter loud in their complaints of British subservience to American policy which inevitably followed. It was in these circumstances that the Labour Government set out on its task of providing the better life demanded by the electorate.

Meanwhile, on 6 August, a new world had been born. An American atomic bomb was dropped on Hiroshima, killing between 70,000 and 250,000 people. Attlee, deputy Prime Minister in the coalition Government, had been told nothing of the atomic project, and thought it was just another big bomb.

Laurence Thompson

The mushroom that would haunt mankind. On 6 August 1945 the world entered a new era. An atomic bomb was dropped on Hiroshima. It knocked Japan out of the war and brought a new nightmare to mankind.

With His Wife in the Garden of their Cambridge Home
Lady Russell, who is the philosopher's third wife, was previously his secretary. Though christened Marjorie, she is known to everyone as "Peter." They married in 1936.

BERTRAND RUSSELL
on the
PROBLEMS OF PEACE

One of the most provocative thinkers of our time analyses some problems of the post-war world, and suggests the kind of approach which will avoid another world disaster.

Photographed by K. HUTTON

A Fireside Recital
In slippers by his fireside, Bertrand Russell reads poetry to his wife.

AT the end of the German war, and again at the end of the Japanese war, vast and formidable problems will confront the victorious nations. These problems will be partly economic, partly political; both kinds must be solved, and it would be a mistake to consider either more important than the other.

Let us take the economic problems first. There will be, to begin with, the necessity of keeping populations alive until agriculture can be revived in regions devastated by the war. This is a problem for UNRRA, and we must hope that it will be efficiently handled. It will demand for a time—probably about two years—a continuance of rationing in Great Britain and America, which may be unpopular, especially if some of the supplies for the sake of which we shall still go short are sent to ex-enemy countries. It is probable that Germany and Japan, at first, will be allowed only very meagre rations, but it is to be hoped that the obligation to prevent wide-spread starvation will be recognised even in relation to those countries. If the victors are wise in their other economic measures, the world's food supply ought soon to become adequate.

Making good the enormous destruction and deterioration of goods and industrial capital will be a stupendous task. The Russians plan to achieve it in Russia by means of German forced labour, but this plan cannot be adopted in capitalist countries. Outside Russia, reconstruction will involve investment of capital, and the United States is almost the only country that has much capital to invest. If American capital is to be available for Europe, it will be necessary to curtail the natural inclination of Americans to spend their money on supplying their own wants. And if the capital is to be invested by private enterprise, the interest will have to be guaranteed by the American government, since European governments will not be trusted by investors in the United States. This means government control over both investments and expenditure, and considerable interference in the economies of European States. Such a policy will rouse political opposition. But any one who considers the vast destruction of houses, bridges, rolling stock, factories, oil wells, etc., not only by enemy action, and not only in enemy countries, must become aware that reconstruction is impossible within the limits of an old-fashioned *laissez-faire* economy.

I hope we may assume that governments have learnt how to avoid the cycle of a frantic boom followed by a world-wide depression involving large-scale unemployment. Economists seem to be agreed that this cycle can be prevented by governmental control of expenditure and investment, without a complete abandonment of free enterprise and private

A Lion of Controversy Finds Pleasure in the Simple Things of Life
In the last war he suffered prison for his unpopular pacifist views and was deprived of his lectureship at Cambridge University. But he was invited to return to Cambridge last year.

The Seer of Trinity: At 73, Bertrand Russell is still the Protagonist of Fresh and Stimulating Ideas
Lord Russell—he likes still to write under the name of Bertrand Russell—is the third Earl, and grandson of Lord John Russell, who piloted the first Reform Bill in 1832. He has championed scores of unpopular causes and suffered persecution because of his intellectual loyalties.

capitalism; but it certainly cannot be prevented without a degree of governmental interference which will be very repugnant to the belated adherents of "rugged individualism." Foreign trade will have to be controlled, not merely by tariffs designed mainly to minimise it, but by more detailed agreements aimed at directing it into the most useful channels. All this will be needed, at first, to enable devastated countries to become self-supporting; but over a longer period it will be still needed to prevent a collapse of the economic mechanism such as afflicted the whole world after 1929.

Poor Countries Are Bad Customers

Except in Great Britain during the free trade era, it has been a universal maxim of statecraft, ever since the sixteenth century, that the economic interests of different countries conflict. There is, of course, some truth in this, but there is less than is often supposed. A rich country is not only a competitor, but also a customer; a poor country is not likely to be a good customer, but may, owing to a lower standard of life, become a dangerous competitor. In the years after the war, it will be important to realise the identity of economic interests between different countries, wherever it exists. This will apply, in the long run, to Germany and Japan as well as to other nations. It will no doubt be necessary, for military reasons, to curtail their heavy industry, but it will not be desirable to keep them poorer than surrounding nations if ways can be found of making them prosperous without increasing their potential strength in war. For we must hope that they will in time be content with their legitimate place among the nations, and to this end prosperity will be the most potent means.

But no measures of economic reconstruction will long avail unless a solution is found for the political problems which will remain as possible causes of war. It may be assumed that, for some twenty years or so after the end of the present war, weariness and the tasks of reconstruction will prevent any large-scale conflicts. But the process of rebuilding our shattered world will be a futile one if, as soon as it is more or less completed, we proceed to demolish the structure afresh. So far, in the pronouncements of statesmen, I have seen no evidence that anything of importance is being done to avoid another big war as soon as the Great Powers have had time to recuperate. Perhaps at the moment it is politically impossible to do much; but it is to be hoped that, at the end of the war, some better effort of constructive statesmanship may bear fruit.

The problem may be divided into three parts : first, the treatment of Germany and Japan; second, the smaller Powers; and third, the relations of the Great Powers.

Germany and Japan must, of course, be disarmed, and must for a considerable period, be deprived of the means of re-arming. This means that their heavy industry must be controlled and directed by the victorious nations. But this policy is not one which can be prolonged indefinitely. It must be supplemented by a long-run policy designed to make Germany and Japan willing partners in a world-wide system designed to prevent aggressive wars. This will require care for their economic welfare, and considerable control over their educational system; also a willingness to relax restrictions gradually when they appear to be no longer necessary. Two complementary principles must guide the policy of the victors : first, to show unmistakably that aggression is to have no chance of success; second, to make it clear that a co-operative spirit will receive its due reward.

As regards the smaller Powers, the plan outlined at Dumbarton Oaks may be adequate in protecting them against each other; if it is carried out, it will prevent such occurrences as the Polish seizure of Vilna and the Graeco-Turkish war. This is all to the good, and, since small wars may develop into big ones, it can on occasion be important. But there is nothing in the plan to protect small Powers against great ones. We can therefore hardly expect a warm welcome for the plan from any but the major Powers who are jointly to rule the world, or severally to fight over it.

A Retrogressive Step

As regards the Great Powers—Russia, the United States, Britain, France and China—each of them is to have a veto on any measures proposed to be taken against itself as aggressor. In regard to them, therefore, the situation will be exactly what it would be if no international authority existed. This is a retrogression from the League of Nations, which, however ineffective in practice, did, in theory, make every aggressive Power subject to sanctions. The new plan leaves the world, so far as formal agreements are concerned, completely and unrestrainedly at the mercy of the most powerful countries.

The Dumbarton Oaks plan has not yet been definitely adopted, and it is not impossible that the vehement opposition of all the smaller Powers may cause it to be modified or abandoned. If it is abandoned, the field will be clear for something better at a later date; if it is modified, it is scarcely possible that it should be modified for the worse. We are supposed to have gone to war because we objected to German aggression, and yet the three major victors solemnly propose to the world an international constitution which sanctions in advance similar aggression by themselves, while severely condemning aggression by nations too weak to be likely to be guilty of it. We thus proclaim to the whole of mankind that it is not aggression that we object to, but only aggression by our enemies. Could anything be more pitiful as the outcome of six years of endurance on the part of the millions who believed that some important principle was at stake?

It may be that, in the present temper of the world, nothing better was possible. I am not concerned to find fault with this or that statesman, but only to consider what, if nothing can be done now to amend this very unsatisfactory proposal, is the best hope of avoiding another great war within a generation.

For the moment, the only method proposed is the very unsatisfactory one of spheres of influence. If the whole world could be neatly mapped out into separate regions, each under the tutelage of one of the five Great Powers, a precarious peace might last for a considerable time. At present, the Russians do what they like in Poland, and we do what we like in Greece. But in practice the delimitation of spheres is apt to be a very controversial matter.

Clearly, if the world is not to drift towards war, something better will have to be found during the next few years. All immediate sources of conflict should first be eliminated by careful treaties, and then the field would be clear for the creation of a permanent structure designed to preserve the peace of the world for a long time.

Three Steps to Security

The first step is to create the necessary state of feeling. For this purpose, it should first be emphasised, by all the force of official propaganda, that great wars are a folly, and that, on a calculation of self-interest, a give-and-take agreement on disputed points is always more advantageous to both parties than a war. It is true that an agreement which is all give and no take may be worse than a war, since it may lead to subjection to a foreign Power: but a very moderate degree of sanity in statesmen should prevent demands for such one-sided arrangements, given a general belief that war is to be avoided if possible.

The next step will be to allay the mutual suspicions which have unfortunately existed between Russia and the Western Powers. So long as the Soviet Government hoped for communist revolutions in other countries, it was natural that the governments of those countries should feel hostile, and this hostility in turn bred distrust in the Government of Russia. But there has not, for a number of years, been any reason for this state of feeling on either side. Since the fall of Trotsky, the Soviet Government has ceased to support revolutionary movements in other countries, and co-operation between Russia and the West should now be as possible as between Mohammedan and Christian countries.

The third step—which can only be taken after the other two—will be to establish a genuine and effective League against aggression, in which the Great Powers, as well as the others, agree to settle disputes by peaceful means, and to resist aggression even when perpetrated by a Great Power. Only in this way can peace be made fairly secure. If the evils likely to result from another great war are adequately apprehended, we may hope that the years of reconstruction will be used, not only to repair material damage, but to save the world from disaster by the creation of effective governmental organs of international co-operation. If this is not done, mankind will inevitably continue to travel along the downward road to barbarism and chaos.

A Grandstand View of Man and Manners
The Fellow of Trinity, who has surprised two hemispheres into new thought on society, politics and sex, gives his views on the way the post-war world can find peace.

BERTRAND RUSSELL : A PIONEER OF MODERN THOUGHT

"I NEVER conducted a nudist colony in England. I never went in for salacious poetry. Such assertions are deliberate falsehoods which must be known to those who make them to have no foundation in fact." In these words Lord Russell denied charges made against him which resulted in the revocation of his appointment at City College, New York, on the grounds that he was not fit for the position because of his "immoral and malicious attitude towards sex." This was only one phase in Bertrand Russell's long struggle against mis-representation of his progressive views, many of which have since come to be accepted as part of our daily life, though the old slanders still attach themselves to his name in the backwoods of trans-continental thought.

To-day Bertrand Russell is a Fellow of Trinity College, Cambridge, with a salary of about £300 a year—the University where, as a brilliant mathematician, he began his career. Though he is chiefly known for his philosophical and social writings, it is his achievement in mathematics which he rates most highly. Among approximately forty (he cannot remember exactly the number) books which he has written, he values most his *Principia Mathematica*, published by the Cambridge University Press, in which he collaborated with Dr. Whitehead.

At the age of seventy-three, exasperating the complacent with his fresh and progressive ideas, invoking his patron saint, Voltaire, to clarify the muddles of the mystics, he feels content, as he greets his fellow Dons on the Cambridge Backs, that, after being deprived of his lectureship for heterodoxy in the last war, he is honoured by his College if not as a prophet, at least as a philosopher.

The End of An Excursion

The Last Resort of a Desperate Enemy
With the Siegfried Line cracking, von Rundstedt's battered army falling back under the impetus of the
Allies' Western Offensive, the Germans fight for a little more time by flooding the battlefields.

A BATTLE WITH THE RHINE

By flooding the flanks of the British positions east of Nijmegen, the Germans try to maroon our forward troops. But a spectacular amphibious operation by the Canadians beats the menace of the waters.

"IT makes me feel damp just to talk about it," said the Canadian, "but it happened like this: Our lot, east of Nijmegen, were given the job of assaulting a dyke and pushing about a kilometre across country to one of those little Dutch villages which look like a collection of doll's houses and are called by a name which sounds like a bad word.

"We attacked the dyke across open water in assault boats, buffaloes and ducks. Then we got on dry land again—or what's called dry land in Holland:

Covered by a Smoke Screen, Amphibious Vehicles Race Along the Dykes to Pick Up the Troops Cut Off by the Flooding
Only six hundred yards away, on the other side of the river, the enemy are sniping at our columns. But the smoke screen gives enough cover to allow our rescue force to move along the top of the dyke wall almost to the area where forward troops are surrounded by the rising flood-waters.

anywhere else, you'd call it a swamp—and we pushed on to our objective, this little village, and dossed down for the night.

"Jerry didn't counter attack but we weren't surprised by that because, these days, he's not nearly so sensitive as he used to be. But trust him to get up to something if he's got a chance. During the night, we heard some explosions. And, sure enough, he'd blown the dykes again and we'd got the river flooding down on top of us.

"Well, when a dyke goes, there's nothing you can do about it except shin up a tree and wait, like Noah, for the waters to subside, which may take days or weeks. The point is that, if nature had her way, all that area of Holland round Nijmegen and Arnhem—what we call "the island"—would be under water most of the year. Because most times the level of the river is higher than the level of the surrounding landscape. The only way the Dutch have kept the water out is by building great arti-

ficial walls along the banks of the rivers. By the way, the dykes are the actual walls not the gutter through which the water runs. And there are usually two, one behind the other. The front one is the summer dyke. The back one, which is much higher, is the winter one.

"And keeping the water under control is a tremendously complicated business. Each district in Holland has its own Waterways Engineer, and the whole economy of his area depends on how he

THE FLEET WHICH IS WINNING THE BATTLE OF THE FLOODS: *"Buffaloes" and "Ducks" Crawl, Run, Paddle and Swim O*

manages the sluices—because you have to let some water in to irrigate the land—and how he cares for the pumps and dykes. You see, even in peacetime, they get floods occasionally because, if the river rises above the level of the dykes, you've had it.

"So every year in Holland, round about November, people are inclined to get windy. They show you all the records of the water levels for hundreds of years. And if there's a heavy fall of rain, such as we've had this year, everybody keeps an eye on the winter dyke. They need to.

"About this time of year, the water in the rivers—the Waal, the Neder Rhine and the Maas—is running twenty feet or more above the level of the surrounding countryside. So you see how easy it is for Jerry. All he has to do is to blow a charge in the dyke and the river spills over the whole landscape. That's what happened to us, and that's what's been happening, on and off, ever since we started fighting in Holland.

The Rescue Force Makes Contact With the Marooned Men
Yesterday, when our troops captured it, the village was on dry land. Then, during the night, the Germans blew the dyke wall. Now, the whole place is submerged under several feet of water.

The Waterborne Troops Go Into Action
The Germans believed that the water defences of the Siegfried Line would smother our offensive. But the Allied Armies have learnt to float.

"Of course, the water subsides in time. As the level of the river falls in dry weather, the irrigation mechanisation starts to work again. Each field drains into a ditch, each ditch into a bigger ditch, then into a canal and finally back to the river and the sea.

"Apart from that there are pumps, but you can't do much with pumps in the sort of flooding were up against now. You simply have to wait till the level of the water gets low enough to mend the dykes.

"Meantime, the only place where you can keep your feet dry is on the top of the dyke walls. Fortunately, the whole countryside is trellised with big and little dykes; every poldar—as they call the fields—has a dyke of sorts. And, with a fleet of amphibious craft, you can keep going.

"When they washed us out of that village, they didn't stop the offensive. They slowed us down, that's all, while the ducks and buffaloes were retrieving the infantry (us included). The point is

Flooded Fields, Muddy Swamps, and Broken Dykes of What Were Once Called "The Impassable Water Defences of Holland."

177

WE WIN A BATTLE WITH THE MOST TERRIBLE ENEMY OF ALL : *Like Noah's Arks in a Desolated World,*
The houses in the village are submerged up to the first floor. Only the tops of the trees can be seen above the water. For miles around, the whole country
fleets of ducks, buffaloes and assault craft which have been assembling for months and years to meet just such an emergency. As the wa

The Rescued Men Take Their Last Look Back
Shivering and cold, soaked to the skin, the marooned Canadians, in their winter overalls,
are taken aboard the rescuing Buffaloes.

now that, when Jerry floods an area, he can't keep us out because our amphibious craft can keep us moving. But he himself can't make a come-back because he's stopped by his own flooding.

"Mind you, this water war is tough on the infantry. Some of us Canadians were only just beginning to feel dry after the Walcheren show. And now we're up to our necks in it, soaked through to the skin all over again. What is it you read in the Bible? 'The waters prevailed exceedingly.' I know now what those words mean. And we've all seen some of the things that the Bible story talks about too. Water is a terrible ruthless thing.

"You see, the worst of the flooding isn't the hold-up it causes in our offensive—we can beat that—it's the suffering it brings on the Dutch. That's bad enough now, but its effects will go on for years. Their homes, their farms, their villages, their churches are ruined. Their beasts and poultry are all drowned. The labour they've put into their land for generations is swept away. And all to give the Nazis a few more weeks' or months' grace before we finish 'em. It's a helluva war."

...faloes Ride Triumphantly Over the Flood Which the Enemy Has Turned Loose on Our Advancing Armies in Holland.

...ake. The enemy, unable to resist any longer by force of arms, has blown the dyke walls and done his best to drown us. He hasn't counted on the ...to rise, the amphibious columns are already on the move. By nightfall, our troops have been picked up and brought back to dry land.

The Isolated Church
The battered church steeple rises like a lighthouse out of the flooded fields.

The Dutch Village That Was Submerged
For hundreds of years the villagers have struggled to keep the dyke walls strong and the water from their homes. But, after all, it ends like this.

Picture Post, 20 May,

WITH ALL HIS BIRDS COMING HOME TO ROOST IN HIS OWN RUBBED-OUT CITY, THE SELF-STYLED "GREATE

THE LAST TWO PHOTOGRAPHS?

THE final scene, Gotterdammerung itself; here is the Fuehrer's last appearance on this or any stage. These two pictures, only now discovered, conclude Adolf Hitler's rendezvous with history. One of his personal photographers took them at the door of that famous Bunker in the Wilhelmstrasse where, very soon afterwards, the topshot Nazis died. Here, with his Aide-de-camp, Obergruppenfuehrer Julius Schaub, the ruffled and beleaguered Adolf Hitler emerges in a lull, surveys the bomb-wreck and the bric-a-brac of his Chancellery. The Russians are at one gate, the Western Allies at the other. All that is left of the Thousand Year Reich is this. These prints, found at last in a Berlin suburban laboratory, are the last ever taken of the man, alive or dead. They were made on his birthday—April 20, 1945. Ten days later he was dead.

HITLER AND HIS LAST AIDE-DE-CAMP

GERMAN OF ALL TIME" POSES FOR THE LAST TIME

"To Moscow, Not Munich": says Bevin
Labour would have sent its Foreign Secretary to Moscow in 1939. He stands for collaboration with Russia.

"Great Changes in Our Time": Morrison on Home Policy
Labour's Five Year Plan can be carried through by a Five-Year Parliament with a working Labour majority. There will be no co-operation with the Tories.

Labour Makes Its
PLANS FOR POWER

Photographed by K. HUTTON

A NEW spirit has taken hold of the Labour Party. You felt it in the first hours of the Blackpool Conference. It expressed itself in the faces and voices of the delegates who came to the microphone. It communicated itself to the Executive. It made itself heard in the speeches of Labour's leaders. Labour has recaptured its old evangelical fervour. More than that, Labour has won the will to win.

What would have been the reply of the young delegates—the soldiers, the factory workers, the doctors, the teachers—to the old jibe that Labour isn't fit to govern? They gave it in so many words : if Labour was fit to help in winning the war, Labour is fit to govern. Gone was the "sea of white heads" which a member of the Executive once complained was his bird's-eye view of the Conference floor. The men and women, who eagerly came to the microphone to give their constituency or Trade Union view were young, fresh from the factories, the farms and the Forces. They willingly accepted Mr. Churchill's challenge to fight

In the Chair, Ellen Wilkinson
She dominates the Conference with her masterly handling of the delegates.

At the Rostrum, Clem Attlee
Though overshadowed by his colleagues, he co-ordinates the Party.

The Scene in the Empress Ballroom
The vast hall is crammed with delegates wh all, and peace for all, recei

a General Election. They, better than anyone, knew that the credit of victory belongs to the people who worked and fought as much as to any one leader. They were the representatives of a reinvigorated Party, the Labour Party, the Party of the ordinary men and women of Britain.

"We've time to finish our game of bowls, and beat the Spaniards," said Miss Ellen Wilkinson, the Chairman. The Tory Armada was in full sail, but the well-rigged galleons of Churchillian self-righteousness, and the craft of Lord Beaverbrook, now clearly visible, failed to frighten the delegates.

Where were Mr. Churchill's "Left-Wing, stay-at-home intellectuals"? Certainly not at the Conference; they must have stayed at home. These men and women were not academic planners. From the Labour Ministers on the platform to the most modest Ward-secretary on the floor, all had taken some active part in production, in war-organisation or in the battle. Never in its history had the Conservative Party been faced by such a united Labour

Representative of Labour's Young Men, Major Healey Makes a Passionate Speech
He has just flown back from Italy. "The struggle for Socialism in Europe," he says, " has been
hard, cruel, bitter and bloody. . . . After paying this price, our comrades won't let go."

"What D'you Think of Him, Harold?"
Two Executive members, Hugh Dalton (left) and Harold Laski, size-up the new men.

Party as at Blackpool, never was Bevin so close to Bevan, never was Brockway so nearly affiliated, never were the Socialists so enthusiastically persuaded, and the Tories so unhappily convinced, that Labour is able to govern.

It was the new men, the young men who helped to win the war, rather than the venerable, white-haired idealists who alarmed Lord Beaverbrook. In search of easy game, he fell on Ian Mikardo, delegate and candidate for Reading. Let us forget his columnist's jibes at Mikardo's name. They

are jibes, which like those of Lord Northcliffe after the last war, make up in poison what they lack in wit. Ian Mikardo is an industrial consultant; he advises business men how to run their businesses; he knows the inside story of the vast-scale legalised profiteering which has gone on, under the protection of Trade Associations; he knows that Britain's basic industries nationalised would be more beneficial and productive to the British people than under the present system of private ownership; he is not intimidated by Big Business nor willing to com-

Blackpool, Where Over a Thousand Delegates Assemble for the Most Enthusiastic Conference Labour Has Held for Many Years
...sten attentively to fighting speeches, both from the platform and the floor. Morrison and Bevin, stating Labour's programme of jobs for all, houses for
...remendous ovations. The Conference eagerly accepts Mr. Churchill's challenge to fight a General Election, and ends with a Victory fervour.

THEY DISCUSS LABOUR'S PROSPECTS : *At the Hotel*
Aneurin Bevan, M.P. (left) continues to talk politics over tea with Lord Stansgate (centre). He is confident of victory.

At Blackpool's Casino, the Fabians Expect a Hard Fight
Margaret Cole, honorary secretary of the Fabian Society, talks to John Parker, M.P., secretary (left) about his chances at Romford.

promise with it, like some Trade Unionists who have had no experience of management. Mikardo, in short, represents the tens of thousands of Labour's new technicians who are able to put into operation Labour's plan for socialism. The very reverse of Lord Beaverbrook's ideal "little man," he was undisturbed by the charge of being middle-aged (which he is not) or of being a smaller version of Ernest Bevin (which he is). In his speech, he courteously thanked the *Daily Express* for advertising his resolution on nationalisation which last year's Conference adopted; and Lord Beaverbrook, having scratched Mikardo and discovered the full-blooded policy of a powerful Party, will now, no doubt, go hunting for easier victims.

Labour is, indeed, far less vulnerable electorally than at the end of the last war when it had a large

Pacifist wing. Major Healey, candidate for Pudsey and Otley, who had flown back from Italy, stated in his speech the view of the Socialist serving man on foreign policy. "Its crucial principle," he said, "must be to help the social revolution in Europe . . . The upper classes in every country are selfish, depraved, dissolute and decadent. These are the people who look to the British Army to protect them against the just wrath of the people."

For the first time in many years, the Executive didn't act as a brake on the Conference. It heard the delegates call for action, and Morrison, hotly followed by Bevin, rose up, and shouted "Forward!"

Between them they answered those who had asked "Where are the men to lead Labour?" The choice of the electorate is not between the colourful,

dynamic Mr. Churchill, full of glory and accomplishment, and Mr. Attlee. Their choice, as far as the actual government is concerned, is between Mr. Churchill and his colourless Cabinet (supported by sundry Lords as junior ministers), and Bevin and Morrison with expert representation in the departmental ministries by men like Cripps—the whole under the Chairmanship of Attlee. The Conference showed that Labour had the cordial collaboration of two of its biggest men—Morrison and Bevin—once assumed to be rivals. The reception that Morrison received when he spoke on domestic policy, and Bevin when he spoke on foreign policy, announced both their popularity and the fervour which the Labour Movement has recaptured.

"I am not a recent convert to friendship with the

AT THE LORD MAYOR'S RECEPTION : *Mr. Morrison's Victory Dance*
His partner is Barbara Castle, candidate for Blackburn. He takes part in the fun, and is as popular at the social events as he is on the platform.

Some Like to Dance
Philip Noel-Baker, ex-Minister of War Transport, dances grimly for the whole evening.

Some Like to Read
She's a journalist who rests from her labours at the Conference by reading what others write.

In the Tea Lounge, the ex-Minister of Labour is Optimistic
Ernest Bevin is amused by a press report of the Conference. Mrs. Bevin and Andrew Conley share the joke.

In Conference, a Bristol Candidate is Earnest
Sir Stafford Cripps (right) re-admitted into the Party, finds Blackpool more congenial than Southport, where he was expelled.

Soviet Union," said Mr. Bevin. "If we'd been in power in 1939, we'd have sent our Foreign Minister to Moscow." He was in favour of a Round Table Peace Conference, with cards on the table, face upwards." Labour will have nothing to do with the secret diplomacy beloved of the Tories; it wants our dealings with our Allies to be open, for all the world to see. Every speaker on foreign policy, including those in the services, urged the friendship with the Soviet Union which Bevin supported. He proved that Labour had a leader with a grasp of world affairs—including a policy for India—and a programme to give the world a political stability which the anti-Russian, anti-Irish, anti-French, anti-American, anti-Resistance section of the Tory Party is working so hard to prevent.

Some Prefer to Sing
Ellen Wilkinson draws the number in a raffle for whisky. She joins in the song of the miners.

And Everybody Wants to Eat
The buffet is crowded ; miners rub shoulders with knights and ex-Cabinet Ministers.

A Greeting for Every Delegate at the Lord Mayor's Reception
The Lord Mayor and the Lady Mayoress, together with Miss Wilkinson and Mr. Attlee, shake hands with each delegate. The delegates will go home, proud and happy.

On domestic policy, Herbert Morrison made the clearest and most rousing case for Labour that has been heard for many years. Dealing with the control of industry, described in the pamphlet "Let us Face the Future," he said :

"If control goes, with the consequences that luxury mansions come before cottages . . . there's going to be a row." That was his answer to the Tories who want to make house-building a free-for-all. Morrison knows that if building were de-controlled, there'd be even fewer houses built than at present under the control of the inadequate Ministry of Works; and that those built in a system of private speculation would go, not to the ex-Serviceman in search of a home, but to the rich.

As Labour's most experienced administrator, Morrison didn't want to entrust matters like nationalisation to a timid Civil Service, frightened to stand up to Big Business. He wanted a reformed Civil Service of experts, "able to talk to business men in their own language." He would not tolerate "big industries being built into totalitarian monopolies." They would be socialised on the basis of suitability and urgency.

By the time the Conference ended, the programme of the Party was being summarised in a few phrases : jobs for all, homes for all, and, after victory in the Far East peace for all. "The election after the last war," said Morrison, "was a triumph for vested interests and reactionary forces. Its evils pursued us till the outbreak of the present war." With a vast majority, the Conservative Party failed to give Britain work, failed to give Britain houses, failed to give Britain peace. Now, says Labour, it's our turn. Capitalism has proved that it benefits only the few. We have a policy to benefit the whole nation. In the confidence that Labour's Five Year Plan will build a new and better Britain, the delegates—civilians and serving men—returned to the constituencies to win the election.

MAURICE EDELMAN.

Hindsight by Maurice Edelman

And that's how it was. A thousand delegates at the Empress Ballroom in Blackpool cheered Clem Attlee when, with the stiffening of Bevin , he decided to break the Coalition and fight Churchill at a General Election.

Earlier in the day, I had seen him in his hotel, fretful and insecure, tormented by self-doubt, walking alone up and down the corridors, mentally composing the letter accepting or rejecting Churchill's proposal that the Coalition should continue. Now at last the decision was made, and with Ellen Wilkinson in the chair the Conference was dressed for action with the speakers of the New Britain — young soldiers like Denis Healey and John Freeman — coming to the rostrum to give their testimony.

Reassessing my 1944 article, there's nothing that even hindsight would want to make me change. Before the war, Party Conferences had been dominated by white-haired veterans, retrospective and anecdotal, of the working-class struggle. At Blackpool, the mood was forward-looking. The men in uniform and the young factory workers wanted change in the doctrinal aspect of Socialism, apart from the basic tenet of nationalization of the key industries which, Ian Mikardo reaffirmed, was secondary. Above all, the Party Conference was interested in the qualitative differences between Socialism and Toryism.

A fascinating constellation of Party strong-men and the young lions gave the Conference an authority in the post-war world that pre-war Labour had never had. Bevin was a powerful national figure whose importance as a trade unionist and a Minister of Labour was acknowledged far beyond the Party. Morrison as Minister of Home Security was the man who beat the blitz, a social democrat who hated Communism, an empiricist who spent his political life resisting the Party idealists. In a curious way, the democratic, middle-class, cricket-loving qualities of Clem Attlee gave confidence to the football-watching workers he led, and a respectable sanction to their rejection of the aristocratic descendant of Marlborough, the Swordsman Winston Churchill. For the first time, the Labour Party at Blackpool in 1945 seemed to me to be a national party and not a class party, and one equipped to govern.

I arrived at Blackpool a journalist; I left it, in embryo at any rate, a prospective Parliamentary candidate. Within a few months, I was elected M.P. for Coventry West, swept in by the irresistible Labour tide that turned heavy Tory majorities into equally heavy losses. For five years, the impetus of that great Blackpool Conference enabled the Labour Government to build the Welfare State and to carry out its basic nationalization programme. Post-war deprivation, austerity, the nagging of the Housewives' League, the coal shortage — none of this was able to destroy Labour's profound faith in its cause. But by 1950 when most of its 'Let's Face the Future' manifesto had been translated into Acts, the Party had begun to run out of steam. Having exhausted its programme, it lost its self-confidence. Though it won the following election with a small majority, the Labour Party was already in the wilderness, led by old, tired and dying men.

When it returned to power in 1964 it was a pragmatic and revisionist Party. But by 1970 it was once again looking for a framework of principle, with its ideologists yearning for the spirit of 1945.

The Abyssinian Delegate
Jomo Kenyatta asked for an Act of Parliament making discrimination by race or colour a criminal offence.

The Nigerian Trade Unionist
Chief A. S. Coker, represents unions with a membership of half a million workers. He demands full franchise for the negro worker.

The Liverpool Welfare Worker
Mr. E. J. Du Plau, is responsible for hostels and centres for negro seamen. "Negroes are social exiles in Britain," he maintains.

AFRICA SPEAKS IN MANCHESTER

Delegates from many parts of Africa and the United States to the first Pan-African Conference talk for a week—of freedom from the White Man, of the colour bar, of one great coloured nation, of force to gain their ends.

Photographed by JOHN DEAKIN

THE dance was a mixed affair—mixed in trade, from the stoker to the anthropologist; mixed in class, from the £3 a week labourer to the rich cocoa merchant; mixed in dress, from the baggy grey flannels to the suit of tails. But above all it was mixed in colour, from the blonde white to the midnight black. This dance, held at Edinburgh Hall, on the corner of one of Manchester's drab and soot-blackened streets, was the first gathering of delegates to the Pan-African Conference. They chose Manchester because its people have less curiosity or hostility to colour than the people of any other English city. Certainly, there was no self-consciousness among the white women who partnered their negro husbands or friends through "jive" to the last romantic waltz. Their attitudes varied. Some had approached the colour bar problem intellectually, others from a Christian viewpoint and others from simple human values.

Typical of the last attitude is the mixed marriage of Mary Brown to John Teah Brown, and before the conference got down to the more serious problems of the negro peoples, I went to their home to see a successful black and white marriage in its own domestic setting. Mary Brown was left stranded in Liverpool with her child when she met John Brown, a donkeyman on a merchant ship. He married her, gave her overwhelming affection, and saw that her child was properly educated.

I listened to John Teah Brown's story—a story which in many ways put in terms of one human being the resolutions and speeches of the whole week's conference. John Teah Brown was born in Sierre Leone and is a member of the Kroo tribe. He was educated at a mission and brought up a Roman Catholic. He was devout and sincere in his religion until one day in a church at East London, South Africa. He went in to pray but a priest came up to him and told him it was a white man's church and he must get out. He has not been inside a church since, though he remains true to the Christian faith, practising it, he thinks, with rather more sincerity than the priest who turned him away from the altar.

He left Sierra Leone at the age of fifteen, for he

A Mixed Marriage That is a Success
Mr. John Teah Brown, with his white wife, Mrs. Mary Brown, in their Manchester home. He says the negro must earn the respect of the white man to merit full citizenship.

In Conference: A White Man Urges the Negroes' Cause

John McNair, General Secretary of the I.L.P., addressing the delegates, says: "I object to the idea that the white people have anything to give to the black. There is, on the other hand, a debt which the white people owe to the coloured races: a debt which must and shall be paid."

felt that the discrimination, segregation and low standard of the negro's life there cramped his spirit. His escape was to the sea and for thirty years he has been in the Merchant Navy.

"The negro," he says, "must not only clamour for the help of the white man, he must also learn to help himself. The negro is not only exploited by white men—he is often exploited by the rich and wealthy negro traders. When we learn to help each other, then we shall merit citizenship and freedom from the white man."

The moral of his and similar stories was the motive force at the conference. George Padmore, leading negro journalist, maintained that a negro's skin is the passport to an oppression as violent as that of Nazi Germany's oppression of the Jews. "We don't need yellow armbands in Africa—just black skins," he maintained.

But this is the extremist's view of the problem. There will be little sympathy with the overstated case put forward by Mr. J. E. Appiah, delegate for the West African Students Union. In a noisy, impassioned speech he declared: "The only language the Englishman understands is force. Others plead for more diplomatic negotiation but I am for firmer action. Only force will take us out of our disgraceful plight . . ." and so on and on.

More reasonable and more likely to succeed was the case put forward by the Labour and Trade Union leaders, the real strength of this Pan-African movement which seeks to unite all Negro Associations. They claim that the real force to be used is that of organised labour. They point out the success of the recent Nigerian strike, when thousands of negro workers came out to demand a minimum for all workers of 2s. 6d. a day. But for their constructive speeches, the conference would have produced merely a deluge of abuse and violent oratory.

On certain principles they are united. They demand strong representation on the legislative councils which govern the various territories. This already applies in certain areas but is restricted to negroes with an average income of £50 a year, which disfranchises the majority of coloured workers.

They ask for the principle of equal pay for equal work to be established, regardless of colour, race or creed. They ask for improved medical and educational services, for an end to the Uncle Tom shack, and the compound system of segregation.

Mr. Peter Abrahams, chief propagandist for the federation, told me that they did not intend to stop at merely organising the peoples of African descent. They planned to go on further and mobilise the whole of the Non-European nations, comprising over three-quarters of the world's population. Left Wing members of the Federation oppose this idea. "They accuse us of chauvinism," he said, "but the white workers of Europe have let us down and we must now all get together to fight for our rights and freedom." In other words, a reversed colour bar.

A few delegates admitted a positive side of our rule in Africa. There is a maternity hospital at Accra, capital of the Gold Coast, where a native woman can have a child for 1s. or nothing at all. In the Tanganyika sisal factories there have been established excellent factory welfare workers. In Uganda an enormous university, with mixed black and white staff, has been opened and negro students are helped with fees. A younger and more vigorous type of white civil servant has lately been sent out to the West Coast and their conscience and goodwill is showing results. On Britain's side we plead that six years of war has robbed us of much chance to put into operation White Paper proposals. It was Wallace Johnson, the negro Trade Union leader, who put the whole case most sanely.

"We turn," he said, "to the British Labour Movement to help us, and thereby help themselves. We do not want to be cheap labour, driven in competition against British workers.

To such reasoning, this country will not be unsympathetic. But to creating a black bloc, to the use of force advocated by hotheads of the Federation, there will be immediate white hostility.

HILDE MARCHANT.

The American Red Cross Worker
He comes from Washington and cares for his own people in Britain. He suffers no colour humiliation.

The Barrister from Lagos
Mrs. Renner urges the need for a great raising of the standard of education and knowledge among African women.

The Founder of Pan Africanism
Dr. Du Bois is the head of the American Negro Association. He opposed the extremist idea of a new "nationalism of colour."

Hindsight by Tom Hopkinson

In October–November 1945, only a few months after the end of the Second World War, a conference was held in Manchester. Though it attracted no great attention at the time, it has since become historic — a landmark in the story of African liberation.

This is due partly to the tremendous impetus given to those working for African freedom by the discovery that there were other workers in territories far away from theirs just as determined as themselves, sharing the same ideals, and equally prepared to face hardship and sacrifice to make them real. And partly to the fact that among the 200 delegates were a number who would become the founders of modern Africa.

The joint political secretaries for the conference were Kwame Nkrumah, a little-known student of law and politics at the London School of Economics, and George Padmore, a West Indian. Only twelve years or so later when I visited him in Accra, Padmore was the political theorist and close adviser to the first Prime Minister of the newly independent state of Ghana, Kwame Nkrumah.

Nkrumah recalls in his Autobiography how '. . . we worked night and day in George's flat. We used to sit in his small kitchen, the wooden table completely covered by papers, a pot of tea which we always forgot until it had been made two or three hours and George typing at his small typewriter so fast that the papers were churned out as though they were being rolled off a printing press.'

The assistant secretary was a farm-worker from Sussex. Named Jomo Kenyatta, he was destined to become first President of an independent Kenya. S. L. Akintola, future Prime Minister of Western Nigeria, was a delegate. The publicity secretary was a South African Coloured, Peter Abrahams, whose 'Tell Freedom' would become a seminal book in the struggle against racism.

Presiding over the conference was the almost mythical American Negro leader, Dr W. E. B. DuBois who had flown over from New York at the age of seventy-three. Back at the start of the century, when the white races could see no challenge to their supremacy anywhere in the world, DuBois had made the extra-ordinary prophecy that colour was to be the great problem of the twentieth century. DuBois, as Padmore later wrote, 'had done more than any other to inspire and influence by his writings and political philosophy all the young men who had forgathered from the distant corners of the earth'.

Even the choice of Manchester was significant. It had been picked, said the chairman, Peter Milliard, a doctor from British Guiana who had been practising successfully there for twenty-five years, as being 'the most liberal city in England'. And he recalled how, during the American Civil War, the Lancashire cotton workers had sacrificed themselves to help the Negro. The North was blockading the ports of the South on whose raw cotton the mills of Lancashire depended. But when the mill-owners pressed the British Government to send warships to break the blockade, the mill-workers resisted to a man.

Though the resolutions passed might today seem matter-of-course, they had a profoundly stirring and inspiring effect upon the delegates. The nature of these delegates also was important, for they were farmers, workers, trade unionists, cooperative society organizers, students. In the words of Nkrumah, they 'were practical men and men of action and not, as was the case of the four previous conferences, merely idealists contenting themselves with writing theses'. Also, he remarked, since 'the preponderance of members . . . were African, its ideology became African Nationalism — a revolt against colonialism, racialism and imperialism in Africa — and it adopted Marxist socialism as its philosophy'.

So the delegates were men of action. Their programme was an action programme aimed at Africa. But above all the time was ripe. As another African leader, Ndabaningi Sithole, now in prison in Rhodesia, wrote in his *African Nationalism*:

World War II had a great deal to do with the awakening of the peoples of Africa. During the war the African came in contact with practically all the peoples of the earth. He met them on a life-and-death-struggle basis. He saw the so-called civilized and peaceful and orderly white people mercilessly butchering one another just as his so-called savage ancestors had done in tribal wars. He saw no difference between the primitive and the civilized man. In short, he saw through European pretensions that only Africans were savages. This had a revolutionizing psychological impact on the African.

But more than this, World War II taught the African most powerful ideas. During the war the Allied Powers taught the subject peoples (and millions of them!) that it was not right for Germany to dominate other nations. They taught the subject peoples to fight and die for freedom rather than live and be subjugated by Hitler. The subject peoples learned the lesson well. . . .

Looking back on Hilde Marchant's article with the hindsight of more than twenty years, one can see how much was left out. The article was written from the white standpoint natural at the time. There were mistakes. We called it the first Pan-African Conference, when in fact it was the fifth. We had never heard of Kwame Nkrumah, and we evidently supposed Jomo Kenyatta to be an Ethiopian. But the important thing is that the article was written at all, and that it was by no means unsympathetic.

In laying the story out for the magazine, I never dreamed that I would myself spend nine years in Africa and talk to many of its leaders — from Lumumba to Luthuli, from Mboya to Azikiwe — on the subjects covered by the conference. And no more, I suppose, did Joe Appiah, when he declared 'The only language the Englishman understands is force', foresee that he would become a victim of force and spend long years in prison. Not as a prisoner of the English, but of his fellow-delegate, Kwame Nkrumah.

1946

The Conservatives made a quick recovery from their greatest electoral disaster for forty years. Their newly-appointed chairman was not only an able organizer, but a man whose self-made background was a standing advertisement of the party's claim to encourage careers open to the talents. Viscount 'Uncle Fred' Woolton fitted oddly into the Conservative pantheon of Burke, Bagehot and the Marquess of Salisbury, but he deserved his niche in it all the same. The Conservative Research Department under R. A. Butler recruited several able young men with their way to make. Born a generation earlier, Reginald Maudling and Iain Macleod would have been Fabian Socialists. Enoch Powell – lucid to the point of incomprehensibility, as a colleague described him – was a lost pro-consul on the Curzon model, though with the obligatory middle-class background from which the others also sprang. They contributed a lively flow of progressivist ideas from the thirties, the most dangerous being filtered out at a higher level by enlightened paternalists like Oliver Lyttelton. Only one indomitably unfashionable figure marred the Conservative New Look. In August, Eden, an ageing heir-apparent, was writing anxiously to Halifax that Churchill seemed in the mood to proclaim his intention of leading the party at the next election. 'Disastrous', noted Halifax – a view widely held in select circles, though little talked about.

Labour, on the other hand, staggered from crisis to crisis. Shortage of dollars caused rations to be cut even from their wartime level. The Minister of Food, John Strachey, was an intellectual whose political progress, from belief in Sir Oswald Mosley to a Popular Front with the Communists, spoke of the unfailing optimism he demonstrated by his faith that the shortage of fats could be overcome by growing groundnuts in virgin East African bush. In July, the nation suffered the traumatic experience of bread-rationing, which had never been necessary in the darkest days of two world wars. Luxuries like nylons, whisky, chocolate, were mainly for export only – a fact unfailingly rubbed in by anti-Labour advertisers. Almost the only experiment on which Attlee had ventured in forming his Government was to give responsibility for housing and health to a volatile Welsh rebel, Aneurin Bevan, who engaged in a long struggle with diehard doctors over the formation of a national health service, and had little energy to spare for the other half of his task. As few houses were being built, the homeless drew attention to their plight by taking over deserted army camps, empty houses and Central London hotels.

Abroad, Jewish guerrillas blew up the King David Hotel in Jerusalem, and kidnapped and flogged a British officer and three N.C.O.s in retaliation for the whipping of a Jewish youth. This and later outrages led to outbreaks of anti-semitism, and even riots in Liverpool and Manchester. It was not yet widely known that something like five million Jews had been murdered by the Germans. The withdrawal from Empire proceeded no more smoothly in the Far East, where Indian Muslims refused to accept an independence which placed them under Hindu domination. In Europe, negotiations over the peace treaties dragged on, while both sides consolidated the division foreshadowed at Tehran and Yalta.

In a speech at Fulton, Missouri, Churchill signalled the declaration of the Cold War by voicing widely held suspicions of Russian intentions. Independent political research and frank political memoirs being luxuries the Soviet Union cannot afford, there is no way of knowing what Stalin's real intentions were, but there seems reason to suppose that he was acting defensively from weakness, rather than aggressively from strength. Russia had lost perhaps twenty million dead in the war, many of them the young and active. Her industry had been wrecked, and the 1946 harvest was ruined by drought. Stalin was kept well-informed by Communist sympathizers of the progress of American atomic capability, and there were many in the West who went further than Bertrand Russell's proposal that the threat of atomic war should be used to make Russia less intransigent.

It was not until the end of 1947 that Ernest Bevin's 'Now 'e's gone too bloody far' marked a real break in British attempts to reach agreement with Russia; but the British Foreign Secretary was playing a difficult and what can be seen with hindsight as a misguided hand. He tried to convince the world that Britain still belonged in the league of the Big Three, which she patently did not. He was afraid of an American withdrawal from Europe, as after the first World War, leaving a weakened Britain as the only counterpoise to Russian expansion. And there was the threat to British independence shown by the ganging-up between Russia and America at Tehran and Yalta. The British decision to make the atomic bomb was influenced as much by fear of an anti-Socialist America as of Russia.

By the end of 1946, Beveridge and the better life seemed as far away as the Siegfried Line in 1940. But Government and people hung on, and things did, though slowly, get a little better.

Laurence Thompson

June 22, 1946

PICTURE POST

LEADERS IN WAR
AND PEACE

HULTON'S NATIONAL WEEKLY   VICTORY SPECIAL   4^D

JUNE 22, 1946   Vol. 31. No. 12

Holiday Making by Numbers: Mass 'Keep-Fit' at a Butlin Camp
Nearly half-a-million people will pay £5 15s. 6d. a week to have a holiday in one of Butlin's camps this year. They are expected to take part each morning in army style keep-fit exercises. They do so. And they like it.

LIFE IN A HOLIDAY CAMP

Photographed by K. HUTTON and CHARLES HEWITT.

The Human Alarm Clock

She calls the 3,000 campers at 7.45 a.m. through fifty loud speakers. When she isn't announcing, the gramophone floods the camp with music.

Prompt Answer to the Summons to Enjoy Themselves
It's the start of an exhausting day. Chalets for the guests are strictly utilitarian—two beds, one chest of drawers, one wardrobe. For families there are double-decker beds, similar to ship bunks.

MOST things in Butlin's holiday camp, Filey, go in straight lines, from the sauce-bottles to the chalets, from the dining-tables to the flower-beds. Should a chair or a vase of flowers get out of place, then the dining-room supervisor calls the head waiter, who calls the station waiter, who summons a waitress and the line is reformed. The trouble, said one of the waiters, is the people. Some are fat, some are lean, some sit straight in their chairs, others wriggle. People will behave differently, even in a well-organised camp.

That, in a sense, is the reply which Mr. Butlin gives to those who deride his mass-produced, conveyor-belt holidays. He says that, within such a highly-organised setting, the individual gets a greater opportunity for self-expression. Handling half-a-million people, as he will next year, demands a routine and orderly procedure, very similar to that of an army camp. But, apart from such mass classifications as whist, snooker and tennis players, or children, lovers, marrieds and middle-aged, he says, he merely provides the framework and within that Butlin framework you can create whatever holiday pattern pleases you.

Individual Attention for Female
Ex-army P.T. instructors give a camper a work
out. Butlineers have to be prepared for a lot of
boisterous, unsolicited, fun.

Individual Attention for Male
The beach is two hundred yards away, but there's
no need to go all that way. Butlin's supply bathing pool, lake and playgrounds in the camp.

The Camp Picks Its Weekly 'Butlin Beauty'
Weekly beauty contests among the campers have developed into a nation-wide contest. Number
34 was the week's winner. There are also prizes for crooners, the knobbliest knees and the
broadest smile. Bashfulness is the cardinal sin.

"I don't compete against the sun or countryside," he says, sitting in the sun lounge under a
plaster tree with plastic leaves, "I just provide
everything to keep the campers happy. There are
no rules and no compulsion."

As he talked in the model Viennese Inn, swallows dived over his head, under the pale blue glass
roof and into the plaster eaves. Mr. Butlin did not
organise the swallows and sparrows that have come
to the ready-made nests of the beer garden—
'absolutely accurate copy of the real thing'—but
once they arrived, proper accommodation was provided in the way of plaster nests, baths with clean
water and wired tree branches for singing in the
early morning. Nothing like the song of birds to
give the authentic touch to the chemically-green
raffia lawns and the plastic beams of old Vienna.

As with the birds, so my friends K3 and K4, were
having everything provided for them. This code
number represented a typical family, who were
being checked through at the camp reception office
which everybody refers to in army slang as 'Admin.'
They collected a number for their chalet, a number
for their dining-room position, a number for their

Concerted Attack Upon the Country
Some people like to go hiking by themselves. But not many of that sort go to Butlin's.
The more hundred people you can get to join you on the ramble, the better.

Only the Horse Gets Bored
There is one member of the staff to every ten campers. It's the staff's
duty to keep the party jolly and constantly on the move. The old retainer
does not seem to have heard the Butlin order—'Keep smiling'.

And the Sea's Thrown In
These children like the authentic beach, but Butlin provides sand-pits
and paddling-pools in the camp for those who don't want to walk as far,
or who feel lonely and unprotected when they get outside.

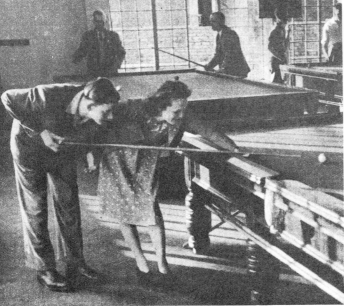

Even Billiards Can Be Shared
On wet or sunny days, the 24 billiards tables are in big demand. Games,
theatre and cinema are all included in the fixed rate for the week's stay.

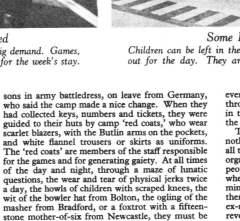

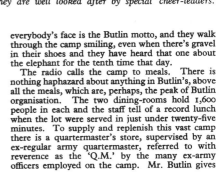

Some Butlineers Start Young
Children can be left in the charge of staff entertainers while parents go
out for the day. They are well looked after by special cheer-leaders.

luggage and an overall name for the house they are going to belong to during their stay.

The last is most important for, as in all the best boarding-schools, the members of Kent or Gloucester house eat together, play together and compete together against other units in such competitions as the knobbliest knees, the camp 'lovely' and the mass keep-fit exercises. The house captain, a member of the Butlin staff, is chosen for his jollity and talent as a mixer, and at frequent intervals rallies his house over the camp radio with such calls as 'Hi-di-hi.' The house responds 'Ho-di-ho.' Mr. Butlin indignantly denied a newspaper report that if a camper refuses to respond he is penalised.

K3 and K4 were a party of eight, including two sons in army battledress, on leave from Germany, who said the camp made a nice change. When they had collected keys, numbers and tickets, they were guided to their huts by camp 'red coats,' who wear scarlet blazers, with the Butlin arms on the pockets, and white flannel trousers or skirts as uniforms. The 'red coats' are members of the staff responsible for the games and for generating gaiety. At all times of the day and night, through a maze of lunatic questions, the wear and tear of physical jerks twice a day, the howls of children with scraped knees, the wit of the bowler hat from Bolton, the ogling of the masher from Bradford, or a foxtrot with a fifteen-stone mother-of-six from Newcastle, they must be worthy acolytes of the Spirit of Fun. A smile on everybody's face is the Butlin motto, and they walk through the camp smiling, even when there's gravel in their shoes and they have heard that one about the elephant for the tenth time that day.

The radio calls the camp to meals. There is nothing haphazard about anything in Butlin's, above all the meals, which are, perhaps, the peak of Butlin organisation. The two dining-rooms hold 1,600 people in each and the staff tell of a record lunch when the lot were served in just under twenty-five minutes. To supply and replenish this vast camp there is a quartermaster's store, supervised by an ex-regular army quartermaster, referred to with reverence as the 'Q.M.' by the many ex-army officers employed on the camp. Mr. Butlin gives

They All Fall Down Together
Roller-skating, like most other Butlin pleasures, is taken communally. Instruction is given free.
Chain formation gives them confidence.

An Approach to Privacy
There are plenty of bars, tea rooms and lounges. But no
reading or writing-room. Nobody wants one.

ex-army men preference in running the sharply
departmentalised organisation, because it is work
similar to that they have become used to and they
can give orders and ensure discipline.

On the shelves of the camp store most things are
stored by the gross—plugs for wash basins (a dozen
are taken home each week), door handles (twenty a
week is an average replacement), right down to
blank key shapes (about a hundred campers forget
to leave them every week).

The normal day at Butlins begins at 7.45 when
the camp radio gives a hearty rise-and-shine call to
the camp. The voice is cheerful, but relentless, as
it recites : "Good morning, campers. It is a lovely
day and the sun is shining (or, the weather has let

Tribal Rites of the Butlineers
Most popular dances are marching parades like the Lambeth Walk, or action dances
like the Hokey Cokey. Even the shy lose their self-effacement under the spell.

A Lady Plays Solo
*There are a few quiet spots where older people
can get away from the mass jollity and enjoy a
moment's peace on their own.*

The Rebel
*She's decided to entertain herself somewhere where
nobody will tell her to do P.T. or sing.*

Two Who Find Quiet even in Butlin's
*You needn't always join in the organised fun. Quiet retreats along the coast are plentiful. The
camp, in fact, is popular with honeymoon couples.*

us down), so show a leg you lads and lasses, rub the sleep out of your eyes and prepare for another grand day of fun, another Butlin's jolliday."

From that moment on, the radio keeps up a perpetual chant over the whole camp. It is informative, briefing the campers for the day's whist-drive or gymnastics, it plays waltz time as the mass hike sets out for the villages around, it follows you round with song or, towards sunset, pours out the pink romance of a violin solo. It leaks through every door and window. It calls, croons, marches and agitates all day, until the final dance.

Billy Butlin is lucky in his name. It is simple, yet sufficiently unusual to be remembered should you not have noticed it on the crockery, the tower, and the staff. It seems somehow to bespeak good humour, warmth and friendliness, and suggests, hale-fellow-well-metery. While some of his staff call him the 'C.O.' and others 'B.B.', he prefers the more matey ring of 'Billy Butlin.' He is a frank and friendly man who thoroughly enjoys the week-ends he spends at the camp.

Most of his campers are working-class, North Country folk, with a common bond of accent, hard work done, money saved for play. They know the community life of mill, mine and factory, and they happily absorb the pleasure of one another's com-

pany. They love dancing together, and in the evenings they pack the theatre for community singing—hearty humming when they don't know the words, tapping their feet, completely spontaneous.

And even the most superior critics who think it all slightly vulgar, intended for the mass-minded who have no individuality or peace of spirit—must admit that the campers go back to work thoroughly refreshed. The weary mother has had her children well cared-for in the nursery, the lonely have been partnered in a dance or at tennis, the pale have been well-fed and caught the sun, the vain have been admired on the top step of the diving-board, and fathers have escaped from the nag of domesticity to the snooker-hall.

Mr. Butlin is not worried by the critics. He turns down 600 applications every week for the summer, and now the campers have asked him to provide winter clubs for them. His shares have risen, and he has no staff difficulties because he pays excellent wages and bonuses.

"They come back year after year. That is my test," he says. And he and his family wouldn't dream of spending their own holidays anywhere else but in a Butlin's camp.

HILDE MARCHANT.

THE HAPPY ELEPHANT

Yes, he's heard of the atom-bomb. He knows all about the breakdown of the Conference—of all the conferences. You can't tell him anything new about bun-rationing. But just now the elephant's thinking of his holiday. It's a good many years since he had the last one, and he means it to be good.

Photographed by WERNER BISCHOF

THE hard-working creature that pulls the heaviest loads. The gentle creature that gets pushed around because, though he's so massive, he's so mild. The patient creature that goes plodding on, when the others have stopped to argue as to why they came this way at all. The tolerant and timeless beast who's often so much wiser than his master, but who makes so much less noise about it. That elephant —the ordinary mass of simple human beings—has been having a pretty thin time lately. Nothing has gone at all as he hoped, and everything only too much as he expected. The war, he hears, is ended —but it's quite uncertain if and when there will be any peace. The war ended in a loud bang; and the main concern of everyone since has been as to when and where the next bang will go off. Proposals for stopping bangs altogether have so far proved to be only the occasion for fresh arguments and threats. The elephant loves a quiet life, and so far he's had to work harder than ever in his life before—or just

as hard. But he refuses to despair, perhaps things will turn out better than they look like doing. The elephant loves his food, and he hoped, when war ended, there would be an extra basinful all round. Instead, he's had to go shorter still, to leave something over for the other animals. The elephant is not very happy about this arrangement, but he accepts it for the reasons given him by those who know better than he does. However, there's one thing the elephant has quite made up his mind about—and nobody is going to interfere with him on that. The elephant means to take a holiday this year. The elephant hasn't had a holiday for some years, and there are some members of his family whom he scarcely knows by sight. This year he means to get away and get to know them. For a week or a couple of weeks, you can count him out. He'll be down by the sea or in the country, rolling in the water, basking on the sand. For a week, or a couple of weeks, he won't be worrying—and the best thing anyone can do about it is just to let him be

Picture Post, August 3, 1946

The Man the Crowd is Waiting For: Wally Hammond 'pads up'
Twenty-six years since he first played for Gloucestershire. Twenty-one years since his first
Test. Yet, today, in 1946, his average is still around the 100 mark.

ENGLAND'S CAPTAIN

**The first M.C.C. side to visit Australia for ten years will be led by
the first ex-professional to captain England—Walter Hammond.**

Photographed by CHARLES HEWITT

The Face of a Gloucestershire Legend
From Cheltenham down to Bristol, they speak of him
in the same breath with 'W.G.'

Hindsight by John Arlott

Cricket in England in 1946 was a symbol of return from the war to an England of peace and normality. In that year, and the sunny Compton—Edrich summer of 1947, people crowded nostalgically and excitedly to the grounds where the first-class game was played. Since then a more technically informed, but less generous, approach by players has coincided with declining public interest in the three-day game. Nowadays there are large attendances only for Tests, touring sides' fixtures, and the one-day matches of the Gillette Cup and Sunday League.

Walter Hammond was made captain of England in 1939 when he became an amateur. In 1951, Tom Dollery, first professional captain of Warwickshire, led his county to the Championship. In 1952 Leonard – later Sir Leonard – Hutton, a professional who was never appointed captain of his native county, Yorkshire, became captain of England who never lost a series under him. In 1962 the distinction between amateur and professional was abolished and English cricket began to take a new, but still not final, shape.

RESEARCH would probably prove conclusively that, over the last quarter-century, the two phrases most used by the newspaper-reading, wireless-listening, match-spectating people of Gloucestershire have been these : "Hammond's in !" and "Hammond's out !" For Walter Reginald Hammond, although, as a soldier's son, he spent his early boyhood in Malta and Dover, was educated at Cirencester Grammar School, and, ever since he played his first match for the county in 1920 at the age of 17, he has been part of the Gloucestershire legend. In the minds of the Bristol docker, the Cotswold farmer, the old Cheltonian, he is bracketed with the most formidable cricketer of all time— W. G. Grace.

Wally Hammond was, in fact, only 24 when he equalled one of W.G.'s records by scoring 1,028 runs between May 1 and May 28 in the season of 1927—two years after playing his first match for England. Since then he has been on three Australian tours and has created a precedent by being selected, in 1938, as the first ex-professional to captain England. (In that year he joined the board of the Marsham Tyre Company.) And now, once more, Wally Hammond has been selected to lead the first M.C.C. side to visit Australia for ten years.

In terms of figures, everybody knows Hammond. Every schoolboy can tell you that it was way back in 1935 that he completed his hundred 100's in First Class cricket; that it was in '33 and '37 that he made thirteen individual centuries. But, statistics apart, Hammond is a little-known figure; though his outward appearance is familiar and memorable to anyone who has ever once seen him at the crease or in the field. The dark blue St. George-crested cap drawn over the right eye; the rock-footed stance; the lofty back-lift of the bat; the punch of the bull shoulders; the catapult momentum that comes from the wrist.

There are things you don't forget. In particular, nobody who has ever bowled against Hammond will

The Shoulder-work of England's Most Forcing Batsman
The ball explodes to the boundary as though it had been fired by a human, self-propelled gun. Hammond makes his drives off either foot as he feels inclined.

know is that there's been a flash and a dive, and the fellow has somehow managed to get his hand between the ball and the ground, and you've had it.

Power and mastery : those are the qualities which invest Hammond on the field. Reserve and disinterestedness : those are the qualities which in the pavilion isolate him—not from his colleagues and his friends, but from interviewers, photographers and other publicists. He himself admits to being allergic to pressmen, confesses that he's 'always been that way.' But among his own kind he starts to be himself—frank, full-blooded, robust,

The Unorthodoxy of Genius
The flat sweep off the leg-stump. A stroke for which every schoolboy would be chided, and which would be fatal for you or me.

ever forget the sensation of being faced by an immovable, morale-destroying mass, solid with mastery. Bowling into that mass feels like tossing peas against Everest. And if you're a batsman and Hammond is fielding close-in, the sensation is no more comfortable. You feel as if you were encircled by this one man, who is standing in the military 'at ease' position, hands behind him, rocking policeman-like on his heels, head back, studying the clouds. Then you make your stroke. The ball travels hard, only six inches above the carpet, and yards clear of Hammond. But the next thing you

The Certain Four to the Long-leg Boundary
It's for Hammond's superlative drive through the covers that most of his admirers remember him. But he's equally firm on the on-side—absolute master of the hook, the glide and the drive wide of mid-on.

Hammond, the Most Effective All-rounder of Our Time
Fascinated by the number of runs he still makes, some people forget how many wickets
he used to take in the '20's and '30's, and the pace he used to get from the pitch.

Hammond the Selector
A conference with Colonel Henson, Gloucestershire C.C. secretary. As a county and England
captain, Hammond has plenty of paper work.

genial; no teetotaller; enjoyer of the good things of
life; brilliant driver of fast sports cars; accomplished ballroom dancer. His sense of fun is school-
boyish; his laugh is big. He has the temperament
that goes with his talents and his taciturn moments
as well. But, in this Narcissistic age, was there ever
a hero less vain?

Hammond's own book, *Cricket My Destiny*,
should be out next month. Modestly, it covers the
field—nearly every ground from Leeds to Cape
Town, New Zealand to Jamaica. And this winter
Hammond returns once more to Australia. During
the war he served six years overseas with the R.A.F.
No cricket to speak of, then. Yet this year, with
only a few weeks of the 1946 season still to go, he
has an average of around 100.

Wally Hammond now talks of retiring on his return
from 'down-under.' See him while you can. The
chances are there'll never be anyone quite like him
again, and your grandsons will feel you have let
them down if you didn't see Hammond on their
behalf.

Not that there's any likelihood of Wally Hammond adopting a wholly sedentary life when he
gives up first-class cricket. It's true that he is an
effective company director and a competent
writer. But his out-of-door activities have never
been confined to cricket. He used to be a Bristol
Rovers footballer. He still plays a good game of
golf. He's above the average at squash and billiards.
When he was at school he knocked out his own
boxing instructor.

Today, among a certain section of the Press and
public, Hammond is coming to be referred to
occasionally as 'the Old Man.' Look up his record
again in 'Wisden'. It's true you'll find from the
dazzling logarithmic table of his records that he's had
a full twenty-five years of it, on all kinds of wickets
—turf and matting—in all varieties of climate, and
against every type of bowling. During that period
he has happened to accomplish probably more than
any other single person towards dissolving the distinction between amateur and professional at home.
On tours abroad his personality has always been
potent in the cause of Imperial unity and friendship. The Old Man, indeed! Was there another man
in Britain who, this year, could have been a sensible
alternative to Wally Hammond as the man to lead
England in Australia? But then, perhaps the title
of Old Man has little to do with age, nothing to do
with decrepitude, and everything to do with the
affection and admiration that Englishmen feel for one
of their finest sportsmen.   PATRICK CAMPBELL.

With Another Century in His Pocket, England's Captain Goes Off Home
Next winter he'll be leading the M.C.C. team 'down-under'—his fourth Australian tour. When
that's all over, Wally Hammond thinks he may feel like retiring.

Picture Post, August 10, 1946

William Empson: News Editor, Eastern Service
Born in 1906, Empson has been a lecturer in English Literature in China and Japan. He returned to this country in 1939. His poems are inclined to be cynical and fatalistic, at times almost wilfully obscure. Often his work has a tragic beauty, especially when he is concerned with emotions rather than with ideas. But it is usually complex and intellectual.

Roy Campbell: Talks Producer, British Service
A South-African, Campbell was born in 1901, and has lived in France, Spain and Portugal. In his latest book he answers criticism of his sympathies with Franco during the Spanish Civil War. Many feel his law of force 'Let nobody deride the Donkey's jaw,' out of place in poetry. But he is a master of words.

'A NEST OF SINGING BIRDS'

Even a bad novelist can often live on the money his books bring in. But poets, even good poets, find they have to have jobs as well. A number of them feel that the B.B.C. offers the kind of jobs they like.

POETS are not such addicts of solitude as they are sometimes thought to be. Like painters, they have a tradition for getting together in groups. As far as one can ascertain they don't do it to talk about poetry, any more than plumbers to talk about pipes, or plovers to jostle feathers over the growing menace of egg-collectors. In the sixteenth century they found themselves together in the Mermaid Tavern; in the early nineteenth century they gathered round the lakes; in the early 1900's they seemed to take to the Civil Service; at present they are inclined to gather in and around B.B.C. offices and studios in London.

There they get about their jobs as producers, script-writers, news-editors, or whatever they are paid for doing in an ordinary workaday way which earns them their bread-and-butter—and beer. And all along they go on being poets. "How do they do it?" you may ask. "I always thought poets needed lots of time to themselves to sit about and dream; that they were the kind of people who were useless once they left their ivory towers and stepped out into the steel and concrete world."

Patric Dickinson, Poetry Editor at the B.B.C., has something to say in answer to that. He maintains that it is more difficult to be a poet at the present time than ever before in the history of literature. He finds that when he wants to write he is forced by the routine nature of his job to do something else. He is responsible for the 'Time for Verse' programme, which goes on the air every Sunday night, and for other regular programmes to do with poetry. He has more-or-less fixed office hours, during which he has to read through published and unpublished poetry, answer correspondence, contact readers for his programmes, arrange rehearsals of his programmes, and generally tie up all the administrative ends which fringe his job as poetry editor. But in spite of this and having to leave his flat in Notting Hill at a fixed time every morning, he still writes poetry. To him, and to the other poets at the B.B.C., as with most modern poets, it's a question of carrying a poem around until it must be written. Dickinson's words could well be spoken by most poets. He says "I do not write a poem unless I passionately feel I want to write it. It is carried around with me

everywhere rather like an unborn child. Then, if it is to see light of day eventually, it makes its own birth. It will be written, in spite of everything, if I feel its body grow in the imagination with sufficient urgency.

"To begin to write a poem is the hardest part of all. There is so much to be said, and one doesn't always know where to begin. That is a sign that the poem is not yet ready to be born. Once the poem is begun, the rest follows—as a rule—comparatively quickly." Dickinson's main work, *Theseus and the Minotaur*—a dramatic poem for radio production—was in his mind for nearly a year before he set pen to paper. After that he worked during every free evening until it was finished, always re-writing and correcting. Other things continually interfered with his writing, and the mundane ends would soon have tangled if he had said "I must write my poem first." But at last it was finished and produced on the radio—successfully. Patric Dickinson's instance is typical of many poets—inside and outside the B.B.C. They have to do two jobs at once. For poetry is the least remunerative of all the fine arts.

John Arlott : Talks Producer, Eastern Service
At 32, Arlott writes about things everybody can see—country fairs
or cricket matches. But he is fundamentally concerned with the
impressions ordinary things make on his mind. His most recent work
is a sequence of sonnets on a Roman Clausentum near Southampton,
his home until 1945. He broadcasts cricket commentaries to India.

Dylan Thomas : A Non-Staff Reader and Writer
Born in 1914, Thomas made a reputation as a poet before he was twenty.
He has written for newspapers and films. He is one of the few modern poets
proclaimed as a genius by critics generally. His themes are the old poetic
themes of birth, love and death which he regenerates in exciting language
which has a lot of the Bible and the singing of his native Wales in it.

Rayner Heppenstall : Producer
Yorkshireman, born in 1911, Heppenstall has
an ease of style which is deceptive. His interests,
witchcraft and anything with mystery about it
are reflected in his poems. He has written two
novels and a book on ballet. and he came to
the B.B.C. from the Army ranks a year ago.

Louis MacNeice : Producer
Irishman, classical scholar, university lecturer,
born in 1907, his poems are typical of that
written in the 1930's. They reflect the tragedy
of modern life, with its political and social
uncertainty. He has worked as feature-
writer and producer at the B.B.C. since 1941.

James Monahan : Assistant Director
Born in 1912, a journalist before serving in
the Commandos, Monahan now works in
the European Service. Much of his poetry
has a quiet, retrospective, unwarlike quality.
He believes his being a poet saved him from
becoming 'a mental casualty' of war.

Patric Dickinson, in Charge of B.B.C. Poetry Programmes, at a Broadcast: Flora Robson, the Actress, Goes Through the Script

Born in 1914, Dickinson left Cambridge to
be a schoolmaster. Badly injured in the war,
he was invalided out of the Army. He wrote
war propaganda for the B.B.C. Foreign
Service before entering his present job.

Geoffrey Dearmer: Assistant Director
A war poet of the pre-atomic era, born in
1893. He saw trench warfare in a way which
resembles that of Wilfred Owen, the poet
concerned with 'the pity of war.' Apart
from verse he writes novels. He's been
examiner of plays to the Lord Chamberlain.

Valentine Dyall: 'The Man in Black' as a Poetry Reader
His voice is well known for its sinister and ominous qualities. But he can feel the emotions in the
poetry he reads. He's a friend of most of the poets at the B.B.C. and likes meeting them as much as
possible. But has less chance to do so than when he worked with the B.B.C. Repertory Company

Picture Post, October 12, 1946

HOW LAURENCE OLIVIER PLAYS
KING LEAR

The Old Vic Company presents ' King Lear ' at the New Theatre, London. Laurence Olivier produced the play and acts himself the difficult and tremendous part of Lear. In doing so this great actor adds another to his list of masterly Shakespearian portraits.

Photographed by K. HUTTON

The First Betrayal, and the First Fear of Madness
Cordelia is banished; Goneril has betrayed him. Lear kneels and prays: "O, let me not be mad, not mad, sweet heaven! Keep me in temper: I would not be mad!"

The Op
Lear has launched his grotesque and c
tions, and Cordelia (Joyce Redman), wi

THERE were times when the whimsical fancy of the essayist Charles Lamb would turn his head a little. He wrote, and Hazlitt quoted him respectfully, that "the Lear of Shakespeare cannot be acted. The contemptible machinery with which they mimic the storm he goes out in is not more inadequate to represent the horrors of the real elements than any actor can be to represent Lear."

This is nonsense. For one thing, a man has just done it. But the superstition is not dead, and a good many people have come to the same conclusion as Lamb on the way home from seeing a good many Lears. And, since in many ways the part of Lear is not more difficult than Hamlet, or, if it comes to that, Cleopatra, it is interesting to ask what all the to-do is about. For these very people who doubt whether the play is playable insist at the same time that it is one of the four 'great' tragedies, and probably the greatest of all.

The trouble is that the admirers who cry : "It's a wonderful play—don't touch it !" have seen a whole string of Lears that did not convince. The stage performance has affected them less than when they read the play at school. And so, rather than conclude that Shakespeare slipped, or that Mr. So-and-So did not know what he was doing when he played it, they have decided that it is the very magnitude and poetic power of the part which defeats the puny efforts of man. It is too 'sublime,' too 'titanic.' Canonise it. Promote it to holy writ. Make a Tales-from-Shakespeare version for the children, to teach them filial piety. But better not try acting it.

In fact, *Lear* is of all plays the most in danger of being killed with kindness and smothered with holy awe. And when every ambitious actor or producer decides that the time has come when he must take

Picture Post, October 12, 1946

ene In Olivier's Production of 'King Lear': Cordelia Makes the Speech That Banishes and Disinherits Her
npetition to discover which daughter loves him most. Goneril (Pamela Brown) and Regan (Margaret Leighton) have delivered their extravagant protesta-
k of her father's obstinacy, says simply: "I love your majesty according to my bond; nor more nor less." Kent (Nicholas Hannen) intercedes for her in vain.

One Daughter Taunts Him

Regan is insolent. "O, sir, you are old; Nature in
you stands on the very verge of her confine. . . ."

Another Listens Unmoved to His Curses

Lear storms at Goneril: "Turn all her mother's pains and benefits to laughter and contempt;
that she may feel how sharper than a serpent's tooth it is to have a thankless child!"

The Unique Quality in Laurence Olivier's King Lear: the Touching Gentleness with Which he Plays the Quieter Scenes
Lear—now mad—with the Earl of Gloucester who has been blinded for befriending him when he was driven out into the storm by his daughters. To moments in this scene, to the scene in which Edgar feigns madness, to some of his scenes with the Fool and with Cordelia, Olivier brings a really beautiful and touching quietness, which throws up the splendid high-lights of his rage.

a swing at it for the sake of his reputation, he has to do so in the teeth of a prejudice that it can't really be done at all.

All that is necessary to make nonsense of these arguments is for somebody to start from the assumption that the matters with which the play deals are not incomprehensible, find out what they are about, or at any rate evolve a coherent version, and then act it. And most people would agree that Laurence Olivier has done it, and magnificently. To say it can't be done in the face of this performance would be like denying the giraffe before your eyes. To say it can't be done by anyone of much less than great actor's stature is another matter, and, I should say, the whole point. The trouble is that you can no more dissuade a man from trying to act Lear, if he thinks he understands the play and can play it, than you can stop a fat lady from wearing slim lady's clothes if she refuses to believe she *is* fat.

Obviously it is the part of King Lear himself that worries people, not the general body of the play, which is no more unplausible or unactable than most Elizabethan plays. And obviously it is the madness in the part, and the feeling that royal dignity doesn't go with gallivanting about in storms, and behaving like a lunatic. When the madness moves on the grand scale, when it raves and shouts for nature's moulds to crack, that is all right. It may fail, either dismally or spectacularly, to move or terrify, but at least it isn't embarrassing, not indecent exposure of the soul. But when it comes to the level of dodderings about mice and toasted cheese; when it is suddenly ludicrous in mid-tragedy ('Ha ! Goneril with a white beard !'), or when the old king goes cavorting unregally with senile giggles into the wings, it becomes a most delicate affair for the actor, a matter of his sensitivity or lack of it, which will certainly communicate itself to an audience ready to be put off by the first wrong note. To be an obstinate old fool, a man much sinned against, and

at the same time every inch a king is the proposition before him.

Some think Olivier just misses the heights, or sacrifices them to what, for some reason, they consider the mere levels of the part, and that he fails to convey regality. It is difficult to see where Shakespeare provides for conveying regality except indirectly in the terrifying process of Lear's losing it. And in fact it is never really lost. One does not doubt that he is a king, any more than one doubts that he is also a very foolish, fond old man. The play has hardly begun before those about him are shaking their heads over the increasing signs of dotage, which his own behaviour quickly confirms. So that, if he is to be regal, it has got to be more in his manner of speech than in his words.

For Olivier, Lear is a Problem Solved

What seems certain is that Olivier has solved, for himself at least, and therefore for the audience while it sits there, the problem of what *King Lear* is *about*. And one gets the impression that the first step to solving it was to assume that Shakespeare, after all, knew what he was doing, that he was not so 'fairly caught in the web of his own imagination' that he wrote a play when he had a poem in mind.

Also, it was right not to assume that 'lower key' scenes are the easiest, or the least impressive and significant. One of the most striking scenes in the play is the fifth scene of Act 1, when Lear, after his bitter quarrel with Goneril, flaying her without mercy, has cast her off, and sits in the palace court-yard with his Fool. It is the beginning of betrayal, the setting-in of the rot. And it is, after all, the scene which ends with "O, let me not be mad, not mad, sweet heaven ! Keep me in temper : I would not be mad !" Olivier plays the scene in such a way that it leads logically and movingly to that climax. Lear knows already, though he has not admitted it to himself, that he has wronged Cordelia. He has a

last hope that Regan will not turn against him, but he is not over-confident. Since it has been his life-long habit to allow himself to be diverted by jesters, he involuntarily turns half an ear to his Fool's attempts to wake him to his folly. And, since neither he nor the jester are much in the mood for jesting, the effect is extraordinarily touching, not least because Alec Guinness is a very touching Fool.

For the production as a whole one cannot say quite as much. Of course it is always adequate, and sometimes it is magnificent. Though the settings are not highly imaginative, and occasionally rather cardboard Gothic, they serve. But the main weakness is simply that there are not enough first-class actors in the world, or in the same part of the world at the same time. The perfect cast is a phenomenon that does now and then occur, but this is scarcely it. That the audience is not suitably stirred, for instance, by Edmund's self-introduction and the progress of his plot, is no doubt partly due to the fact that nobody today is as preoccupied with bastardy as the Elizabethans were. But it is also because Peter Copley, though he manages bravely, has not the infernal spark that Edmund needs. That he was not entirely credible would not have mattered had he been more of an irresistible force.

The most impressive performances—apart from Olivier's own—are those of Pamela Brown and Margaret Leighton as Goneril and Regan. That they are never credible in cold blood is no matter at all, for they seldom permit one's blood to get much below boiling-point. And they do not play as identical twins of wickedness. Goneril is played by Pamela Brown with a cutting edge that glints through even when she melts for Edmund. Margaret Leighton puts into Regan a sort of soft sadism, a flabby-graceful sensuality that breaks into gross brutality when she is stung by jealousy of her sister. If Lear is cruelly treated, Olivier is well served.

LORNA HAY.

Lear at the Height of his Madness: One of Shakespeare's Most Overwhelming Scenes Gets the Acting it Demands
Too many Lears rant their way through, tearing themselves to fragments over their interpretation. Olivier moves through this exacting part with power, but power always in control. He has great dignity—but it is the dignity of a humble man who is a king, not the assumption of royalty by a hollow shell.

1947

On 1 January 1947 plaques were placed at the entrance to every British coalmine, announcing 'This colliery is now managed by the National Coal Board on behalf of the People'. It was an emotional moment for veterans of the Labour Party, who had spent a lifetime working for this. To the miner, it meant only that 'the boss', now serving a remote organization in London, seemed less able to take decisions than before nationalization. The miners were a tired and ageing force, with a stormy industrial history. There was a great deal of absenteeism among them.

Snow, which had begun falling in December 1946, went on falling through the first weeks of January. By the end of the month the country was paralysed by drifts fourteen feet deep, transport was at a standstill, and the inadequate stocks of coal at power stations were virtually exhausted. It became an offence under the Defence Regulations to keep the home electric fires burning at times when factories were working. Early in February, industry in the south, the midlands and the north-west had its electricity cut altogether. Unemployment rose temporarily over the $2\frac{1}{2}$ million mark. Exports fell to practically nothing. The Big Freeze lasted until the middle of March, to be followed by floods which devastated arable land and drowned thousands of cattle. Over the previous year, inflation had led to a substantial rise in American prices, and by June 1947 only £250 million remained of the American loan, and £125 million of a later dollar loan from Canada. In July, under the terms of the loan agreement, sterling had to become a convertible currency.

In February, as the probable development of events became apparent, Britain warned America that she could no longer continue the economic aid to Greece and Turkey without which it was feared they would collapse into the Communist camp. On 12 March President Truman appeared personally before Congress to announce the Truman Doctrine, not only of American aid for Greece and Turkey, but for any free people 'who are resisting attempted subjugation by armed minorities or by outside pressures'. Three months later, the American Secretary of State, General Marshall, offered aid to any Government willing to assist in the task of recovery. The offer was eagerly grasped by Western Europe, rejected by the Soviet Union and its eastern European allies.

The effects of Marshall Aid were not immediately apparent to a Britain drying out in a golden summer after the winter of freeze and flood. Convertibility doubled the drawing rate on the dollar reserves, and had to be suspended after only a month. Drastic cuts were made in dollar imports of tobacco, petrol and newsprint. The meat ration fell to 1s. 2d. worth a week. Attlee told the Commons 'We are engaged in another Battle of Britain', and his Chancellor, Hugh Dalton, reinforced the point by raising the price of cigarettes from 2s. 4d. to 3s. 4d. for twenty.

Abroad, Attlee hastened the pace of disengagement in Asia by setting a time-limit for the bickering Indian leaders to reach agreement about partition. On 15 August King George VI laid down the imperial Indian crown, and power passed to the self-governing dominions of India and Pakistan. Communal massacres broke out, in which half-a-million people died, but war had hardened men's minds to death, and the massacres passed almost unnoticed as a regrettable necessity. Burma and Ceylon followed India and Pakistan to independence, and Burma formally withdrew from the Commonwealth.

In Palestine, a United Nations Special Committee — to which Britain had passed this troublesome baby — recommended an end to the British mandate as soon as possible, and partition between Arab and Jewish states which would be politically independent, though economically interdependent. The Arab countries showed what they thought of this optimistic solution by preparing to sweep the Jews into the sea as soon as the British withdrew. The Jews made their own preparations, which proved more adequate.

On the whole, the British withdrawal from empire passed more smoothly than that of the French, fighting a costly war to hold Vietnam and Laos, or the Dutch, with their brutal 'police action' in what became Indonesia. But there were Churchillian thunderings about 'scuttle' and 'surrender' which added to the miasma of discontent spread by increasing austerity and a rising cost of living.

At the end of the year, the British received some much-needed reassurance that their world had not changed out of all recognition. Six reigning monarchs, and ex-monarchs and princelings innumerable, assembled in London for the wedding of the heir to the Throne, Princess Elizabeth, to Lieutenant Philip Mountbatten R.N. It was one of the largest gatherings of royalty of the century, and a distinguished foreign guest was able to tell the world that 'A country which can throw such a party as that will never go under'.

Laurence Thompson

Europe's problem of the refugees. Millions of people displaced by the war are still milling about in Europe. They are collected into vast camps from which they will slowly be returned home or resettled.

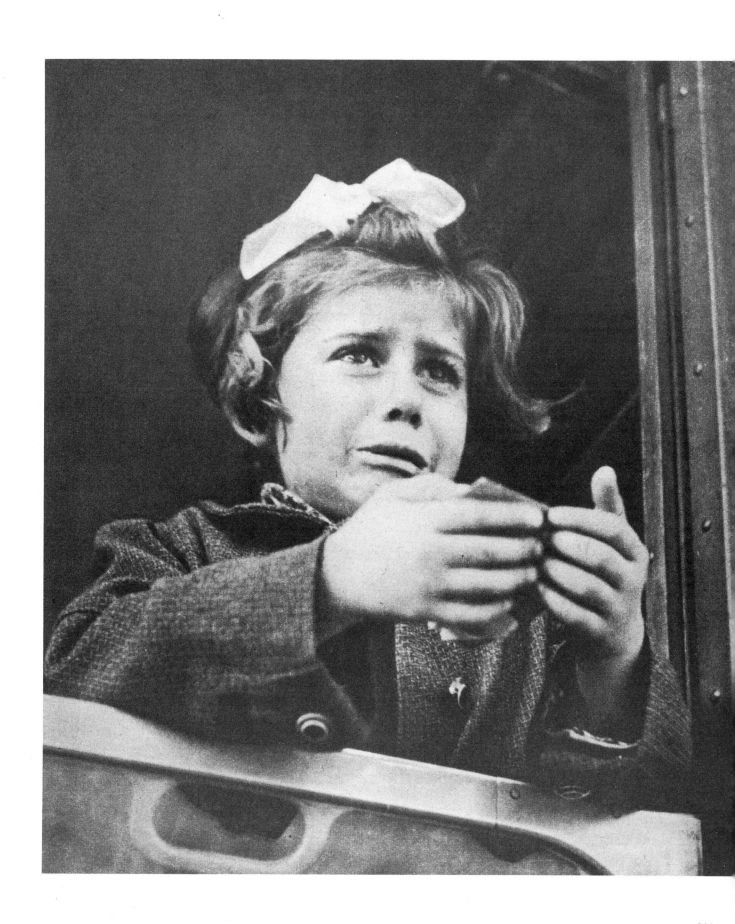

PICTURE POST

A Symbol of British Industry Today? Steam-roller on a Coal-Site after one of Winter's Many Snowstorms

AFTER THE THAW, THE PROBLEM REMAINS

The snow goes and comes again—and goes. Slowly British industry thaws out. Slowly the machine gets under way again. But what kind of a machine is it? And how is it going to get us through the next few years?

ONLY in July of last year was the American Loan approved. By February 24 of this year, with a large part of British industry at a stand-still, well over a quarter of the total amount of £937,500,000 had already been spent. Precisely how the £250,000,000 had gone was anybody's guess, because figures of amounts spent by Britain in U.S. on particular kinds of goods include dollars earned in the course of trade. What was clear was that, in the year 1946, Britain had spent £55,000,000 on American tobacco, £43,000,000 on American dairy produce, and £18,000,000 on American films. Out of the loan's £250,000,000 used up in seven months, not more than £5,000,000 had been spent on machinery, and about £3,000,000 on ships. From these figures two facts stood out a mile. First, that at this rate the loan would scarcely last two years. Second, that British industry would be little, if any, better off when it was gone. The sole reason which had induced many doubters to accept the idea of the loan was that it was to be spent in re-equipping Britain's basic industries. The cost of re-equipping the cotton industry alone has been reckoned at something like £50,000,000 at pre-war prices. The sum needed to restore British industry merely to its 1939 level has been estimated at £885,000,000. Instead of being used for these essential purposes, the loan was being puffed away in smoke, gaped at in films, eaten in scrambled-eggs, and even chewed away in gum.

Meantime, the machinery of British industry—battered and bombed, over-worked and under-tended during six years of war—was being called upon to produce as never before. The employers, managers and directors of British firms—facing every possible difficulty in acquiring supplies of any kind—were being urged to raise output far above anything yet achieved. The workers of Britain—tired and not far from hunger—were being asked to surpass their own war-time efforts. And the grim fact is that all these demands are necessary.

Clearly there have been Government muddles. How was it possible—men asked angrily—for a Government with a plan to go on filling the shops with electrical goods when power stations for electricity were heading for a crack-up? How could a Government see so short a distance ahead that on Thursday it should be a man's patriotic duty to work all out, and on Monday his patriotic duty not to go to work? All this was true, but beside the point compared to the tasks that face us all. Government, employers and workers have now to find a line on which they can pull together as they have never pulled before. Our industries have got to be modernised—and modernised while working at top-speed. The days in front will in some respects be tougher than the days behind. The alternative? A few more months of smoke-puffing and gum-chewing—followed by 'austerity' on a scale unknown here for a hundred years.

Vol. 35. No. 2

PICTURE POST

April 12, 1947

In a Furnished Room in Brixton a Deserter Prepares to Surrender
His name is Frederick Madigan. His age is 24. He was an Army driver. During the Western
Front fighting he came home on leave, found his father's house bombed, and deserted. This morning
he has decided to give himself up. His wife makes his shaving kit up into a parcel.

ONE OUTLAW RETURNS

**In January of this year a Government announcement called
on the 20,000 deserters to give themselves up. Eight weeks
later, 837 had done so. Here is the story of one of these few.**

Photographed by CHARLES E. HEWITT

"WANT your hair-cream along with you, Fred?"
asked the trim young woman in the spotless
bed-sitting in Brixton. The wireless-box, which
relayed music from the shop round the corner, was
churning out Rita Hayworth's song from *Cover Girl*
—'Long Ago and Far Away'. "Sure," said Fred,
who had been far away himself. "What'll they want
to send you to Germany for?" asked Mrs. Fred.
"That's where I dropped out from, that's where
they'll send me back to, that's the Army," said Fred

equably. Mrs. Fred got up and looked out of the
window, along the ledge of which lay a line of green
tomatoes waiting for the sun. "I believe you *want* to
go to Germany, I believe you've got some fräuleins
there," said Mrs. Fred, with a gallant smile. "Those
tomatoes shouldn't be too long ripening-up now,"
said Fred. He had been a greengrocer, and he knew.
"Not if they don't go bad, meantime," said Mrs.
Fred. The calendar on the wall showed March 4,
1947—the D-Day of Fred's own choice. The alarm

He Arrives at Scotland Yard
When he left home, he walked in to the first
guardroom he saw—and was directed here.

Under Close Arrest He Gives His Particulars

For a quarter of an hour in Scotland Yard, after he has announced that he's a deserter, he has an escort. Then he is given a railway warrant to the transit camp.

Under Open Arrest, He Makes His Own Way to the Transit Camp

No escort. No indication of any kind that he is not an ordinary passenger. At any point on the journey from Liverpool Street to Harwich, he could change his mind if he wished.

A Hot Meal in the Mess-Hall

There's a hot meal laid on for him at Harwich, and there's Cook Corporal D. Guest to serve it.

clock on the mantelshelf went ticking on towards his H-hour—10 o'clock. "Long ago and far away, I dreamed a dream that you were here beside me," sang the yearning voice from the wireless box.

That wireless box had been important in Fred's life. For it was that which had uttered the broadcast report of the Defence Minister's statement to the House of Commons on the subject of deserters. And it was that, in turn, which had first prompted Fred to consider giving himself up. That had been January 22, 1947. Mr. Alexander had said that there were nearly 20,000 deserters outstanding. The

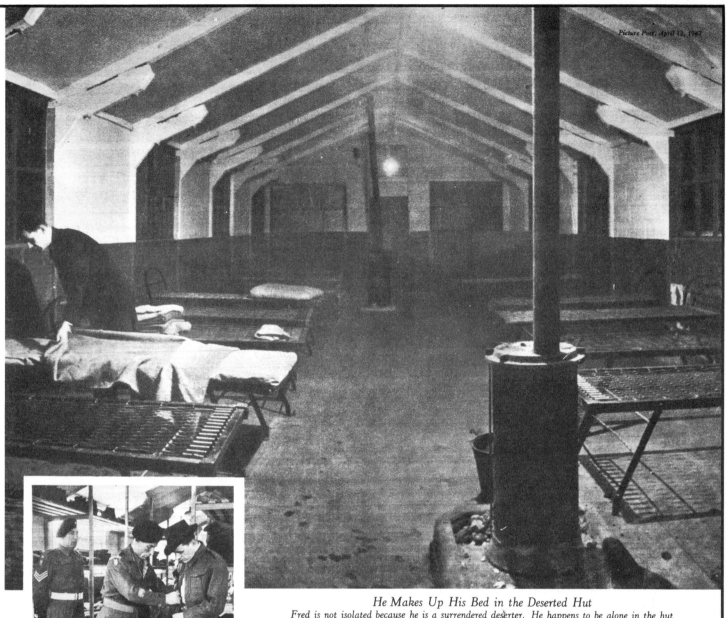

He Makes Up His Bed in the Deserted Hut
Fred is not isolated because he is a surrendered deserter. He happens to be alone in the hut because the last batch of leave-men have just gone out, and the next batch have not yet come in. The only difference between Fred and them is that he must not leave the camp.

He Gets Kitted Out Once Again
R.Q.M.S. L. Miles matches his battledress, while Provost Sgt. J. F. Reddan looks on.

Government had already announced that there could be no amnesty for them, since that would give them preferential treatment. "But," said Mr. Alexander, "it is to the advantage and well-being of the men themselves and of the nation as a whole that they should take steps now which will enable them eventually to resume normal lives as free citizens. ... Those who surrender voluntarily by March 31, 1947, will have this fact and any other mitigating circumstances taken into account when their cases are determined."

In other words, most deserters had been a dead

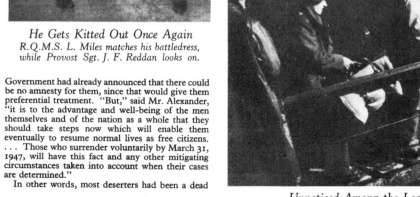

Unnoticed Among the Leave-men, He Embarks for Germany
On Tuesday he gave himself up. On the evening of Wednesday he goes on board at Harwich. At 5.45 a.m. on Thursday he arrives at Hook of Holland—still without an escort.

Back Again After Two Years, the Absentee is Taken Before His C.O.
It was when his unit was in North-West Europe that Fred Madigan went absent. His unit has since been disbanded; so he is ordered to report to a Reinforcement Holding Unit. The C.O. decides that there is a case to answer and remands Madigan for a 'summary of evidence.'

loss to their country during the war; and the Government was now trying to face the question of whether or not it was inevitable that these men should continue to be a dead loss to their country, world without end, in peace.

That was the nation's problem. Mr. Alexander's statement represented the Government's attempt at a solution of that problem. Was it really a solution? In the case of Fred, for instance? Fred himself clearly thought it might be. His own instinct was to give himself up. But for several months now he'd been hoping, privately, to marry a girl who was working in NAAFI. He'd known her about a year. Half-way through that year she'd found out about Fred's 'past' from his sister. So now, when Fred heard the Government's announcement, he went along and talked it over with the girl he wanted to marry. The girl agreed that the best thing for him to do was to surrender. She agreed, too, to get married. On February 15th, they got married. On March 4 she packed his shaving kit neatly in a small brown paper parcel and watched him walk out through the front door into the dree Brixton morning. He strolled along at leisure, heading down Battersea way, making for the first place he could remember where there were soldiers. He went in through the barracks gate and stopped at the guardroom door. "Yes, mate?" said the guard corporal. "I've come to surrender," said Fred. "You've come to *what*?" said the corporal. "I'm a deserter surrendering," Fred elaborated. "Cor!" said the corporal. He jerked his thumb at Fred towards the guardroom stove, and went off himself to find a higher level.

The higher level directed Fred to the Garrison Sergeant-major at Scotland Yard, where, for a quarter of an hour, Fred found himself under close arrest. Then, after he had given particulars about himself and his old unit, he was placed under open

A Fortnight After His Surrender, He Gets His Court Martial
Madigan has had a long session with his defending officer. Now he faces trial by a court consisting of a major, as President, with two captains from another unit.

Picture Post, April 12, 1947

arrest—i.e. the escort was withdrawn—and he was given a warrant to a transit camp at Harwich, and sent off by himself on his journey to the Rhine.

In the same railway carriage as Fred, on the trip from Liverpool Street to Harwich, were three young soldiers going back to Germany from leave. Two of them wore the France and Germany star. As they talked, the familiar military phrases—the 'guards' and the 'fatigues' and the 'caps-offs' and the 'curtains'—rattled, like a shower of hail-stones, against Fred's corner of the carriage. It's true that they didn't know about Fred. But the people at the Transit Camp—from the C.O. to the R.S.M. and thence to the men in the cookhouse—did know about him; and their attitude was entirely matter-of-fact. Most of them were detached, impartial, and quite unwilling to prejudge him. A few were curious. Curious about why he'd deserted: even more curious about why he'd given himself up.

And why had Fred deserted? His own account of his reasons for doing so was as inarticulate as his picture of the Normandy campaign was incoherent. But it seems that Fred was a driver in a mortar platoon. When his unit were up in Holland, some months after the Second Front opened, Fred got his normal privilege leave to England. He came back to Clapham to find that his father's house had been bombed, and that his father and fifteen-year-old brother were carrying on existence among the rubble of the bottom floor of the house. Fred's mother (she had eleven children in all) had been killed in a car smash shortly before D-Day. "There seemed to be trouble all round," said Fred. "Somehow I didn't seem to care what happened." So he decided to stay "and help father." He "had never minded" the Army. And, when he left Holland to go on leave, he had no intention of deserting.

Yet now here he was, living in a furnished room in Stockwell at an address which he concealed even from his father. Still, father had had plenty of callers. First, a red-cap Sergeant; then the police.

As for Fred, he managed to live, for a week or two, on his leave money. Then he met a man in the local who offered him a partnership in his green-grocery. Fred started to serve in the shop in the Waterloo Bridge Road and to pass the time of day with the policemen who came in for a pound of apples. He had never had his photograph taken in his life. He had burnt his A.B.64 and all his other Army documents. He had given his battle-dress to his brother. He had no ration book; but he ate a lot at cafés. No identity card; but, in two years, he was never asked to produce one.

After several months, Fred and his partner parted company. He borrowed a pair of scales, hired a barrow from Clapham, bought fruit from Covent Garden and started selling it outside cinemas, moving on whenever a policeman appeared, so as to keep in step with the law. When fruit became scarce, Fred bought soda wholesale at about 1½d. a pound, and sold it for 2d. a pound in Brixton market. That's how he lived for over two years, and that's how he was earning a living nearly up to the time he gave himself up on March 4.

Fred's court-martial was fixed to be held in Germany on March 19, 1947. He was found guilty of desertion and sentenced to two years' hard labour. The following morning the sentence was reduced to eighteen months by the Convening Officer, and it was 'promulgated,' i.e., announced, to Fred that afternoon. The sentence will now be reviewed periodically, at least once every three months, and the question of suspending it considered.

Between January 22, 1947, the day when the Government announcement was published, and March 19, 1947, the day fixed for Fred's court-martial, 837 deserters surrendered. During the same period 440 were apprehended. 75 per cent. of sentences during the period were for six months and under. 25 per cent. were for a longer term than six months. Of these 25 per cent., the majority were men who had been apprehended.

Still, 837 men giving themselves up out of a total of nearly 20,000—it hardly makes the Government 'offer' sound like the answer to the problem.

Though that, of course, is not to say that the Army's new procedure with deserters is not quick and efficient. It is. The period from the day when Fred gave himself up to the day when he knew his fate was only a fortnight. And, of course, much of his sentence is likely to be suspended. But, as Fred remarked to himself when he first heard what he'd got: "Is this supposed to encourage the others?"
LIONEL BIRCH.

The First Week-end of the 18 Months' Sentence
He is taken to the Unit's 'cage'. After the week-end he will go to the detention barracks. His sentence will be reviewed at least every three months. Much of it is likely to be remitted.

THE FOUR WHO DISCUSSED THE PROBLEM:

EDWARD ATIYAH: *Secretary-General of the Arab Office, London*

Has held his present post since its creation two years ago. The Arab office is sponsored by various Arab Governments and the Arab League, and acts as their mouthpiece in London. A Lebanese Christian, he is 43 years old, was educated at Victoria College, Egypt, and Oxford. Before taking up his present job, was Public Relations Officer to the Sudan Government for 19 years. Has contributed a number of articles on Arab affairs to the British and U.S. press, and last year published a book "An Arab Tells His Story." Attended the UNO meeting in the United States last November.

THOMAS REID: *66 year old Labour M.P. for Swindon*

His detailed knowledge of Palestine dates from 1938, when he was a member of the Commission which was formed to prepare a detailed plan for partition. The Commission eventually rejected partition, and the Chamberlain Government dropped the idea, adopting the White Paper policy which restricted Jewish immigration and prohibited land sales to Jews in large areas of Palestine. Previously Reid had gained wide experience of Colonial affairs from 25 years in the Ceylon Civil Service. In 1933 he was appointed Financial Commissioner to report on the Seychelles Colony.

CONVERSATIONS ON WORLD PROBLEMS:

PALESTINE: CAN DEADLOCK BE BROKEN?

On these pages we begin an entirely new journalistic experiment. We are inviting leading authorities on controversial problems to come together and try, in talk, to hammer out the greatest common measure of agreement. We are asking them to leave fixed opinion behind and come to the discussion with an open mind—hoping to convince, but willing to be convinced. We begin with perhaps the toughest problem of all—the controversy between Jews and Arabs over the right to live in Palestine. We believe readers will find here—as we did—not only an exceedingly high level of discussion, but a notable readiness to understand the other man's point of view.

Photographed by FELIX H. MAN

CROSSMAN: Shall I put briefly forward how I see the problem, having been on the 18th Commission? Tom Reid was on about the 15th. Let me list the facts as I saw them. First the most provocative—the co-existence of two nations. People might tell me Jew and Arab get on socially and individually. That is true. So did Sudeten Germans and Czechs, but here are two nations who assert the right to the whole country; whatever their politicians say, emotionally and traditionally they feel their absolute right to the whole country. Point No. 2: Each nation feels that because of the political situation in the Middle East it is not justice which prevails but force, and therefore each feels it must preserve to itself the right to use force. Thirdly, the gradual deterioration of law and order to a point where you have now a régime which has the consent of neither community. The existence of a British ghetto with the British officials driven into it, is the symbol of the British position in Palestine.

ATIYAH: *I agree with this statement of the factual position. The most crucial fact is that you have two peoples existing side by side, each claiming the country as by right. The Arabs maintain irrefutably that the two peoples do not stand on the same footing as regards the justice of their claims to the country. The Arabs are the indigenous population. They*

have been there for centuries; as Arabs for nearly 1,500 years, since the Moslem conquest of the 7th century. But they have an older claim in the sense that they are the descendants of the very first population of the country, before the original Jewish. . . .

BUBER: So far as I'm concerned, I cannot acknowledge the identity of the Arabs of today with that population, which was before the immigration of the Hebrews from Egypt to Palestine.

CROSSMAN: *So we have to record the fact that the two communities both put forward a long historical tradition. We have to record that there is a divergence.*

ATIYAH: From my point of view it is quite enough to say that in 1917, when the whole problem was created by the Balfour Declaration, Palestine was inhabited by a population which was 90-per-cent. Arab in the sense that it was part of the whole Arab community that inhabits the Middle East, that it was Arab by language and culture, and that this population had been the indigenous population of the country for centuries.

BUBER: *I cannot accept that the position has been created by the Balfour Declaration.*

R. H. S. CROSSMAN: *Labour M.P. for Coventry East*

Was a member of the recent Anglo-U.S. Commission on Palestine, whose report recommended continuation of the British mandate and immediate admission of 100,000 Jews. Has since written a book on the Palestine problem. During the war he served on the Psychological Warfare Division of Eisenhower's headquarters in Europe, and in Algiers. He had a brilliant academic career at Oxford, where he was a scholar of New College, with a First in Moderations and Greats. He was a fellow and tutor of New College, 1930–37, and is at present Assistant Editor of the *New Statesman and Nation.*

PROF. MARTIN BUBER: *Professor of Sociology at Jerusalem University*

Is at present making his first tour of Europe since the war. Renowned as a writer on religion and ethics, who has made a special study of the Jewish mystic sect, the Chassidim. Came under the influence of Dr. Herzl, the founder of modern Zionism 46 years ago, and has been a prominent Zionist ever since. Was Professor of Ethics and Religion at Frankfort University from 1925 until the advent of Hitler, when he retired, but remained in Germany for some time as a leader of Jewish affairs. At one time editor of *Der Jude,* the monthly organ of Jewish European intellectuals.

REID: When Edward said that at the end of the first World War the population was 90 per cent. Arab, I think he was leaving out the Bedouin who come and go from Palestine. Of the 10 per cent. Jewish population, about one-third were recent emigrants since 1890, so I think what Edward says about Palestine really being an Arab country is correct.

CROSSMAN: *We are all agreed that it was Arab in 1917.*

BUBER: Statistically I agree, but it does not say it is an Arab country.

ATIYAH: *It seems to me there is only one criterion which establishes the right of any people to the country they inhabit, and that is long and continued possession. If length of occupation does not give a people a right to its country, can you point out any other criterion, in international morality, by which such a right can be established?*

CROSSMAN: You have raised a point on which Tom Reid and I, as Europeans, are in difficulty, because it concerns overseas settlement. The British went to Australia, New Zealand and Tasmania, and the Americans went to America. Many of these occupations took place within the last hundred years, so I suppose every European has, in a sense, a split conscience on the subject of overseas colonial settlement.

BUBER: *I agree.*

CROSSMAN: Europeans have gone overseas and taken other peoples' territories, and I have often put it to myself that perhaps the ironic bad luck which asserts itself with the Jews is that they should be almost the last of the white overseas settlers and therefore get it in the neck.

ATIYAH: *I see a false analogy creeping in.*

REID: I think that in civil and international law, prescription is the only claim that can be made to a country. Now in the case of Palestine, before the first World War the people who owned it were the Turks. They owned it for 400 years. They gave it up at the end of the war by treaty, and the question was, who owned it then? In my opinion, there is no getting away from the fact that the Arabs had been there during the Turkish occupation and were practically the only occupiers for 1,300 years, except for a handful of Jews.

CROSSMAN: *Reid has tacitly claimed that the Balfour Declaration,*

whatever advantages it had, committed an injustice on the lawful owners of the country.

REID: Yes, especially as it was done behind the backs of the Palestine Jews and the Arabs. I think it was an iniquitous document. But it was issued for strategic motives to get allies in America and elsewhere.

BUBER: *My own point of view is not a legalist one. I am asking myself this question only: what has been done by these peoples in this land? What co-operation has there been between the land and the people? What were the fruits of this co-operation? The particular link between the people of Israel and this land is the link of a unique productivity. This is not a legalist point of view, but for me it is the decisive one. If a people in a certain land was creative, as Jewish people have been in Palestine, in the days of old, and our days, too, it constitutes a special right. It is the manifestation of the spirit.*

CROSSMAN: Now we have this: Atiyah says, "Ours is the right of prescription," and Buber replies, "I claim on what the Jews have accomplished since 1918."

BUBER: *I do not mean 'since 1918' only. I mean 'since the beginning of the relation between this people and this land.'*

REID: Are you basing your argument not on political grounds, but on moral grounds?

BUBER: *I am basing my argument on the fundamental facts of the history of the human spirit. It is more than morals.*

ATIYAH: I have three comments to make. First, concerning what Reid said about Palestine having belonged to the Turks. Under Turkish suzerainty the Arabs were not a subject people, but partners with the Turks in the empire. Second, on what I considered was the false analogy—when Crossman said the Jews were unlucky in that they were, as he put it, the last comers into the field of overseas settlement. He mentioned Australia. I would point out that the Arabs in Palestine do not belong to the same category as the aborigines of Australia. They belong to what was once a highly-civilised community, and before what you call overseas settlement in Palestine by the Jews was begun, the Arabs were re-awakening into a tremendous intellectual and spiritual activity after a period of decadence, so there can be no comparison between the two cases.

217

PALESTINE: CAN DEADLOCK BE BROKEN?—Continued

CROSSMAN: *Tom, what do you think were the real mistakes of British policy which led up to what we all agree is an intolerable situation?*

REID: The British Government during the first World War had induced the Arabs, who were in revolt against the Turks, to come in and fight on the Allied side. We made them a promise in the McMahon Declaration and then, without their knowledge, invited the Jews to come in and establish a national home. That was unwise and wicked. As I understand it, the idea of the British Government was that the Jews should come in and gradually become a majority. That was a secret understanding and was doubly wicked.

CROSSMAN: *We ought to note it was not only the British Government, but the League of Nations as well.*

REID: That came later, in 1923. In 1918 there was an Anglo-French Declaration which promised the Arabs a Government in Palestine evolved from the will of the people. I hate running down my own country, but really the treatment of the Arabs in Palestine was disgraceful. They were promised time and again their independence. The British should have done what commission after commission has asked them to do: to give a clear definition of their policy in Palestine. They never did. They did nothing but vacillate. They hoped the Arabs would eventually tacitly consent to Palestine becoming a Jewish State in fact.

ATIYAH: *I think the basic trouble in implementing the Mandate has been that the Mandate and the Balfour Declaration provided for two incompatible things—for the protection of the rights of Arabs on the one hand, and for handing their country over to the Zionists on the other.*

BUBER: I think the Balfour Declaration was not too much, but too little. It did not make clear enough that it meant for the Jewish people free access to the soil of Palestine and an autonomy sufficient to build there a life of its own.

CROSSMAN: *So we can get agreement on this point, that in the past the failure has been the failure of the British Government and the League of Nations to face up to the issue in Palestine one way or the other, and if we do not face up in the future to the fundamental issue we shall not add anything to the solution of the problem, which ever way it goes. There has been a great deal of discussion about an agreed solution between Jew and Arab. Is it sheer moonshine for a statesman to say that he is looking for an agreed solution between the existing organisations on both sides?*

ATIYAH: I think an agreement between the Arabs and the Zionists is absolutely impossible.

BUBER: *I think it is now somewhat difficult, but not impossible.*

ATIYAH: It is quite impossible because the conflict is between the indigenous people of Palestine who are in the majority who are determined to keep their country and want independence immediately, and a group of Jews—not the whole of Jewry—who regard Palestine as theirs by right and who want to come in in unrestricted numbers and have a Jewish National State. Between the two armies there can be no compromise.

BUBER: *Political organisations can be changed, and can change their opinions. The real question is not one of organisation but of reality. Nor is it a question of majority and minority.*

CROSSMAN: You do not believe in counting heads in Palestine?

BUBER: *No: nor in any other country. But there is an urgent need to find a new political form for the living and working together of two peoples.*

CROSSMAN: The question we put to you, put bluntly, is, if we wait for an agreed solution between the Jewish Agency and the Higher Committee of the Arab League, have we got to wait till Domesday?

BUBER: *If you put the question so, I have no answer to it. I think what is the real obstacle is the morbid obsession with purely political terms, which does not allow these two people to come to an understanding on the basis of their real common interests.*

REID: It is quite hopeless to expect political Zionists and political Arabs to agree. It would not pay them politically, from a narrow point of view, to lower their demands to outside powers.

ATIYAH: *It is not only the Arab politicians who would never agree to a Zionist solution, but the whole Arab people.*

CROSSMAN: Do you feel that on the basis of an imposed solution, co-operation might be possible?

REID: *I have said before that you won't settle the Palestine omelette without breaking eggs. If an imposed solution is imposed, one side or the other will resist it, unless independence is given to Palestine at once.*

BUBER: Everything depends upon the kind of solution. If it is a sound one, bringing the two peoples together in their common interest, a solution, even if imposed, will do what must be done.

ATIYAH: *It is not only an imposed solution that offers a chance of co-operation. There is one alternative, that every foreign influence should be withdrawn completely from Palestine and the Arabs and the Jews left alone to come to terms or fight it out. This may not be a very desirable solution, and the condition it involves may be unrealisable, but if it could be tried a natural equilibrium would be reached, possibly after a fight. If*

the Zionists could no longer depend on foreign armed assistance they would realise that it was essential for them to cultivate the goodwill of the Arabs.

REID: Dick, do you agree with the view that we have expressed, that it is quite impossible for political organisations on both sides to agree?

CROSSMAN: *Completely. And furthermore, I think we are all agreed that if there were a sudden and complete withdrawal of British troops, there would be bloodshed and disorder. This brings us now to our concluding stage of asking ourselves what, in our view, is the sort of solution which a commission could give, and which the Great Powers could impose. Readers will want to know what sort of solution could be, first, just and second, feasible.*

BUBER: A solution giving to either side the right of domination would lead to a sudden catastrophe. The only solution that would not lead to a catastrophe, but only to a difficult situation for some time, is the creation of a bi-national state. That is, putting Jews and Arabs together in a kind of condominium and giving them the maximum of common administration possible in a given hour. They would have equal rights, these two nations, as nations, irrespective of numbers.

CROSSMAN: *In a State where there was such a parity there would be deadlock on any vital issue and that would mean no Jewish immigration, because every issue over which there was a deadlock would be one on which no action would be taken.*

BUBER: I mean the constitution of the State should be based on the right of immigration by the Jews until there is an equal number, but there should be equality at once, not only of individuals, but of nations.

REID: *On what grounds would the Professor justify immigrants coming into a country until they were equal in numbers with the indigenous population?*

BUBER: I think that Judaism cannot live without becoming an organism with a living centre, and not only for itself, but for mankind it should live on. For Arabism there is no similar alternative.

ATIYAH: *I think a bi-national State on the basis of absolute parity is either unnecessary or impossible, because unless there is enough goodwill on both sides such a State will end in deadlock and complete paralysis. If there is enough goodwill there is no need for such an elaborate scheme.*

BUBER: Then the question of majority arises and that is what I am trying to avoid. In the last 30 years the possibilities of an agreement between Jews and Arabs have deteriorated as a result of growing politisation. I do not see any solution other than depolitisation as far as possible. This means replacing the slogans on the site of reality and building upon it.

ATIYAH: *The first condition of a just solution is that the Palestine problem should be solved in relation to the welfare of the people of Palestine—and not by reference to extraneous factors such as Zionist national aspirations or the plight of Jewish refugees, however grievous, or American public opinion, or the oil and strategic interests of the Great Powers. This, for justice, is essential. Second, you must decide which of the two claims to the country—the Arab or the Zionist—is morally valid. If these two conditions are applied, the only solution is that the country should be given the independence to which it is entitled and which it has so far been denied, and that a democratic Government should be set up for the whole population, and Arabs and Jews given equal rights as the citizens and a share in the Government in proportion to their numbers; that immigration should be stopped until the country has its own Government to decide its immigration policy like any other Govern-*

Atiyah is positive; Reid is positive

ment. It would be quite possible for such a State to enter into treaty relations with Britain.

REID: I have been greatly impressed by the sincerity and moderation of the professor's views, but he said earlier that he does not believe in counting heads to get a majority, and yet when he comes to a solution he insists that emigration must go on until Jews equal the Arabs.

BUBER: *I am not interested in formulas. You can say if you prefer: the Jews have a right to immigration as far as the economic conditions allow.*

REID: I think abstract justice in practical politics cannot always be implemented. It is quite wrong in any country, whether India, Burma or Palestine, to say "our interests and nothing else," because the world is inter-dependent. While I agree the interests of the people of Palestine should be a primary consideration, the problem is really an international one. It was said Palestine should be considered with reference to the appalling fate of the Jews elsewhere. The Arabs have accepted, against their will, it is true, five hundred thousand Jews into Palestine, and it is utterly wrong to try to settle the problem of displaced Jews by dumping them into Palestine, which has already done its share. Britain is not bound by any promise to set up a Jewish State in Palestine. The Jews, in 1917, asked for a State and the British Government did not grant it. What they did, without any right to do so, was to recommend the setting-up of a Jewish cultural national home, now established. That did not bind the Arabs, and what the Jews have been trying to do is to turn that national home into a Jewish State, mainly by bringing in immigrants. The doctor has recommended an independent bi-national State. Mr. Atiyah has recommended independence. In my opinion there is no way out. If we are going to face the facts, I think there is no solution except independence.

CROSSMAN: *In the near future.*

REID: That is the correct way to put it. That, of course, would cause violent reaction on the part of some of the Jews. In 1923 the French wanted the whole of Syria and the British did not want them to have the southern part, Palestine, and in carrying out the dictates of power politics the French took the northern part and we took the southern part. That was a most unjust act and economically a disastrous one. In my opinion, if the Arabs were wise, and with friendly pressure, I think they could be induced to undo the partition of Syria.

BUBER: *A Federal State?*

REID: It should have one Government, federal or unitary.

BUBER: *With what degree of autonomy?*

REID: I have not gone into the details of that. In my opinion that would do a great deal towards solving the immigration question, because the Arabs, the indigenes, would be in the majority. It is no use Mr. Atiyah saying Palestine can go on on its own. It must have relations with other States. Palestine is the bridge between Asia and Europe. It is a key position in the world. Before the settlement is made, this little State of Palestine should in its own interests enter into a treaty with Britain or America or UNO for protection against outside aggression. It will lead to trouble, but, as I said before, you won't make a Palestine omelette without breaking eggs. If this solution is adopted, you will have some opposition from the extremists, but the average Jew in Palestine will accept it.

CROSSMAN: *I personally think that Dr. Buber's solution, the so-called bi-national State, is a figment of the constitutional imagination. If they work together, you don't need it, and if they don't work together the constitution doesn't work. With regard to Mr. Atiyah, I happen to agree that the immediate objective has got to be independence, but for both Jews*

and Arabs. The difficulty I see is this. If we grant immediate independence, the withdrawal of our troops will mean a de facto partition whether you like it or not, and there will be some bloodshed. You will get a de facto and illegal partition of the country because I do not think the two communities would work together. I regard the so-called solution of an immediate independence as merely a form of splitting the country between existing warring groups. In the second place, any solution likely to be effective will not be carried out by only one power. The British have been put in the intolerable position of having a world problem on their shoulders. But a sound solution has got to have not only the backing of British forces, but also of the forces of other powers as well. There will have to be a token American and Russian force—if Russia would agree—or else there will be no chance of success, for no one Government can stand the strain. That is the second principle: an international solution with full international backing, and I think that is the position the British Government will adopt. Thirdly, a greater Syrian unity has got to be the final objective. I do not like partition because I think it is wicked to divide that small country, but I see no other way of getting responsibility into the hands of Jew and Arab, and of recognising the rights of Jewish immigration into Palestine. I regard partition as a short-term policy, something that you do in order to lead on to the integration of Palestinian Jews and Arabs into the Middle East. Partition is bound to fail if it is only partition, and is not accompanied by a complete revolution in our attitude to the Middle East, and if it does not lead to a Jewish State telling the rest of the world that there can be no unlimited immigration.

REID: Let us see if we are clear. Three of us recommend independence. You favour partition. In my opinion, if partition were established it would simply mean that the Jews, with their superior education and money, would buy up the land and swarm across the Arab boundaries, and there would be strife from the word 'go.' We examined partition thoroughly in 1938. We decided in the end that economically, strategically and politically it was quite impossible. It would be unjust to hand over the sovereignty of part of Palestine to immigrants because Jews had a State there 2,000 years ago.

CROSSMAN: *I do not conceive of an Arab and a Jewish State, but of one State exclusively Arab and one at the beginning fifty-fifty Jew and Arab, and later achieving a Jewish majority.*

ATIYAH: What does that solve? Nothing at all. You are merely cutting off the purely Arab part of the hills and leaving the main part populated by Jews and Arabs to become a Jewish State. It is the most important and richest part of Palestine. Can you see the Arabs accepting that?

CROSSMAN: *Any solution demands force and involves people outside Palestine. If we use force against Jews we are using it against all the Jews in the world, and if we use it against the Arabs we use it against the Arabs of the whole Middle East. What you do in Palestine reacts over the whole world and is unjust either to Jews or Arabs or both. I seek not perfection but lesser injustice, and believe that to be partition.*

BUBER: Unfortunately, time is not sufficient to discuss the question of partition. I am against it because I am for a living and productive Palestine.

CROSSMAN: *Would you rather have partition than an Arab independent state?*

BUBER: Of course, but only because I think it is the lesser evil. You said a bi-national state in your view would not work. This is an argument that has been used many times against that kind of thing. Secondly, I am for, and not against, a bi-national Palestinian state entering as an autonomous member into a Syrian confederation.

CROSSMAN: *On the Syrian Confederation at least we have reached agreement.*

Hindsight by Richard Kershaw

What prophecy from the Holy Land!'... It is not justice which prevails but force, and therefore each feels it must preserve to itself the right to use force.' Ten months after Dick Crossman said this the first Arab–Israeli war started. It is still going on: 1956, 1967, and the fighting that goes on at this moment are all parts of one war, fought about the same issue – the issue which Crossman, Reid, Buber and Atiyah failed to agree about (as they would fail were all still alive now).

'Have we got to wait till Domesday?', the question was asked about a settlement for Palestine. Twenty-three years is not eternity; but as the war continues, and as the greater powers supply the two sides with more and more sophisticated military apparatus, it seems at times as if Palestine itself might drag the world into the Domesday of a global conflict.

Perhaps *Picture Post*'s quartet was ultra-clear-sighted. Or perhaps the conflict and the situation have always been simple enough for anyone to parse, while no one can solve it. But their forebodings were borne out quickly: 'If there were a sudden and complete withdrawal

of British troops, there would be bloodshed and disorder.' Ten months later, British troops were withdrawn, Israel declared itself to exist, and on 15 May 1948 the fighting started. A *de facto* partition indeed took place. The boundaries have since changed, Palestine has disappeared as a cartographical entity – yet it has survived, and even recrudesced in the last two years, as a political force and idea.

In between there was Suez ('... if we use force against the Arabs, we use it against the Arabs of the whole Middle East', as Crossman saw so clearly). And Martin Buber's argument, that the Jews had acquired permanent title to part of Palestine by their 'unique productivity', has not only remained Israel's boast as it makes the desert grow oranges and melons, but has also been proved in their eyes by unique military prowess; the young men of Mordecai Hod's air force are now the heroes of militant Zionism, just as the *fedayeen* are the symbol to Arabs that Palestine survives. Edward Atiyah really said it all in 1947: 'I think an agreement between the Arabs and the Zionists is absolutely impossible.' I am afraid that is not only still true, but may be true two decades hence.

Picture Post, September 27, 1947

In autumn 1947 Paris launched the 'New Look'. All through the war, woman's dress had been drab, economical, military in cut. Now all that was to be swept aside. At one blow woman was to become feminine, mysterious, above all luxurious. Costly materials — velvets, brocades, furs and lace — used lavishly and often with the most intricate cut, were the marks of the new styles. The new look was inaugurated by a new genius, Christian Dior. Corsets, bustles, padded hips and busts were back as well. . . . But in Britain clothes were still severely rationed. And over most of Europe they were unobtainable.

T.H.

One of the Skirts Which Ignores Europe and Starts a 'Civil War' in America

Paris has its eyes on the American market in launching fashions which use more material than Europeans can afford. They decree narrow shoulders, exaggerated busts, pinched-in waists, padded hips, skirts fantastically full or hobbled, to cut the calf, or reach the ankle. Even America has started to object. Most of the clothes on these pages are by the leader of present-day Paris style, Christian Dior.

PARIS FORGETS THIS IS 1947

Photographed by SAVITRY and GEIGER

Straight from the indolent and wealthy years before the 1914 war come this year's much-discussed Paris fashions. They are launched upon a world which has not the material to copy them—and whose women have neither the money to buy, the leisure to enjoy, nor in some designs even the strength to support, these masses of elaborate material.

A Step Backwards
If a twenty-yard skirt is too wide, you can be just as chic in this long crippling hobble.

Outdoor Clothes are Fur-trimmed
Besides padded hips, this black suit has a taffeta ruffle beneath the peplum. The marmot-banded deep blue coat on right has the new hour-glass line.

WITH an Arabian Nights' splendour of rich regal velvets, brocades like shimmering moonlight, glittering gold and silver and pearl-encrusted embroidery, rustling taffetas covered with cobweb-fine black lace, and the most lavish and extravagant use of fur, Paris dress designers have introduced their much-talked-of new winter fashions. Entering the salons of the *haute couture* from the chestnut-lined boulevards, where the average Parisian woman looks no better-dressed than her London counterpart, one steps back into another age. Here are the hobble skirts of just before World War I, the Victorian bustle and crinoline, the tightly-corseted waist, the padded hips and exaggerated bust, the only-just-visible ankle, the extreme *décolleté*. We are back to the days when fashion was the prerogative of the leisured wealthy woman, and not the everyday concern of typist, saleswoman or housewife.

By these spectacular collections, Paris is attempting to re-establish her position as the world's centre of fashion. During the war American designers evolved a brand new type of casual clothes, easy to wear and to mass-produce, and both practical and functional in design. After the Liberation extravagances of 1944, Paris tried making simpler clothes on these new American lines. But the American buyers were not interested. Why pay extravagant prices and heavy custom duties for models similar to those already being made back in New York? Meantime, the American designers, delighted with their own success, liked to think of themselves as entirely independent of Paris. While before the war, there were few who did not cross the Atlantic each year, there are many today who have not been since 1939. Some indeed still refuse to have French fashion magazines in their showrooms.

It was actually the clothes shown at the previous and very first collection of the new designer, Christian Dior, which were chiefly responsible for the revolutionary—or rather reactionary—fashions causing such widespread concern today. Formerly an art dealer, Dior was until last year one of Lucien Lelong's bright young men. There can be few of the Paris houses which have not been influenced by his first collection, and it is hardly too much to say that the spectacular clothes being shown at the moment are largely the development and adaptation of his ideas. Today, Dior's clothes are the most talked-of in Paris, London or New York. He is a season ahead of everybody else. The chief dictator of the very

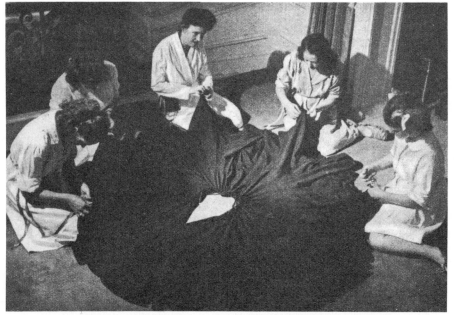

An Enormous Skirt Which Surrounds an Eighteen-inch Waist
This afternoon dress takes nearly fifty yards of material. For British women it would require the hoarded coupons of several years.

An Echo of the Tzars
Ilex green velvet, leopard skin and spark-
ling gold and silver beaded pockets; narrow
shoulders set off another enormous hem-line.

An Echo of the Avenue du Bois
The sloping shoulders, long jacket and hat are
pure period, though in those times, Piguet's
skirt would have seemed shockingly short.

An Echo of Edwardian Elegance
Is it the muff-like draping, or the giant
chenille spot on her veil? Piguet lines the
mushroom-pink coat with sealskin.

long skirt, even his tweed suits and coats are only ten inches above the ground, while more formal day clothes are ankle-length. His new silhouette has narrow shoulders, a rounded bust emphasised by padding if necessary, a wasp waist and fantastically full skirts falling in a flower-like curve over padded hips and stomach. A dress with an eighteen-inch

waist has nearly fifty yards of material in its skirt. Even his day dresses have twenty to thirty yards of flute-pleated tweed in their voluminous skirts. Under an ankle-length taffeta afternoon dress, several petticoats will rustle. Yards and yards of pleated tulle are used for evening crinolines, while velvet and satin gowns have an immense fullness

swept behind and draped into enormous bustles.

Jacques Fath causes as much sensation as Dior with his crippling hobble skirts, so tight and so long that his mannequins can hardly walk. With them go neat little Edwardian jackets, with fur-edged basques flaring out at the back like the one on our cover.

FOR INDOORS: *Accent on Hips*
The draped skirt is pulled tight to cut just below
the knee. A gigantic bow enlarges the hips.

Dinner Dresses are Briefer
Many have whale-bone instead of shoulder-
straps. And the skirts are only ankle-length.

The New 'Little Dress'
Its simplicity is deceptive. It has an inner story
of intricate cutting and fitting.

An Echo of the Eiffel Tower
Some coats have tremendously full, many-gored skirts. Carven drops the length to low calf level with a deep band of fur.

Dior's Day Coats are Ankle-Length
No more 'spiv' shoulders, but a tightly-belted waist and a full skirt falling over padded hips.

The Woman With a Secret Assignation
She is dressed for what, beneath her all-concealing great-coat? Fur is used lavishly. Evening dresses have fur trains and halters. Numerous skins of silver fox make a ground-length evening coat.

Balmain's skirts are often seven inches from the ground and, though his shoulders are narrow, the hips fit smoothly without padding. Piguet's clothes have a lovely echo of Edwardian elegance. Even the fur which he uses lavishly for lining coats and suits is the period black sealskin.

The materials used throughout the collections are of exquisite quality. The favourite colours are subtle shades of grey and brown, with very much black, and many dark greens. Besides the long skirt and the accentuated curves, another feature seen everywhere is the elaborate embroidery. The bodices of many cocktail and dinner frocks are completely covered with silver and gold, pearl and Victorian jet embroidery. Prices are fabulously high. Starting at about eighty pounds, many of the embroidered and fur-trimmed models are selling for as much as £250, and in spite of this there are said to be many more overseas buyers in Paris this year than last.

The fact remains that these romantic frivolous clothes have such a seductive appeal that your eye is 'in' remarkably quickly. Their utter femininity recalls the splendour and elegance of the Avenue du Bois before the 1914 war. Only in Paris could these clothes have been made; only in Paris could such a daring experiment have been undertaken. But whether you see in it a sensational bid to recapture the American market, or a cynical disregard for the world-wide shortage of textiles, there can be no question about the entire unsuitability of these new fashions for our present life and times. Already in America demonstrations have been staged in revolt against the return of the long skirt. In this country they are simply an economic impossibility.

But even if the many thousands of yards of material were available, and every woman had enough coupons for an entire new wardrobe (the changes are so drastic, that no compromise between old and new is possible), can anyone seriously contemplate hopping on to a bus in a hobble skirt? Try lifting a bale of tweed—and imagine voluntarily adding to the fatigue of standing in the fish queue by having twenty yards of it hanging from one's waist. Think of doing housework, or sitting at a typewriter all day, or working in a factory, tightly-corseted, and encumbered and constricted with layers of hip-padding and petticoats. Our mothers freed us from these in their struggle for emancipation. And in our own active workaday lives there can be no possible place for them.

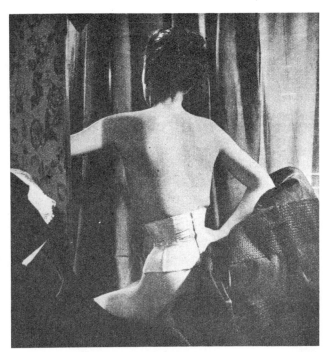

A RETURN TO 1870 AND ALL THAT
First stage in dressing for the evening is a whale-boned corset like the one Grandmama wore.

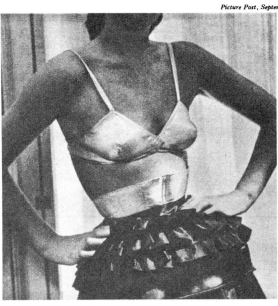

A Frilled Ruff Enlarges the Hips
A ruff of taffeta over the underskirt further emphasises the tiny waist. Dior alters your shape to fit his clothes.

The Petticoat Adds Shape
With deep bands of horsehair stiffening, it has a big protuberance to support the bustle of the dress.

Before the war, as soon as a new line was shown in Paris, it was immediately copied and adapted by all the small houses and the little dressmakers. The Parisian woman seemed to be *à la mode* overnight. Today her skirts are as short as ours, and although material is not rationed in France, it is in short supply, and so fantastically expensive that the new fashions could almost be labelled 'For export only.' But most countries export successfully only the commodities they perfect in usage themselves. The best publicity for English tweeds is to see an Englishman wearing them; similarly, no amount of advertising could popularise French wine more effectively than the restaurants in France where it is served with discretion. Designing these sensational new fashions, it would seem that the *couturiers* have forgotten that they need the ordinary Parisian woman to show the world how to wear them. But, like ourselves, the ordinary Parisian woman has neither the leisure nor the money for clothes such as these.
MARJORIE BECKETT.

The Shape That Paris Would Like to Give You
An enormous amount of fullness is draped and looped at the back to form the bustle, while in front the skirt bulges over the taffeta frills to give the fashionable pregnant look.

Vol. 36. No. 8

PICTURE POST

AUGUST 23, 1947

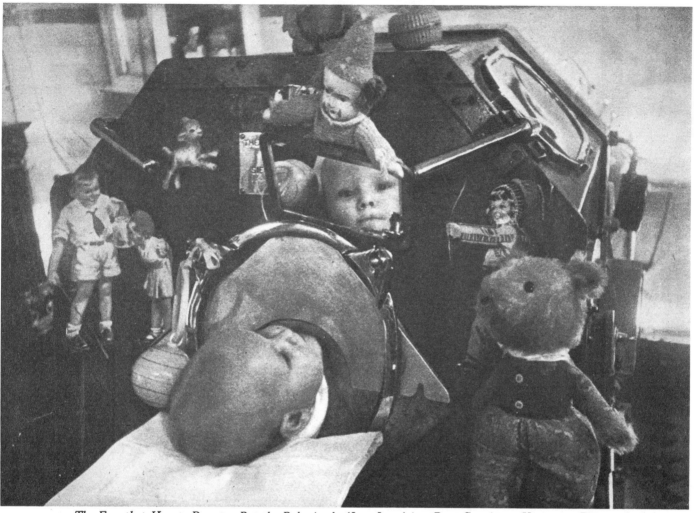

The Fear that Haunts Parents: But the Baby in the 'Iron Lung' is a Rare Case in an Uncommon Disease
Baby John, 16 months old, has lived like this for two months in the Western Fever Hospital, Fulham, London. But this is infantile paralysis at its worst. In most cases there is no paralysis at all, and, where there is, a large majority will recover wholly or partly. In two months Baby John has improved so much that he breathes naturally for six hours a day, and his paralysed limbs are regaining some movement.

NO NEED FOR PANIC ABOUT
INFANTILE PARALYSIS

The daily press gives little but the barest figures about the present disturbing outbreak of infantile paralysis. To allay unneccessary anxiety among parents, Picture Post has carried out an investigation, and is able to report that, terrible as the disease can be in a small minority of cases, it is usually not nearly as serious as people imagine. 50 out of every 100 cases make a complete recovery; a further 30 are left with only minor muscular defects.

Photographed by K. HUTTON

FOR thousands of parents infantile paralysis has thrown a shadow of fear over holiday time. In this country, never as badly affected as the United States and Australia, people know little about the disease, and that little is usually the worst. They remember with affection a great victim—and moral conqueror—of infantile paralysis, Franklin Roosevelt. They remember the publicity given to rare 'iron lung' cases. They may have seen *Sister Kenny*, the film based on the life of a notable woman who has done more than anyone else to direct attention to this disease. And every day people read the latest figures in the rising total of notified cases.

It is not surprising that in the absence of balanced information there has grown up a sense of helpless fear sometimes amounting to panic. It is time to look at infantile paralysis calmly.

There is almost always some infantile paralysis in Britain, but the peak incidence is in late summer or early autumn. Since 1912, when statistics were first kept, there have been between 600 and 800 cases a year, except in 1926 (1,159 cases) and 1938 (nearly 1,500 cases). The present outbreak will almost certainly make 1947 the worst year yet, for the increase began two months earlier than normally, and the disease shows every sign of increasing, as usual, until the warm weather ends. This disturbing fact has been trumpeted, but almost no publicity has been given to the mild nature of so many cases, and the simple truth that in a population of 46,000,000, even 2,500 cases would hardly be reason for panic.

The popular name of the disease is itself terrifying and a little misleading. Infantile paralysis (acute anterior poliomyelitis) is not confined to infants, and paralysis is so far from being an inevitable result that it can fairly be called the exception rather than the rule. Probably at least two out of three cases among those who show undoubted (meningeal) symptoms of poliomyelitis, recover without any paralysis, even of the most minor and temporary nature. A safe estimate is that of every 100 cases, 50 recover completely, 30 are left with very minor muscular defects which probably will not interfere with normal activities, 15 are permanently disabled, and five die. Because early diagnosis is difficult, and because paralysis is consequently often the symptom that gives certainty, the percentage of paralysis among notified cases—that is, those covered by the

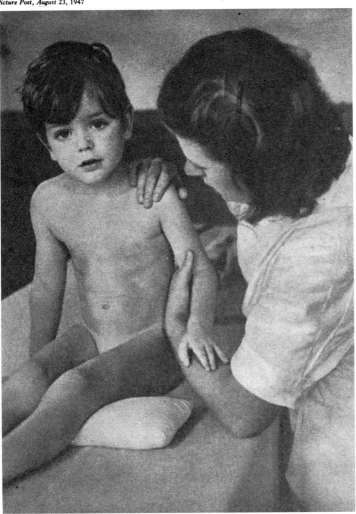

The Paralysed Arm that is Almost Mended
*In the Queen Mary's Hospital for Children at Carshalton, Surrey, a physio-
therapist manipulates Christian (4), whose affected arm is almost recovered.*

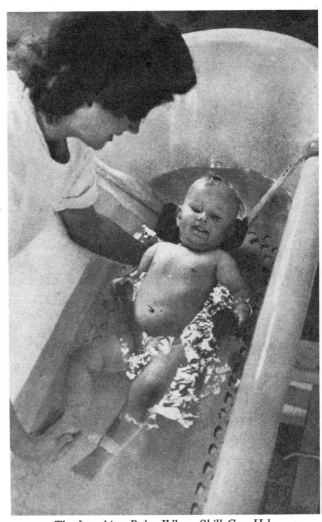

The Laughing Baby Whom Skill Can Help
*Fifteen-month-old Dennis is exercised in water, which supports the
limbs. His back, neck, leg, and feet muscles are affected, but improving.*

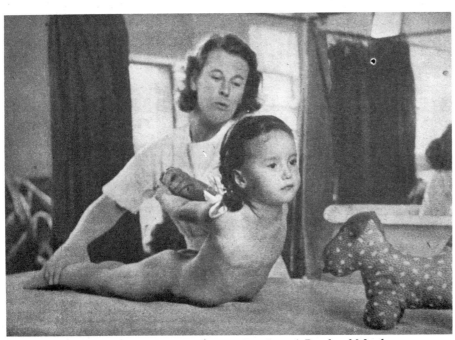

Special Exercises, Controlled Rest, 'Re-educate' Paralysed Muscles
*Betty is four, and has mild paralysis of the neck muscles. She is improving, as most do after the
peak of paralysis. Improvement can continue for six months, in some cases for two years.*

official figures published in the newspapers—is
probably as high as 70. But even among notified
cases there is hope of recovery in a 'large majority.'
Two cases in a family are rare, and one attack,
however mild or abortive (without paralysis), gives
immunity.

Yet so far no serum or vaccine or drug has been
found to combat this disease, which is caused by
a filtrable virus. The accepted theory is that the
virus injures that part of the spinal cord that controls
muscle movement. The harm is all done in the
early acute stage, and if paralysis develops, it is
believed that its severity depends upon the degree
of injury to the spinal cord. Fortunately in most
cases paralysis lessens after its peak.

Before 1930 it was believed that little or nothing
could be done to relieve or recover paralysis after
poliomyelitis. Patients were kept in bed with as
little movement as possible, and this, with heavy
splinting, is thought to have been the cause of
much crippling and deformity. In the early
'thirties, poliomyelitis began to share the benefits
of new theories and techniques in orthopaedics
and physiotherapy ('physical medicine'). Fewer
and lighter splints were used, and movement
was encouraged as soon as possible after the acute
stage. But the big impetus to a new outlook and
improved techniques came from the work of Sister
Kenny, the Australian nurse whose personality
overshadows the whole subject.

Sister Kenny, a keen observer who had studied
poliomyelitis intensively, had encouraging and
sometimes startling results by new methods which,
if she did not altogether pioneer, she established
surely and carried further. But wider trial of her

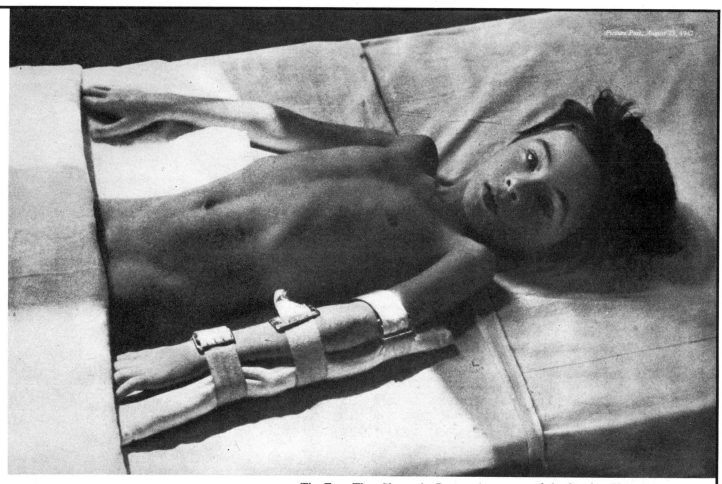

The Face That Shows the Patient Acceptance of the Stricken Young
Like all the children pictured so far, Terry (8), is a victim of the present outbreak. Both arms were at first paralysed. Already he can move his right arm, and there is hope for his left.

Harry Takes His Medicine
Screwing up his eyes is prescribed exercise for this eight-year-old with facial paralysis.

methods counselled a more cautious optimism, and induced Sister Kenny to modify her claims and ideas. Some of her theories are certainly hard to justify. No one, for example, can detect, or understand what she means by, the 'shortening of the skin' which she regards as a significant symptom, and she holds that paralysis is caused by local factors (that is, in the affected muscle or group of muscles) and not by 'central' damage to the spinal cord. Confronted by post-mortem signs of damage to the spinal cord, she has latterly admitted that central damage may cause the local paralysis in ten per cent of cases. Where she formerly claimed to be able to cure, she now claims only to ameliorate. Stories of obstruction and persecution by the medical profession are, at the least, exaggerated. At the Queen Mary's Hospital for Children at Carshalton in Surrey, for example, she was given

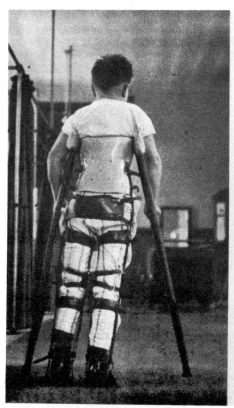

The Boy Who is Crippled
Helped by this specially designed support, Brian learns how to walk again.

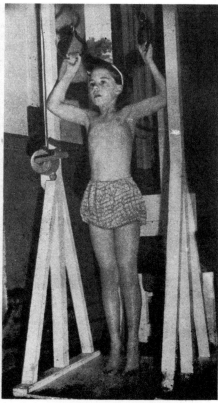

The Girl Who Escaped
Madeline (10) strengthens once-paralysed muscles in the gymnasium.

Infantile Paralysis is Not Confined to Infants, and Two Cases Out of Three Have No Paralysis

Late comer to a picnic party at Queen Mary's Hospital. Most of these children have leg paralysis. The majority of patients improve, many recover. And of all those who contract infantile paralysis, the large majority recover without any paralysis at all. Most victims are under 14, about one-third are between 14 and 35.

equipment and staff and full authority for a year (1937-38), and the committee which afterwards assessed her results, found only a slight advance on results obtained by the hospital's own methods. Yet no one can deny that Sister Kenny has stimulated medical interest in this disease, and forced new techniques, as no one else has. Probably the truth is that her admirers claim more, and the medical profession allow less, than Sister Kenny's due credit.

But no one who has visited Carshalton, where L.C.C. cases of poliomyelitic paralysis are treated, or the Western Hospital, Fulham, which is the chief London receiving hospital for acute cases, could imagine that the doctors there would allow any bias to interfere with the best possible treatment. The Carshalton staff are there because they like children, and this is reflected, as it always is, in their young charges, whose patient and happy acceptance of disabilities is moving and merciful.

In America, where much research has been done, doctors believe that poliomyelitis is spread almost wholly by direct contact, not necessarily or even commonly from victim to victim, but through a chain of carriers, themselves immune. By direct contact they mean by droplet infection (by sneeze or other violent exhalation), by kissing, or from drinking vessels. Since the virus is found in faeces and has been found in flies, the disease may be spread by drinking water or food, but there is no reliable proof of this, and the 'pattern' of the present outbreak is not that of a food- or water-borne disease. There is presumptive evidence of relation to climatic temperature; but the 1938 outbreak here, and the bigger American epidemics, seem to dispose of the belief that post-war 'chronic undernourishment' is responsible.

Here is advice to parents : insist on great personal cleanliness, never allow food to be handled with dirty hands, wash dishes well, keep flies from food. See that children have adequate rest, for fatigue seems to increase the likelihood of infection—this, and the possibly true belief that victims are oftenest the brighter children, are unexplained mysteries. In areas where poliomyelitis has occurred, postpone if possible operations on throat or nose, for they increase danger. Don't forbid play with regular companions, but keep children from crowded places, for apart from the greater chance of contacting a carrier there, it is wise for everyone's sake to avoid 'making new herds.' And having taken these precautions, forget about infantile paralysis, which will largely die with the summer.

FYFE ROBERTSON

What Every Doctor Doesn't Know—the Value of Physiotherapy

Poor circulation is one result of infantile paralysis. To improve it, Malcolm (7) gets hot and cold showers before his water exercises. The benefits of physiotherapy are not yet fully appreciated.

Picture Post, August 23, 1947

Postscript to Hope: A Permanently Disabled Boy Learns to Walk Again in a New Way

Bobby has been at Carshalton for two years. It is unlikely that his paralysed left leg will improve any more, and until January he was bedridden. Now with iron support—and the confidence inspired by his physiotherapist teachers—he has learnt to walk in a slightly different way, using different muscles.

229

1948

In the summer of 1948, an official of the Conservative Central Office, actuated no doubt by the highest patriotic motives, called on the head of the Criminal Investigation Department at New Scotland Yard to acquaint him with distressing rumours of wholesale corruption at the Board of Trade. The police investigation came to the notice of the President of the Board, the Rt Hon. Harold Wilson, who, acting with characteristic speed and circumspection, asked the Lord Chancellor to set up an inquiry. The result was a tribunal under Mr Justice Lynskey which sat for several weeks and produced a 50,000-word report that uncovered a spectacular mare's nest. It also introduced to an austerity-weary public the charismatic figure of Sidney Stanley.

Stanley had come to England as a refugee from Poland before the First World War, had entered his own idiosyncratic kind of business when he was sixteen, and had shortly achieved his first bankruptcy. After the Second World War, he acquired a flat in Park Lane and, describing himself as a 'business agent', let it be known that he had influence in Government circles which, for a consideration, could be placed at the disposal of businessmen short of the Government permits which were necessary for most activities except breathing. He added verisimilitude to an otherwise bald and unconvincing narrative by scraping acquaintance with the Parliamentary Secretary to the Board of Trade, an ex-railway clerk named John Belcher, and other minor Labour stalwarts. He entertained them, bought them suits, gave Belcher a gold cigarette-case, and in a characteristically exuberant flight of ambition sent Ernest Bevin some cigars — though the Foreign Secretary's roars of denial that he had ever received them could be heard as far away as Moscow.

Promoters of football pools, importers of amusement machinery and similar figures appeared before the tribunal to describe their dealings with Stanley, who was able to convince them that he was paying Belcher £50 a week, had the austere Sir Stafford Cripps in his pocket, and was addressed by Dr Dalton as 'Dear Stan'. The credulousness of businessmen excited much comment. The tribunal found that most of the rumours had no basis outside Stanley's Arabian Nights imagination; but that Belcher had received small gifts and favours from Stanley and others, and had intervened in their favour in a number of cases. Belcher, of course, was ruined and had to resign. Stanley sold his memoirs to the *People* for a reputed £10,000, and shortly transferred his talents to the new state of Israel, where, sad to relate, they were not appreciated.

It was perhaps inevitable that a largely anti-Labour press starved of newsprint should devote more space to Sidney Stanley than to the genuine achievements of the Labour Government. Aneurin Bevan almost wholly diverted the headlines from the setting-up of a National Health Service by choosing its inauguration to proclaim his hatred of the Tories responsible for the deprivations of his boyhood who 'as far as I am concerned are lower than vermin'. But by the summer of 1948 the foundations of the Welfare State had been firmly laid in a series of social security acts and the Government could genuinely claim that the worst extremes of poverty had been abolished. There was full — too full, said the economists — employment. New houses were being built at the rate of 200,000 a year, and New Towns were coming into being which had their defects, but which did enable mostly young skilled artisans and their wives to raise families in an environment far removed from the twilight rows of urban cottages. Rationing was still severe — though bread rationing ended in July — but subsidized milk and orange juice lavished on sometimes reluctant children were producing a race fitter than ever before.

This had been accomplished against a background of almost unbroken crisis which continued throughout the year with war between Arabs and Jews in Palestine, Communist guerrilla campaigns in Malaya and Burma, civil war in Greece. In February, Czechoslovakia vanished behind the Iron Curtain after a Communist *coup d'état*. In June, Yugoslavia emerged from it, having been expelled from the Cominform for deviationist heresies.

The barriers throughout the world built up: the Warsaw Pact, the beginnings of a North Atlantic Treaty, the Organization for European Economic Cooperation to administer Marshall Aid, unofficial talks about a United Western Europe, supported by Churchill, rejected by Attlee on the grounds that it cut across plans for Atlantic unity.

In June, the Western allies prepared to perpetuate the division of Germany by setting up a West German Federal Government. The Soviet Union retaliated with an attempt to cut off supplies and fuel from the Western sector of Berlin. For a short time, it seemed that the West would either have to withdraw from the city, or go to war, but the R.A.F. and the American air force mounted an airlift which maintained a modicum of supplies to Berlin for almost a year, until the Russians somewhat sheepishly lifted what had never been more than a partial blockade.

At the end of June, fears about Russian intentions led to an American request to station atomic bombers in Britain, a move which not unnaturally excited the

A future British Prime Minister talks about European Union. Harold Macmillan, a Conservative M.P., visits
The Hague to talk about European union. But he is overshadowed by Winston Churchill, and few see him as a
future Prime Minister.

gravest alarm in Russia. The Americans were apprehensive about British public opinion, but Bevin immediately accepted the request on the British people's behalf, and the bombers arrived in mid-July.

In fact, Bevin's four-square, John Bull stance to the Russians probably delighted his fellow-countrymen as much as Philip Snowden's anti-French stand had done twenty years before. But it antagonized the always articulate Left Wing of the Labour Party, which has traditionally provided many of its most active workers. The introduction of selective military service in the United States was followed in November by raising the period of conscription in Britain from a year to eighteen months. Forty Labour M.P.s voted against the measure, and about a hundred more abstained.

On the home front, also, the Cabinet was suspected of being 'soft' on steel nationalization, which had been left until last in carrying out the party programme, and which was believed to be opposed by Morrison and the leaders of the steel unions.

By the end of the year a Government of weary men – many of whom had been continuously in office through five years of war and three years of scarcely less exacting peace – was beginning to show, for all its massive majority, obvious signs of decay, if not yet of disintegration.

Laurence Thompson

Sir Oswald Mosley Speaks at the Formation Conference of His Union Movement

WHY SHOULD ANYONE STILL FOLLOW MOSLEY?

Seldom in man's history has any creed proved more obviously disastrous to its followers than Fascism. Even if they have no regard for mankind as a whole, surely they might learn from what has happened to their fellow-Fascists! Yet here is Mosley starting up again. How is it possible for anyone still to believe in such a leader? How is it even possible for the 'leader' to believe in himself? This is a subject not for political invective but for scientific invest-igation, and Picture Post has asked a well-known Harley Street psychologist to try and find the answers.

Photographed by CHARLES HEWITT

THE other night my wife suddenly sprang up in bed. She was talking in her sleep, but her nightmare was not only hers. "There is something wrong!" she said. "I know there is something wrong! What is it? You must put it right at once!" It was about two o'clock in the morning—zero hour. Why should I be disturbed? I said,

"Oh, it will be all right. Go to sleep. We will see about it in the morning." I was not to be bothered. She fell asleep beside me, oblivious again; but I remained awake long enough to think twice. I thought—"Well, this is our problem. There is something wrong, and plenty. But the nightmare of our zero hour is that someone *will* get

up and do something about it, in too much of a hurry!" And then I thought again—"Yes, and you will go on sleeping like the others, while the wild ones run all of us over the precipice."

"Well, there are only two alternatives, aren't there," I said to myself rather petulantly in the dark: "You can either do something or you can do

Faces of Delegates in the Audience at a Mosley Meeting in the Year 1948

nothing. They can't *both* be wrong." And even though I was half-asleep, I knew that both alternatives were on the wrong track, as two opposites so often are, with their squabbling between who is right and who is wrong, and which one ought to be 'liquidated.'

Of course there is a third alternative, which is neither appeasement nor compromise. It is a way of paying attention carefully, with good humour and good-will, to both sides of the controversy and then coming to an understanding through experience, patiently. So when we are truly sane do we accept the inevitability of action at the right time and after considering all the circumstances.

We are all suffering more or less at this time from frustration and a feeling of despondency. What with the war and the price of war's all-round destruction, we are in a mess. How are we to get out of it, and who will lead the way? The sheep want a shepherd, the weak listen for the word of power, and the children are glad to surrender to the authority of the Father-Mother figure who is always right. Tired, anxious, impotent—we become urgently—and dangerously—ready for someone to save us and to put us all in his bag.

Of course, having found him, we know that he is 'right,' and those who differ must be 'wrong.' We know that the wrong must be destroyed, because we learnt in the nursery, in school and Church, that it was simply so. Evil and ignorance, it seems so clear, must be pursued to their destruction. The time is short. Right and wrong are as clearly divided as our world is split in twain : we have found both Leader and scapegoat, and the hunt begins. We are on the right side, and we have the power at last to prove the other wrong, and therefore there is no doubt he ought to disappear.

But, in fact, all argument on these lines is nursery stuff—and nonsense! On this level of thought and behaviour, we are no more than unweaned babies seeking for omnipotent mothers to exert their benevolent tyranny on our behalf—and obliterate our opponents with a smack. The moral tyranny is false which states, "because I am right, therefore I am entitled to compel you to change—or die !" In truth, we have no title to exercise this power over one another. In truth, the conviction that I am right and you are wrong does not entitle me to interfere with you at all : you and I remain equally free to exercise our choice about alternatives, despite my own conviction, and even despite my being right. All moral tyranny makes nonsense of free will, which is our human right.

And yet the moral exercise of so much free will as individual responsibility requires may seem to impose too heavy a burden on us, especially when we are tired and confused by the confusing clamour

" We Are All Suffering More or Less from Frustration and a Feeling of Impotency"

MOSLEY IN ACTION: A SET OF PICTURES WHICH DESERVES CLOSE STUDY

of alternatives. Many look back with longing to their privileged world of infancy, and its promise of escape. When our new Nannie, in the person of our Leader, calls "*You ought and you must !*" then Father-Mother-God (or is it only Lucifer ?) assumes an earthly throne, and moral tyranny must reign supreme. Hitler, Mussolini, Mosley—and all would-be Saviours who have plagued us in their time—are really only bolstered Nannies who bully, more or less benevolently, those children who prefer to regard them as divine.

The Longing for an All-powerful Parent

Let's face it. Many of us—and some part of all of us—have not quite grown up yet. We are still bound to 'mass' and 'mother,' collectively unweaned. Especially when in difficulties, we still look for some composite, all-powerful parent-figure to provide unlimited privilege for those who will accept the moral pressure of a benevolent authority. By composite parent-figure I mean a kind of super-human He-She-It which seems to combine in one person all the desirable attributes of Father, Mother and God. In our hearts—when unchecked by our powers of thought and reason—we are still looking for a saviour, a leader into a material Promised Land, who will be father, mother, country, God, and into whose hands our person, our very self and soul may be surrendered. This mythical and monstrous person must be, of course, on our side and all-powerful. In return for his willingness to do all this for us, we must on our side do all for him, abased in moral self-surrender. It is not only the declared Fascists who feel the need to be strengthened and comforted by being drawn, tight-laced and uniformed, within their leader's 'bundle.' There is *something* of this urgent but half-realised longing to be found in all of us. In essence, it is a longing to find *home*, and therefore appeals especially to those whose homes have somehow failed them in the past.

What was your own home-life like ? Was it secure in all the love and nourishment for heart and mind that the good home can provide ? (Mosley's parents separated when he was five years old.) Did you ever have trouble with your Dad, or were you despised by him, perhaps, as Mosley was ? Have you ever felt that you knew all the answers, and that if only 'they' were not so wrongly in the way, you would know just what to do and be able to get on with what you wanted in life ?

The Mosley boys are typical of all such deep-seated and unconscious craving for the unweaned joys of being done up in a mysterious and miraculous bundle, like babies restored to the basic comfort and protection of the womb again. Totally uncritical, their claim for power and privilege 'bundles'—into the single person of their leader—love of mother, power of father, and privilege of child, with a scapegoat conveniently thrown out. But Mosley's emotional appeal is not only to those suffering from an intolerable feeling of inferiority, to impatient egotists and frustrated adolescents looking for security and comfort. They are not the only ones who are looking for mother and father rolled into one in the person of their beloved Leader. Nor is it only to the childhood victims of unhappy homes, where father and mother did not play their honoured and respectful parts. His appeal is also to those who know and seek the colour and pageantry, the passionate purpose of living and dying for a worthy cause. Where life is dull and times are tedious, false hopes seem better than no hope at all.

Have you never burnt with resentment at the slowness, stupidity and inefficiency of other people, and felt how much better you could do it yourself ? Have you never felt fed-up with boredom and frustration, so that you wanted to smash something, almost anything, to get free ? Have you never felt uncertainly and passionately young, longing for some cause to share or ideal to follow, so that life might be full of wonder and glory ?

The Appeal to Discontent

No, the appeal of Mosley's leadership is not *only* to those who resent the frustration and responsibility of independent birth, nor to natural hooligans and thugs. It is also most dangerous for all who feel the need for more abundant life : and it is our job—the job of those who understand this youthful longing but appreciate its dangers—to see that such idealistic discontent is not deceived by false leaders and their specious promises.

Unity, urgency and heroics comprise a rich bait to trap the eager but unwary adolescent. What else are we to offer ? It is no use being negative. It is no use fighting Fascism simply with anti-Fascism, for the one leads inevitably to a strengthening of the other. The best way to deal with the Mosley boys is not the Mosley way of "You ought not!" and "You must !" That is the answer on the nursery level. The best way to counter a bad proposal is not by a blow, but by the offering of something better.

Our human rights and needs, when analysed, comprise a sufficiency of security (which includes all that nourishment means, and implies good mothering) : encouragement to experiment and adventure in the way of our own free choice (which is father's job); and opportunity for every child to grow, according to his needs and capacity. These are the right alternatives to Mosley's monstrous appeal for collective unity, urgency and heroics.

The Alternative: Happier Homes

The stress is laid upon personal responsibility ("Mind your own business !") and not upon the benevolent tyranny of an over-ruling authority; upon freedom of choice in regard to several alternatives, without which humanity is lost; and upon right relationship with persons and with things (such as machines) instead of the mere accumulation of power and property. For this purpose, a Government needs to use a minimum of directive (and obstructive) authority, and a maximum of decentralisation, so that power is invested in the people, the homes and the factories—which are the functional units of society present before our eyes—and not in the clerical armies of unseen bureaucracy. The creative alternative to Mosley is not increased overall planning and administrative efficiency, which owes a similar allegiance to the monster of collective Power. The real alternative is happy homes and contented workers, where all feel free to bear their share in making their own small world work better, and the whole great world a better place in which to live. But, above all, the welfare of the home and the fitness of parents is the foundation, as it is the training-ground, for a well-organised society.

The collective term 'we'—which is Society—is made up of many separate individual 'I's.' We all know the difficulty of relating the one that I am, to the many that we are, and of fitting in *my* will in such a way as to integrate it within the complexity of *ours*. To decide that 'I will' is comparatively simple. But to decide 'we will' is another and altogether more complicated matter. There are three alternative ways of making 'I' into 'We,' or three meanings which may belong to this small word 'we.'

First, there is the way of the *bundle*—which is the original meaning of Fascism. As a bundle of separate sticks may be stronger when bound together in a common tie, so many can be collected and bound up together in the common purpose of loyalty to one leader. Simple and powerful as this bundle may seem to be, it is essentially primitive and feeble, because the individual suffers obliteration in total subservience to the will of the whole as represented by the Leader. We are

234

unweaned again, returned to the womb of the Leader, who is our Father-Mother-God. In spite of its specious appearance of combining efficiency with felicity, this uncomfortable arrangement has been proved a fallacy by recent history.

Second, the term 'we' may refer to a *muddle*, an accidental congregation of the unrelated, who are bound together by no deeper tie than a shared desire to see a football match, or win some larger war. There is no cement to hold their unity together, as the time of 'peace' will prove.

Third, there is the 'we' of an *organic group*, in which the separate rights and differences of all are each respected within the fabric of the living whole. Such is (or should be) the principle of family life, but the same good system may apply in any human partnership. Thus capital can marry (but not exploit!) Labour, as the wedded partners of efficient industry.

Wherever many are concerned, Fascism solves the problem of unruly wills by reducing all to one, within the person of the Leader. There is no alternative, and so no freedom. But the solution of right relationships allows no such destruction of individual will and responsibility. Organic partnership, or 'marriage of the opposites,' exploits neither but includes both within the common ring and shared purpose of the welfare of the whole. The Fascist system is a throw-back in the long course of human history to primitive conditions, in which power exploits love to power's advantage. Our human heritage, so painfully acquired by countless years of suffering, becomes increasingly the way of love which uses power only for love's advantage. And to Christians the idea of love is, of course, the idea of God.

Why, you may ask, bring God into the argument? He is in it already, implicit in the Fascist belief and behaviour. The Leader is deified, as his enemies are diabolical. The worst feature of all atheistic creeds is the way in which they inevitably deify something, or someone, who is totally unworthy of such high office. Either persons or things, such as guns, tractors and machines, may receive this utmost promotion out of all good sense and good humour, by virtue of the surrender to them of that intrinsic and mysterious worth which belongs secretly within each one of us. Mosley and Co., in common with other more domestic tyrants, have put God in the bag along with the rest of us, and He, like us, must do the Leader's will. The argument is not a theoretical one, as to whether you

THE CLIMAX OF AN HOUR'S DENUNCIATION

or I believe in God. Either we do or we do not. In either case, surely He should not be bagged by any precocious, jumped-up saviour, who pretends to know His will and seeks to usurp His power!

But, in fact, do we believe that any man can save another man? To push the same question a stage further, do we believe that we, you and I, can even save *ourselves*, apart from the presumably more difficult task of saving one another? Does the doctor heal the wound and mend the broken bone, or does he only prepare the way for a more mysterious Healer? Does the politician lead us to the Promised Land, or does he only clear the ground over which each one of us must singly travel? Can we come nearer Heaven by pulling at our own belts?

It would greatly simplify our lives together on this awkward planet if we could accept the fact that we are all members of one great family, brothers and sisters, children of one Father. But if we cannot yet put our trust so simply in Him, need we promote our very earthly brother to be our Heavenly Father, expecting *him* to save us?

What an Hour of Mosley Does to His Audience
They have cheered whenever their leader has raised his voice to sustain abuse or defiance. Now they stand to cheer and chant again and again an incantation of M-O-S-L-E-Y. Some, remembering the 'old days,' give the Fascist salute.

Picture Post, November 20, 1948

The Life of a
PRISON OFFICER

Our prison system is out-dated. Public and prison officials agree. But with prison populations doubled by post-war crime wave, any progress demands more prison officers. And recruitment is tragically slow.

Photographed by BERT HARDY

He Fingerprints a Newcomer
Most convicted persons are fingerprinted every time they come into prison. Some say "Scotland Yard could make wallpaper of my prints."

THIS is the cruellest season in gaol, when summer is over and the prospect of Christmas seems cheerless. Each morning, at the six-thirty rising bell, is darker and colder than the morning before; and inside the big old prisons like Strangeways, Manchester, life seems ugly to the waking inmates. Most English prisons have an unreal look, like sets for an eerie film, laid out as they are with long, long rows of concrete galleries, radiating spoke-like from the hub of the control centre. In Strangeways the air of a bad dream is heightened by the Moorish-Gothic-Manchester style of the architecture.

On these raw mornings, Prison Officer Davidson

At 6.30 a.m., Strangeways Prison Has a Dead and Ghostly Look
Prison Officer Davidson, just arrived on duty, surveys his dominion. Row on row, the cells are silent. At any moment, the dreams of 880 prisoners will be shattered by the rising bell.

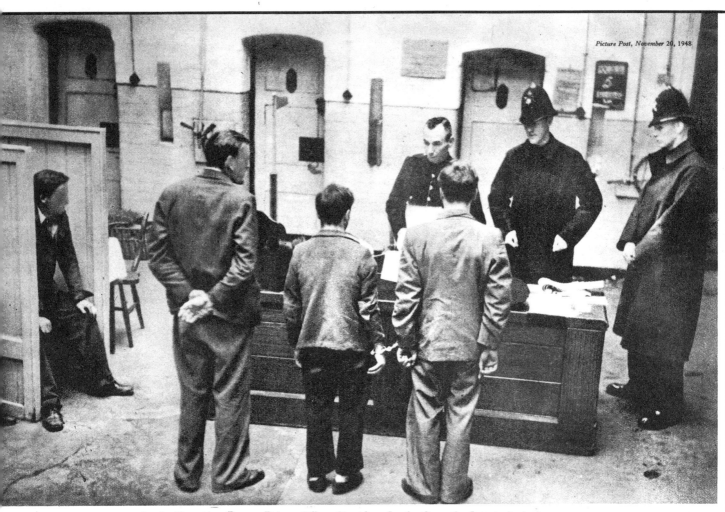

Picture Post, November 20, 1948

In the Reception Room, Prison Officer Davidson Looks Over the Latest Arrivals

Some are new faces. Some are old. Some are wild faces. Some are gentle. Some are faces showing bravado, remorse, indifference, or plain hangover. The owners of the faces have been brought in from local courts for a spell in gaol. The prison officer reads the warrants, classifies the men, allots them a uniform (grey for convicted men, brown for remanded men or debtors) and a cell. New arrivals are crowding out prisons at the rate of 47,000 a year.

and his colleagues need to be on their toes as soon as they unlock the cells for the first business of the day, the 'slopping out,' when the prisoners line up along the landings to empty their night-slops and fill their water jugs. Prison officers know that if tempers are ragged or feuds are in the air, the crowded 'sanitary recess' is a likely place for settling scores; and batterings and stabbings, so early in the morning, are not unknown. Already this year, three murders have been committed inside local prisons. None of them happened at Strangeways, and Davidson and his friends don't expect that sort of trouble on their hands. But they have their worries.

The main trouble with gaols is that too few officers are trying to look after too many prisoners. The prison population has doubled itself over the last nine years. War nerves, broken family ties, black-market prices that make robbery almost worth-while, have meant a startling rise in the incidence of crime. In pre-war times there would be about ten thousand prisoners in prisons and Borstals on any given day. Now there is about twenty thousand. The gaols are overcrowded, and just over 2,000 prisoners are sleeping three in a cell (it must be one or three; you can't have two men in a cell for reasons of love or hate). Officer Davidson can't remember any time during his ten years' service when the work was as exacting as it is today.

Davidson is one of the eighty discipline officers in charge of Strangeways' 884 prisoners. He is a typical prison officer (don't call them warders; the name went out twenty years ago), and a typical prison officer is not what folk on the outside might expect. He is a quiet, reasonable and sympathetic man, interested in his job and good at it, who can keep order without raising his voice or showing his muscles. He has the average sensual man's interest in rummy and the pools, and he is the branch secretary of his trade union—the Prison Officers' Association—which has a hundred-per-cent. mem-

His First Duty of the Day: 'Slopping Out'

Early in the morning comes the hated job of emptying night-slops. Officers need extra vigilance, as the 'sanitary recess' is sometimes a setting for violence among feuding prisoners.

One Way to Pass the Time
Some prisoners spend hours untying knots—
'Strangeways love-knots'—in Post Office string.

Thrice a Day He Turns Waiter
Some eat in company. Most eat in their cells.
The officer serves each man on his landing.

The Tedious Hours Creep By
Prisoners' dreariest job is making mail-bags. Officers' dreariest job is watching them do it.
Wire netting stretches across the landings to prevent prisoners' suicide-falls.

bership in Strangeways Gaol.

Like all prison officers, he works a long day, and sometimes a varied one. Perhaps, for instance, he receives prisoners into gaol; or he may supervise the visits of prisoners' relatives (in Strangeways they still keep to the old system of obliging prisoners to talk to their visitors from behind a glass partition in a cubicle); or he may be busy part of the time paying out prisoners' 'wages' or censoring their letters; or a hundred other tasks, intricate or simple, interesting or boring beyond measure. He says he has never dared to tot up the hours spent standing around, watching the long grey rows of prisoners untying the tangles in Post Office string (they call them 'Strangeways love-knots'), or slowly shredding mattress fibre, or bent over mail-bags, stitching their time away, eight stitches to the inch, two thousand seven hundred and eighty-four stitches to the mail-bag, two mail-bags every seven hours and forty minutes (that is the quota, and for every hour's work above the quota, the prisoner is paid a third of a penny, up to a maximum of 1s. 5d. a week). Supervision of mail-bag and workshop parties is likely to be a boring, nagging job; and at the same time officers know that any lapse of

vigilance may well be serious, where folk of violent nature are handling tools that can cut a man's flesh or batter his bones.

Not that most prisoners are violent, nor even remarkably wicked men. Prison officers know better than most, that the bulk of gaol inmates only differ from the rest of mankind in that they happen to have been caught. You do find officers who are martinets, just as, in the army, you come across bullying N.C.O.s. They are the exceptions. Most prison officers look on their charges with far more sympathy and tolerance than even prisoners realise. But the system common to many prisons imposes a behaviour-pattern that means secret and endless conflict between gaoler and gaoled. In the wide world outside, life is a battle for power or love or some such godlike thing. In the narrow world inside, the absorbing struggle is for a fag-end, a library book, a sheet of writing paper. For the prisoner, the weapons of the struggle are guile and artfulness; and whether he wishes or not, the gaoler must bring his scale of values down to the fine focus of the gaoled. For either, it is the pettiness of prison life that is the wearing thing.

For one hour of the day—usually between two

Picture Post, November 20, 1948

He Teaches a New Boy an Old Prison Art
Habituals know it well. 'Star' prisoners (first time in) have to learn the mailbag art. Eight stitches to the inch; 348 inches to the mailbag; two mail-bags every day. Week in, month out.

and three in the afternoon—Officer Davidson will march his working party into the prison yard to join others for exercise. Four officers will supervise a single party of some two hundred men. The exercise yards in Strangeways are set in the angle of the prison wings. They are a maze of concrete, with sad oases of earth, where a few soot-covered flowers turn their defeated faces to the Manchester sky. Here the prisoners walk round and round and back and forth, clockwise and anticlockwise, as if in a crazy squirrel-cage. All look remarkably alike to the eye of the stranger, who can't help wondering why, with prison greys, the jackets are *always* several sizes too loose, while the trousers are several sizes too tight.

The prisoners are supposed to circulate at an even pace, in twos and threes, at a distance of two yards apart (so that they don't hold up the files, the cripples take their exercise alone, hobbling along the margin of the yard, away from the rest of their comrades). Nowadays, with overcrowding, the two-yards rule is relaxed, and, indeed, quite a lot of latitude is allowed the prisoners.

The exercise-hour is often the prisoners' best opportunity for what is called in prison language 'association.' And, if the discipline officers are not vigilant, it is one of the times when the 'barons' do their business. A baron is a prison aristocrat, who rises to his eminence by trading in 'snout'—the prisoner's word for tobacco. What he does is to save

A Familiar Scene: The 'Rub Down' at the Prison Centre
Every time a working party comes into the prison centre, they are searched for scissors, knives, razor-blades, anything that might cut a fellow's flesh, or make a hole in a prison wall.

For One Hour Every Day, the Prison Officer Guards the Prisoners at their Exercise.   They Walk Between the Sooty

his weekly workshop earnings till he has enough money to buy, say, half an ounce of tobacco and a packet of papers. From this he will roll 60 cigarettes, to bring him in at least 100 per cent. profit. With that money, he buys more tobacco, rolls more cigarettes, accumulates more profit. In a short time, if the baron is a skilled operator, he will have a whole host of prisoners in his debt, buying tobacco for him from the prison canteen (for he dare not draw attention to his own affluence), collecting the week's takings from other prisoners, even beating-up any welshers or slow-payers, on the baron's behalf. Such ganging as exists inside prison is likely to centre round the personality of the baron, so one of the things that prison officers must watch for, during exercise-time, is the furtherance of the baron's business. He is a kind of parable version of the big monopolist, and the horror of it is that, un-checked, he will assume the power of life and death over his less talented comrades, for the sake of a few shillings a week.

About five o'clock, the prisoners put down their mail-bags, switch off their looms, check in their tailor's scissors and their cobbler's knives, and are marched back to their cells. The officer in charge of the landing unlocks the cell door, the prisoner walks in. The door is slammed to, and locked. Standing in the prison centre, you hear the echo-less crash of door after door, till finally there is no more. Still, for Officer Davidson the day is not done. His last job is to supervise the serving of tea along his landing. Two orderlies carry the stuff. Officer Davidson unlocks each cell, hands in to the prison-ers a cob of bread weighing one pound, a one-ounce pat of margarine, a pint of tea (the bread and margarine is to last for breakfast as well); and then the cell-door is shut again, and for most prisoners it will not open until the next morning. Officer Davidson descends the iron stairs, signs (for the *n*th time during the day) the register certifying that every man in his charge is present, and lines up with his comrades, ready to be dismissed by the Chief

Officer. By 5.30 most of the prison officers will be away, except for the few who are working overtime or on night patrol. A bleak silence falls on the prison, disturbed now and then by the fluttering of stray pigeons who have crept in some open fanlight, and who fly up and down the galleries in the dusk. Davidson says they're the souls of departed 'screws' ('screw' is the old prison slang for a warder). By nine o'clock the lights are out. The lonely officers on night duty pace the landings in a silence that is heavy with the dreams of eight hundred men.

Prison officers find their profession is a queer mixture. About half of them work, like Davidson, in local prisons. The other half work in Borstals, Training Centres, Convict Prisons; and for them life is rather different. But the basic factors remain the same. Anything to do with prisoners has a special fascination; yet the routines of the business are rather dull. The wage-rates, on the whole, are unimpressive; yet the job is unusually secure, as slumps don't affect it, and it carries a

Flower Beds, with the Prison Walls Around and the Manchester Sky Above. It is the Nearest Thing they have to Freedom

pension at fifty-five.

Davidson says what he likes best about the job are the things that break the monotony—especially escort duties, which may involve bringing a prisoner to London, say, or some such far-flung place. He enjoys the work of receiving prisoners, and of letter-censoring. What he likes least is standing around doing nothing but watch the men at the mailbags, the looms, or the toy-soldier moulds.

As a good trade unionist, he has his views about 'conditions.' At present, a prison officer works 84 hours a fortnight plus a compulsory 10 hours' overtime (called the 'Morrison hour'). The basic pay is £4 18s. a week, with nine yearly rises of 3s. a week. On top of that, free unfurnished accommodation is provided, or a rent allowance in lieu (in London, the rent allowance is 22s. 6d.). There is always the chance of promotion up to the rank of Chief Officer, with a top salary of £9 10s. a week, or even to the rare and dizzy height of Governor. At 55, officers retire on a pension whose

amount depends on length of service. The full pension is half-pay.

The Prison Officers' Association is trying to negotiate a 20 per cent. rise at present; and one of the arguments they put forward is that, with living costs as they are, the officer is likely to be tempted to raise a little extra cash by smuggling 'snout' to prisoners at fancy rates. The practice is dangerous, for once an officer starts trafficking, prisoners may blackmail him into going on with it, and what began as a relatively tame bit of tobacco-smuggling, may end with the officer handing the prisoner lethal weapons or even keys.

In a sense, the future of Britain's prison system depends a great deal on this simple hours-and-wages question. There is still some doubt among prison officials as to why men are sent to gaol. Is it to punish them? To keep them out of harm's way? To reform them? The most-favoured view is the latter; and though existing gaols are not designed for the job, the Prison Commission has made a

, genuine attempt to turn some of them into reformative institutions where prisoners can learn something which will be of practical value to them as citizens, and wage-earners, when they are released. The régime of most prisons has considerably mellowed over the past few years, and prison governors are often found to be progressive and intelligent people. Meanwhile, all the extra 'freedoms' and reforms have quite changed the prison officer's job, and though much of his work consists of unlocking doors and searching cells and counting heads, he is nowadays much more than a mere turnkey, and in many prisons he is expected to be a fellow who can help to make a prisoner's existence bearable, and to aid him to feel there is a worthwhile life in front of him when he comes out. But the notion of educating men in gaol and giving them a sense of purpose, is winning small success because prisons are overcrowded (so that rooms for leisure are turned into cells), and there just aren't enough prison officers to tend men outside their cells after tea-time.

Picture Post, November 20, 1948

The Five O'clock Scene That Means the End of the Prisoner's Day: the Moment Before he Enters His Cell for the Night
Most are in their cells already. Soon Officer Davidson will unlock the doors for his men. Then the doors will slam to again, with that echo-less bleakness that prison sounds have. Silence will fall, broken only by the footsteps of the night-duty officer. Most prisoners will not leave their cells again till morning.

The Spy-hole Check-up
Observation-glass is its polite name. There's one to each cell. Officers can see if a man is escaping, committing suicide, falling sick.

Many feel with Officer Davidson that to put the humanitarian prison reforms into action would necessitate a double shift of prison officers, and present staffing doesn't allow it. The only chance is by quicker recruiting and training; and with the national shortage of man-power, quicker recruiting can only be got by an improvement in pay, housing, and other conditions. As it is now, he says, staffs are strained to the limit and supervision is getting less efficient, so instead of prisons being healthier places than before, they are distinctly rougher. Prison officers have reported at trade union conferences that gangs are growing among the prisoners, rackets are developing in fancy forms, and razor-slashings—even murders—are on the increase inside prison.

The last Report of the Prison Commissioners, issued in July this year, and covering 1946, shows 606 cases of violence against the person in local and convict prisons; attempts to escape (the nagging fear of all prison officials) numbered 343. (1936, a 'normal' pre-war year, showed 482 cases of violence, 15 attempted escapes, though it should be remembered that the prison population was only half the present size, and outside working parties were fewer.) One result of all this has been that, instead of prisoners getting more rehabilitation training, workshop hours have had to be reduced so that prison officers may give more time to searching prisoners and their cells. Like his colleagues, Officer Davidson wants to see our prisons made happier places. He believes it can be done. But, he says, far more prison officers than we've got at present will be needed if the prisons are to be run as decent folk feel they ought to be.　　　　A. L. Lloyd

An Important Part of a Prison Officer's Job: the Cell Search
It happens every now and then. A man's cell is turned upside down. Bolts and bars are tested. Bedding is carefully gone over. The prisoner is stripped down for a thorough search. Officers look not only for tools and weapons, but also for money or tobacco—evidence of racketeering.

Hindsight by C. H. Rolph

One sentence of this 1948 article could well be the opening for mine.

> The notion of educating men in gaol and giving them a sense of purpose, is winning small success because prisons are overcrowded (so that rooms for leisure are turned into cells), and there just aren't enough prison officers to tend men outside their cells after tea-time.

That picture is not much changed except that, now as then, cells which might once have been 'rooms for leisure' have always started out as cells – and had to come back to that.

What changes *would* prison officer Davidson find if he came back to the Service now? The 2,000 men sleeping three to a cell have become 6,000. It's no longer true, in all prisons, that 'exercise hour' is the prisoner's best opportunity for 'association': there's much freer association today wherever it can be arranged – with T.V. and cards and table tennis and educational classes – even among the hard-nut prisoners. The tobacco barons are still there, but they rule smaller empires because cigarettes are more accessible; they could be got rid of altogether if we allowed free cigarettes and tobacco as in Californian prisons. In a 'local' prison, namely one that takes remands and short-term sentences as well as long-timers awaiting allocation, many visitors still have to be talked to (or shouted at) through a glass-and-wire-mesh screen; and as a rule you have to do it standing up. Letters are still censored. Mailbags are still stitched. The prisons have changed rather less, in fact, than the prison officers, among whom there are probably fewer bullies (there are about as many as you find in any other job) and more 'sympathy and tolerance' than twenty years ago.

To tell the truth, I thought the whole scene had changed more than it has. Reading this 1948 account is a bit depressing. But reading history always is, for the only thing we ever learn from it is that we never learn from it.

The Youngest Winning Jockey We Can Remember
He is Lester Piggott, twelve years old, four feet six, and a straw-chewer with the best of them. At Haydock Park recently, he showed he can ride winners too. But so far it's only a holiday pastime. He won't be a serious jockey till he leaves school.

An Illustrious Grandparent
One of Lester's grandfathers was Ernest Piggott, thrice National winner (twice on Poethlyn, above). Other grandfather won a Derby.

Even the Horses Have Their Eye on Him
Riding is in his blood. Horses are all his life. His out-of-school time is spent helping in his father's stables at Lambourn, Berks.

HOLIDAY JOCKEY

At twelve Lester Piggott has won his first big race. Just now, it's only holiday work. Crack jockeys may look out when Lester leaves school.

WHEN Lester Piggott booted home a horse called The Chase at Haydock Park the other week, he was cheered as the youngest boy to win a flat race within living memory. At twelve years old, he had beaten some of the craftiest jockeys in the North, to gain his first victory in five races this year.

Riding is in Lester's blood. His grandfather, Ernie Piggott, was a well-known steeplechase jockey who won three Grand Nationals. His other grandfather, Tom Cannon, rode his first winner at the age of nine, and won the Derby on Shotover in 1882.

For Lester Piggott, jockeying is a bit of holiday fun. Despite the attention gained by his win, he will not take up racing seriously until he is fifteen, and has done with school.

Vol. 41. No. 4.

PICTURE POST

OCTOBER 23, 1948

A Cockney Shows His Star the Town
Before Ingrid Bergman leaves for a short holiday in Sweden, Film-director Alfred Hitchcock, who was born within sound of Bow Bells and was married at Brompton Oratory, takes her round his London.

Ingrid's Last Look at London

Ingrid Bergman was here to shoot her new film 'Under Capricorn.' It is a story of an uneasy triangle, whose other corners are Joseph Cotten and Michael Wilding.

Photographed by K. HUTTON

WHEN Ingrid Bergman arrived in London, three months ago, to work under Alfred Hitchcock's direction on the latest Transatlantic Pictures film, *Under Capricorn,* the first thing she noted with pleasure was that nobody bothered her. Wherever she moved in California, she had been aware of being watched and reported. But here, in restaurants and night-clubs, nobody cared. "You can go and dance where you please, and though people may notice you as you walk in, they don't worry you; and

there's nothing in the papers next day."

When we took Miss Bergman on a sight-seeing tour of London, we saw what she meant. There was scarcely a passer-by who batted an eyelid. But it occurred to us that the reason for this consistent courtesy lay, perhaps, less in the profound and proverbial diffidence of the British bobby-soxer and film-fan, than in Miss Bergman's own personality. Because the first thing you notice about her is that she doesn't talk like a film star. She doesn't walk like a film star. She is not

Busy People in a Busy Street
Lombard Street on its weekly day-off. And Bergman and 'Hitch' on their first real day-off for months.

245

"This is Where the Police Force Began . . ."
Hitchcock, the first director to make the English policeman a convincing figure on the screen, takes Miss Bergman along to Bow Street.

"That's Where Heads Used to Roll . . ."
On Tower Green, Hitchcock shows off the site of the scaffold where so many famous English men and women were beheaded.

made up to look like a film star. Nor is she made up, in the manner of some continental screen-actresses, to look as unlike a film star as possible. She is not made up at all. Neither made up, nor stuck-up. On the other hand, she is refreshingly reluctant to pretend to be interested in things that bore her. But when she *is* interested, either in a building or a view or a person, her face and expression take on the keen, tremulous alertness of a setter. At such moments, it would be almost impossible for anyone to guess her nationality. She could easily be from Scotland or Northern Italy or Austria or Jugoslavia or Scandinavia or Hungary. Maybe that is why film-goers of so many nations feel that they have a special claim on her, and why she comes nearer than any other living screen-actress to the thing which ought to be meant by the words 'universal appeal. But if her appeal is universal, her personality and identity are very much her own. When, for instance, after a long morning's sight-seeing she said : "Now why don't we go to a pub ?" we couldn't help recognising that she didn't say it because she thought film stars ought to go to a pub to show how human they are, nor because she wanted to creep away and drink and forget; but because she quite simply liked pubs and pubbishness. And for us, too, that made a change.

"So He Said: 'Shoot . . .' "
"You play darts ?" asked Hitch. "No, but Gary Cooper taught me to shoot," said Bergman.

"So I Picked up the Rifle . . ."
"He said 'Just pick it up and point it straight at the target, that's all'."

"And it Went Into the Bull . . ."
"The first time was fine. But after that I could never hit a haystack."

Conversation-piece in 'The George,' at Southwark: "That's Another Thing About the English: They Like Warm Beer"
'Under Capricorn' is the third film in which Alfred Hitchcock has directed Ingrid Bergman. The other two were 'Spellbound' and 'Notorious.' This is the second film—'Rope' being the first—that Hitchcock has made for Transatlantic Pictures, which is owned by himself and Sidney Bernstein.

1949

On 22 January 1949 Chinese Communist troops entered Peking – an event little noticed in the West, preoccupied with its own crisis over Berlin. Shanghai fell in May, and by September the red banner with its five-pointed gold star representing the Communist Party, and its arc of four satellite stars representing workers, peasants, petty bourgeoisie and national bourgeoisie, waved over most of mainland China. On 1 October the People's Republic of China, with Mao Tse-tung at its head, was formally proclaimed before a crowd of two hundred thousand in the Square of the Gate of the Heavenly Peace in Peking. The Nationalist Chinese Generalissimo Chiang Kai-shek withdrew to Formosa, announcing that the Third World War had begun.

The new Government was immediately recognized by Russia, whose technicians and military experts were already at work in the country, and in mid December Chairman Mao was received by Stalin in Moscow with every appearance of friendship, though with many private reservations. Britain and Norway alone of the Western countries recognized Mao's China, and a request for recognition by the United Nations was refused. The Russian representative on the Security Council was thereupon instructed to take no further part in its work while the Nationalist Chinese representative remained – a decision which was to have important later consequences.

On 22 September the American, British and Canadian Governments announced that Russia had recently exploded an atomic bomb. The news was not unexpected, but the Russian Government denied the announcement, saying that it had only been engaged on large-scale blasting operations. The chairman of the American Joint Chiefs of Staff, General Bradley, forecast that if no agreement on international control of the bomb could be reached, America would have to invest in defensive measures on a vast scale; and reports spread, officially confirmed early in the following year, that the Americans were making a hydrogen bomb a hundred to a thousand times more destructive than the atomic bomb.

Throughout the latter half of 1949, the apparent solidarity of the Communist front was broken by the trial and execution of Eastern European Communist leaders on charges of spying for Yugoslavia and the Western imperialists. Less publicized was Stalin's purge of 'enemies of the people' in Russia itself, which included the chief economic planner of the Politburo, and almost engulfed Stalin's eventual successors, Malenkov and Khrushchev.

In the West, a German Federal Republic was formally proclaimed, with Dr Konrad Adenauer as its elected Chancellor, and Dr Ludwig Erhard as Minister of Economic Affairs. The German economic miracle had begun. Proclamation of the East's German Democratic Republic followed in October. East and West accused each other of rearming their own half of Germany, indignant denials followed, and both East and West Germany were presently rearmed.

In Britain, there was a springtime of mild euphoria. The end of sweet rationing was triumphantly announced in April, followed by a holiday bonus of petrol, and the President of the Board of Trade proclaimed a 'bonfire' of controls which removed the need for nearly a million licences and permits a year, including those over such exotic items as hairnets and veilings, pine oil, and raw goatskins. It was revealed that export targets for 1948 had been exceeded, and Sir Stafford Cripps, the Chancellor, celebrated by taking a penny a pint off beer in his budget, though he added a halfpenny on a box of matches. He also spoke ominously of the need for some special charge on the health services, to bring home to users that they had to be paid for out of taxation. The cost of the services had risen by forty per cent over the original estimates, and went on rising.

Springtime did not last. In April, a series of strikes began in the docks and on the railways, which held up the flow of exports and led the Government to proclaim a state of emergency, with the use of troops to unload perishable foods. The Prime Minister and others found in the strikes evidence of a Russian-inspired plot to sabotage British economic recovery. The small British Communist Party did in fact exercise an influence out of all proportion to its numbers, through the willingness of its members to attend union meetings and undertake the routine work of organization at shopfloor level. Without them, and the political opposition they stirred up, the British trade union movement would have been even more moribund than it had become; but for this the Communists received no gratitude.

In any event, British recovery was sabotaged less by strikes than by a minor American recession which hit dollar exports and caused what the Minister of Fuel and Power, Hugh Gaitskell, called 'a day of supreme crisis for the Government'. The gold and dollar reserves plummeted by £66 million. The Government met the crisis by reintroducing sweet rationing, and once again cutting dollar imports of tobacco, timber and paper. Sir Stafford Cripps denied that there was any question of devaluing the pound, and a thirty per cent devaluation two months later consequently came as no great surprise. Most of the Western world followed the British devaluation, so that the advantage was lost almost immediately, and with the autumn came another crisis. Sir Stafford announced

The Spring everyone has waited for: for the first time the Nation is having a slightly easier life.

cuts in housing, education and capital investment, together with a shilling charge on National Health Service prescriptions. Sir Stafford had assured a large radio audience that devaluation would not alter the internal value of the pound; but prices rose, and Sir Stafford proclaimed a policy of wage restraint, which the T.U.C. loyally accepted on behalf of eight million trade unionists who had not been consulted and turned out to have different views.

Astonishingly enough, the Government had not lost a by-election during its four crisis-haunted years of life, and it began its preparations for a General Election with a confidence unshaken even by the events of the summer. A new programme was presented to the Labour Party conference, under the condescending title *Labour Believes in Britain*, which included proposals for nationalizing industrial insurance, cement, the sugar industry, and water supplies. The list seemed to stop

some way short of what Aneurin Bevan called the commanding heights of the economy, and did little to inspire party workers disillusioned by the party's rightward trend. But it did stir up forthright opposition from the industries concerned. Very shortly, the Man from the Prudential, with bluff man-to-man honesty, was assuring the reader of advertisements that private insurance delivered the goods, and few housewives could escape the blandishments of an engaging character called Mr Cube, who appeared on every pack of Tate & Lyle's sugar putting a voter's cross through the 'S' in 'State'. Morrison voiced solemn warnings that the large sums spent on these campaigns might be held to infringe the Representation of the People Act, but Mr Cube only thumbed his nose unrepentantly, and the Government did nothing about it.

Laurence Thompson

Photograph by Baron

FIRST PUBLIC APPEARANCE: *Prince Charles in his Grandmother's Arms After His Christening on December 15*

The Queen smiles at her little grandson as his nurse, Sister Helen Rowe, comes to carry him back to his nursery after the christening. The nursery is simply the old school-room of Princess Elizabeth and Princess Margaret into which a cot and nursery fittings have been moved.

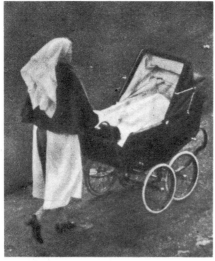

FIRST OUTING: *Three Weeks Old*

His nurse wheels him in the palace grounds— snapped by a cameraman with a tele-lens.

THE BABY: HIS FIRST

JUST six months ago, on Sunday, November 14, 1948, Princess Elizabeth's child was born. A Royal Prince, second in succession to the throne, his birth was heralded by salutes of guns, peals of church bells, loyal addresses and deep and wide national rejoicing.

On December 6 large newspaper headlines announced that the baby Prince had had his first outing. Miss Helen Rowe, the nurse who had attended his birth, pushed him in his pram—the one used by his mother 22 years before—in the pale winter sunshine around the grounds of Buckingham Palace. He was still the 'baby Prince'—no name had been announced for him—and though various suggestions were made about long-range cameras being trained on the gardens of Buckingham Palace, there were still no photographs to be seen of him. Ridiculous rumours were even printed suggesting that something must be wrong with the child's health as no photographs had appeared. It was only

on the day on which he was christened that it was announced that his mother and father had chosen to call him Charles.

On December 15, at a silver-gilt lily font made for Queen Victoria in 1840, in the White and Gold Music Room of Buckingham Palace, the infant prince was given the names Charles Philip Arthur George. Wearing the Royal christening robe of white silk and Honiton lace which was worn by all Queen Victoria's children, he was carried into the room by his nurse. The service was simple and attended only by the King and Queen, members of the Royal Family, and a few of their close friends.

Later in the day Prince Charles posed for his first press photographs. The photographers' descriptions of "a model baby, healthy, blue-eyed, wispy-haired and as well-behaved as babies usually are," published with many of the photographs, made front-page news all over the world.

On January 5 the Royal baby made his first

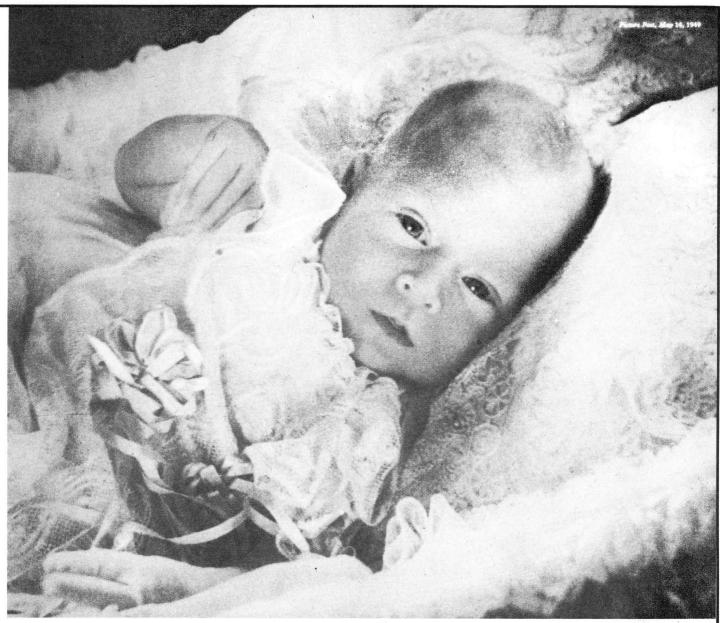

Photograph by Cecil Beaton

FIRST CLOSE-UP PORTRAIT: *'The Royal Baby' has Just Become Prince Charles Philip Arthur George of Edinburgh*
His christening has just taken place in the White and Gold Music Room of Buckingham Palace. They have used a silver-gilt lily font made more than a hundred years ago for Queen Victoria. He wears the traditional Royal Christening robe of white silk and Honiton lace.

SIX MONTHS

public appearance, and had his first glimpse of the English countryside when he went by car to Sandringham. As he left the Palace, thousands of women saw the seven-weeks-old baby sleeping peacefully in his mother's arms in the back of the black saloon car which was one of Princess Elizabeth's wedding presents. At the wheel, like any other father, was the Duke of Edinburgh.

On March 4 Prince Charles held his first court, when he was seen and admired by thirteen of his grandfather's Privy Councillors, five from the House of Lords and eight from the House of Commons.

Such is the official life of the Royal baby. His private life is much like any other baby's. It consists of sleeping and eating. He is, perhaps, a little more travelled than most babies of his age, as his first six months of life have been spent in three different homes—Buckingham Palace, Sandringham, and his parents' country house, Windlesham Moor, near Ascot, in Surrey. But, like all babies, it is of

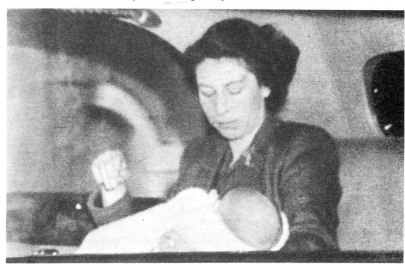

FIRST CAR RIDE : *He Leaves for Sandringham*
The seven-weeks-old baby sleeps peacefully in his mother's arms on his first journey. His father is at the wheel of a car given to them as a wedding present.

Photographs by Baron

FIRST INFORMAL SNAP : *He Discovers the Joys of Necklace-Grabbing*

Now five months old, the baby has discovered his own hands and feet. He likes holding on to his mother's finger, can make a shrewd grab at a necklace and hang on. Princess Elizabeth has decided that his upbringing is to be as simple and quiet as she can make it.

little importance to him whether the pearl necklace he plays with is worth thousands of pounds or a few shillings, as long as its wearer is a loving mother. At present he is just a baby, crying when he's hungry and uncomfortable, chuckling when he's warm and well-fed, and instinctively wanting little else than loving care and affection.

All too soon a public position will be thrust upon him. Realising, no doubt, the enormous benefits she

herself derived from the normal childhood and family life insisted upon by her own parents as Duke and Duchess of York, Princess Elizabeth has from the moment of his birth resisted any efforts to have her baby drawn from the kindly seclusion of the nursery. And the arrangements made for his nursery in Buckingham Palace are typical of his mother's outlook. Though various descriptions were published of rooms lavishly decorated with

fairy-tale animals and figures from nursery rhymes, in actual fact the room in which Princess Elizabeth and Princess Margaret had both done their lessons was simply cleared of its schoolroom furniture, and a cot and nursery equipment was moved in. Princess Elizabeth had no illusions about a newly-born baby—Royal or otherwise—being able to appreciate decorated walls or furniture. Her son's upbringing is likely to be based on the simplicity which

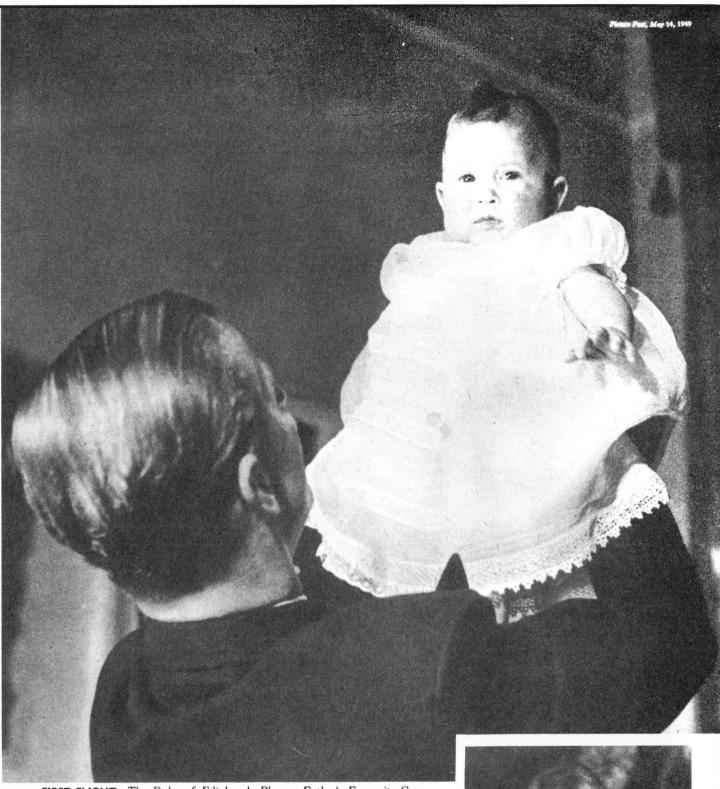

FIRST FLIGHT: *The Duke of Edinburgh Plays a Father's Favourite Game*
The airborne game, favourite of all fathers with their children, and reported to be the favourite game of most small babies with their fathers.

guided her own. Even some of her toys have been saved for him. When, as Duke and Duchess of York, her parents visited Australia in 1927, Princess Elizabeth was nine months old. The thought of the baby daughter left at home here in England appealed to the imagination of the Australian people. Not one, but thousands presented the Royal couple with toys for their little girl. Many of these toys were given to hospitals, but of those kept for Prin-cess Elizabeth herself, several have been saved and will in turn amuse her baby son.

Princess Elizabeth's charm of character endears her to everybody wherever she goes. However inherent this may be, such a manner is undoubtedly encouraged by environment and upbringing. And to-day she in her turn wishes to give her son the natural childhood which meant so much to her, and to which any small boy in our country is entitled.

FIRST RECORDED SMILE
Imagined smiles begin at birth. Real smiles can start any time after the first few weeks.

Hindsight by Robert Kee

At first sight it is the changes in the colour situation which stand out after twenty years. It now seems almost incredible that it could have been possible seriously to raise the question: 'Is There a British Colour Bar?' when the total coloured population of this country was only about 25,000. Today that population is about a million and a quarter. Where in 1949 it was possible to talk of only two 'large' concentrations of coloured people – 7,000 in Cardiff and 8,000 in Liverpool – today there are concentrations in every growth area of Great Britain, but principally in Greater London, in the south-east generally, in the West Midlands, and in the West Riding of Yorkshire. And, by comparison with 1949, they are really large.

Since so much of today's argument about coloured immigrants is concerned with figures it is important to have today's figures straight. Mr Enoch Powell – though for subconscious reasons he may be inclined to exaggerate – is basically correct when he suggests that the present figures will be much greater still. They will be at least double at the end of twenty years. This is not because of continued immigration. Though many people still have the impression that immigrants are pouring into this country at a 'dangerous' rate, immigration has of course been legally restricted by the Labour Government. Only 7,500 work permits a year are now available to citizens of all Commonwealth countries, and as these are only issued to the highly skilled, only about 4,000 a year are taken up. However the wives and children of immigrants already legally here are still allowed in. These amounted to some 50,000 last year. In the nature of things this annual figure will fall sharply as the number of those legally here with work permits barely increases. But Mr Powell, in the figures at least of his forecast, may still not be so far wrong, for in another respect 'the nature of things' takes a decisive hand. The majority of those immigrants legally here with work permits are young people who will marry and have children here. The situation is in terms of figures of a totally different dimension from twenty years ago.

And yet fundamentally it is the same situation. For if difficulties are caused by integrating coloured immigrants into a white society of over fifty million when there are only 25,000 of them, then clearly the causes of those difficulties have little to do with numbers at all. It is in high-lighting this point that this article seems to have some modern relevance.

Apart from the question of numbers, some details of the situation are today 'better' – if one accepts integration as desirable –, some worse, many the same. Today we have positive legislation against racial discrimination such as was then only envisaged as a remote possibility, but it is still true that 'the problem is too fundamental to be solved by mere remedial steps'. A Race Relations Board exists to assist the law in positively prohibiting an official British colour bar. But the invisible colour bar has become more subtle and now even has its visible advocates. Prejudice continues to beget counter-prejudice, but I think few coloured people would say today as they did then, that an outright colour bar like that in South Africa would be preferable to the state of affairs here. On the whole the article's rather optimistic note – a little too glib perhaps when numbers did not put it to the test – has, I think, been borne out. Where white and coloured people are together they get on well together. It is when conditions keep them segregated in our society that things are not so easy, and the fact that so many new Pakistani immigrants speak no English has undoubtedly been a temporary complicating factor.

Though prejudice is, with ignorance, one source of opposition to multi-racialism, on both sides, I think I laid too much simple emphasis on this. Today I see the question of whether or not one wants an integrated multi-racial society as more clearly a matter of deliberate choice about life itself. Do you find the continually changing nature of life and society in itself something interesting, or something dreadful? I happen to find the spirit of life as expressed in Bert Hardy's picture on the last page of this article an ideal to be worked for rather than a 'danger' to be feared.

Picture Post, 2 July, 1949

IS THERE A BRITISH COLOUR BAR ?

Photographed by BERT HARDY

Britain stages Colonial Month—a campaign to stimulate popular interest in the life and people of the Colonies. The King attends the opening ceremony. But there are more than 20,000 Colonial people who live among us. What do we know of them—of their work, of their living conditions, their hopes and grievances? Picture Post conducts a survey into this dangerous and important question.

IT is not possible to find out the exact number of colonial coloured people in Great Britain. There is no registry of people with black skin, any more than there is a registry of people with black hair. And there you discover the first important fact about the colour bar in Britain : officially it does not exist. For the purpose of the law and the administration of Britain there is no distinction whatsoever made between white and coloured British subjects—they are all just British subjects. And the same official lack of discrimination is echoed categorically by all government departments, professional organisations and trade unions. But offices and organisations are run by human beings, and inside the minds of human beings, both in and outside offices, strange fogs of ignorance and prejudice can be at work.

Although there are no official figures, the coloured population of Great Britain is estimated by both the Colonial Office and the League of Coloured People at about 25,000, including students. This total is distributed over the whole of Britain, but there are two large concentrated communities : one of about 7,000 in the dock area of Cardiff round Loudoun Square, popularly known as 'Tiger Bay', and the other of about 8,000 in the shabby mid-nineteenth century residential South End of Liverpool. These came into existence largely as a result of the immigration of colonial coloured people to work as seamen, soldiers and factory hands in the First World War. They were supplemented during the Second. Smaller coloured communities are found in all the main ports including London (there is one of about 2,000 in North and South Shields), in Manchester and the industrial areas of the Midlands. The prosperity of these different communities varies.

The term 'colonial coloured people' is, of course,

On the Curb of a Liverpool Pavement a Coloured British Subject Expresses the Indignation of His People
Officially there is no colour bar in Britain. But from restaurant-keepers and landladies, employers and employees, even from the man in the street, says Nathaniel Ajayi, he and his people meet with considerable colour prejudice. Ajayi has lived in five European countries, was a British Prisoner-of-War in Germany, but says he knows of no European country where the coloured man is treated with more unofficial contempt than in Britain.

Picture Post, 2 July, 1949

Unestablished Seamen Sit Hoping for a Ship in a Seamen's Pool Canteen
They view life simply. In the war, when voyages were dangerous and Britain needed men, they could always get a ship. Now they need a job, but Britain has no ships for them.

a vague one. It covers people of different races from more than fifty colonies, with different historical backgrounds, different emotional temperaments and of different social status. For the purposes of this survey colonial coloured people may be broken up into Africans, West Indians (whose ancestors were, of course, Africans brought to the West Indies as slaves), Somalis, Adenese Arabs—and their descendants. The Somalis and Arabs are almost all seamen. They are fairly regularly in employment. The Somalis—who in addition to any colour disadvantages often have the additional one of being able to speak little English—have a special technical grievance against the Colonial Office, inasmuch as they are officially described only as 'British Protected Persons.' But the majority of the colonial coloured people of this country are Africans or West Indians.

Before examining them in individual social groups it is most important to remember that all colonial coloured people, of whatsoever origin or class, have been brought up to think of Britain with the greatest pride and affection as 'The Mother Country.' (West Indians even talk of Britain as 'home'.) Thus any disappointments or rebuffs they may receive here on account of their colour are bound to find them doubly sensitive. Not only do they suffer the natural humiliation of being resented for a purely

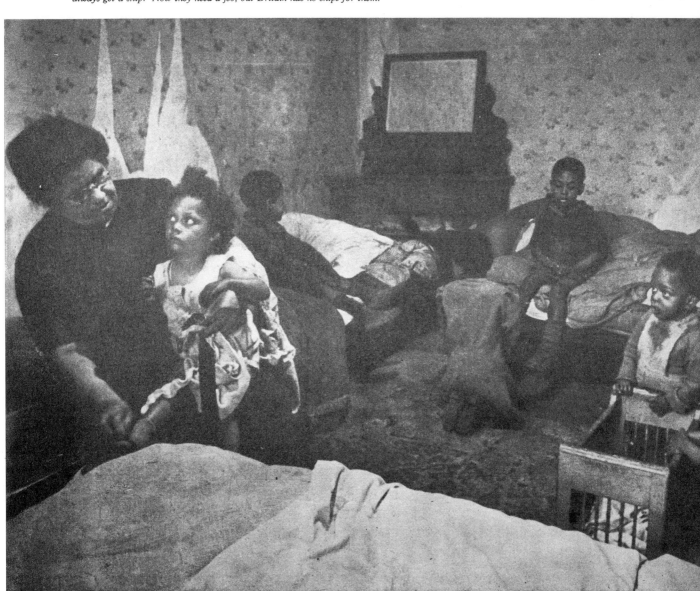

The Overcrowding that is Typical of Conditions in the Coloured Quarters of Some British Towns
Mrs. Johnson lives with two daughters, whose husbands are seamen, and eleven grandchildren. She and six grandchildren sleep in three beds in this room: Mrs. Johnson and two children in the bed, top right, three children in the bed on the left, and an older grand-daughter in the bed in the foreground.

personal characteristic: a deep emotional illusion is being shattered for them as well. This is particularly true of the West Indians, who no longer have the tribal associations and native language which can still provide some fundamental security for the disillusioned African. The West Indian disillusioned with Britain is deprived of all sense of security. He becomes, quite understandably, the most sensitive and neurotic member of the coloured community, and may be the most inclined to drift into bad ways.

The aristocrats of the coloured community are the students, of whom there are about 3,500. A third of them hold scholarships; the rest have private means, sometimes considerable. The Colonial Office Welfare Department makes special arrangements for them to be placed at a suitable British University, or equivalent—the most popular studies are medicine, law, nursing and engineering, in that order—and colonial students may also if they wish be put up for virtually as long as they like at one of the Colonial Office's student hostels. Compared with the rest of the coloured community, the student is relatively well-off.

And yet he voices many convincing grievances, which throw a light on the general colour problem. In the first place none of these hostels are luxurious places. Where an enlightened warden is in charge,

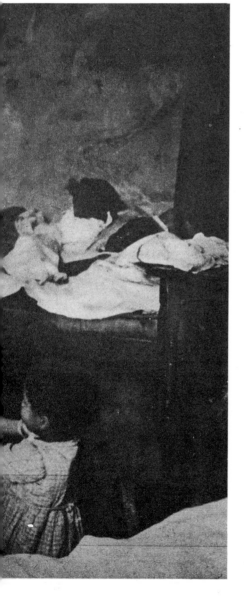

The Stowaway Sees His Dreams Begin to Crumble
He stowed away from Lagos to realise his dream of working in the 'Mother Country.' The police gave him Service clothing, the Colonial Office gave him temporary lodging, the Assistance Board gave him £2 a week. But no one in Liverpool can give him a job. The danger is that he may drift.

as at the Balmoral Hotel in Queen's Gate Gardens, there is a reasonably cheerful and civilised atmosphere, in spite of the barrack-room type furniture. (This could only be improved if the Treasury were prepared to make the Colonial Office an increased grant.) On the other hand there is a hostel in Wimpole Street which is distinctly unsatisfactory. It is in need of decoration and repair. There is the minimum of furniture. Some students have to sleep in dormitories of eight. The dining-room is in a dark and depressing basement.

But more important—because less material—student grievances bring one nearer the heart of Britain's colour problem. In principle, coloured students dislike living in hostels. They come to England because they have admired England and English life from a distance, and want to know it from close to. But they cannot do that if they live in hostels full of their own people. Why then do they stay there? The answer is distressingly simple : because it is often extremely difficult for any coloured man—student or not—to find a furnished flat or room in England. Even the Colonial Office often has difficulty in placing a coloured man in lodgings.

The operation of this particular unofficial colour bar is almost always the same. A coloured man, perhaps with a name like Smith or Murdoch, will write or ring up in answer to an advertisement and be told to call to see the room at a certain time. The landlady, when she sees him, will usually say quite politely that the room has just been let. In many

cases a check carried out by a white friend immediately afterwards will prove that the room is still available. From a social survey made just before the Second World War, it was estimated that up to 60 per cent. of landladies, boarding-house keepers and private families in England would refuse to take a coloured person into their homes. Most landladies explain their attitude in a manner characteristic of English colour prejudice in general: "I wouldn't mind for myself. But there's no telling what the other lodgers might say."

The other grievance which coloured students have is more vague, but even more symptomatic of the whole colour problem in Britain. Coloured students find it extremely difficult to get to know white people outside the hostels. So they form defensive cliques and are accused of 'not mixing.' This dangerous spiral of segregation is found all down the social scale.

The coloured student's problems become severely practical when he graduates. There are, of course, a few coloured professional men working successfully all over Britain. But these—if one excludes the entertainment profession, where colour is often an asset —are mainly doctors, most of whom are very successful and highly-praised by their white patients. Many students want to return to the colonies to cash in professionally on the prestige of an English education. But others who would like to stay here have to reckon that colour prejudice would be too strong against them in their profession.

Picture Post, 2 July, 1949

Two Men Happy At Their Work: The Paper-Baler . . .
It's fairly easy to get unskilled work, except in Liverpool. Paper-baler Benson has worked happily for a London Council for two years.

. . . And the Student of Medicine
William Jorsling, from Trinidad, reads medicine in a Colonial Office hostel in Kensington. Students are the aristocrats of the coloured population.

The British colour bar, one might say, is invisible, but like Wells' invisible man it is hard and real to the touch. (Many coloured people say that they would honestly prefer an official colour bar, such as that which exists in America or South Africa.) And it is when you get lower down the social scale that you find it hits the hardest.

A large number of those seamen, men for the R.A.F. and skilled technicians who came here during the war, stayed on. Many now—especially if they live in a bad area like Liverpool where the total unemployment figure, white and coloured, is nearly 25,000—have difficulty in finding suitable employment. This is partly due to changing economic conditions in England, but this type of coloured man is not likely to be content with a lesson in economics, and anyway, the invisible colour bar is undoubtedly against him in ways which we shall examine. In addition to these coloured workers there has been, ever since the war, a further influx mainly from the West Indies, but also from Africa, of men coming voluntarily—even enthusiastically—either in large self-organised boatloads such as the 'Empire Windrush' of last year or the 'Georgic' of this year, or as stowaways. (There were 500 stowaways to Britain last year.) These have come here partly because of the economic impoverishment of their own country (the unemployed figure for Kingstown, Jamaica, alone is 70,000), partly because of the reports they have read in the colonial press of England's labour shortage. Many have had fanciful letters from coloured friends in England about how well they are doing. All are convinced that they will find the streets of England paved with gold.

Because, officially, there is nothing to distinguish them from other British subjects, there is little official machinery for dealing with them. The Colonial Office Welfare Department can give temporary lodging to a stowaway, and he will receive National Assistance Board money, but that is all, and the Welfare Department's official activities could be expanded a great deal in this direction. Unofficially there is some commendable co-operation between the Colonial office and the Ministry of Labour. In midland towns like Birmingham and Wolverhampton there are several hundred coloured workers working happily and successfully in factories, and these areas could absorb more. But it is almost impossible to find accommodation for them. There is little point in telling an unemployed coloured man in Liverpool to uproot himself from there and go and get a job in the Midlands, if you can't gaurantee him anywhere to live.

But a more important difficulty still, because it relates to the general social problem, is the initial reluctance shown on all sides to welcome coloured workers. The coloured man meets prejudice in connection with his employment from all classes. It may come from an ignorant Ministry of Labour

White and Coloured Share a Problem
In work these Englishmen might have resented the introduction of a coloured worker to their factory. But the common experience of unemployment breaks down colour prejudice.

A Marriage That Can Lead to Difficulties
Herman McKay who, as Alfonso Perez, runs a dance band, is married to an
English girl. Such marriages can cause social difficulties on both sides.

Social Segregation That Can Lead to Trouble
In most big towns coloured people live together in close communities.
In such communities grievances are brooded on more bitterly.

clerk, who will be reluctant to submit a coloured man for a job. It may come from a reactionary employer who states categorically that he will not employ coloured labour, or from an employer, who, like the landlady, says he doesn't mind himself but he doesn't like to risk the effect it may have on the other workers. Very often, in fact, it will come from the white workers themselves.

The coloured worker arriving in this country with many illusions will find that he has not only to deal with a different labour situation from that which he anticipated, but also a threefold prejudice (social, in housing, and in employment). It is not surprising that if he meets with these in a particularly virulent form he himself turns bitter and fills with prejudice. He will forget, if he lives in a slum, that there are white people who live in one too. He will see the whole social system as a conspiracy against his colour.

The prejudice which the coloured man meets, and which in its turn begets counter-prejudice, is almost always based on ignorance. A great many people who express feelings of dislike or mistrust of coloured people have never seen any, and where these feelings are professedly based on experience—as sometimes in the case of employers and factory workers—they have usually been based on the experience of an embittered coloured man, or of individual trouble such as sex rivalry which gets mistakenly attributed to the coloured man's being coloured rather than to his being a man.

The ignorance which breeds prejudice is caused, quite literally, by not knowing the coloured man. A tentative survey made during the war estimated that 95 per cent. of Englishmen had no first-hand knowledge of coloured people. In the last few years, thanks partly to a lead given by the Government, coloured people have begun work in many different trades and industries. Coloured workers are found in responsible positions in the G.P.O., the Mint, the Ministry of National Insurance, the Mines, British Railways, and in many well-known private firms such

as Dunlop and the General Electric Co. Very gradually—much too gradually—they are becoming integrated fully into our working society, and as this happens prejudices dissolve. Wherever in Britain white and coloured people get to know each other and live together on equal terms, the same sort of atmosphere exists as is to be found in the mixed schools—where coloured and white children play and work together, instinctively

relegating colour differences to their proper insignificance. But there is still not enough first-hand contact in adult society for the prejudices of the majority to be dissolved, and progress is slow. By a strange emotional leap many coloured people look to Communism to release them from their social humiliation.

One of the most permanent and symbolic obstacles to progress is perhaps the existence of

Half a Pint That Can Only Lead to Friendship
Wherever white and coloured people live continually together, there is little colour feeling.
In a Cable Street, Stepney pub, white and coloured customers are on the best of terms.

Picture Post, 9 July, 1949

Where Society Knows No Colour Prejudice: Liverpool School-children at Play

On the roof of the Windsor Street County School, in the South End of Liverpool, white and coloured children play naturally together. They attach no meaning to differences in colour. A white and coloured child will often be 'best friends.' From such children society can learn a valuable lesson.

segregated communities. The close coloured communities of Cardiff and Liverpool may give a sense of defensive security to the coloured people who live in them. But, quite apart from the danger of their becoming forgotten communities where conditions, such as housing, can deteriorate without the white community feeling responsible (because they are out of sight), this situation fosters ignorance and thus prejudice. It encourages the coloured man to brood on grievances, real or imaginary, and grow bitter. It encourages the white man to fall back on the crude absurdities absorbed in his youth (the pictures of 'funny' savages in geography books; the threats of a stupid nurse : "the black man will come and fetch you if you don't behave"; the general notion that somehow coloured people are not like other human beings) and grow smug.

For Britain's colour problem there are a few practical and remedial steps that can be taken. One recently suggested in Parliament was that the Government should be given powers to deal with landladies showing racial discrimination similar to those which the Ministry of Food (by means of licences) possesses against restaurant keepers. But as a whole the problem is too fundamental to be solved by mere remedial steps. It can only be solved by a true integration of white and coloured people in one society. And for that to take place there must be some sort of revolution inside every individual mind —coloured and white—where prejudices based on bitterness, ignorance or patronage have been established.   ROBERT KEE

Where Society Suspends It: Sport
Learie Constantine has had 'colour bar' trouble. But when recognised, he is accepted.

And Entertainment
Miss Elizabeth Welch, the well-known singer, whose colour is all part of her success.

Vol. 44   No. 9.

PICTURE POST

27 AUGUST, 1949

At the Council of Europe in Strasbourg, Meet Two Illustrious Fathers of the Movement for Greater European Unity
Edouard Herriot was associated with Briand from 1925 onwards, in his drive for European Unity.   Now, at the inaugural session, he acts as
Provisional President of Europe's Consultative Assembly.   He is greeted by Winston Churchill, today's most resounding advocate of United Europe.

EUROPE: DARE WE FACE REAL UNION?

Photographed by FELIX H. MAN

A real Union. Not simply a continuance of the present loose co-operation in economic affairs, in which the sovereign States need only co-operate while it suits them.   But a real political Union, leading to a real European Government, to which all states would surrender some of their sovereign rights. Who is for such a Union? Who is against? And could any such Union be any good at all without Germany? And—without *which* Germany?

WE stood at the reception desk of the hotel, fiddling with our Travellers' Cheques and looking round at the transfigured pictures—the innocent water-colours of Strasbourg—on the walls. "What have you been up to with The General?" we asked the hotel. When we were last here, in May, the unforgettable face of General de Gaulle had come at us from every wall and alcove of the hotel. De Gaulle standing and de Gaulle sitting; de Gaulle fulminating and de Gaulle sedating;

de Gaulle serious-to-grim and de Gaulle giving his formidable impersonation of a merry old soul. And now he was nowhere to be seen. The hotel changed the subject. "What have *you* been up to with The Pound?" they asked, eyeing our travellers' cheques without love. "We haven't touched the Pound," we said. "Then why is it being devalued, Monsieur?" "But it isn't being devalued." "In France," said the hotel, "the physical pound-note sterling is already invested with the aroma unmistakable of

devaloriꞩation." "Well, fancy," we said, and tried not to smile. All the same, these two pieces of dialogue had once more forced upon our attention the fact that it is still, even now at this late stage, impossible for any one partner in the European firm to know which way any other partner in the European firm is going to jump next, either politically or economically. In other words, the sovereignty in these two matters of all the States involved is still absolutely intact. In O.E.E.C., the Organisation

THE FIRST ANXIETY: WOULD THE COMMITTEE OF MINISTERS ALLOW THE CONSULTATIVE ASSEMBLY FULL SCOPE FOR EFFECTIVE DELIBERATION?

for European Economic Co-operation, the Western Nations co-operate 'by consent'—that is, for as long as, and as far as, it suits their own sovereign economic policies; but the first stage of the *qualitative* change from European *co-operation* by consent-so-long-as-it-suits to European *union* by obedience - to - majority - decisions - even - when - it - doesn't-suit, has not yet begun. It's impossible to understand what has really been happening at Strasbourg, unless one is absolutely clear about this. We have started to *co-operate*; but we haven't even started to *unite*.

But, then, one reminded oneself, that's more or less what we are all here present in Strasbourg *for*. 'More or less'—because, as will appear later, there are present quite a number of advocates of 'European Unity' who simply don't want to unite, but who would just like to go on quietly 'co-operating,' until such a time as the informal Socialist International or the informal Tory International—as the case may be—looks to be certain of a permanent majority in any future legislative Assembly of Europe.

Still, here we are. But who exactly—in this epoch when the constituent elements of this diminished thing called Europe seem to change from year to year—are 'we'? From the number of flags on the flagpoles near the University building, you can conclude that, on the first day of this first session, we are ten. And if you are one of those Europeans who can tell one national flag from another, then you will know that 'we' consist today of Belgium, Denmark, France, Great Britain, Ireland, Italy, Luxembourg, Netherlands, Norway

M. Schuman Gives a Private Dinner to the Committee of Ministers
On the first evening, France's Foreign Minister acts as host to the Foreign Ministers of Belgium, Denmark, Ireland, Italy, Luxembourg, the Netherlands, Norway, Sweden and Great Britain, and to a few distinguished local Frenchmen such as this one.

The Foreign Ministers of Norway and Italy in Session
Dr. Lange, left, and Count Sforza. To them and their colleagues in the Committee of Ministers falls the task of deciding which subjects the Assembly may debate.

The Elite of Europe's Statesmanship
Under the chandeliers in the Palace of the Prefect, the original ten Foreign Ministers meet.

Sweden, Great Britain and Denmark Find They Speak the Same Language
M. Osten Unden, left, Mr. Ernest Bevin and M. Gustav Rasmussen. Mr. Bevin gets an
interested reception from the people of Strasbourg, and a special welcome from the Mayor who
believe it's to Mr. Bevin that credit is due for the choice of their city as a 'capital.'

Luxembourg's Foreign Minister
M. Bech, elder statesman of the Grand
Duchy, and a personality of Benelux.

and Sweden. On the following day, 'we' shall be
thirteen; because we shall have expanded our
democratic borders to embrace Greece, Iceland and
Turkey. The Swiss, who are busy with their own
neutrality, will not be with us. But, at some later
date, we may conceivably be joined by the Germans
—always provided that some of the French don't
continue to press, successfully, for the inclusion of a
delegation from the Saarland. If that happens, Dr.
Schumacher has declared in his usual challenging
tones, then Germany simply won't play. The joke
about this, if you can regard it as such, is that any
future delegation from the Saarland would very
probably vote along the same lines as any future
delegation from Germany. And yet it is the
Germans who passionately oppose the idea of a
Saarland delegation, and it is some of the French
who passionately advocate it. In such farcical
knots as these have the strings of nationalism
tied-up the sovereign organs of Europe.

However, here we are; and these thirteen are, for
the moment, *who* we are. Well, then, what are we
here *for* ? The Statute which created the Council
of Europe lays it down that the aim of that Council
is to achieve "a greater unity among its Members for
the realisation of their common ideals and for the
facilitation of their economic and social progress."

That is the allotted job. The tools allotted for that
job are a Committee of Ministers and a Consultative
Assembly. The Assembly is consultative, advisory,
deliberative only. It can deliberate on such political,
economic and social subjects as the Committee of
Ministers approves. It cannot discuss questions of
defence at all.

The aim is greater unity for the realisation of
ideals and for economic and social progress. It is
the fact that there are at least four main schools of
thought and feeling as to *how* this greater unity can
best be achieved. That accounts for the friction—
both the destructive and the creative friction—
which animated the early meetings of the Assembly.

Members of the first school of feeling want to
start off by procuring agreement on one or two pieces
of practical European symbolism. They would have
liked to begin with a European Charter of Human

The Man on Whom Relations Between Ministers and Assembly Depends
M. Spaak of Belgium, right, starts as a member of the Committee of Ministers, then
becomes President of the Assembly. Left is Sir Gladwyn Jebb, of Britain.

The Conservative Economist
Robert Boothby, M.P., advocates a supra-national planning authority to integrate Europe's production of essentials, e.g., food, coal, steel and transport.

The Labour Leader
"Let the Assembly" says Mr. Morrison "think of itself as an institution of a parliamentary character, and not as a Conference or Demonstration."

Federalists: Two Who Stand for a Rapid Advance to a Real Union
Dr. Hendrik Brugmans, President of the European Union of Federalists, and Professor at Utrecht University, left, with R. W. G. Mackay, M.P., of Britain. Federalists say Europe's economy can only be integrated through a European political authority, that is, a European Government; and—says Mackay—a European currency, for a start.

Rights; but, failing that, they would go for a European passport, or a European flag, or a Channel tunnel or a tunnel under Mont Blanc, or any other symbolic tunnel. If they got any of these, a fair number of European Conservatives and Liberals would not ask to see the distant scene; one step would be enough for them.

Members of the second school of thought include a number of European Conservatives and Liberals for whom one such step would certainly not be enough—if only because it could hardly have the slightest bearing on the sick economy of Europe. These people—having studied the present wasteful and unprofitable system whereby the industries of a dozen miniature European countries are all trying to make themselves self-sufficient by 1952, instead of dividing the labour among themselves and con-

centrating on producing the things that they could produce best—would now be prepared to advocate a supra-national authority which should direct the integration and expansion of various essential European products : for instance, coal, steel, transport and food. What ! Do you mean to say that it's some Conservatives, rather than most Labour people, who are in favour of a supra-national planning authority? That is so : for the reason that the Conservatives calculate that, as 80 per cent. of Europe's industry is still privately owned, the supra-national planning authority would have largely to be directed by private enterprise.

The third school of thought consists of people who calculate that that is, indeed, exactly how any supra-national authority would be directed at present, and who, therefore, shy away from the idea

of any supra-national authority. Most prominent in this school are the orthodox Labour members of the British Delegation. These are the advocates of the 'functional' approach to greater unity in Europe. That's to say, they will continue to 'co-operate by consent' in the O.E.E.C., and any other similar industrial organs that may emerge, but they will not, if they can help it, abandon any portion of their economic sovereignty. In other words, they will co-operate; but they won't unite—or not, anyhow, until the informal Socialist International looks like having a majority in the Assembly, which could then be safely transformed from a Consultative Assembly into a legislative one.

The fourth and last school of thought includes most federalists, many continental Socialists and one or two British Socialists like Mackay, who say, in

Functionalist : One of the Chief Spokesmen of the British Labour Party, Which Believes in 'Co-operation by Consent'
Rt. Hon. Hugh Dalton, right, and Aidan Crawley, Labour M.P. It was Dr. Dalton who, in 1948 at Scarborough, expressed the Labour Party National Executive's attitude to European Federation and a United States of Europe. "Let us keep our feet on the ground," he said. "It must be made quite clear, I think, that we are not going to have chance majorities of reactionaries who might be thrown up from any part of Western Europe having the power to decree that we in Britain shall go back to the inter-war years of trade depression and all the rest of it."

effect : "That's fine, that last argument. But how about if the Socialists don't look like having a majority before the next war starts to arrive?" These people argue that one of the things most likely to postpone or prevent the next war is the economic integration of Europe : that this cannot be achieved by the functional approach, because no-one, certainly not O.E.E.C., can compel one nation to revise, e.g., its steel programme, if it doesn't want to consent to; that it cannot be achieved, either, by any supra-national economic planning authority unless that economic authority is backed by a supra-national *political* authority—in other words, a European Government, whose first job, in Mackay's view, should be the introduction of a common European currency. The instant that currency was introduced, each of the dozen hitherto boxed-up coun-tries of Europe would find that, for its best products, it now had a market twelve times the previous size; competition, in this new kind of free trade area, would become a real thing once more; and the two essentials for the economic life of Europe—increased productivity per man-hour and lower costs and prices—would follow.

Such were the four main groups of midwives who were standing-by for the delivery of the infant Europe. During the first few days, it seemed at least possible that the impassioned natterings of the midwives in the corridors might actually drown the first life-signalling yelps of the new infant. However, there was one thing about which practically all the midwives could agree : the fact that the new infant Europe could never grow into anything economically sound—or, as some whis-pered, militarily respect-worthy—without Germany.

But the life-or-death question which, at the time we had to leave Strasbourg, had not yet been asked, much less answered, is : "Which Germany?" Up till now, national delegations to the Council of Europe have either been elected by, or appointed from, the national parliaments concerned. Which Germany are we going to clasp to the European bosom? If the majority of all-party nationalists in the German Parliament—themselves elected on the basis of competing nationalist appeals—are given the opportunity of 'democratically' electing their own delegation to the Council of Europe, they will hardly be so stupid as to go and elect democrats and anti-nationalists to that delegation. Leave aside the case of the virulently nationalist Dr. Schumacher, and take the case of Dr. Adenauer, who sometimes

EUROPE: Dare we Face Real Union?

M. Senghor
French delegate. Senegalese. "We need: a decision to pool sovereignty; the incorporation of Germany; the refusal of a nationalist Germany."

M. André Philip
French delegate. "If we can design a proper procedure now, we shall be able to apply the same procedure to any future legislative assembly."

claims in private to be a life-long supporter of democratic European Union. A couple of months ago, Dr. Adenauer went to Switzerland. While there, he received an invitation from some eminent French supporters of European Union to visit Paris and discuss ways of bringing Germany into a United Europe. Adenauer replied that he could not come to Paris before the German elections, because the Germans would think he was a *quisling*. Then, to demonstrate how very far from being a quisling he really was, he proceeded to sound off, there in Switzerland, a speech that was a perfect bugle-call to German nationalism. Immediately after making this speech, he explained privately, to two local supporters of European Union, that he was obliged to do this in order to get a majority over Schumacher, who was gaining support by his resounding nationalist appeal; and that, unless he, Adenauer, went one better in nationalism, then he and his Christian Democrat followers, who deep in their hearts were the only genuine German supporters of anti-nationalism and a democratic United Europe, would be beaten. Well, well.

Which representatives of which Germany are we inviting into European Union? If the peoples of Western Europe want to be sure that the first German delegation that arrives is composed mainly of the democratic representatives of all that is best and most anti-nationalist in Germany today, they had better see that the Council of Europe hand-picks that delegation themselves from among the *proven* German apostles of 'Europa Union,' few of whom are members of the German legislature, and many of whom are not even members of any German political party. "Undemocratic procedure?" "Gross interference in the internal affairs of another country?" It was exactly that argument which gave Hitler his long start. But if the Council of Europe is going, in the name of democracy, to permit the German Parliamentary nationalists to choose and send their own most nationalistic representatives to Strasbourg—well, then, imagine, if you can, that there was already a Council of Europe in 1928, and that its Credentials Committee accepted without demur a duly-elected, unknown German delegate called A. Hitler, of the respectable-sounding National Socialist DEMOCRATIC Workers' Party. And then work that one out for yourself.

But, someone will say, if we non-Germans invite a delegation of certain hand-picked Germans to Strasbourg, then those Germans whom we invite will be looked upon as quislings by a majority of other Germans? That is deadly true —*unless*, in absolute reality, the invitation goes out from the Europeans of one parish to the Europeans of another parish : in which case there can be no question of quislingism.

The Proof of a European Reality

What could convince a sufficiency of Germans that this as-one-European-to-another business is a reality, and not just a trick of words? Could a European passport convince them? Or agreement on a Channel tunnel? Or a functional extension of the activities of O.E.E.C.? I doubt it. Personally, I believe that the only thing that could both convince and *work*, would be 'one spasm of resolve' on the part of Western Europe's peoples and parliaments, resulting in a declaration by the Council of Europe that European political union—not simply continuing *co-operation*, but *union* : in fact, a European Government with legislative and executive power—was the goal; and that the first step ever towards European *Union* would be taken before the end if this year. But . . . "that's *so* difficult to arrange?" Certainly. Nevertheless, the true political *Union* of Europe does seem to be the one great beneficent and magnetic counter-attraction capable of drawing a sufficient number of Germans away from the malign magnet of a resurgent Nationalist Germany. If we don't like the idea of a United European Government, or if it seems *too* difficult to arrange politically, then—for the German reason, if for no other—I'm inclined to think we've had it. Which last is something that is *not* difficult to arrange politically, at all.

LIONEL BIRCH

Hindsight by Lionel Birch

Plus ça change. . . . That bit about the vanishing General and the groggy pound could just as well have been written in August 1969 as in August 1949. And the 1949 verdict 'We Europeans have started to *cooperate*, but we haven't even started to *unite*' still holds good.

True, in the interval, both the E.E.C. ('The Six') and E.F.T.A. ('The Seven') have done a bit more economic cooperating; and at one time it even looked as though The Six were going to start doing a bit of political uniting. But de Gaulle soon put a stop to the federalist fantasies of his junior partners, as well as to their sentimental yearnings for British participation.

Yet, long before de Gaulle reappeared on the field, Britain had been persistently refusing invitations to come and play. Join, in 1951, the epoch-making European Coal and Steel Community? Not bloody likely, said the Labour Government. Join, in 1957, the revolutionary Common Market? The Conservative Government preferred to wait and see.

What they saw by 1961 impelled them to ask if, now, they could come in and play, too – provided that some of the rules could be somewhat adjusted in their favour. Which enabled the General eventually to say: 'Sorry, you're simply not up to the Big League, yet.'

Later, when there were punch-ups on the field between the Frenchmen and the other Five, some British spectators commented audibly that, well anyhow, it was a most un-English game, and one that we were well out of.

So when, in January 1967, Harold Wilson and his *'joyeux petit compagnon'*, George Brown, had another go in Paris, they never really stood a chance; and the devaluation of the pound in November 1967 gave de Gaulle a pretext to make that retrospectively clear. Ironically, in August 1969, the French post-de-Gaulle franc was itself devalued.

The other irony is that, logically, the Italians, Belgians, Dutch, Germans and Luxembourgers, all ardent federalists, ought to have wanted to keep Britain *out*; and de Gaulle, logically, should have wanted to pull Britain *in*. Because all British Governments have always been willing, like de Gaulle, to do a bit of voluntary cooperating, on a hundred per cent sovereignty basis. But they have always viewed political *union* – involving a European Legislative, Cabinet and Defence Force – with the same invincible repugnance as does de Gaulle himself. And as, perhaps (God help us!), do his heirs and successors.

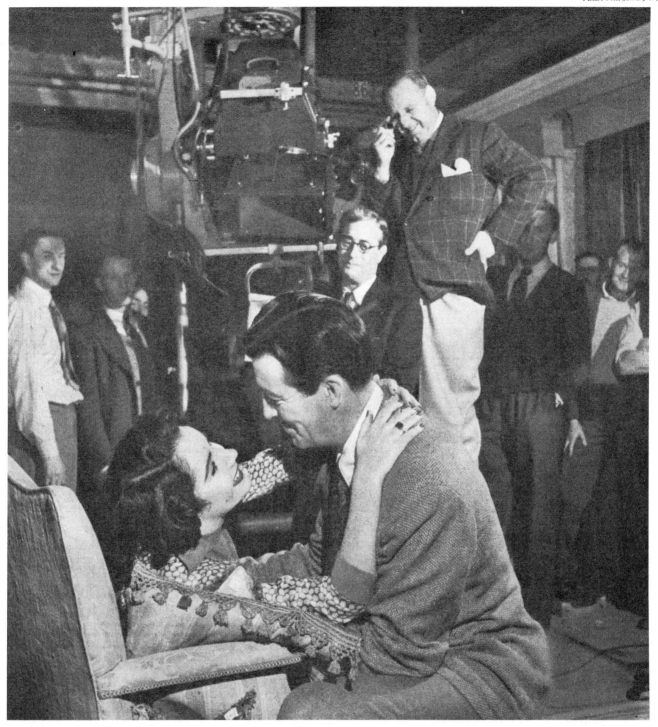

The Girl Who Is a Film Star Only on the Set: Elizabeth Taylor Filming with Robert Taylor
Sixteen-year-old Elizabeth Taylor in the arms of Robert Taylor (no relation) during the shooting of the film 'Conspirator.' Off the set Elizabeth has to go back to her psychology studies. Director Victor Saville (in the check coat) seems pleased with her progress.

ELIZABETH TAKES ANOTHER LESSON

Photographed by GORGE KONIG

Elizabeth Taylor is only 16. She's already a M.-G.-M. star. But she puts in three hours a day studying history, psychology and sociology. And the streets of London have a lot to teach her too.

YOU are on the set of *Conspirator*, the new M.-G.-M. film, based on Humphrey Slater's best-seller, about a young girl's marriage with a Guards' officer, who is also a secret member of the Communist Party. Disregard for a moment the wandering electricians, the enormous stealthy cameras, the army of the apparently unemployed. You are looking through the fourth wall of a rich man's house in Belgrave Square. A pretty, dark girl in a long evening dress runs from the drawing room into the hall to take a telegram. She looks very young, but

There's Always Something to Stare At
A band? The Lord Mayor's Show? Or just another adventurer climbing Eros? A London crowd will
look at anything. But it won't always recognise the film star looking with it.

sophisticated—about 18 perhaps. "Break for tea," shouts the director. Elizabeth Taylor puts down the telegram and walks through the fourth wall of the house in Belgravia across the coils of rubber flex in front to a pre-fabricated two-room shack. There her governess, Miss Birtina Anderson of Los Angeles, is waiting to take her on with her history lesson.

Miss Anderson, a mild, white-haired lady in rimless spectacles, is as pleased with Elizabeth as a student of history, literature, psychology, sociology, etc., as Victor Saville is pleased with her as an

actress who can play both an innocent young girl and a disillusioned married woman. Because Elizabeth is still only 16 her three hours' study a day are compulsory by Californian State law. This prescribes that children must either graduate or stay at school until they are 18. Elizabeth hopes to graduate next year. Until then, three hours a day, snatched in intervals, with full make-up on, in the stuffy little shack on the set, count as school.

Talking to her with a book on social history lying open on the table and her mother resting vigilantly in the little room next door, it is difficult to decide

How Are You in Maths?
Elizabeth talks to two pages outside a London
hotel. She graduates next year.

whether Elizabeth is a star or a high-school girl. Unaffected, honest, perhaps not abnormally absorbed in her studies, she seems like any other charming pretty American of, well, say 17. Her tastes are conventional and enthusiastic. ("I just love literature—Shakespeare, etc." "I love music too—I wish I could play something.") And yet there is that sophisticated mask of film make-up. And the astonishing knowledge that in a few minutes she will walk on to the set and act a difficult part, opposite a world-famous film-star, with as much competence and self-assurance as an actress twice her age.

Ration Books for Mother and Daughter
Elizabeth's mother goes with her everywhere. And, as even a film star and a film star's mother
have to have ration books, they get theirs together from Westminster Food Office.

The Order They Were Glad to Obey
A party of troops entering Buckingham Palace gets the order "Eyes left." Elizabeth Taylor last saw London when she was seven. She's American, but her family used to live in England before the war.

How Are You in Botany?
She buys a gardenia at Piccadilly Circus. Only the young and the old buy their own flowers.

Before the war, Elizabeth went to a kindergarten in Highgate, London. Although she is an American, the daughter of Americans, her parents lived in England for some years and her father, Francis Taylor, kept an art gallery in Bond Street. Every year the Taylor family travelled to America to see Elizabeth's grandparents. In 1939, when she was only seven, they prudently decided to stay there. This is her first visit to London since then. And since then, without any let-up in her educational programme, she has established herself as a star with her role in *National Velvet* and other films.

Now She and Her Mother Can Put Their Feet Up
She's walked the streets of London till her feet hurt. She's seen the sights, the crowds, the processions and she's even waved a flag. It's the end of yet another lesson.

1950

The 1950 General Election is notable as the last to be contested without benefit of television. The announcement of polling day was accompanied, amid ribald Conservative cries, by the news that the bacon ration was to be increased from four to five ounces a week, and the sweet ration from four to $4\frac{1}{2}$ ounces. Almost simultaneously, the West German Government announced the abolition of petrol rationing and an end to all food rationing except that of sugar. Not for the first time, the British people wondered audibly who had won the war.

Polling day, 23 February, fell almost exactly on the fiftieth anniversary of the founding of the Labour Party. It had travelled a long way from the obscurity of the Farringdon Memorial Hall, and John Burns's ringing declaration that he was tired of working-class boots, working-class houses, working-class margarine and working-class parliamentary candidates. The party in 1950 would not have disappointed him. The Prime Minister himself was Haileybury and Oxford, 255 of the party's 617 candidates had been to university, and 258 described themselves as professional men. The Liberals, hoping to cash in on the prevailing mood of disillusionment and discontent, put 475 candidates into the field, 319 of whom lost their deposits. A hundred Communist candidates, including one Old Etonian, amassed between them fewer than 100,000 votes. In spite of disappointments, the working-class vote held like a rock in the Labour strongholds of the north – the total Labour poll was actually two million higher than in 1945. It was the middle and lower middle classes of the London suburbs who swung enough to turn the scale.

At the end of the first day's counting, Labour had a majority of sixty. Then came the cliffhanger. As the delayed results came in from the country constituencies, the Labour majority dwindled until by mid-afternoon Conservatives and Liberals combined had drawn level. It seemed that the Government had fallen; but there was a dying spurt, and Attlee crept back into Downing Street with a majority of six.

For the old Labour Party, in which the Prime Minister and most of his senior ministers were rooted, it was the end of the road. The young – healthier, better educated, strangers to mass unemployment, living with their hire-purchase furniture in New Towns and new housing estates – were more interested in the Affluent Society Now than in the Socialist Commonwealth Hereafter. They had many admirable qualities, but they had not yet had occasion to learn the awe-inspiring patience and resilience of their elders in the face of disappointment and defeat.

The enfeebled Government, limping back into power, went on limping from crisis to crisis. During the

excitement of the election, the arrest of an atomic scientist, Klaus Emil Fuchs, on charges of communicating secrets to Russia had gone little noticed. His trial in March was the forerunner of others which sowed distrust in America about the efficiency of British security – indeed, it has been suggested that Fuchs and the others, having served their purpose, were deliberately betrayed with that object in view. It also came in time to provide a plausible background against which the American Senator Joseph McCarthy was able to work his black magic.

Fuchs's trial, and sentence to fourteen years' imprisonment, coincided with the opening of a Washington investigation into McCarthy's allegation that 81 security risks, including 57 card-carrying Communists, were or had recently been employed by the American State Department. The first victim was Professor Owen Lattimore, whose sinister influence and advice were said to be responsible for the loss of China to the Communists – an allegation, some thought, unduly flattering to the importance of that eminent Sinologist. The American Secretary of State, Dean Acheson, was declared a bad security risk by McCarthy, and from these beginnings he proceeded on a witch-hunt which soon made it impossible to voice even mildly Liberal opinions without being declared 'soft on Communism'.

It was in these circumstances that, in the early morning of 25 June, North Korean troops armed with heavy tanks and other Russian equipment crossed the 38th parallel and advanced rapidly southward on the South Korean capital, Seoul.

Korea, annexed by Japan in 1910, had been promised independence after the Second World War. As in Europe, 'independence' took the form of a Russian occupation north of the 38th parallel, and an American one to the south of it. The occupation troops withdrew in due course, leaving a Korean People's Republic in the north and a Republic of Korea in the south, each breathing fire and slaughter against the other and claiming the right to reunify the country under its own domination. Since the withdrawal, there had been sporadic skirmishing along the 38th parallel, and the situation had caused the United Nations some concern. The North Korean invasion, well armed and apparently carefully planned, followed a formal alliance concluded between Russia and China, and led to the plausible supposition in the West that the attack was the result of an agreement reached between them.

America asked for an immediate emergency meeting of the United Nations Security Council, from which the Soviet representative – under orders to boycott the

Audrey Hepburn, aged 20, enjoying the Spring in Kew Gardens

Council because of Nationalist China's presence – was absent. Without the Soviet veto, the Security Council passed a resolution enabling President Truman to send American sea and air forces to the help of South Korea, and to put the American General MacArthur in command of the operation. By the end of July, despite the commitment of American land forces, MacArthur with his back to the sea was holding little more than a bridgehead in south-eastern Korea. He mounted a brilliant seaborne landing behind the North Korean lines, however, recaptured Seoul, crossed the 38th parallel, and headed for the Manchurian border. Russia and China reacted sharply. Russia warned that if Manchurian airfields were bombed, the Soviet Air Force would retaliate. China put 250,000 'volunteers' into Korea, who pushed MacArthur back beyond the 38th parallel. At this point, in answer to questions at a press conference, Truman indicated that America would take whatever steps were necessary in Korea, including the use of the atomic bomb. Five years after the end of one devastating war, the world seemed to be on the brink of another even more destructive.

The British Government had limped some way behind its impetuous senior partner during these events, but at the beginning of December, alarmed by Truman's announcement, Attlee flew to Washington, and apparently dissuaded Truman from extending the war. One says 'apparently' because Truman himself has implied that he was only sabre-rattling, under pressure from MacArthur and American Right Wing opinion.

The war did not in fact extend beyond Korea; but the first half of the twentieth century ended with both East and West employing the triumphs of modern technology to lay waste an already poor country, whose inhabitants were butchered by ideologues on either side among their fellow-countrymen. So much for progress in the centuries since Tacitus's Germans had made a wilderness and called it peace.

Laurence Thompson

Hindsight by Kenneth Allsop

With the advantage of hindsight, it's a hard-hearted question to ask of an ex-colleague and the paper I worked for – but need they have been so fussed? The article's premise was that, unarguably, harm *was* being done by the Film Club sixpenny dreadfuls, the case dramatized by the murals of flinching young faces.

Can we, twenty years later, test that assertion? Not really. Even if one of those children watching Jungle Girl being minced by steel fangs was found now to be a sadistic killer – or a lawn-mower fetishist – that, without analysis of his entire formative pattern, would prove nothing. Home Office tables show a spectacular jump in crimes of violence since those children, now between 24 and 33, were young: a national rise from 3,839 in 1950 to 17,076 in 1967. Convictions of the Saturday matinée age group quadrupled. But such figures should be set in the context of population increase, and anyway some criminologists believe they reflect not an increase in delinquency but improvement in police efficiency. Moreover, the Saturday matinée generation was soon outstripped. Wrongdoing in the 14 to 17 age group went up eightfold, and among the 17 to 21s tenfold. These were the teenagers who had kicked the habit of yesteryear – or added to it the double-dyed addiction of television.

Even with those crime statistics seemingly speaking in his favour, Derek Monsey would doubtless point out that he wasn't saying that a weekly intake of crude celluloid horror was necessarily going to manufacture law-breakers, but that he was concerned about a corruption of their values, about their inner as well as outer life. Also he could claim that in 1950, when television was but a flicker on a few sitting-room walls, he was unwittingly scrutinizing a virus about to become a plague. The weekly outing to the local Essoldo of 750,000 youngsters now seems a piddling problem against television today reaching into ninety per cent of British homes and ninety-nine per cent of the population having access to a set. But Mr Monsey might warrantably observe that it is, *mutatis mutandis*, the same problem in blow-up.

Much gloomy anxiety is expended upon this. Jungle Girl hasn't, to my knowledge, yet made those cosy B.B.C.2 archive programmes as a charming curio of film fare. As moralists complain, the quality of television content has not risen in ratio with technical virtuosity. Is there a causal link between violence on the screen and violence on the street? Even serious current affairs coverage, whose rightful function is transmitting man's activities – not infrequently riot and war and assassination – may have a stimulating effect, one feeding the other in intersecting spirals. But the focus of the disquiet is the beatings-up, bootings, karate chops, throttlings, face-punchings, stabbings, shootings and torture in run-of-the-mill entertainment. In America, where it is calculated that the air waves project a violent incident every 16·3 minutes and a killing every 31 minutes, a Presidential Commission has been studying the correlation between portrayed and committed aggression, and the Noble Committee has been spending six years investigating these influences in Britain. Of course, the *crime d'imitation* has always existed and every magistrate in the land hears the ritualized saw-it-on-the-telly-sir excuse, but there has been a distinct change since those relatively innocent days of 1950.

Derek Monsey disregarded a possible enjoyment those children were wringing out of their terror – perhaps each hyping it up to demonstrate that his blood was curdling best. Maurice Ambler's camera did not follow them out of the cinema. I wonder what they did. Run off to a bomb-site for a game of football? Get out a skipping-rope? Perhaps some did have nightmares. Perhaps, though, the Saturday morning goosepimpling was assimilable. At that age myself, I watched with rapt relish Scarface slicing men down with a tommygun and Frankenstein's monster strangling a small girl, and didn't want to become a gangster or a pioneer transplant specimen. Perhaps I, and those London kids of 1950, knew it all to be pretend creeps: Ruritanian Grand Guignol, Prohibition Chicago and the land of Jungle Girl were all too remote and fantastical for real-life acting out.

That does not apply to most televised roughstuff: therein the difference. Sophisticated 'realism' has made the commonplace urban setting the new open theatre in which television characters are easily identifiable and identified with – not only in their alert recourse to solving problems by smashing the opposition, but in the sham-smart glamour of their poncey lives. The viciousness, blandness and amorality, and the vacuity behind the shimmer, could be far more pervasively harmful than the galumphing melodrama of the pre-telly Stone Age.

Incidentally, *Picture Post* may have reformed those Saturday morning saturnalias. The manageress of my local cinema says they dropped theirs because of shrinking attendance. What sort of stuff was shown? 'No horror films', she said. 'Cowboys and comedies; Tommy Steele, or Laurel and Hardy, Shirley Temple.'

Was that why the little customers stopped coming – because there was stronger meat and zingier poison at home on the telly?

Vol. 47   No. 6

PICTURE POST

6 May, 1950

Part of the Children's Audience at a London Cinema Waits For the Start of the Saturday Matinée
Every Saturday they come along to the local cinema. Every Saturday there is something supposed to be funny, something supposed to be interesting, something supposed to be exciting. And every Saturday, when the lights dim and they stop whistling, they lean forward in their seats.

FILMS YOUR CHILDREN SEE

CAN'T WE DO BETTER THAN THIS?

Photographed by MAURICE AMBLER

Five to fourteen year-olds go to Children's Matinées at the local cinema every Saturday morning. A photographer attends one, and takes pictures of them watching a typical 'suitable' programme. He uses infra-red, so the children are unaware that he is photographing them.

IT is a difficult sum to do, but it has been worked out that somewhere around 750,000 children go to the 'children's matinée' at the local cinema every Saturday morning. That is a large number of youngsters between the vastly different but extremely impressionable ages of five and fourteen. What they see on the screen must be of considerable importance : what is given to them should be a great responsibility, weighing on exhibitors and parents alike. 'Must be' and 'should be'; but, with certain exceptions, is not considered to be.

Let us have a look at the elementary facts and the fundamental difficulties. In forty years of progress, the film has become the most effective social weapon for good or evil the world has known since the era of religion. In Britain alone, about thirty million people buy seats at the cinema every week. What they see in black-and-white or glorious technicolor is, if repeated often enough, what they come to believe in. Seeing *is* believing. The social habits, the speech, the dress, the ideas of high life, low life, love and violence, of the last two generations have

been influenced by that too often distorting-mirror, the screen. That statement is fact. You can prove it, if you won't admit it, by reading the newspapers and by watching and listening to the people in the queue or coming out into the foyer after the show. And if grown-ups, or so-called grown-ups, are affected to *any* degree by canned entertainment, it seems unnecessary to argue that the effect on children must be considerably greater. The child *is* father to the man, whatever you may think of Wordsworth; the kind of men or women we

TWO SHOTS FROM THE FILM THEY WERE SEEING

'JUNGLE GIRL': IT'S CONSIDERED AN EXCITING SERIAL

The end of one week's thrilling instalment. Three death-dealing harpoons point at the children's heroine. Next week we'll see who sets her free. Is this the way to train young children's minds?

'JUNGLE GIRL' MEETS ANOTHER HORRIFYING CLIMAX

She is unconscious on the ground: the terrible 'machine' is almost on her. One of its spikes has already gashed her leg. Children—remember this! Next Saturday, maybe, you'll see how she gets free.

CHILDREN'S FILM MATINEE: WHAT AN INFRA-RED PICTURE SHOWS

become depends to an almost fantastic degree on what we learn to fear, love, respect and admire between the ages of seven and fourteen.

Seeing is believing. Watch the faces of children at the cinema. The reactions, the immediate response of a child, is spontaneous and uninhibited. Boredom, interest, amusement and excitement pass across faces that are almost perfect mirrors to the emotions experienced. An adult is conditioned to a greater or lesser extent in his reactions : he will watch a film that bores him without showing much outward sign of lack of interest. He will watch a 'Horror' film that horrifies him, with a sort of self-induced phlegm, a resolute air of 'I can take it.' He does *not* boo the villain and cheer the hero. He has acquired at least a mask of self-control. But go to a 'children's matinée' and see the difference.

The programmes are generally 'planned' on fairly definite lines. The children come in, take their seats, change them, put their feet up, shout across to one another, scream, whistle and kick up

Some cover their eyes, some peep, some pray, some get right out of the picture. Some bite their fingers, some don't care, some stand rooted to the spot. This is the sort of reaction you get for sixpence. This is where your children could walk out, but won't. This is where somebody's child might get the idea for a first-class nightmare, where somebody else's child might meet with a shock that won't quickly be forgotten.

the usual children's idea of heaven and grown-up's ideal of hell. Then they join half- or whole-heartedly—it depends on the song—in community singing. They begin to roar for the 'picture.' They get, first, a cartoon. It may be a good Disney or a poor imitation, but always it is short: it holds their interest, a rather casual interest; it sometimes makes them laugh, often smile. Next comes a 'documentary.' This again, if it is *very* good, may hold their interest even if it is long. If it is *not* good, three or four minutes will have them whispering, then talking and laughing, and soon booing and hissing. Pea-shooters and catapults come out, lemonade and sweets. The same happens during the Western that usually follows. The reaction is intense, so long as there is shooting, chasing, something positive and preferably active going on. It slackens immediately the pace drops. Love scenes leave them cold and generally chuckling or whistling hilariously. And poor (though short) love scenes, poor dialogue, scenes in cabins and sheriff's offices, all in broad

'cow-boy' Americanese, split up the action. Finally, there is generally a serial. This, in the conventional serial technique, begins with the hero or heroine on the spot where they were left last week, gets them out of it (or off it?) and leaves them on a different spot at the end. Then they roar out of the cinema while The King is being played, and give hell to the policemen on duty in the street outside.

It is this spontaneous reaction, this shrill, unself-conscious criticism of a children's audience, that points the problem. Children, speaking generally, demand excitement, adventure, above all, action. And they know what that means, or *should* mean. For these 750,000 are not *only* Saturday-morning film-goers. P. J. Mayer, who has made research into the subject of children at the cinema his especial study, reckons that the age groups 5 to 14 represent 20 per cent. of our total national cinema attendance. Which gives a staggering figure of six million children a week seeing, many of them, 'A' films with their parents and 'U' films generally selected indis-

criminately. Naturally, when they go to the Saturday morning 'Film Clubs,' any suggestion of condescension to age is liable to cause a violent reaction. On the other hand, exhibitors are themselves in a difficult position. They must only show 'U' films, but apart from that 'suitability for children' hardly exists as a definable classification. 'Horror,' and 'harmful to morals' are supposed to be out. But whether 'love' is more harmful to morals than 'murder', or 'sex' than 'slugging', seems, in view of some of the films that *are* shown to children, to become a debatable point. And where 'horror' begins for an exhibitor—and where for a child of six or seven—is even more debatable. But the exhibitor has another problem. Not all of the 'U' films are available to him. The 'Film Clubs' are generally non-profit making: the charge is seldom more than sixpence. He cannot, under the present system of distribution, afford to rent 'good' films until they are several years old. He must, instead, take the cheap and shoddy. And he does.

Picture Post, 6 May, 1950.

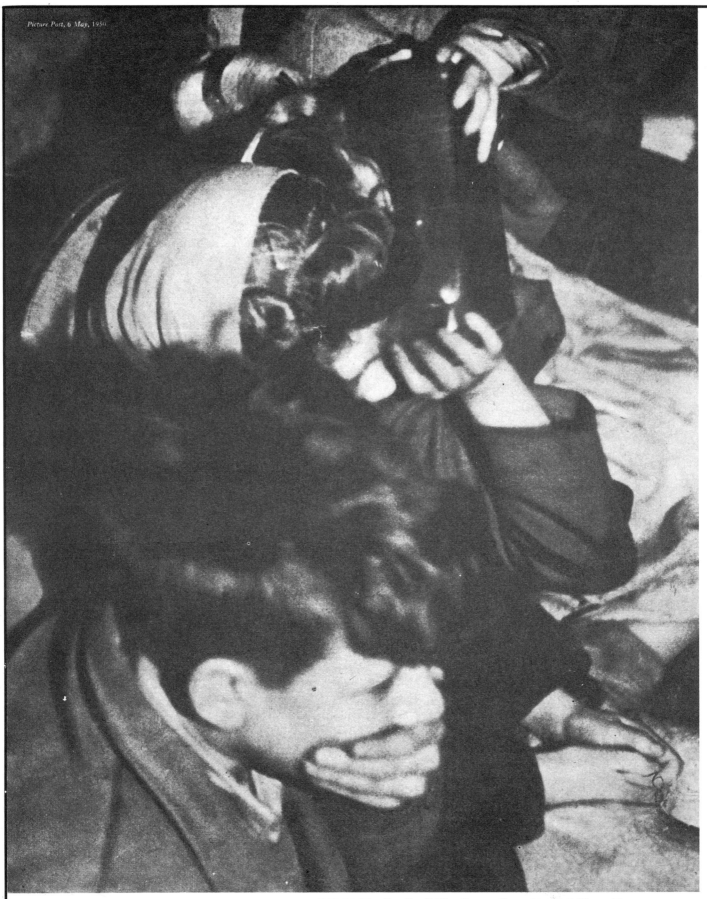

CLOSE-UPS IN THE AUDIENCE OF CHILDREN: *One Small Handbag to Cover Up Four Young Eyes*
Children know very exactly what they like and what they don't like. In films, they like action and excitement. They do not like murder and horror.
But when something frightening comes on they feel they have to sit through it. Though many will go to any lengths to try and hide themselves away.

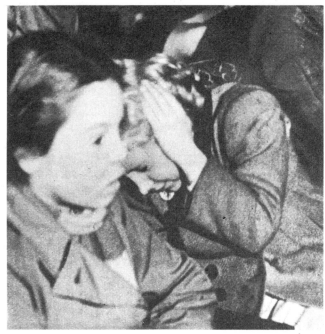

One Tries To Take It : One Can't Even Try
Some children sit it out; hands clenched, nerves keyed up. Some,
like the other little girl, cover their ears and hide their faces.

One Who Is All Alone In Terror
No-one pays any attention to him. The others have their own fears
to worry about. He just puts his head down and waits for it to end.

Two Feel They Must Try To Be Brave
Their faces show how real they feel the film is; how hard they must
try not to give way to fear. The little girl, centre right, sat with her
coat in her hands throughout, ready to cover her face.

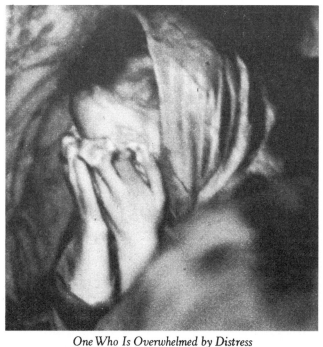

One Who Is Overwhelmed by Distress
She went to the matinée as usual on Saturday morning. Some of it
she enjoyed. This part she didn't want to see. But even if she did
want to see it, should she really be encouraged to ?

Arthur Rank has tried, through the 400 Odeon and Gaumont clubs that are within his own organisation, to keep the selection of films on a reasonable level, and to raise the level by producing special children's films—features, as well as shorts and serials. But, though it is a considerable achievement, he has only produced about one-eighth of the material necessary for his own clubs, and with varying success. Inside his organisation, despite his own personal understanding and religious idealism, the quality of entertainment necessarily varies. Outside it, the number of absolutely bad and unsuitable films shown *specifically* to children is frighteningly large.

If we admit the power for good or evil that the cinema has upon the development of a child between the impressionable years of 5 to 14, and on adolescents up to at least 17, there is a strong case to be made out for a far more rigid system of censoring. 'A' and 'U' are purely arbitrary classifications : they seem in very few cases to be based on anything more than sexual content. A love affair, treated in exquisite taste, may get a film an 'A'; a murder, or a piece of quite horrifying sadism, may possibly be the climax of a 'U' film. In any case, both classes of film may be shown in the same programme. And, *in any case* again, exhibitors are fairly lax in enforcing the ruling. We need a classification of 'suitable for children' based on a careful psychological *and* aesthetic understanding of what *is* suitable. But until we get it, we should at least demand that cheap, horrifying films that have the nightmare effect on boys and girls shown in the pictures on these pages, should not be given at children's matinées. There should be *some* limit to the amount of harm parents *and* film exhibitors are prepared to do to the minds of our next generation. DEREK MONSEY

Hindsight by James Cameron

I do not much like looking back on stories in the past. It always seems to me (a) that they were notably badly done, or (b) they were so much better than I can do today; in either case the conclusion is dispiriting. The Inchon story is curious in that I have no recollection of writing it at all. I have intense memories of living it, of watching it, of surviving it, but when I managed to put the words together I cannot imagine. Those were *mouvementé* days. In any case Inchon was overtaken so quickly by other aspects of the Korean war, more personal involvements with the wretched Syngham Rhee and the general conduct of the war, controversies that finished off Tom Hopkinson and me on *Picture Post*, and by and by *Picture Post* itself. The Inchon invasion was a terrific *coup de théâtre*, but it was strictly a brief bloody melodrama that scared me to death but didn't leave the same scars as other things did around that period.

Like everything else that seems to happen in a war, it had little intelligent meaning for us at the time. Later, Fleet Admiral Bull Halsey was to call the landing 'the most masterly and audacious stroke of all history', which seems to be a bit thick; nevertheless it was the second biggest seaborne invasion ever (only Normandy five years earlier had been more immense); it did completely change General MacArthur's strategy from long inglorious retreat to even more alarming pushfulness; it took the war to the Yalu river, brought in the Chinese, and finally cost MacArthur his job. I suppose those September days of 1950 do indeed qualify as a climacteric. But for me, and I dare say the soldiers, it seemed at the time just one more development of a campaign that was becoming every day more disagreeable, cruel, perilous and incomprehensible.

I do remember how the preparations for this huge adventure took on, among the tensions, some of the elements of black comedy. The whole United Nations force was then corralled in all that remained to us of Korea, the toehold enclave of Pusan that looked more and more like turning into a Dunkirk. It was clear that something of importance was up, and every day it became more obvious, to the simplest-minded, what it was. The operation, I wrote later, was a military secret so closely-guarded that no one knew of its development except perhaps every living soul within ten miles of the harbour, where our preparations for the great surprise were attended by all the reticence of a three-ring circus. As the accumulation of warlike gear piled ever higher on the docks it was examined, recorded, and tabulated at leisure by processions of spies. The impending hammer-blow became known, resignedly, as Operation Common Knowledge.

Nor were our misgivings much assuaged by the information that of all imaginable locations for a seaborne landing, the most improbable and unpropitious was Inchon harbour. We were told that its enormous tides were the second-highest in the world, that its mudbanks extended for 6,000 yards, that what was not full of mud was full of mines, that if we missed the precise moment of landfall we should never get in, and that if only some of us got in we should never get off, and a variety of similarly useful facts. 'Take every conceivable natural and geographical handicap,' said the spokesman brightly, 'Inchon has them all.'

General MacArthur's attitude to this unpromising state of affairs was sanguine: he argued that the whole Inchon proposition was militarily so preposterous that the North Koreans would decide that even we could not be fools enough to try. The historical analogy was General Wolfe, who succeeded at Quebec just because his men had scaled cliffs that the defending Montcalm knew for certain could not be climbed. Thus morally reinforced, we shambled into battle in a landing-craft marked PRESS.

As it turned out, of course, the General was right; the story describes, though does not explain, how the North Koreans somehow let us get away with it. It was not, however, the way I would choose to spend my holidays.

I feel now that I must always have cut a rather futile figure as a war-correspondent, however often I was obliged to pose as one. For one thing I was almost continually afraid. Not particularly, I think, of getting killed, which seemed to be happening to most people, but of getting maimed and invalidated and left hanging around with legs or eyes and balls shot off; I never in the least fancied that. On the Korean assignment, as on many others, I was fortunately reinforced by my old mate and colleague Bert Hardy, and one of the good things about that was that Bert was no more of a John Wayne type than I. One of the daunting things in those days was to be attached to a cameraman with heroic instincts, who would follow the sound of the cannon as I follow the sound of the clinking glass, and who would shame one into dramatic gestures of great unwisdom. Bert was, I am sure, as alarmed as I was, but there was one signal difference in our roles: he had to take the pictures, and it was long ago established that one way you cannot take pictures is lying face-down in a hole. I spent considerable periods of time doing that. Bert, on the other hand, was plying his trade upright in the open, cursing the military exigencies that had organized this invasion in the middle of the night. One of my enduring memories of that strange occasion is of Bert Hardy on the seawall of Blue Beach, blaspheming among the impossible din, and timing his exposures to the momentary flash of the rockets. That is the difference between the reporter's trade and the cameraman's. His art can never be emotion recalled in tranquillity. Ours can – or could be: the emotion is easy; the tranquillity more elusive.

As for Inchon – for me, the record stands.

Vol. 49   No. 1   7 OCTOBER, 1950

PICTURE POST

Thirty Minutes Before H-Hour, in the First Great Counter-strike of the Korean War
Into the Bay of Inchon, 262 ships of the Allied navies have disgorged their amphibious tanks and tracked vehicles.   Now the vehicles skid round
in the water and the troops wait for the high tide that will rumble them up against the sea-wall.

INCHON

A little before dusk on the evening of September 14, the most formidable Allied landing force ever assembled since the invasion of Normandy, fought its way ashore at Inchon. Inchon was the port of Seoul, and Seoul was not only the South Korean capital, but the key communications centre for all North Korean armies attacking in the south. The United States 1st Marine Division were the first to go in at Inchon. With them went James Cameron and Bert Hardy, the only British journalist-cameraman team to get themselves on to the scene at this tremendous climax of the war.

The Rocket-launching Ships Go in to the Kill
Salvoes of five-inch projectiles tear into the beaches about to be
stormed, and into the town about to be liberated.

Picture Post, 7 October, 1950

FIFTEEN MINUTES TO GO: *The Whole Coastline Kindles, and the Boats Swing Their Noses Towards the Shore*

The sun is going down; and the tide, which will cover the mud-flats, is coming up. Suddenly the landing-craft, which have been buzzing about in all directions, start heading off in one direction. Once the tide starts running out again there can be no reinforcement—and no retreat.

THE challenge, when it came, was too loud, the effect too abrupt; it was not reasonable to fight a war so noisily. We had indeed been waiting for some time. Nevertheless, however you anticipate the stage revolver-shot, it always makes you wince; so I suppose invasions are always more startling and uproarious than you expect.

This was, after all, the biggest seaborne assault of all, after Normandy. This was the operation to end the war. This was the payoff to take the Thirty-Billion-Dollar Police Action out of the red at last. This was MacArthur's final argument in his personal one-man deal with destiny. This was the top-secret business for which we had been lurking furtively in

Pusan, of which everyone in Korea appeared to know almost everything, even us. Then, when it came, it stunned, for a while. All the fear came first. Perhaps we shall never understand exactly how it came off as it did, nor why the enemy failed to do any of the three things that could have crippled the whole enterprise. Anyhow, God was on the side of the big battalions; they were even that big.

We had sailed out in a fat Naval freighter, full of stentorian metallic commands and whistles in the dark, deck-loaded with big and little landing-craft, nesting inside each other like Chinese boxes. We weaved in a curious pattern over the Yellow Sea until we met more ships, and then a few more, and

in three or four days more yet, all in the silent off-hand manner of a casual encounter. Very soon there were a hundred and fifty of us, of incalculable variety of shapes and purposes, slowly converging on the port of Inchon. I would never have believed how tedious it could be. It would not have occurred to me that a climactic moment of such emotional intensity and concentration of nervous activity could have been preceded by such days of numbing boredom.

Up until D-Day eve the Marines still kept up the jesting, the special exclusive badinage of soldiers before battle, the protective flippancies . . . this was of all landing-points the most unsuitable, with a

The Start of the Journey to the End of the Night

There is now no more day and night, as designed by nature. There is now only blackness shot with redness, as made by man. But somewhere in that blackness there's a sea-wall. And, somewhere in that sea-wall there are other men. We shall be with them before long, we hope.

The Last Man of the First Wave of the Assault Climbs Down Into his Landing-Craft

Visibility is going. Audibility has long since gone. There are no more separate noises. The shrieking of the rockets tearing-up the air, the grinding of the engines shaking the sea to pieces, the drumming of the naval guns, have all merged into one vast demonic noise. It is now too late for words.

Picture Post, 7 October, 1950

A FOOTHOLD IN HADES : OVER THE SEA-WALL AND INTO THE NIGHT GO THE LEADING MEN OF THE UNIT

thirty-foot fall of tide that, should anything upset our schedule, would give us a three-mile stumble through waist-deep mudflats under the shore batteries; the enemy was obviously prepared for us; the sea-wall on Blue Beach presented unmapped hazards. Everyone laughed briefly. Then at blackout they settled down to write to their wives. So we came in a great sombre regatta past the Tokchok-kondo islands and dropped anchor in the Inchon channel between the plains of silt, exactly one fortunate half-degree below the Thirty-Eighth. That night the thing happened as everyone knows—with a result, moreover, that everyone now knows, too, though as I write this I can only guess. On that evening of haze and filmy rain among the hills it was like an Argyllshire sea-loch, somehow steam-heated and washed with pastel grey. In no respect, and in no circumstances, can Korea be called lovely, nor even barely likeable; yet at this moment, in the especial dusk of doubt, it came more nearly to being beautiful than I had ever seen before.

The guns began erratically, an hour or two before H-Hour—half past five—with a few crumps from the cruisers, an occasional bark of five-inch fire, a tuning-up among the harsh orchestra. At what point the laying of the guns merged into the final barrage I do not know; so many things began to take place, a scattered series of related happenings gradually coalescing and building up to the blow. All around among the crowded walls of the fleet the landing-craft multiplied imperceptibly, took to the water from one could not see exactly where, circled and wheeled and marked time and milled about, filling the air with engines. There seemed to be no special hurry. We could not go until the tide was right; meanwhile we lay offshore, in serene insolence, under whatever guns the North Koreans had, building our force item by item, squaring the sledge-hammer. The big ships swung gently in the tideway, from time to time coughing heavy gusts of iron towards the town. It began to burn, quite gently at first. What seemed to be a tank ashore sent some quick resentful fire back, but it soon stopped. Later, we found that one ship had tossed a hundred and sixty rounds of five-inch amunition at the tank before it had finished it; the economics of plenty in action.

Quite suddenly we saw the floating tanks, those extraordinary seagoing hunks of amphibious hardware. They crawled awkwardly out of the hull of the mother-ship; she spawned them out in growling droves, a grotesque mechanical parturition. Like a flock of rattling turtles, they lurched out of the ship and began to crawl over the surface of the water; a spectacle utterly surrealist.

As the light faded the noise rose in key, the intervals shortened between the explosions, which now broke out from unexpected places; the din grew suddenly less discriminating and more vicious, abruptly hard to endure. We got into our landing-craft—by no means, as it happens, the easiest thing in the world to do, enveloped in rolls of lifejacket like the Michelin Man, with the helmet rolling over the nose, scuffling and dangling down a rope-ladder in the rising sea. When we headed for the shore, the concussion of shells and bombs was no longer a noise, it was a fierce sensation, a thudding jar on the atmosphere, on the hull of the boat, on the body itself. The waterfront of Inchon began to disappear under a red-shot screen of smoke; it seemed to vibrate. Then the rocket-ships let go. That was the most

The First Steps Into the Edge of the Inferno

Beyond the sea-wall there had been a North Korean trench. But no men in it—only a machine-gun, 80 yards away. And when the Marines had probed for 80 yards, there were still no men. Only another machine-gun, 80 yards away.

ATES FIRST MARINE DIVISION

appalling noise of all; the ships burst into violent pyrotechnics, with a new and ghastly sound, the round of a tremendous escape of gas, the roar of a subway; the projectiles arc-ing through the air and crashing into the beaches; when soon one prayed for it to stop for just a moment it screamed out once more.

At last, as the hundreds of troops began to surge towards Inchon, with what seemed to be powerful express trains howling through the sky overhead, it reached the stage where individual sounds ceased, the bangs and thuds blended into a continuous roll of intolerable drums. The town, and what remained of its quarter-million inhabitants, was gaudy with rushing flames, with more explosive pouring into the flames; one more inconsiderable little city, one more punch-drunk town, one more trifling habitation involved by its betters in the disastrous process of liberation.

Now the twilight was alive with landing-craft, tank-landers, marshal-craft, ammunition-carriers, things full of cranes and guns and lorries and bull-dozers and Marines, more Marines—forty thousand

The Last Curtain of a Lethal Day

They are there! No mines, no frogmen, no aircraft came against them. Maybe, the North Koreans didn't have enough men to go round, when the day began. When it ended, they had fewer still.

Picture Post, 7 October 1950

D-Day Plus One: It's All Quiet Down at the Beaches . . .
The war has gone on ahead, up the road to Seoul. But the war needs to be fed daily, with guns and bulldozers galore. And the beach becomes a fabulous marshalling-yard.

IN THE STREETS OF INCHON:

The Foreshore's Being Cleared

Everyone's Proving Their Identity

Everyone's Busy With Something
Walls for a new house, to replace the one that got blasted away last night.

men on Operation Inchon, twenty-five thousand to be put ashore—tall boats and squat boats and bad-dream swimming tanks, all whirling round in an intricate minuet—and in the middle of it all, if you can conceive of such a thing, a wandering boat marked in great letters 'PRESS', full of agitated and contending correspondents, all trying to appear insistently determined to land in Wave One, while contriving desperately to be found in Wave Fifty. The LC bounced and heaved through the spray; I found to my bewilderment that I was not, as usual, rolling in nausea; I decided that I was too frightened to be seasick, the counter-nervous-irritant. It was a hard matter to rationalise at that moment.

We headed into the heavy bank of smoke, and there we were. By some extravagant miscalculation we

reached the sea-wall ahead of the Marine assault-party, who came blazing in behind us, making retreat quite out of the question. I scrambled ingloriously up the stones and over the parapet and instantly fell flat on my face into a North Korean defence trench most happily empty of North Koreans. There seemed to be a field ahead, and a tidal basin, and beyond that the town, surging with smoke, jarring to the bombs; a place—it must have been—of stark despair. That was the landing, anyhow. The fact that in our flurry we had reached an unscheduled area, that we had in fact hit entirely the wrong beach, were considerations that moved us only when we were told, some time later. At the moment it seemed merely fantastic; the smoke and dust and flames on the one side and, on the other,

WHAT DAYBREAK SHOWED

Suspects Are Being Grilled

And No-one's Taking a Chance

And Every Shop is Suspect
Every house and shack is searched. Every
hiding-place is destroyed.

. . . But Higher Up, the Town is Sizzling Still
Tomorrow turns out, after all, to be another day. After the night of destruction, Koreans
come out to pick their way through their smoking and twisted city.

picking that instant with outrageous theatricality, the sun set in a black-and-vermilion blaze that was too intensely dramatic, too exactly appropriate to be true.

In effect, that was the taking of Inchon, the hammer-blow to the heart, the smashing of the gate to Seoul, the turning-point. The rest was to come at next day's light—the consolidation, the flattening of ruins, concealment of corpses, tending of wounds, the turning of Red Beach into a fabulous marshalling-yard of heavyweight war-machinery. And, somehow, the handling of the Koreans who had survived that terrible night, the sifting of the friends from the enemies, the quick from the dead, the simple from the suspects. As we edged into the charred town they came stumbling out, some of them sound, some

of them smashed, one or two of them quite clearly driven into a sort of bomb-happy dementia by the night of destruction. They ran about, capering crazily or shambling blankly, their only gesture a frantic hands-up; some calling their one English phrase as a kind of password : "Sank you !"; a macabre piece of irony. It was the job of the ROKs, the South Korean militia, to mop up and secure the town; this they did with violent and furious zeal, rounding up householders, searching them with great toughness, herding them around, ancient crones and baby toddlers too, with the strange venom of the Korean, which is that of the armed adolescent; the hoarded anger of the dispossessed returning. Once again there was the phenomenon everyone has remarked before in all

Picture Post, 7 October, 1950

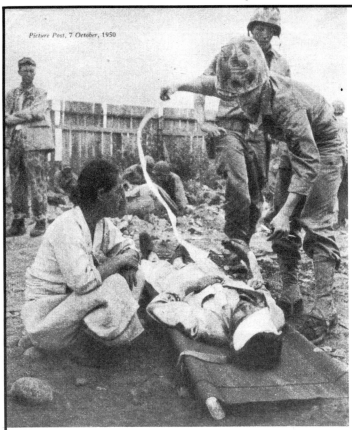

The Human Bric-à-Brac of Victory
The morning after the morning-after. Now the process of sorting friends from enemies, and quick from dead, can begin in earnest.

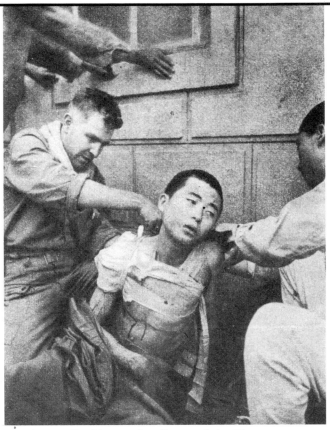

Patching-up One Corner of the Chaos
While the troops fan out from the town on the task of "mopping-up," an American doctor does his kind of "mopping-up"—for both sides alike.

The Ones Who Spoke Out of Turn
The Marines have passed on ahead. Now the R.O.Ks., the South Korean militia, zealously undertake the rounding-up of suspects.

The One Who Can't Get a Word Out
Most of the inhabitants are still feeling beaten-up by the bombardment. But the victors have to separate the simple from the suspects, somehow.

THIS IS WHAT HAPPENS TO HUMANITY WHEN IT IS LIBERATED TWICE WITHIN THREE MONTHS

When humanity gets given 'the works,' in mid-twentieth century style, it passes beyond tragedy. Its old ones caper round like crazy goats, its young ones put out more crazy flags in a confused desire to please, its crazy infants surrender in advance, and its spokesmen utter their final crazy verdict: "Sank you!" Which, being interpreted, means that humanity, with the best will in the world, can stand no more liberations like this.

captured towns : the inexplicable appearance of the victors' flag all over the neighbourhood; from almost every roof and window there was some version of the South Korean flag or the Stars and Stripes. One shopkeeper had gone so far in broadmindedness and lack of prejudice that already he had hung a sign "Wellcom U.S. Forces !", while forgetting to complete the gesture by removing the Communist Red Star that hung beside it.

So began the drive to Seoul.

That was the taking of Inchon. Why the North Koreans did not resist more forcefully I do not know, unless the obvious reason be true : they had too few troops there and could not disengage forces quickly enough from the south. That they did not mine the channel, that they did not scrape together even a squadron of planes, however decrepit, to sprinkle bombs on that congested roadstead, that they did not send fireboats or saboteurs down that dense lane of shipping on the rushing ebb, that in fact they behaved with a hopelessness and irresolution they had never shown at any time before—

these are matters that no doubt will be explained one day. They lost their beachhead, they lost their town, they lost their lives, in numbers, and with them the lives of many simple people who shared the common misfortune of many simple people before them, who had the ill-luck to live in places which people in War Rooms decided to smash. It seems clear they could have hurt us more than they did, but the hammer was too hard.

But there it is. Sitting here, one is glad to be alive—a bit ashamed, maybe, but glad.

How Many Do You Recognize?